MACROECONOMICS

Second Edition

For
Susan and Veronica

MACROECONOMICS

Theory and Policy in the UK

Second Edition

DAVID GREENAWAY and G. K. SHAW

Basil Blackwell

Copyright © David Greenaway and G.K. Shaw, 1983

First published 1983 by
Martin Robertson & Company Ltd.
Reprinted in 1984 and 1986 by Basil Blackwell Ltd,
108 Cowley Road, Oxford OX4 1JF, UK

Second edition 1988
Reprinted 1989

Basil Blackwell Inc.
432 Park Avenue South, Suite 1503
New York, NY 10016, USA

British Library Cataloguing in Publication Data

Greenaway, David
    Macroenomics: theory and policy in
the UK—2nd ed.
    1. Macroeconomics   2. Great Britain—
Economic policy—1945 –
I. Title   II. Shaw, G.K.
    339′ .0941   HC256.6

ISBN 0–631–15763–8

Library of Congress Cataloguing in Publication Data

Greenaway, David 1952–
    Macroeconomics: theory and policy in the UK.

    Bibliography: p.
    Includes index.
    1. Macroeconomics.   2. Great Britain—Economic
policy—1945 –   I. Shaw, G.K. (Graham Keith),
1938–   II. Title.
HB172.5.G75   1987   339′ .0941   87–20831
ISBN 0–631–15763–8 (pbk.)

Printed in Great Britain by
Billing & Sons Ltd, Worcester

Contents

Preface to the First Edition

There are many intermediate macroeconomic texts, a number of which are to be highly recommended for the serious student of economics wishing to obtain a more specialized insight into the controversies, theoretical and otherwise, deriving from modern macroeconomics. However, the vast bulk of this literature is distinctly American oriented, and the policy issues as well as the supporting empirical evidence and findings reflect the American scene. Not only is the American perspective on economic issues understandably different from that in the UK but also the institutional constraints upon policy formulation differ, and differ substantially, in a country with a federal system of government and where the party constituting the executive may have a minority voice in the legislature. Constraints upon policy formulation exercise subtle but persuasive influences upon areas of current interest and research. Comparisons of British and American academic journals offers an interesting commentary in this respect.

This book evolved as an attempt to produce an up-to-date macroeconomic text at the intermediate level which would take full account of the policy issues and controversies in the UK economy. It attempts full coverage of recent developments in macroeconomic theory and deals with the newer schools of economic thought but attempts to relate them specifically to the UK context. Thus particular emphasis is given to monetarist, new Cambridge and neo-classical supply side macroeconomics. At the same time, considerable attention is devoted to the changing status of fiscal policy in the UK, reflected in the importance attached to monetary targets, the public sector borrowing requirement and medium-term financial strategies. Finally, the theoretical exposition contained in this book attempts to assess the importance of the revolution in rational expectations as it impinges upon macroeconomic policy formation in the UK.

Although the book deals with these topics and their implications for economic policy, it is none the less the case that the traditional methods of analysis have been retained. In particular the authors have retained the well-known *IS/LM* framework, partly because they are convinced that this conventional analysis can be developed and extended to illustrate many of the topics just described. The importance attached to the budget constraint and the debate over the crowding out controversy provide a striking example of how the traditional apparatus can be manipulated to yield richer insights into the functioning of the economy than previously imagined. Whilst it is no doubt true that the *IS/LM* framework has been unjustly utilized to provide caricatures of extremist Keynesian, classical or monetarist positions, which inevitably distort the true stance of the protagonists in the debate, it is none the less of great pedagogical value when used sensibly – that is, when it is recognized as being but a tool of analysis derived from a number of mechanistic simultaneous equations, with all the qualifications that this implies.

The book itself falls naturally into three parts. Thus, following upon a general introduction indicating the nature and purpose of macroeconomic modelling, part I examines the individual macroeconomic sectors which collectively comprise the macroeconomy. The principal sectors here are the commodity market, comprising both consumption and investment goods, the money market, the labour market and the government sector. Each sector is examined in turn in relation to specific theories which attempt to account for its behaviour. Part II then examines how these various economic sectors can be analysed together under alternative economic systems of general theories. Thus, part II deals with classical, Keynesian and neoclassical/monetarist interpretations of the economic system as a whole with particular attention being given to the analysis of the open economy. This ordering – the examining of individual sectors in detail before proceeding to the analysis of economic theories dealing with the functioning of the economic system as a whole – is the one which appeals as the most logical to the authors. However, one can readily understand that there may be readers and instructors who would prefer the alternative approach – an analysis of broad economic systems followed by the analysis of the individual sectors. For those preferring this methodology there is no reason why the material of part II cannot precede that of part I. Regardless of which approach is preferred, part III then applies the analysis to the current policy problems confronting the UK economy, with particular attention being devoted to employment, inflation, balance of payments and economic growth. Each chapter is supplemented with suggestions for further reading which offer a guide to the more advanced literature.

It must be emphasized that this book is an intermediate text aimed at second- and third-year students. Accordingly, it assumes that the reader has already become familiar with macroeconomics at a more elementary level and that he is fully conversant with the standard 45° Keynesian model and with elementary concepts of measurement, national income accounting and so forth. These topics will not be examined in the present work.[1] It is also assumed that the reader will have acquired the necessary technical competence to be able to follow the elementary algebraic manipulations and simple differential calculus which accompany the formal analysis. The mathematics has been kept to a minimum and is used principally to fill out what is primarily a diagrammatic presentation. Nevertheless, it adds a certain rigour to topics which are often treated only intuitively (and which are therefore never fully appreciated) and fortunately the mathematics employed here is now commonplace in any university economics course which proceeds beyond the first year.

Any venture of this kind must inevitably be eclectic. Whilst we believe that there is some original material in these pages, such is the nature of a textbook that it must draw upon several sources. Hopefully, these sources are fully acknowledged in the text and in the references for further reading. The authors have also drawn upon their own previous publications in certain parts of the presentation. We are also indebted for constructive comments from a number of our colleagues in the field, including in particular Rod Cross of the University of St Andrews, Bob Elliott from the University of Aberdeen, Chris Milner from the University of Loughborough and Mike McCrostie from the University of Buckingham.

Several generations of former students have left their own mark upon the volume and have certainly been responsible for improving the exposition. No acknowledgement would be complete which did not mention the cheerful and painstaking secretarial contribution of Linda Waterman, of the University of Buckingham. Finally, we would like to acknowledge the constructive support of Michael Hay of Martin Robertson and his patience and understanding as the book developed both in content and in size. One is reminded of Pascal's famous dictum:

La dernière chose qu'on trouve en faisant un ouvrage, est de savoir celle qu'il faut mettre la première.

DAVID GREENAWAY
G. K. SHAW

---

1 For a relatively detailed discussion of measurement problems and national income accounting in the UK context, see Parkin and Bade (1982).

Preface to the Second Edition

The response to the first edition of *Macroeconomics* exceeded our expectations. Whilst there were, of course, critical comments and valid objections raised by colleagues and reviewers in the field, none the less, the overall reaction was most pleasing and hopefully justified the decision to update the volume. In the present edition we have tried to take account of the criticisms made and to eliminate major sources of error as well as updating both data and references. In this regard the detailed comments of Jim Taylor (Lancaster University) and Alan Marin (London School of Economics) were particularly helpful. In addition, however, we have also extended the exposition in a number of areas. The initial introductory chapter has been extended in essentially a non-technical manner in an attempt to illustrate recent policy controversies in the UK. Also, extra material has been introduced to expand the importance attached to expectations formation in macroeconomic policy and contract theory in the analysis of employment. Elements of growth theory have been introduced into the final chapter to provide a more relevant framework against which growth policy might be evaluated. More weight has also been given to the open economy and the constraints upon policy generated by external influences. The policy sections have been updated to take account of developments since the first edition was written. We have kept faith with the original structure of the first edition as we believe this to fit well with the way intermediate macroeconomics is taught in universities and polytechnics in the UK.

We are indebted to former students who served as guinea pigs as the original volume developed; many of them diligently discovered typographical errors in the first edition. As always we are grateful to Mrs Linda Waterman for her outstanding secretarial assistance and we appreciate the efforts of Mr Ivan Araya-Gomez, who helped in the task of updating the data and checking data sources. Finally, our thanks to Basil Blackwell for their continued encouragement and confidence.

DAVID GREENAWAY
G. K. SHAW

1

The Nature of Macroeconomics

The subject matter of macroeconomics is the performance of the economy in the aggregate and the underlying relationships between broad *economic aggregates,* and how those relationships alter over time. It is to be contrasted with *microeconomics* which focuses primarily upon the rational decision-making processes of the individual unit, whether it be the consumer, the unemployed, the producer, the firm, the industry or even the market. An alternative way of making this distinction is to say that microeconomics looks at individual decision-making situations – how, for example, a representative firm might react to the imposition of a value added tax (VAT) – whereas macroeconomics would examine the same issues from the highly aggregative stance of all firms throughout the economy. At the risk of oversimplification, macroeconomics deals with three broad market aggregates and their interrelationships; these aggregates are the labour market, the market for goods and services, and the financial market, where the last is understood to encompass the money market as well as the market in alternative assets.

In one sense, of course, the micro/macro distinction is inappropriate since the whole is of necessity the sum of its parts, and hence any microeconomic decision must exert a macroeconomic impact no matter how negligible. Indeed, when the individual decision-making unit is, let us say, the British Steel Corporation, the impact upon crucial macroeconomic variables such as the price level or the balance of payments may be by no means insignificant. Moreover, it is rapidly becoming accepted that many of the deficiencies of modern macroeconomic theorizing stem from inadequate attention to the microeconomic underpinnings of macrotheory. This has been shown to be especially true with regard to theories involving expectations, search theories of unemployment and so forth. Equally, some very important macroeconomic concepts, such as the 'natural' rate of unemployment, are fundamentally determined by microeconomic forces and constraints.

Moreover, recent supply side economics in both the USA and the UK attaches considerable importance to the free play of competition in individual markets, and in particular to the power of relative price changes to generate efficient resource utilization and also to eliminate the obstacles to, and provide the incentives for, the full utilization of resources. In this view, dismantling the barriers to competition and permitting the flexible functioning of free markets is essential to the overall co-ordination of economic activity and to the attainment of macroeconomic objectives.

None the less, the traditional distinction between macro- and microeconomics is conceptually appealing and useful partly for historical reasons. Microeconomics, developed largely during a period when Utilitarian philosophy was very much in the ascendancy, tended to emphasize almost self-evident postulates of maximizing behaviour even though such theories did not lend themselves to empirical testing and in some cases were incapable of refutation.[1] In contrast, modern macroeconomics was a much later development and focused not so much upon premises of rational utility maximization but rather upon the formulation of aggregate hypotheses which would lend themselves to empirical testing. The Keynesian consumption function was undoubtedly a prime example of the latter approach and provided tremendous stimulus to empirical research and developments in applied econometrics.

Perhaps the most important reason for maintaining the traditional distinction between micro- and macroeconomics, however, is that assumptions which appear valid in a microeconomic setting may not be tenable when transferred to the sphere of macroeconomics. Thus variables which are correctly judged to be exogenous from the microeconomic standpoint of a single firm – as, for example, the general price level – would be very much endogenous variables to be explained from the macroeconomic vantage point. In a similar vein, the individual firm under perfect competition, adjusting its output by moving along its upward sloping marginal cost curve, could very sensibly look upon existing factor prices as a datum. For the economy as a whole, however, attempts to adjust aggregate output are hardly likely to leave factor prices unchanged.

For these reasons, this book accepts the prevailing micro/macro dichotomy and considers its primary objective to be to provide an exposition of the functional relationships of aggregate economic behaviour and their implications for policy formulation and control. The major concern, therefore, will

---

1 The theory of consumer behaviour provides a case in point. The consumer is assumed to act so as to maximize his total welfare. If his income increases and he increases his consumption of a certain good it is assumed that he is acting in accordance with the theory. However, if he decreases his consumption it is still assumed that he is maximizing his satisfaction, and now the good is deemed to be 'inferior'. In short, whatever the observed outcome, it remains consistent with the underlying hypothesis which accordingly cannot be refuted.

be with the determinants of employment, output (national income), the general price level, its rate of change over time (inflation), and the overall balance of payments. In the examination of these issues, particular attention will be paid to such topics as the determination of the money supply, the rate of interest and similar variables that exercise or are believed to exercise a dominant influence on the major economic aggregates. At the same time, the book is not concerned with fundamentally microeconomic issues, such as relative price changes between competing sectors of the economy, or with regional considerations, competition policy, equity and the like.

Methodology

Having indicated, along fairly broad lines, the major concerns of the book, it is perhaps appropriate to add a word about methodology. In this respect it is important to perceive the distinction between macroeconomic *theory*, which seeks to explain the structure and functioning of the economy – what *is* – and macroeconomic *policy*, which is concerned with normative issues – what *ought to be*. The latter cannot be derived from the former, for even if a complete consensus prevails on how the economy behaves, differences will still emerge about the competing priorities of alternative goals. Thus, for example, two economists with broadly the same view of how the economy actually behaves may differ substantially over the extent to which employment goals should be sacrificed to the objective of price stability; such disagreements reflect different value judgements as to the relative costs associated with inflation and unemployment, and differences which cannot be reconciled by objective enquiry. Whilst differences in political and moral judgements will make for disagreements between economists concerning the appropriate policy action, in many cases what appear to be normative differences turn out on closer examination to spring from differences concerning the structure of the economy.

If it is indeed the case that fundamental differences between economists reflect different views of how the economy behaves, then the obvious question which arises is, how does one correctly appraise competing theories? If monetarists take a distinctly different view of the functioning of the macro-economy from that advanced by Keynesians, for example, then surely there should exist some rational basis for choosing between them and determining which is the more relevant to the UK economy? In principle, the answer to this question is in the affirmative and based upon the *positivist* approach to economics. Useful theories should be capable of generating predictions which can be compared with observable evidence to either verify or deny the prediction. In this way, theories which perform well – generate predictions borne out by events – are to be preferred to theories generating predictions which are denied by the evidence. On these grounds a useful theory must be capable in principle of being refuted or falsified and a theory so refuted or falsified is to be discarded.

Unfortunately, whilst this criterion is acceptable in principle, there are considerable differences about it in practice. One problem arises from the measurement difficulties relating to the evidence which is used to test the theory. The measurement problem is especially acute for the social sciences. Second, an intriguing problem arises over whether it is meaningful or sensible to test single hypotheses. For example, suppose a theory predicts that a 10 per cent growth in the money supply will imply 10 per cent inflation. Suppose the evidence subsequently falsifies the theory. It may still be possible to discover some additional auxiliary hypothesis linking monetary growth with output growth which then renders the original thesis fully consistent with the observed evidence. This is but one version of the *Duhem–Quine* thesis which argues that it may always be possible for sufficient auxiliary theses to exist such as to render the original hypothesis irrefutable. (For an elementary introduction to the Duhem–Quine thesis see Cross, 1982a.) Arguments along these lines have led naturally to the attempt to appraise distinct competing schools of thought as opposed to single hypotheses. Although the analysis is conducted issue by issue in this text, it is nevertheless useful to briefly consider the salient and distinguishing features of the principal macroeconomic schools in the UK.

Principal Macroeconomic Schools in the UK

Traditional Keynesianism

The traditional Keynesian school derives from the *IS/LM* portrayal of Keynes which will be examined in considerable detail later in the book. The essential belief is that output and employment are determined by expenditure flows and that the government, by operating upon monetary and fiscal policy, can effectively so regulate these demand flows as to generate the required degree of income and employment. Hence this school of thought is identified with politics of *demand management*, a belief in the ability to *fine tune* the economy and a general interventionist philosphy. In the main, the traditional Keynesian school, at least in the UK, has emphasized the supremacy of fiscal over monetary policy – often discounting the latter almost entirely. This emphasis has been accompanied by a general tendency to dispute any causal link between the money stock and inflation and to argue that the latter is caused essentially by sociological influences, trade union militancy and so forth and can be controlled by appropriate prices and incomes policies.

New Cambridge

The controversial new Cambridge school of macroeconomics, closely allied with the Cambridge Economic Policy Group, claims to be Keynesian in orientation but is largely disillusioned by the poor record of demand management policies over the post-war period. It still attaches primary importance to the role of aggregate demand in determining output levels and employment, but none the less contends that government fiscal policies aimed at controlling demand generate perverse results. In particular, budgetary deficits occasioned by attempts to stimulate the economy are self-defeating and merely translate into balance of payments deficits with the main demand impetus being transmitted to overseas output. This analysis recommends the imposition of import controls to ensure that domestic fiscal stimulus is directed towards domestic output and employment. Such advocacy is often linked with the so-called alternative economic strategy favoured by the left and the trade union movement and is often associated with calls for withdrawal from the EEC.

Monetarism

This is a comparatively recent term coined to summarize a set of ideas whose origins are far older, dating from the earliest statements of the classical *quantity theory of money,* but which were reformulated in the 1950s as a theory of the demand of money. From these ideas is derived the proposition that changes in the money stock are the principal causes of changes in nominal national income. The reformulation of the quantity theory of money as a theory of the demand for money, primarily under the aegis of Milton Friedman of the University of Chicago, sought to demonstrate that the demand for money was a relatively stable function of a few key variables. The implication is that the velocity of circulation of money was relatively constant; if this is the case, then it follows that an increase in the money stock would imply an increase in nominal national income and would not be countered by velocity changes as many Keynesians had claimed. However, the monetarist doctrine goes beyond a simple assertion of a link between money and nominal income. Although allowing for monetary influences upon the volume of real output in the short run, it is part and parcel of the revised theory that in the long term output and employment will attain their *natural* levels, determined essentially by microeconomic influences and constraints; consequently the monetarist doctrine becomes one of claiming that the rate of monetary expansion determines the rate of inflation.

The doctrine also has important implications for the balance of payments. In particular, it is argued that maintaining a regime of *fixed exchange rates* implies loss of control over the domestic money supply and thus the rate of inflation, which will then be determined by world inflation rates. In contrast, *flexible exchange rates* allow control over domestic monetary expansion and hence control over domestic inflation, with insulation from world inflation. In either case, if inflation is essentially a monetary phenomenon then again, in contrast to Keynesian theories, prices and income policies are at best an irrelevancy and at worse may imply serious resource misallocation.

Rational Expectations

This school of thought, of which Patrick Minford of Liverpool University is a leading exponent, accepts the monetarist interpretation of inflation but departs from the monetarist stance on the formation of *expectations*. Monetarist economics relies upon expectations being formed *adaptively* for many of its conclusions concerning natural rates of employment, output and so forth.[2]

In contrast, the rational expectations thesis assumes that individual agents use all available information, including policy announcements by government, in as efficient a manner as possible in forming their expectations about the future state of the economy. The surprising and in some respects disturbing conclusion which emerges from the rational expectations literature is that, if individual economic agents correctly anticipate government stabilization policies, they will effectively negate them. The government thus becomes powerless to influence output and employment by the pursuit of business cycle policy. Only random or unanticipated policy measures will generate *real* effects. In this scenario, real magnitudes are determined primarily by microeconomic forces in market clearing conditions, and consequently any measure aiding the free functioning of competition and market adjustment is conducive to improved macroeconomic performance.

---

2 Adaptive expectations assume that individuals learn from their past experience and mistakes. Thus if last year's expected inflation was 5 per cent and inflation turned out to be 10 per cent then this year's expectation will be equal to 5 per cent plus a fraction of the error made last year, that is

$$EP = 5 + \alpha(10 - 5)$$

where EP is this year's expected inflation rate and $0 < \alpha < 1$. If the rate of inflation suddenly became 10 per cent and remained at that level indefinitely, then this approach would possess the merit that individuals' expectations would progressively approximate the true inflation rate. If inflation is escalating, however, this approach performs badly in that expectations become increasingly falsified.

Supply Side Macroeconomics

Conventional Keynesian economics holds that output and employment are *demand determined*. In stark contrast, and reminiscent of Say's famous Law of Markets, the supply side school of macroeconomics maintains exactly the opposite. Output and employment are determined by the conditions of *aggregate supply*. Once determined, aggregate supply is assumed to be perfectly inelastic and thus Keynesian type fluctuations in aggregate demand have impacts only upon the general price level. Hence it is the supply side view that expansionary demand management policies are likely to be inflationary. Although aggregate supply is held to be completely inelastic with respect to demand stimulus, policies do exist which can promote a favourable outward shift of the aggregate supply curve and hence of output and employment. Essentially, these policies influence the microeconomic environment which determines the position of the aggregate supply curve.

The supply side school of economics has links both with the rational expectations school in providing an explanation of output determination and with monetarism in providing an explanation of the ultimate determination of the 'natural' level of output and employment. Although it has served as a useful antidote to Keynesian oriented demand management policies, its policy prescriptions require an act of faith on the part of its adherents in the absence of any firm convincing empirical evidence.

The Evolution of Ideas

It is perhaps useful, in this introductory chapter to indicate some aspects of how the leading schools of thought have evolved with regard to policy prescription within the United Kingdom. In what follows, we will proceed in a none too rigorous manner, the reader being assured that these issues are taken up in considerably more detail and at a more technical level later in the volume. In particular, we will invoke elementary diagrammatic expositions whose precise underpinnings are for the moment assumed. The attempt is merely to convey an outline of the leading ideas and how they have impinged upon policy debate.

Consider, for example, figure 1.1 which depicts the supply and demand curves for labour, drawn as a function of real wages, and which shows that at the prevailing real wage W/P_1, unemployment prevails. In other words at the existing wage, there are more people seeking jobs than there are job vacancies – we have a situation of excess supply of labour. Now in such a situation two possible remedies suggest themselves if the objective is the securing of full employment. Upon the one hand, we could resort to a *classical* remedy of

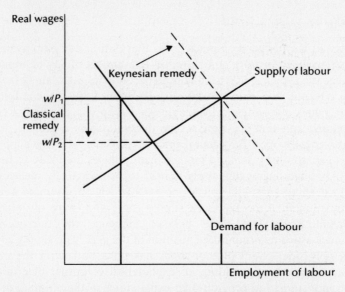

Figure 1.1   Classical and Keynesian remedies for employment creation

reducing real wages which would extend the demand for labour whilst simultaneously inducing some people voluntarily to leave the workforce. If wages were to fall to W/P_2, unemployment would be eliminated. Alternatively, one could invoke a Keynesian solution and enlarge the level of demand possibly by increased government expenditure until full employment is secured at the prevailing wage; this solution is indicated by the hatched line in figure 1.1.

Now of these two remedies – assuming they are both equally available – it is clear that the Keynesian alternative is to be logically preferred. This is because it is consistent not only with a higher level of real output and hence employment but also because it implies a higher real wage. In contrast, the classical remedy secures its objective partly by reducing wages sufficiently so that part of the workforce no longer wish to undertake remunerative employment. None the less the classical solution is the preferred solution – and in many respects is the only solution – both for the classical economists and more recently for the Thatcher government because both are convinced that the Keynesian measure does not and cannot work. The classical rejection of the Keynesian policy proposal is summarized in the philosophy of the so-called Treasury View – which in current jargon is a version of crowding out. In this view, any attempt to raise public sector spending in the interests of promoting employment would involve a transfer of resources from the private to the public sector. Thus any net gain in employment would be small, and would depend upon the possibility that public sector employment was intrinsically more labour intensive. In contrast, although very similar in spirit, and in many respects in substance, the Thatcher government's rejection of Keynesian demand management strategies is based upon a belief in a natural rate of employment to which the economy inherently gravitates together with a certain view as to the means of expectations formation. Implicit in this approach, is the belief that Keynesian-type demand management strategies succeed only in generating higher prices and are incapable of generating any long-term improvement in real output, and indeed, the strict version of this thesis would simultaneously deny the possibility of any short-term gains as well. In order to illustrate the essence of these ideas we will invoke the concepts of aggregate supply and demand analysis whose precise construction is to be analysed in more detail later in the volume.

Consider, for example, figure 1.2 which we may think of as embodying the

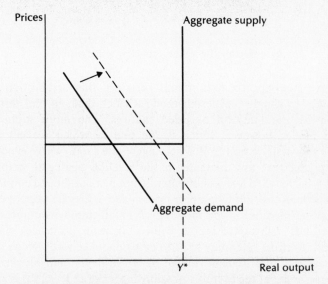

Figure 1.2   Aggregate demand measures to raise output and employment with zero price effects in the naïve Keynesian model

spirit of naïve Keynesianism. In this diagram the aggregate supply curve is drawn with perfect elasticity with respect to price until full employment output or capacity output is reached at Y^*. Before this point is attained, any increase in the level of aggregate demand as indicated by the hatched line exerts its entire impact upon output and employment with no impact upon prices. In conditions of extreme unemployment both of labour and capital assets which characterized the conditions of the 1930s, this may not be a too

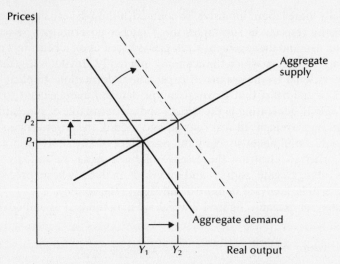

Figure 1.3   Aggregate demand measures to raise output and employment with positive
price effects in the sophisticated Keynesian model

unreasonable first approximation and certainly this assumption was a
commonplace in simple Keynesian models which dealt in real terms and
assumed away the question of price changes. The more sophisticated
Keynesian model, however, which is the one to which Keynes himself
ascribed, is shown in figure 1.3. Here, the aggregate supply curve is positively
sloped implying that any increase in the level of aggregate demand as
indicated by the hatched line would generate not just output and employment
effects but would also impinge upon prices. The aggregate supply curve is
positively sloped because as you move closer to full employment income, less
efficient and less well trained labour will be taken on, bottleneck shortages
may appear, overtime rates may need to be paid and so forth. None the less,
the implication is that demand management strategies can be effective in
raising employment at the cost of a possibly higher price level; the essentially
Keynesian notion of a trade-off between output and prices, epitomized in the
concept of the Phillips curve, is implicit in this construct.

Consider now figure 1.4, which we may categorize as the monetarist
approach and which owes much to the thinking of Milton Friedman and
Edmund Phelps. In the short run, it is essentially similar to the sophisticated
Keynesian model but the difference lies in the long-run adjustment of the
positively sloped aggregate supply curve. To see this, let us assume the initial
situation to be the price level P_1 and the income or output level Y_1 as
determined by the intersection of the aggregate supply and demand curves.
Let us now assume that an increase in government spending raises the level of

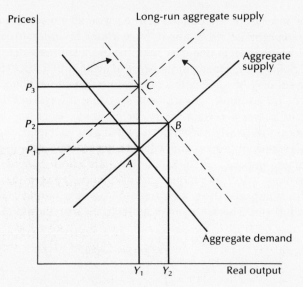

Figure 1.4 Interdependence between aggregate supply and demand schedules, the monetarist approach and distinction between short-run and long-run effects

aggregate demand, as indicated by the hatched line, so that output rises to Y_2 with prices rising to P_2. Essentially, this is precisely the adjustment underlying the sophisticated Keynesian model. However, for the monetarist, such an adjustment will be but short-lived. This is because the rise in prices curtails real wages – indeed it is the fall in real wages which is responsible in part for extending the demand for labour. As labour perceives a decline in real wages it will commence to renegotiate its nominal wage contract so as to restore its former level of real wage consistent with the initial supply of effort reflected in the income level Y_1. Thus, the aggregate supply curve is shifted inwards over time, until the former output level is regained at the former real wage. The trade-off is short-term only, the movement being from A to B to C. The long-run aggregate supply curve is thus vertical above the income level Y_1 which is referred to as the natural level, and a corollary of the above is that the long-term Phillips curve (to be dealt with later in considerable detail) is also logically vertical above the natural rate of employment.

The rational expectations thesis takes this adjustment process one step further to reach what its proponents claim is the logical conclusion. Why should intelligent economic agents wait until their real wages actually decline? Will they not, in the light of their understanding of how the economy actually operates or upon the basis of past experience anticipate that the increase in government spending will generate an increase in prices? As soon as the policy measure is announced or otherwise identified, labour should immediately renegotiate its nominal wage claim in order to defend the existing real wage. Indeed, one may take the argument one step further. If government policy is systematic in the sense of being countercyclical then the policy measures may be anticipated even before they are announced or put into effect. If, for example, government spending always increases when unemployment passes a certain figure, or contracts when the balance of payments goes sufficiently into deficit, intelligent economic agents will recognize this recurrent process and will react accordingly, thus negating any macroeconomic impact. Predictable countercyclical policy becomes impotent. In other words, the monetarist distinction between the long term and the short disappears; there is no trade-off between output and inflation even in the short run. This situation is summarized with the aid of figure 1.5

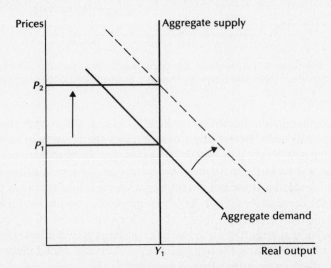

Figure 1.5   Aggregate demand impacts in the rational expectations model: zero output effects and positive price effects

displaying the vertical aggregate supply curve even in the short run. The contrast with the naïve Keynesian approach summarized in figure 1.2 could not be more stark.

In many respects, the rational expectations thesis underpins much of the Thatcher government's philosophy if only implicitly. It explains why conventional Keynesian demand management strategies have been ignored. Moreover, the government's medium-term financial strategy relied heavily upon the announcement of money supply targets even years in advance in the attempt to condition expectations of future inflation rates and in so doing render lower inflation rates more attainable. This is an important feature of the rational expectations philosophy. If the government announces substantially reduced money supply targets, and if the policy announcement is credible to economic agents at large, then inflationary expectations will be swiftly adjusted downwards. These revised inflationary expectations will then form the basis of formal wage bargaining negotiations and output and employment will be speedily restored to natural levels at lower nominal wages than would otherwise have prevailed. In short, providing the policy is credible, chronic inflation can be substantially reduced or eliminated with fairly modest cost in terms of output and employment forgone. This apparently was what the government firmly believed in 1979; the fact that the reduction in inflation was substantially much more painful and long-drawn-out might be construed either as a critique of the rational expectations thesis or alternatively as evidence that the government policy was not credible. Certainly, there were those who believed in and even those who advocated (the 'wets') a 'U-turn' in policy as the number of the unemployed continued its persistent rise to record levels.

Finally, belief in the vertical aggregate supply curve signals not only the death knell of Keynesian-oriented demand management policies but also provides the *a priori* justification for the consideration of supply side policies. Policies to effect a favourable outward shift of the vertical aggregate supply curve thus raising the natural rate of output and employment are consistent with higher growth and greater economic welfare. Such policies are essentially microeconomic in nature and turn upon boosting incentives by tax cuts and arguably lower unemployment and associated benefits, by promoting competition through privatization programmes and trade union reform and similar measures designed to create initiative and a climate of enterprise. As yet, the benefits of such programmes are little in evidence although apologists might claim that the policy measures have still to be fully applied and/or can only yield results in the medium to long run.

Concluding Comments

This taxonomy provides a useful framework of reference which can be invoked when appraising macroeconomic controversies. Although the methodological approach adopted here pursues the arguments on an issue by issue basis, the reader will readily identify the principal contributions of the leading schools of thought as the analysis of macroeconomic sectors, systems and policy is developed.

Further Reading

For a concise introduction to macroeconomic issues in the United Kingdom and for a useful non-technical survey of the leading schools of thought, see in particular Cross (1982a). On methodological issues, the starting-point for any discussion of the positivist approach to economics must still be the classic paper by Friedman (1953a) and the subsequent critique by Nagel (1963) both reprinted in the volume of readings by Breit and Hochman (1968). More detailed analyses of methodological issues in economics and the distinction between the is/ought dichotomy will be found in Blaug (1981), and Hudson (1979). A recent article on the Duhem–Quine thesis and its implications for the appraisal of macroeconomic theories is given by Cross (1982b). A critical survey of the approach of macroeconomic policy in the UK is to be found in Maynard (1982). A simple introduction to recent policy issues is provided by Vines (1986) and Shaw (1987a).

Differences between the various schools of thought often find expression in a comparison of the various economic journals. Thus, for example, the influential *Cambridge Economic Policy Review*, published by the Department of Applied Economics at the University of Cambridge, presents the new Cambridge view; shades of monetarism and the supply side school of economics characterize the admittedly right wing *Journal of Economic Affairs*, published by the Institute of Economic Affairs, London.

PART I

Macroeconomic Sectors

It is difficult to see the picture
when you are inside the frame
R. S. Trapp.

The first stage in constructing a macroeconomic model is to identify the relevant component parts of the system, and understand the behavioural relations involved. In the case of macroeconomic analysis this is especially important since much of the controversy about how the macroeconomy responds to various economic stimuli can be traced to disagreements about the nature and determinants of specific aggregates.

In this first part of the book the aim is to identify the component sectors of the macroeconomy and outline alternative views of the behavioural relations in each sector. Chapters 2, 3 and 4 will deal with the principal components of aggregate expenditure, namely consumption, investment and government expenditure respectively. Chapters 5 and 6 explore the demand and supply sides of the money market respectively. At the end of chapter 6 the three principal components of chapters 2, 3 and 4 will be combined to derive the aggregate demand curve. Chapter 7 analyses the labour market and derives the aggregate supply curve using different assumptions about the manner in which agents behave in that market.

The mode of analysis is essentially partial equilibrium in that each sector is analysed in isolation. Collectively, however, the chapters in this part form the essential background to part II, where complete systems are analysed.

2

Aggregate Consumption Expenditure

When asked what the major influence on consumption expenditure is likely to be, most lay commentators will undoubtedly reply that it is *income*. Indeed this may even be regarded as so self-evident as to obviate the need for thorough investigation. However, the purpose of this chapter is to consider more closely what precisely is meant by income, and how the concept of income is likely to affect aggregate consumption. There are a number of competing candidates to the title 'income'. Attention will be focused on concepts such as *absolute income, relative income, life cycle income, permanent income* and *endogenous income*. Having examined each of these we will then briefly review existing empirical evidence on the consumption – income relationship.

Current Income Theories

The Absolute Income Hypothesis

Keynes viewed consumption expenditures in the aggregate as being primarily dependent on current net income.[1] He contended that, as net income increased, consumption expenditure would increase *but by less than the increase in income*. In other words, some savings will take place. If the *marginal propensity to consume* is defined as the change in consumption which is associated with some small change in income, then this assumption imposes the restriction that the *marginal propensity to consume* (MPC) will lie between zero and unity.[2]

---

1 Net income is here equated with consumption plus *net* investment. Thus, the provision considered necessary for depreciation needs ('financial prudence') is a factor influencing consumption expenditures. Keynes fully allowed for other influences on consumption including windfall gains, interest rate changes and fiscal policy. Modern Keynesians have emphasized the latter influence and in particular have considered consumption to be a function of *disposable* income.

2 As will be seen, the assertion that $0 < MPC < 1$ is not solely the result of armchair theorizing but is also a required condition for the stability properties of the elementary Keynesian model.

As well as imposing this restriction Keynes made two other behavioural assumptions. The first was that at 'low' (but unspecified) income levels, consumption will exceed income, expenditure being financed by dissaving. This amounts to saying that the marginal propensity to consume is less than the *average propensity to consume* (APC). The latter is defined as the ratio of consumption expenditure to income (C/Y). The second assumption was that the marginal propensity to consume ($\Delta C/\Delta Y$) or in the limit dC/dY will itself decline as income increases. If consumption is expressed as a function of *disposable* income, in keeping with modern practice, this consumption function can be formally represented as follows:

$$C = f(Y_d) \tag{2.1a}$$

$$Y_d = Y - T \tag{2.2}$$

$$T = tY \tag{2.3}$$

$$1 > \frac{dC}{dY_d} > 0 \tag{2.1b}$$

$$\frac{dC}{dY_d} < \frac{C}{Y_d} \tag{2.1c}$$

$$\frac{d^2C}{dY_d^2} < 0 \tag{2.1d}$$

where C is aggregate consumption, and disposable income (Y_d) is total income after deduction of direct taxes ($Y - T$). t is the average rate of income taxes. Expression 2.1b describes the marginal propensity to consume, expression 2.1c describes the relationship between the MPC and the APC, and expression 2.1d describes how the MPC will behave as income changes. The last inequality is particularly important since, if it holds, it will ensure that the average propensity to consume (C/Y_d) declines as income rises, and that the APC is more than the MPC. These relations are summarized in figure 2.1 by the function C_1.

The implications of this relationship are worth emphasizing. First, it is clear that if information on the MPC exists, it is possible to predict how consumption expenditure will change in response to a change in disposable income (effected for example by a change in tax rates). Second, it implies that the percentage of income saved increases as society becomes richer. This in turn suggests that in a growing economy a greater proportion of investment will be required to maintain full employment income levels. Third, expression 2.1c suggests that a transfer of income from high-income to low-income consumers will raise the level of aggregate demand, since MPCs differ between the two groups. Thus, implicit in the Keynesian

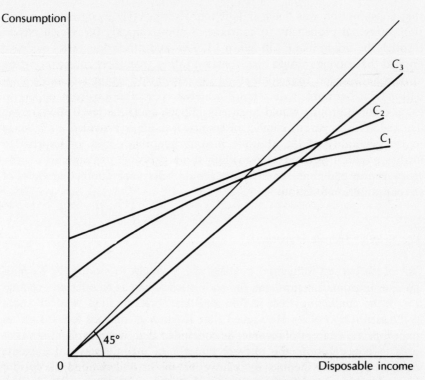

Figure 2.1   Alternative consumption functions

approach is a justification of progressive taxation as a basis of income redistribution in conditions of surplus capacity.[3]

Cross-Section and Time Series Consumption Functions. The Keynesian consumption function provided considerable impetus to empirical investigation. Early studies employing *cross-section budget data* appeared to support Keynes's intuition in almost every detail. Such cross-section data related the level of consumption to income levels for different income groups, and in so doing tended to generate consumption functions remarkably similar to C_1 in figure 2.1, or more accurately, given a linear functional form, similar to C_2 in figure 2.1.

Although the cross-section data lent some support to the Keynesian thesis, a number of early *time series* studies (that is, studies relating observations on consumption and income for specific groups through time) raised fundamental questions. Kuznets' (1946) classic study for example suggested

3 Strictly speaking the opposite conclusion follows in inflationary conditions.

that consumption was a linear function of disposable income with a *constant* marginal propensity to consume of approximately 0.9, which passed through the origin like C_3 in figure 2.1. This and other time series evidence implied that savings would be a constant rather than increasing proportion of national income, thus combatting the pessimistic leanings towards stagnation. Furthermore it questioned whether redistribution from upper- to lower-income groups would have any impact upon the level of aggregate demand. This apparent conflict in empirical findings provided a challenge to the generality of the absolute income hypothesis and an impetus to further research directed at providing some plausible explanation of why cross-section and time series results should offer such conflicting views of the consumption function.

The Relative Income Hypothesis

One of the earliest influential treatises which sought to modify the Keynesian consumption function, and did so in such a way as to offer an explanation of the conflicting cross-section and time series findings, was advanced by Duesenberry (1952). He argued that Keynesian analysis focused on an inappropriate concept of income; he contended that, when explaining variations in consumption, the relevant concept of income was not absolute income but *relative* income. By relative income he had in mind the current disposable income of a consuming unit relative to previous peak income, *and* current disposable income of that same consuming unit relative to the current disposable income of other consuming units. The former of these two relativities is responsible for the so-called *ratchet effect*, that is, the idea that the consumption–income relationship may be asymmetrical in so far as there are downward rigidities to the reduction of consumption expenditure. The latter relativity has become known as the *demonstration effect* and refers to the possibility that consumption decisions may be *interdependent* rather than independent. If both of these effects are taken into consideration, it is possible to reconcile the findings of cross-section and time series evidence.

Duesenberry's Reconciliation of Cross-Section and Time Series Findings. Formally the consumption function can be written as:

$$C_t = f(Y_t,\ Y_t/Y_0,\ \sigma Y) \tag{2.4}$$

where C_t is current consumption, Y_t current income, σY the distribution of income and Y_t/Y_0 the ratio of current income to previous peak income.

Duesenberry's estimating equation took the form:

$$\frac{S_t}{Y_t} = a + b\frac{Y_t}{Y_0} \tag{2.5}$$

that is, current savings are a linear function of the relationship between current income and previous peak income. Since

$$\frac{C_t}{Y_t} = 1 - \frac{S_t}{Y_t} \tag{2.6}$$

then if equation 2.5 is substituted into equation 2.6 the following is obtained:

$$\frac{C_t}{Y_t} = 1 - a - b\frac{Y_t}{Y_0} \tag{2.7}$$

If income were to grow at a constant rate (of say g per cent) without declining, then clearly current income would always represent peak income and the previous year's income will *always* be previous peak income. If the trend growth of income is given as

$$Y_t = (1 + g)Y_{t-1} \tag{2.8}$$

then as income grows along trend

$$\frac{Y_t}{Y_0} = \frac{Y_t}{Y_{t-1}} = 1 + g \tag{2.9}$$

Substituting equation 2.9 into equation 2.7 yields

$$\frac{C_t}{Y_t} = 1 - a - b(1 + g) \tag{2.10}$$

In other words, if income grows along trend, the average propensity to consume and the marginal propensity to consume are constant. The consumption function thus fits the time series 'facts'.

Consider now the situation when income fluctuates around its trend rate of growth. In this situation equation 2.9 no longer holds and the consumption ratio is no longer constant. This would still be given by equation 2.7. Given the negative coefficient on Y_t/Y_0, C_t/Y_t and Y_t/Y_0 will be inversely related. Furthermore, from equation 2.7

$$C_t = (1 - a)Y_t - b\frac{Y_t^2}{Y_0} \tag{2.11}$$

Differentiating gives an expression for the marginal propensity to consume

$$\frac{dC_t}{dY_t} = 1 - a - 2b\,\frac{Y_t}{Y_0} \qquad\qquad (2.12)$$

Comparison of equations 2.12 and 2.7 reveals that the equality of the marginal and average propensity to consume no longer holds. In fact *the MPC is less than the APC*. This implies that when income is fluctuating around trend, the consumption function fits the short-run 'facts'.

An intuitive explanation of how these functions are related is given in figure 2.2. Assume that the typical consumer unit commences at point A. As

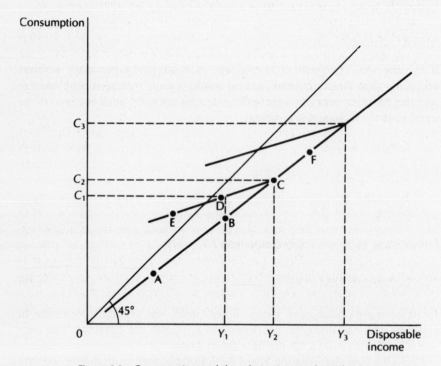

Figure 2.2   Consumption and the relative income hypothesis

income grows along trend, a roughly constant fraction of income will be consumed, with a relatively small proportion being saved. This pattern will continue as income rises through Y_1 to Y_2 to Y_3. The points are on the long-run time series consumption function. The ratio of savings to income will change very little because, typically, consumers strive to attain the standards of consumption set by consuming units in higher-income brackets. As long as the growth of income does not radically affect the distribution of income, once one set of aspirations are fulfilled a new target is set. Thus as the consumer reaches income level Y_2 and consumption level C_2 (for example, one car and one overseas vacation per annum), consumers who were previously in income bracket Y_2 now occupy Y_3 (two cars and two overseas vacations per annum). The maintenance of such targets ensures that savings propensities remain constant and the consumer stays on his long-run consumption function.

Now suppose that at income level Y_2 the economy lurches into recession and average incomes fall. Typically consumers will resist cuts in living standards as set by previous peak income. Thus, rather than moving back down the long-run consumption function, the average propensity to consume from current income will rise, and current savings will fall in an effort to maintain living standards. If income falls far enough, a point such as E may be approached where current consumption exceeds current income – consumption levels are at least in part being maintained by running down past savings. Once the economy recovers and income begins to rise again, the consumer will move back along the short-run consumption function towards C. The APC falls initially as income rises and efforts are made to rebuild savings. Eventually when the previous peak at C is reached and income increases beyond Y_2, the consumption–income relationship returns to its long-run trend.

This stylized description of the adjustment process serves to emphasize the role played by the ratchet and demonstration effects. The thesis has interesting policy implications. As was seen earlier, the simple Keynesian formulation suggested that government tax changes to alter the level of disposable income had a fairly predictable impact. The Duesenberry formulation suggests however that fiscal changes may have an asymmetrical effect. Tax reductions may well stimulate consumption spending. Tax increases may however have a limited impact in curbing demand, in the short run, as consumers attempt to maintain consumption levels.

Duesenberry himself provided some empirical support for the relative income hypothesis, and a number of other studies have provided encouraging support. Subsequent developments in the analysis of aggregate consumption suggested however that one very important variable may have been omitted – namely, the role of wealth, and in particular the part which this may play in influencing expectations of future income. This is a variable which is given much greater prominence in the so-called *normal income theories*, the best known of which are the permanent income hypothesis and the life cycle hypothesis.

Normal Income Theories

Because both the Keynesian and Duesenberry explanations of consumption
behaviour link current consumption closely to current income, they are
found wanting when it comes to explaining consumption behaviour of
groups whose income pattern is highly variable. The farmer (in the absence
of income support schemes), the salesman or the professional gambler all
tend to have fluctuating income. Nevertheless, one may still find that their
consumption expenditure is relatively stable. The solution to the problem is
simple. Individuals are not completely myopic. Thus in the event of a good
harvest the farmer does not increase consumption in line with his increased
income. Nor when times are bad does he reduce consumption to some
irreducible minimum. Over any given period he is aware that his income
will fluctuate. He is also aware however of what on average he can expect
to earn. In other words, he has some idea of his *normal* income, and his
consumption plans are based on this rather than current income. In years
when current income is in excess of normal income he will save, whilst in
years when current income falls short of normal income he will dissave.

Microeconomic Foundations

The normal income approach to the analysis of aggregate consumption has
its roots more firmly embedded in microeconomic foundations than the
current income approaches. A brief elaboration of these foundations is useful
to identify certain characteristics of the normal income approach.

As was noted in the introductory points, the essence of the normal
income approach is that the consumer aims to maximize utility by seeking
the optimal pattern of consumption expenditures through time. If for simplicity the choice is confined to two periods the essential features of the
analysis can easily be developed in a simple geometrical model.

In figure 2.3 consumption and income in period 1 and period 2 are
measured along the horizontal and vertical axes respectively. It is assumed
that the individual consumer receives an income of Y_1 in the first period
and Y_2 in the second period, and furthermore for simplicity that $Y_1 = Y_2$. If
current income were the principal determinant of current consumption the
individual might consume all of Y_1 in period 1 and all of Y_2 in period 2,
ultimately reaching point a in consumption space. If however he can use the
capital market to either deposit savings to finance future consumption
($C_2 > Y_2$) or borrow against future income to support current consumption
($C_1 > Y_1$) his options are rather wider. For instance he could choose to

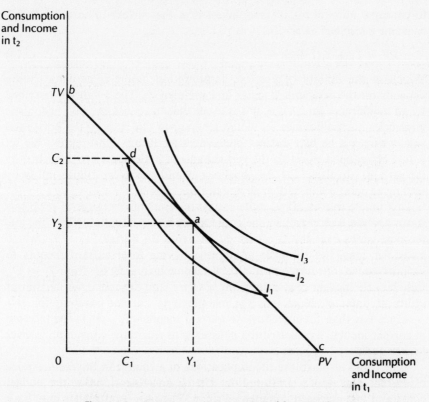

Figure 2.3   Consumption in a two-period framework

consume C_1 in the first period and save $C_1 Y_1$ in order to consume C_2 in the second period, ultimately ending up at point d. There are in fact an infinity of possible combinations of consumption over the two periods which comprise the consumer's *budget constraint bc*. The intercepts of the constraint are determined by the extremes of consuming all income in the first period, or all income in the second period. In the first case the consumer would consume an amount equivalent to the *present value* (PV) of his income over the two periods, where

$$PV = Y_1 + \frac{Y_2}{(1 + r)} \qquad (2.13)$$

that is, his income in the first period and his income in the second period discounted at the current rate of interest (r). Alternatively he could choose to consume none of his income, invest it at the current interest rate[4] and consume a *terminal value* of

$$TV = Y_2 + Y_1(1 + r) \tag{2.14}$$

Which of the infinity of possible consumption points is actually chosen depends on the consumer's tastes and preferences. These can be described by an indifference set.[5] Thus, in the event that the consumer had hedonistic tendencies his indifference set would be mapped out close to the horizontal axis, whereas if he had distinct preferences for future consumption his set would be mapped closer to the vertical axis. If preferences are described by the set I_1-I_3 in figure 2.3 the consumer would clearly maximize utility by settling at point a and neither saving nor borrowing.

This simple framework is quite robust in terms of the range of problems it can analyse. For example, one could apply it to a situation where income received varies over the two periods. In figure 2.4 initially $Y_1 > Y_2$, which leads the consumer to settle at point a, saving from current income to support future consumption. If current income increases, say from Y_1 to Y'_1, this shifts the budget constraint from bc to $b'c'$ and the consumer maximizes utility at point a'. Note that the increment to current consumption ($C_1 - C'_1$) is less than the increment to current income ($Y_1 - Y'_1$). The increase in current income has caused the consumer to rearrange consumption over *both* periods.

One could also explore the implications of a change in the *relative price* of current and future consumption. Up to now the slope of the budget constraint has not been commented upon. The observant reader may have noted that so far it has been drawn at 45° to both axes i.e. with a slope of -1. This was deliberate since the slope of the budget line is given by $-(1+r)$; therefore imposing a 45° line amounts to assuming a zero rate of interest. Suppose, however, allowance were to be made for a positive interest rate. Clearly PV as given by equation 2.13 would fall (discounting at a positive interest rate), whilst TV as given by equation 2.14 would rise (compounding at a positive interest rate). As a result the budget constraint would rotate as

---

4 The assumption that borrowers and lenders face the same interest rate (which is tantamount to assuming a perfect capital market) is crucial to this model, and to the permanent income hypothesis. As Fleming (1973) has shown, if in fact borrowers and lenders face different rates the long-run consumption function which is derived from the permanent income hypothesis is no longer linear.

5 It is assumed that the indifference set accords with the usual axioms of consumer behaviour; that is they are non-intersecting, uniquely ranked from south-west to north-east, and are convex to the origin owing to a diminishing marginal rate of substitution between the objects of choice (in this case present and future consumption).

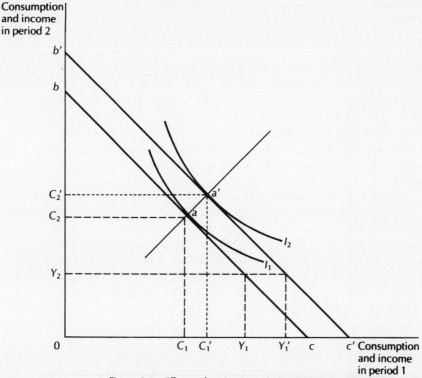

Figure 2.4   Effects of an increase in income

in figure 2.5 with the old and new budget constraints intersecting at the
initial values of income Y_1 and Y_2 (since their current values are unaffected
by the interest rate change). If the consumer's income is held constant and it
is assumed that no change in his preferences occurs, it can be seen that at
the new equilibrium point e the consumer has reduced current consumption
and increased future consumption. Note also that the increment in future
consumption $(Y_2 - C_2)$ exceeds the decrement in current consumption $(C_1 - Y_1)$ owing to the positive return on saving.

This introduction to the allocation of consumption through time has
been brief, but nevertheless it serves to emphasize that there need not
necessarily be any simple relationship between current income and current
consumption. The pattern of consumption expenditure chosen depends in
part on the individual's tastes and preferences. It depends also however on
the pattern of the income stream through time (i.e. whether the individual
expects to receive more in the future than he currently earns) and on the
relative price of present and future consumption as given by the interest
rate.

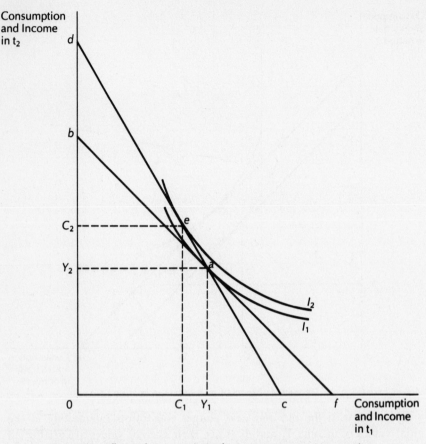

Figure 2.5   Effects of an increase in the interest rate on consumption

Two specific normal income theories will now be examined, namely the life cycle hypothesis and the permanent income hypothesis; it will be found that the postulates deduced in this simple framework are prominent features of these models.

The Life Cycle Hypothesis

The development of this hypothesis is associated with the names of Ando, Modigliani and Brumberg. At its simplest, the hypothesis argues that the individual will maximize his utility by maintaining a stable pattern of consumption throughout his lifetime – in figure 2.6 the trend line C_t. Over the life cycle, income from employment will behave in a fairly predictable way, being relatively low in the early years of working life, zero in retirement,

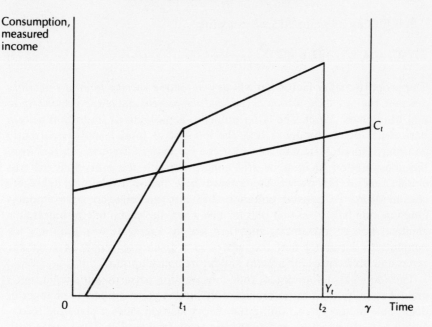

Figure 2.6   Life cycle hypothesis

and relatively high in between. Thus a stable consumption path will be maintained by redistributing resources from $t_1 t_2$ to $0 t_1$ and $t_2 \gamma$. This is accomplished by making use of the capital market, borrowing against expected future income perhaps to finance consumption over $0 t_1$, saving and generally accumulating assets to finance consumption over $t_2 \gamma$.

Following Ando and Modigliani (1963):

$$C_t = \Omega_t V_t \tag{2.15}$$

$$V_t = a_{t-1} + Y_t + \sum_{t=1}^{n} \frac{Y_t^e}{(1+r_t)^n} \tag{2.16}$$

Equation 2.15 tells us that current consumption is some fraction (Ω) of the present value of total resources (V_t) accruing to the individual over his lifetime. Equation 2.16 tells us that total resources comprises three components. The first is any net worth which is carried over from the previous period (a_{t-1}); this may take the form of inherited wealth or accumulated wealth. The second is current income (Y_t), and the third is the present value of expected future income from employment (Y^e) over the remainder of the individual's lifetime, n (where $n = \delta - t$ and where δ is time of death).

Substituting 2.16 into 2.15 we can write,

$$C_t = \Omega_t a_{t-1} + \Omega_t Y_t + \Omega_t \sum_{t=1}^{n} \frac{Y_t^e}{(1+r_t)^n} \qquad (2.17)$$

The proportionality factor (Ω) *will depend on the specific form of the utility function, the rate of return on assets, and the present age of the person* (Ando and Modigliani, 1963). The latter influence is particularly important since a basic tenet of the model is that the amount of total resources currently consumed varies systematically over the life cycle. Of course, in this form the consumption function is still concerned with the individual; as was emphasized at the outset, the interest here lies in explaining aggregate consumption. To convert equation 2.17 into an aggregate consumption function, one has to assume that for any given age group of consumers Ω is identical across consumers, and then simply aggregate age groups. This amounts to assuming that consumers in a given age group have similar tastes and preferences for present and future consumption.

This theory therefore argues that consumption patterns will exhibit much greater stability than those predicted by linking consumption to changes in disposable income. In so doing the theory also provides a plausible reconciliation of cross-section and time series empirical studies. Time series data capture the underlying relationship summarized in equation 2.15, where Ω can be viewed as the long-run marginal propensity to consume, although clearly this MPC refers to *total resources* rather than simply current income. Cross-section data however observes the relationship between consumption and current income for individuals at different stages of their life cycle; Ω differs across these age groups. Thus the typical cross-section will include individuals in the early years of work and in retirement for whom the MPC appears to be greater than unity. Such individuals are dissaving. Those on higher levels of current income, who appear to have a much lower MPC, are in the middle stage of the life cycle and are saving a relatively large fraction of current income to pay off previous debts and make provision for the future.

Before proceeding to the permanent income hypothesis, two difficulties associated with the consumption function as specified in equation 2.17 should be acknowledged. The first is that it is clearly assumed that the factor of proportionality, Ω, is the same for all forms of resources. By implication the individual is indifferent to the form in which resources accrue. A given increase in resources will have the same effect on current consumption whether that increase takes the form of an increase in current income, expected income, or net worth. This seems to imply that switching of assets is a relatively costless transaction (from the consumer's point of view).

The second and perhaps more fundamental problem arises from the difficulties associated with measuring expected income. In equation 2.17 a_{t-1} and Y_t are *relatively* uncontroversial to measure. (As anyone familiar with the literature is aware, they are not uncontroversial *per se*.) Expected income is more problematic; by definition it is not directly observable and its value has to be forecast. The latter is also a problem faced in the permanent income hypothesis; this will be returned to shortly.

To summarize briefly, the life cycle hypothesis directs attention away from current income derived from employment towards a broader concept of lifetime resources. Although this broader concept includes current income, it places much greater emphasis on expected income and wealth. There may be certain empirical difficulties associated with testing the hypothesis, but it is a plausible basis for analysing aggregate consumption, and certainly has more solid microeconomic underpinnings than the Keynesian or Duesenberry approaches.

The Permanent Income Hypothesis

Perhaps the best known critique of the Keynesian consumption function is that advanced by Milton Friedman (1957). This views current consumption as being geared not to current income (whether in an absolute or relative sense) but rather to long-term consumption possibilities, summed up in the concept of *permanent income*. Specifically,

$$C_p = kY_p \qquad (0 < k < 1) \tag{2.18}$$

Permanent consumption is some fraction of permanent income. The precise value which the constant k takes is determined by wealth, age, tastes and interest rates. It can therefore differ between consumers, although it is independent of Y_p. Permanent income is defined as '*the amount a consumer unit could consume, or believes that it could whilst maintaining its wealth intact*'; permanent consumption is '*the value of services that it is planned to consume during the period in question*' (Friedman, 1957). Permanent income can therefore be looked upon as the *discounted value of expected income streams which, if expectations are justified, approximates long-term average income*. Like the life cycle model, this thesis possesses a strong intuitive appeal with regard to those people who experience highly unstable incomes. It differs from the life cycle model in a number of crucial respects, however. It can be seen from equation 2.18 that Y_p refers to *a flow* of resources which the individual consumer unit could consume *whilst maintaining its wealth intact*. In other words, wealth does not enter directly as an explanatory variable, as in the life cycle hypothesis. This is not to say that wealth is irrelevant. Both human and non-human wealth are relevant in so far as they yield a stream of income, which in turn may influence permanent income. Rather it is the actual *stock* of wealth which does not enter as a determinant of consumption. Thus, the life cycle hypothesis relies on a concept of total resources as the explanatory variable, whilst the permanent income hypothesis relies on a flow of income over a somewhat shorter time scale.

A further distinction which can be made is that in the life cycle hypothesis a specific explanation is offered to suggest that the factor of proportionality (Ω) will vary systematically over the life cycle. In the Friedman hypothesis, no such explanation is provided.

According to the Friedman thesis, permanent income and permanent consumption are related to *measured income* and *measured consumption* as follows:

$$Y_p = Y_m - Y_t \qquad\qquad (2.19)$$

$$C_p = C_m - C_t \qquad\qquad (2.20)$$

where the subscripts denote permanent, measured and transitory components. Permanent income can therefore differ from measured income, according to whether *transitory income* is positive or negative. Transitory income refers to windfall gains and losses. Thus an unexpected Christmas bonus would represent a transitory gain, whilst the loss of income arising from an unforeseen strike would represent a transitory loss. The distribution of such gains and losses through time and across consumers is essentially random.

Similarly, permanent (or planned) consumption may differ from recorded consumption owing to transitory gains and losses (e.g. the acquisition of a commodity at 'special offer' sale price in the case of the former, the incidence of unexpected medical expenses on holiday in the case of the latter).

Friedman argues that permanent and transitory elements are related in the following manner:

$$rY_p Y_t = rC_p C_t = rY_t C_t = 0 \qquad\qquad (2.21)$$

where r is the correlation coefficient. The first two correlations assert in essence that transitory components of income and consumption are randomly distributed; this is relatively uncontroversial. The assertion that transitory income and transitory consumption have a zero correlation has been subjected to much closer scrutiny. After all, it seems to imply that if one were to win a substantial sum on the football pools one would be unlikely to buy a new car, or a larger house, or celebrate by taking a holiday in some exotic location. At first sight this appears counter-intuitive. Recall however the definition of permanent consumption – 'the *value of services* that is planned to consume during the period in question'. This implies that the consumer will plan to consume a certain amount of non-durable and durable services over a given period. Purchase and consumption of the former will of course occur in the same accounting period. Where the latter is concerned, however, purchase occurs in one period and consumption takes place over a number of succeeding periods (depending on the length of life of the durable). Thus the purchase of consumer durables is in fact a form of saving, and the increased purchase of consumer durables following an increase in Y_t is consistent with the proposition that variations in transitory income have an effect on the level of savings rather than on short-run consumption. Furthermore, a pools win may cause one to revise estimates of permanent income. When saved, it would yield a rate of return over future periods. In so far as this stream of expected income raises permanent income, it will raise permanent consumption. Note that this does not contradict either of the first two zero correlations in equation 2.21. It is not the transitory gain in income *per se* which has affected consumption; it is the conversion of this into wealth, and the subsequent impact of the return on the latter on estimates of permanent income, which affects consumption.

Friedman's Reconciliation of Cross-Section and Time Series Findings. Herein also lies Friedman's reconciliation of short-run and long-run findings. In figure 2.7, the true underlying relationship between consumption and income is traced out by the long-run function $C_p = kY_p$. Cross-section data will typically capture individuals with positive or negative transitory income. For instance, individual B could estimate his permanent income at Y_p^b, which would result in a permanent consumption level of C_p^b. The cross-section may be taken however when he enjoys a transitory gain of Y_t^b, giving the impression that measured income of Y_m^b results in measured consumption of C_m^b. In fact his savings ratio would be *mn*. This generates future income which may lead him to revise his estimate of permanent income. In the extreme case where the transitory component became permanent (for example, because the initially unexpected Christmas bonus becomes a permanent addition to income), Y_m^b would become $Y_p^{b'}$ and permanent consumption would be revised to $Cp_p^{b'}$, the savings ratio returning to its long-term trend *ms*. The same remarks apply *mutatis mutandis* to the case of individual A in the cross-section who is experiencing transitory negative income.[6]

Clearly, as with the life cycle hypothesis, if this model is to be made operational some proxy for permanent income must be found. Friedman suggested that it was reasonable to presume that individuals would estimate

---

6 Similar conclusions are reached if one reasons from transitory consumption gains and losses.

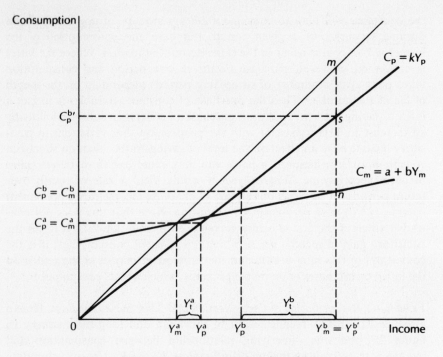

Figure 2.7   Permanent income hypothesis

permanent income from past income. Specifically he argued that

$$Y_{p_t} = Y_{p_{t-1}} + \lambda(Y_t - Y_{p_{t-1}}) \qquad (0 < \lambda < 1) \tag{2.22}$$

that is, permanent income is equal to last year's estimate of permanent income, plus some fraction of the difference between current measured income and last year's permanent income. In the event that Y_t and $Y_{p_{t-1}}$ are identical, no alteration would be made to the estimate of Y_{p_t}. If however $Y_t > Y_{p_{t-1}}$ then the estimate of Y_{p_t} would be revised upwards (and vice versa if $Y_t < Y_{p_{t-1}}$). This is a so-called *error learning process* and implies that the typical consumer unit forms his expectations of permanent income *adaptively*. Of course one might immediately question how an estimate of $Y_{p_{t-1}}$ was arrived at, since this is an integral component of equation 2.22. It too would have been estimated adaptively from $Y_{p_{t-2}}$. Likewise $Y_{p_{t-2}}$ would have been estimated from $Y_{p_{t-3}}$ and so on. Permanent income would therefore be estimated as a weighted average of past incomes with more distant observations being given less emphasis. With a geometrically declining

1   H/ 21110   55225-1   PB H/ 04120

MACROECONOMICS & THE BRITISH ECONOMY GREENAWAY   %147870

BLKW 0181   0631157638   17277019   ECON

0   1   0   0   0   0   0   0   0   0   0   1

1   RE-ORDER QUANTITY   NUMBER IN STOCK

series observations beyond seventeen periods become insignificant and the equation becomes:

$$Y_{p_t} = \lambda[Y_t + (1 - \lambda)Y_{t-1} + (1 - \lambda)^2 Y_{t-2} + \cdots + (1 - \lambda)^{17} Y_{t-17}]$$

$$(0 < \lambda < 1) \qquad (2.23)$$

which can be summarized by

$$Y_{p_t} = \lambda \sum_{n=0}^{17} (1 - \lambda)^n Y_{t-n} \qquad (2.24)$$

Since permanent consumption is some fraction of permanent income

$$C_{p_t} = k\lambda \sum_{n=1}^{17} (1 - \lambda) Y_{t-n} \qquad (2.25)$$

As was indicated at the outset, permanent consumption is dependent on permanent income, which is itself a function of past levels of income. As such it responds only modestly to changes in measured income.

Endogenous Income Theories

Perhaps the most significant contribution of the normal income theories is the way in which they highlight the intertemporal nature of consumption and savings decisions. It is this characteristic of consumption behaviour which serves to break any mechanistic link between current consumption and current income. Although this is an important development – and, within the context of the life cycle and permanent income hypotheses, provided a basis for reconciling the findings of cross-section and time series studies – the approach still leaves one fundamental issue open, namely the precise relationship between consumption and wealth. In the life cycle hypothesis, for example, wealth enters the model as an explanatory variable, that is as a determinant of current consumption. If however one gives a moment's thought to the determinants of wealth, it is clear that this is ultimately a function of consumption. A decision to save now presumably increases future wealth, which in turn increases future consumption. The implications of saving for the accumulation of wealth were not in fact explored by the normal income theories. A number of models which were subsequently developed however recognized and explored this interdependence (for example Spiro, 1962; Ball and Drake, 1963; Clower and Johnson, 1968).

Microeconomic Foundations

Like the normal income hypotheses, the *endogenous income hypothesis* is microeconomic in spirit. It commences from the observation that wealth is endogenous, and that it is a choice variable. When an individual consumer makes a choice between consuming and saving he is effectively choosing between consumption and wealth, since saving is an addition to wealth. Over a given period, therefore, the individual consumer (or more accurately the household) will strive to maximize utility, where utility is a function of consumption and wealth.

In figure 2.8 the objects of choice, consumption and wealth, are plotted on the vertical and horizontal axes respectively. For any given household the constraints on choice can be shown as given by a budget constraint *bc*,

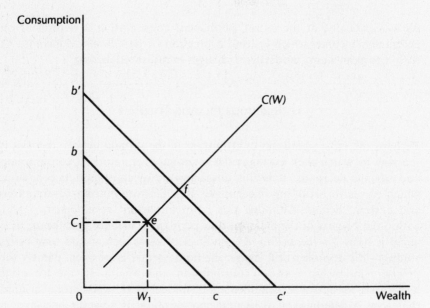

Figure 2.8   Effect of an increase in wealth on consumption

the location of which is determined by the household's total resources. As long as consumption and wealth can be measured in similar units, this budget constraint must have a slope of −1 on the assumption that total resources are used on consumption or wealth (via saving) or some combination thereof, such as $C_1 W_1$.

Suppose the budget constraint is shifted from bc to $b'c'$ by allowing for say a secular growth in income. With a budget constraint of bc the household is in equilibrium at point e. The desired amount of consumption of C_1 is taking place, and the desired amount of wealth of W_1 is held. Since *actual* wealth is equal to *desired* wealth, zero savings take place and current consumption exactly equals current income. If the resources constraint were to shift to $b'c'$, when full adjustment has taken place such that actual wealth is equal to desired wealth the household is settled at point f. When all such equilibrium points are joined up a *consumption–wealth locus* can be traced out. This gives the long-run relationship between consumption and wealth once full adjustments have taken place, and is analogous to the long-run consumption function. It has the characteristics of a zero intercept and a long-run savings ratio of zero. The configuration of the short-run consumption function can be explained by reference to disequilibrium situations.

Consider now figure 2.9. Suppose the initial position is that all households in a given wealth group are optimally adjusted at point e. Since this point is on the $C(W)$ locus, consumption is equal to income and the position is also on the $C = Y$ line in the right-hand segment. Suppose now that one household in the group experiences an increase in its income from Y_2 to Y_4. The resource constraint which it faces would shift as a consequence from bc to df and, once its optimal consumption and wealth combination were attained, equilibrium would be established at point k (and k' in the right-hand segment). In moving towards point k the household has to rearrange its consumption wealth portfolio. Initially it would shift to point g with wealth of W_2 and income of Y_4. At the new level of income, however, actual wealth (W_2) is less than desired wealth (W_4) and savings would take place in an attempt to increase wealth holdings. Initially savings would amount to eg. As wealth increases, consumption increases and the household moves out along the $C(W)$ locus towards equilibrium. An intermediate stage could be at point h where wealth has increased to W_3 consumption has increased to C_3 and savings amount to hj. If this is taken across to the right-hand segment the income–consumption combination of $Y_4 C_3$ is found. By connecting a series of such 'disequilibrium' points a consumption function can be derived like C_1 in the right-hand segment which appears to fit the cross-section 'facts'. Thus the endogenous income approach views the estimated cross-section consumption function simply as a record of disequilibrium situations – in any given cross-section there will be households consuming less than current income as they save to accumulate wealth, whilst other households will be dissaving to decumulate their wealth holdings towards some equilibrium level. In the long run, once all adjustments have taken place consumption will equal income in each wealth/income class and the long-run consumption function will have a zero intercept.

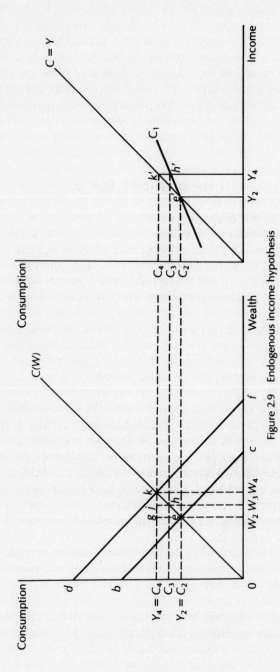

Figure 2.9 Endogenous income hypothesis

Thus, like the normal income theories, the endogenous income approach downgrades the importance of current income as a determinant of current consumption. Also in line with the normal income theories, the approach has solid microfoundations. It diverges from the normal income theories however in focusing on the interrelations between consumption, saving, wealth and income. In ascribing a central role to wealth as the principal determinant of consumption a variable is chosen which is *relatively* more precise than normal income.

Some Empirical Evidence

At an early point in this chapter we mentioned some empirical evidence on the consumption–income relationship, specifically the apparent contradiction between the short-run and long-run consumption functions. From the seminal work by Kuznets and others, a vast literature has now emerged. Comprehensive surveys of this evidence are provided by Mayer (1972) and Leighton Thomas (1984). In this section we shall sketch out the main features of the evidence.

One widely used approach to testing has been to examine the relationship between current consumption and current income. Friedman (1957), for example, followed this approach and estimated that the marginal propensity to consume out of current income was relatively low (0.3), compared with an MPC out of permanent income which exceeded 0.8. Friedman's results have not gone unchallenged. For instance, Wright (1969) used a similar data set to Friedman and estimated a much smaller difference in the MPCs. On the other hand as Darby (1974) has shown, also in the case of the USA, if consumption of durable goods is excluded from consumers' expenditure, Friedman may even have underestimated the difference between the two MPCs.

An alternative way of focusing on the relationship between current income and current consumption is to examine the impact of once and for all changes in income, i.e. explore the impact on consumption of transitory income. This has been tested by reference to a number of cases. Kreinin (1961), for example, assumed that reparation payments from West Germany to Israel constituted a windfall. He then estimated the marginal propensity to consume out of this windfall and found it to be very low, much lower than the MPC out of permanent income. Modigliani and Steindel (1977), using a life cycle model, found that the short-run effect on consumption of an unexpected income tax rebate was also relatively small (though still positive). Blinder (1981) examined the same tax rebate (as well as others), and concluded that temporary tax changes have a much smaller effect on consumption than permanent tax changes (although, again they *do* have an impact). This evidence certainly seems to be consistent with the view that some notion of normal income is more appropriate in explaining consumption behaviour than current income. As Mayer (1972) stated in an early survey of the empirical literature, 'While the more extreme ideas of the full permanent income and life cycle theory are invalidated, the tendency they describe ... is ... strongly confirmed' (p. 350).

One final point on empirical evidence is relevant. During the 1970s, savings propensities in many industrialized economies appear to have risen sharply. For instance in the UK the average propensity to save increased from about 8 per cent at the end of the 1960s to about 16 per cent at the end of the 1970s. Since, as we shall see in part III of this text, the 1970s were a period of accelerating inflation many analysts suspected this may have something to do with changes in the price level, and several studies addressed this issue. For example, one possible explanation is that consumers suffer from 'money illusion'. This is something we shall discuss in greater detail in part II of the book. In the present context it could be used as follows: an increase in the price level is perceived by consumers, but they do not notice the commensurate increases in income and wealth. They erroneously believe real income to have fallen and reduce consumption accordingly. Although Branson and Klevorick (1969) provide evidence to support the money illusion hypothesis, it is not a satisfactory explanation. As we shall argue later it is unappealing to contend that economic agents suffer from complete money illusion.

An alternative possibility was explored by Deaton (1978). He argued that it is the gap between actual and expected inflation which is relevant. In a period of accelerating inflation consumers may make errors in forecasting inflation and as a result they may confuse relative price changes and general price level changes. For example, when inflation turns out to be higher than expected, the consumer may interpret the increase in the price of some product currently being contemplated for purchase as a *relative* price change and as a result may refrain from purchasing. If this occurs across a wide range of consumers then an increase in the APS is recorded. Deaton (1978) offered some support for this hypothesis for the USA and UK, as did Townend (1976) for the UK.

Yet other possibilities have been explored, such as the possibility that increased inflation leads to increased uncertainty and this in turn raises savings. Whatever the precise mechanism, and this is still the subject of ongoing research, it seems that rising inflation does appear to reduce aggregate consumption.

Concluding Comments

The significance of having a clear idea of the determinants of aggregate consumption cannot be underestimated. Consumption expenditure is the largest component of aggregate expenditure. As such, variations in aggregate consumption exert a significant influence on aggregate expenditure. Clearly, if 'normal' income rather than 'current' income is the principal determinant of consumer expenditure, then aggregate expenditure is likely to be inherently more stable. Inevitably much of the empirical evidence is conflicting. What does seem clear, however, is that some notion of normal income or wealth, apart from being intuitively more appealing than current income, performs quite well as the principal determinant of current consumption.

It has to be emphasized that this chapter has not made an exhaustive survey of possible explanatory factors. For example, only a little time has been spent examining the influence of price level changes and expectations of price level changes. Nor has much attention been devoted to interest rate changes. The way in which future consumption can become attractive relative to present consumption was discussed within the permanent income model. Basically it was seen that savings increase following a rise in the interest rate because the return on wealth has increased. It should be noted, however, that the relationship need not be so simple, in part because of the diversity of assets which can be held as wealth, and in part because capital market imperfections may result in different interest rates applying to borrowers and lenders. Furthermore, interest rate expectations may also be important.

The acceleration of inflation in many developed market economies in recent years has resulted in considerable academic interest in the effect of changes in nominal variables like interest rates and the rate of inflation on aggregate consumption (see for example Pissarides, 1978 or Jackman and Sutton, 1982). The tools to explore fully these links have not yet been assembled here, and for the moment some poetic licence must be exercised in noting that evidence is growing that increases in the price level and increases in nominal interest rates do have a contractionary effect on aggregate consumption.

Further Reading

As with any other topic where the subject matter is controversial (which applies to most of the issues raised in this text), the best advice which can be given to students is look to the original sources. In this regard, chapters 6,

7, 8 and 9 of Keynes (1936) develop the principles of the absolute income hypothesis, whilst Duesenberry (1952) is the original statement of the relative income hypothesis. Friedman (1957) is the classic statement of the permanent income hypothesis, whilst the papers by Ando and Modigliani (1963), and Modigliani and Brumberg (1954) constitute the original sources of the life cycle hypothesis. Clower and Johnson (1968) was responsible for initiating much work on the endogenous income approach. Edited extracts from Friedman (1957), Ando and Modigliani (1963) and Clower and Johnson (1968) are to be found in Surrey (1975).

An early survey on theories of aggregate consumption paying particular attention to the normal income theories is Farrell (1959). More recent survey articles are Mayer (1972) and Ferber (1973); the latter can be found in Korilas and Thorn (1979). Bruce Johnson (1971) provides a concise and clear review of the principal hypotheses (although since the book is now out of print it is not easy to obtain). A shorter review is offered by Leighton Thomas (1984).

Good examples of some of the recent work on consumption behaviour and liquidity are Jackman and Sutton (1982) and Pissarides (1978).

The survey papers mentioned above give some details of empirical studies of consumption; for a couple of specific tests in the UK context see Bean (1978) and Davidson, Hendry, Srba and Yeo (1978). Life cycle models have been increasingly attacked in recent years on econometric grounds. See Hall (1978) Sargent (1978) and Eichenbaum, Hansen and Singleton (1984). A recent and notable defence is provided by Miron (1986).

3

Aggregate Investment Expenditure

Investment outlays are among the less stable components in the national income identity, and fluctuations in investment are a major factor underlying fluctuations in the level of economic activity generally. A knowledge of the determinants of investment behaviour, therefore, is important not only to the understanding of national income determination but also to any satisfactory explanation of the business cycle. Moreover, there are many economists who attach considerable importance to the relationship between investment outlays (as a percentage of gross national product (GNP)) and the rate of economic growth of GNP, or who see investment as the vehicle for endogenous innovation and technical change. Unfortunately, despite the undisputed importance attached in investment generally, this is still one of the most unsettled areas in macroeconomics, and one where the available empirical findings are subject to substantial differences in interpretation.

One difficulty arises from the heterogeneous nature of investment spending – a heterogeneity which tends to be masked by the aggregative symbol I in the national income equation. Essentially, four components of the investment aggregate may be distinguished.

Business Investment in Plant and Equipment. This is undeniably the most important and most volatile element in the total of investment spending, and the one which most theories, implicitly or otherwise, attempt to explain. Normally such theories are stated in terms of constrained optimizing behaviour by rational investing agents. Moreover, they tend to assume the profit maximizing motive, and thus are couched in terms of investment being continued up to the point where additional financial returns are just adequate to compensate for the additional costs incurred. As will be appreciated from even a rudimentary knowledge of microtheory, firms may in fact pursue other goals which violate this general principle.

Investment undertaken within the public sector, by public bodies, nationalized industries and so forth, is in complete contrast to the first component. In public sector investment decisions, economic logic may take second

43

place to political or social considerations. The desire to maintain employment, especially in depressed regions, or the attempt to minimize the adjustment problems associated with the secular decline of a traditional localized industry (shipping or textiles, for example), may dictate an investment pattern at variance with that which would be undertaken by private enterprise. Since such investment is essentially political in nature it is unlikely to be explicable in terms of economic theory *per se*. However, it may either compete with investment undertaken within the private sector or be complementary to it; failure to take account of such interdependence may seriously flaw one's approach to private sector investment.

Residential Construction. The decision to purchase a house, and the type of house which one elects to buy, is influenced by a host of factors, amongst the most important of which are government tax and monetary policy. However, house purchase is not necessarily an act of investment from the viewpoint of the national economy; the latter is concerned only with the net addition to the total housing stock. This net addition, new houses minus houses scrapped and depreciation on existing houses, is such a comparatively small portion of total house buying that it is difficult to identify with precision the governing influences. Given the lag between construction and sale, however, it would seem that credit policy must exercise a major role. Also, since house building is predominantly a labour intensive activity, it is of interest to a government concerned with unemployment figures and trends.

Investment in Inventories. Economists have long since recognized the importance of investment in stocks and inventories – indeed, at one extreme, inventory cycles geared to fluctuations in short-term interest rates have been suggested as the major cause of the trade cycle. Rationally, the short-term rate of interest would appear to be an important determinant of the decision to carry stocks. However, other influences undoubtedly enter the picture. Thus, for example, the decision as to the optimum inventory size will depend upon estimates of future demand conditions which may ultimately be shown to be widely inaccurate. This inaccuracy is reflected in unintended investment or disinvestment in stocks and inventory which plays havoc with regression coefficients aimed at explaining *intended* inventory investment decisions.

Whichever aspect of investment theory is of concern, however, there is always one element in common, namely that of time. The investment decision is concerned with suffering a financial outlay, or depletion of one's assets, against the expectation of a *future* income source or *future* augmentation of one's assets. It is because of this time dimension that it becomes imperative to be able to evaluate future returns and compute their present value or worth in order to understand the rationale of an investment decision.

The Cost of Capital and Investment

The Present Value of an Asset

Let a sum of money S_0 be invested at the market rate of interest i for a period of one year. At the end of the year the investment will be worth $S_0 + S_0 i$ or $S_0(1 + i)$. Let this amount be denoted as S_1, where the original *principal* was S_0 and the subscripts indicate the point in time. If the amount S_1 is now reinvested for a second year at the same rate of interest it will subsequently be worth $S_1 + S_1 i = S_1(1 + i)$, written as S_2. But recall that S_1 is merely $S_0(1 + i)$; hence S_2 – the amount that the sum S_0 will be worth if invested for two years at the interest rate i – is simply equal to $S_0(1 + i)(1 + i) = S_0(1 + i)^2$. Proceeding in this way, a sum of money S_0 invested for t years will realize $S_t = S_0(1 + i)^t$.

Let the argument now be reversed and the following question posed. If one knew *with certainty* that one could receive a sum of money in say t years' time by making a given outlay today, what size of outlay would justify the future income receipt? Suppose, for example, that one could be sure of obtaining the amount S_3 in three years' time. Since $S_3 = S_0(1 + i)^3$, the amount S_0 invested at current interest rates would yield the sum S_3 after three years. S_0 is accordingly the *present value* of the amount S_3 to be received in three years time, and it would be foolish to pay more than S_0 to obtain this future receipt. The present value of S_3 therefore is simply $S_3/(1 + i)^3$; in general, the present value of a future receipt S_t to be received in t years' time is simply $S_t/(1 + i)^t$.

This is the essence of the investment decision – the determination of how much it is worth while to pay to obtain an asset which will yield a future income receipt. In practice of course the issues are more complex. To begin with, the future income receipt expected from the asset will not be known with certainty, and indeed its *expected value* may be highly speculative. This will be particularly the case if the income receipt is expected far into the future. Second, the above argument is implicitly stated in real terms with no allowance being made for future inflationary price movements. To the extent that inflation is anticipated the present value of any future income receipt is accordingly reduced. Finally, the problem posed here is that of parting with a given sum of money today in order to receive a fixed sum at a finite date in the future. In practice, of course, the investment decision is

more complex in that it involves the purchase of an asset which will yield
successive income streams over the course of its expected useful life. Thus,
in computing the present value V of any investment asset, it is required to
estimate

$$V = \frac{Y_1}{(1+i)} + \frac{Y_2}{(1+i)^2} + \frac{Y_3}{(1+i)^3} + \cdots + \frac{Y_n}{(1+i)^n} + \frac{J_n}{(1+i)^n} \tag{3.1}$$

where Y is the net income yield in the period of the subscript, n is the
anticipated life of the asset and J is its scrap value. In this manner, it
becomes possible to compute the present value of any investment asset,
making allowance for conditions of uncertainty concerning net income
yields, asset life and so on.

It should be clear from this formulation that distant income streams
exercise a comparatively minor influence upon the present valuation of an
asset and hence upon the ultimate investment decision. The following
example may serve to illustrate this point. Consider an asset with a five-
year life yielding a net income stream of £100 per annum and possessed of a
scrap value of £50. With an interest rate of 10 per cent its computed present
value will be given by

$$V = \frac{100}{(1+0.1)} + \frac{100}{(1+0.1)^2} + \frac{100}{(1+0.1)^3}$$

$$+ \frac{100}{(1+0.1)^4} + \frac{100}{(1+0.1)^5} + \frac{50}{(1+0.1)^5}$$

$$= 90.909 + 82.645 + 75.131 + 68.301 + 62.093 + 31.046$$

$$= 410.125 \tag{3.2}$$

Thus the first year's income stream is worth approximately 50 per cent
more than that of the fifth year; had the asset yielded an income of £100 in
the tenth year its present value would have been £38.551 and in the twen-
tieth year £14.863.

Now consider the same asset possessed of identical yields but assume the
market rate of interest is but 5 per cent. Its computed present value is

$$V = \frac{100}{(1+0.05)} + \frac{100}{(1+0.05)^2} + \frac{100}{(1+0.05)^3}$$

$$+ \frac{100}{(1+0.05)^4} + \frac{100}{(1+0.05)^5} + \frac{50}{(1+0.05)^5}$$

$$= 95.238 + 90.703 + 86.386 + 82.270 + 78.352 + 39.176$$

$$= 472.125 \tag{3.3}$$

The halving of the rate of interest raises the present value of the asset – in this case by approximately 15 per cent. However, the point to be stressed here is that the augmentation of present values in both absolute and percentage terms is greater for the more distant income streams. The value of the fifth year's revenue yield, for example (as well as the potential scrap value) rises by more than 26 per cent compared with the augmentation in value of the first year's receipts of less than 5 per cent.

This analysis suggests that when interest rates are high there will be a marked preference for investment in short-lived assets; alternatively, policies to lower long-term interest rates may influence not only the volume but also the allocation of investable funds, with arguably beneficial impact upon long-term growth rates.

The foregoing has suggested that the present value of an asset is related to the expected net income yield to be derived from ownership of that asset. The question which remains is what determines the expected net income yield. Inevitably a host of influences enter here, including psychological factors such as the state of business confidence which may or may not be grounded on relevant economic criteria. Undoubtedly, however, one of the more objective influences will be the existing stock of the asset in question. If one is contemplating building a hotel upon the Aegean shore one's expected return might well depend upon whether there existed other hotels in competition. Increasing the stock of an asset increases the potential supply of goods and services to be derived from that asset, and thus *ceteris paribus* reduces potential prices and anticipated revenue yields. Hence an inverse relationship might be postulated between the present value of an asset and the existing stock of such assets. Such a relationship is indicated in figure 3.1.

The Decision to Invest

So far the concern has been with determining the present value of an investment asset – that is, what the asset is judged to be worth. Following Keynes (1936) this may be referred to as the *demand price*. But the decision to invest not only involves the demand price but also hinges upon the cost of acquiring the asset. Clearly, if the present value of an asset exceeds the cost of acquiring it then it is rational to purchase the asset; equally, if the present value falls short of the purchase cost of the asset then it would be foolish to acquire the asset. Thus, following marginalist principles and tacitly assuming profit maximizing behaviour, the proposition is approached that investment in any asset will be pushed to the point where the demand price or present value is just equated with its cost.

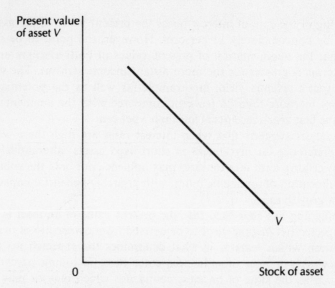

Figure 3.1 · Present value of an asset in relation to the capital stock of the asset

However, it is necessary to distinguish between an act of investment upon the part of an individual and investment from the point of view of society. As far as the individual is concerned, in deciding whether or not to 'invest' he weighs the demand price of an asset against its acquisition costs; in many cases the latter will refer to the sum needed to induce an existing investor to transfer ownership of the asset. The concern here, however, is with investment as it enters into the national income accounting identity, and consequently such transfers of existing second-hand assets are not relevant. By investment is meant the creation of newly produced assets by the capital goods industry, and thus the term 'cost of the asset' should be taken to refer to the price needed to induce the capital goods industry to produce an additional unit of the asset. Again, following Keynes, this cost may be termed the *supply price* of the asset.

A simple statement of investment behaviour may now be presented. If the demand price or present value of an asset, V, exceeds its supply price X, it is rational to invest in the asset. On the other hand, if the demand price falls short of the supply price investment is not warranted. If this argument is pursued to its logical conclusion and avoiding complications arising from indivisibilities and so forth, it is evident that the optimal stock of any capital asset will be determined by the equation of its demand price with its supply price. This situation is portrayed in figure 3.2. The optimal situation is indicated by K^* where V equals X and net investment demand is zero.

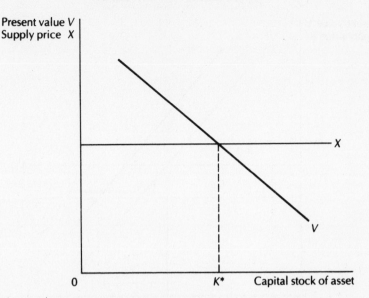

Figure 3.2   Determining the optimal stock of a capital asset

Before this level of the capital stock, V exceeds X, the actual capital stock falls short of the desired or optimal, and *net investment demand* is accordingly positive; beyond this level of the capital stock, V is less than X, the actual capital stock is too large, and there will accordingly be incentives to disinvestment.[1]

It can now be understood why economists have long argued that investment spending will be inversely related to the rate of interest. Whilst the interest sensitivity of investment spending is a matter of some empirical dispute there is no mistaking the underlying rationale of the assertion. A fall in the market rate of interest will, as has already been demonstrated arithmetically, raise the present value of the asset reflected in the upward shift of the demand price. Equally, however, a decrease in interest rates may reduce costs in the capital goods industries and generate a fall in the prevailing supply price. Both influences serve to generate a new optimal level of the capital stock in question, as illustrated by figure 3.3.

---

1 The horizontal supply price of capital schedule derives from the assumption of perfect capital markets. A departure from this assumption, by assuming for example that greater risk is involved in supplying a large amount of capital to one firm as opposed to smaller amounts to many firms, or by invoking differences in physical or subjective supply costs, would be sufficient to generate an upward sloping schedule.

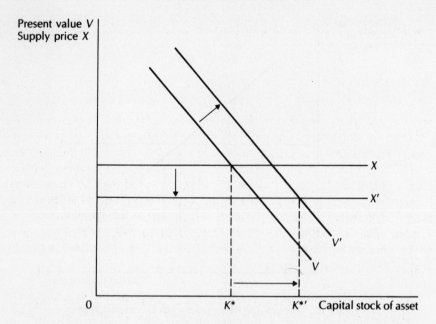

Figure 3.3   Effect of a decrease in interest rates on the optimal stock of a capital asset –
present value approach

The Marginal Efficiency of Capital

An alternative but not identical way of approaching the investment decision
was proposed by Keynes with his concept of the *marginal efficiency of
capital* (MEC). Essentially, the marginal efficiency of capital r is that rate of
discount which will equate the anticipated net income streams to be derived
from the asset to the supply price of the asset. More formally, if X is again
the supply price of the asset,

$$X = \frac{Y_1}{(1+r)} + \frac{Y_2}{(1+r)^2} + \frac{Y_3}{(1+r)^3} + \cdots + \frac{Y_n}{(1+r)^n} + \frac{J_n}{(1+r)^n} \qquad (3.4)$$

Whatever the value of the income streams and whatever the cost of the
asset there is some rate of discount r which can be chosen so as to equate
the two. This is what Keynes chose to call the marginal efficiency of capital.

   It should be clear that the marginal efficiency of capital is in some sense a
rate of return upon the asset in question. To illustrate, consider the simplest
possible example, namely that of an asset which costs £1,000 and lasts for
but one year whereupon it falls to pieces with no possible scrap value. If
during the course of its short life it returns say £1,300, net of labour,

materials, and similar 'user' costs, then its marginal efficiency of capital would be derived from

$$£1,000 = \frac{£1,300}{(1 + r)}$$

and $r = 0.3$. Alternatively, its rate of return over cost may be said to be 30 per cent. As long as the computed marginal efficiency of capital is positive it implies that net revenue yields are sufficient to cover the supply price of the asset. However, this is not sufficient to justify the act of investment, for the money allocated to the purchase of the asset could equally have been loaned out at the market rate of interest. Only if the marginal efficiency of capital is in excess of the going market rate of interest would investment be justified. The rational investment decision, therefore, requires a comparison of the marginal efficiency of capital with the current rate of interest, and the logic of this argument leads to the conclusion that

> the actual rate of current investment will be pushed to the point where there is no longer any class of capital asset of which the marginal efficiency exceeds the current rate of interest. (Keynes, 1936, p. 136)

Diagrammatically, this situation is portrayed in figure 3.4 where once again K^* is the indicated optimal capital stock.[2] The effect of a decrease in the rate of interest i may be examined. Clearly, the interest rate line is lowered suggesting a positive expansion of investment, but if reduced interest charges also lower the supply price of the asset this movement is reinforced by an upward shift in the marginal efficiency schedule. The dashed lines illustrate this combined influence and indicate a new equilibrium at $K^{*'}$.

The marginal efficiency approach may be considered as an alternative to the direct comparison of present value and supply price, and the situation $V > X$ will often imply the condition $r > i$. However, it is important to note that the two approaches will not always give the same result at least from the vantage-point of the individual investor choosing between two alternative investment decisions. This arises because, whilst an interest rate change

---

2 The marginal efficiency of capital schedule is drawn with a negative slope with respect to the capital stock for precisely the same reasons as applied to the concept of present value. As the capital stock is increased so too is the potential supply of goods and services derived from the asset, with a consequent fall in their prices and hence in the expected net revenue yield.

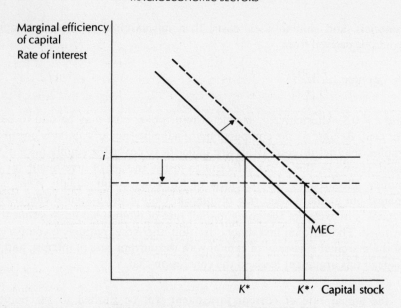

Figure 3.4   Effect of a decrease in interest rates on the optimal stock of a capital asset –
marginal efficiency of capital approach

will not affect the marginal efficiency of capital in any systematic way,[3] it
will exert differing effects upon the present values of assets with differing
time profiles, as has already been noted.[4]

The Rate of Investment

Thus far the concern has been with formulating a simple rule to determine
the optimal amount of any capital asset from the viewpoints of both the
individual investor and the macroeconomy as a whole. In equilibrium, no
asset would have a demand price in excess of its supply price or a marginal
efficiency of capital in excess of the rate of interest. What has not been done,
however, is to indicate how the economy makes the adjustment from one
indicated equilibrium to another. Consider again figure 3.3, where the initial
demand and supply prices of a capital asset suggest the optimal amount of

---

3 Indeed, an interest rate change will leave the MEC schedule unchanged if it
does not affect the supply price of capital assets.

4 Keynes was clearly not aware of this discrepancy and believed that his marginal
efficiency of capital concept was simply a restatement of Irving Fisher's rate of
return over cost. See Keynes, 1936, pp. 140–1. For comment on the distinctions see
especially Alchian (1955).

the asset to be K^*. Suppose that this indicated optimum actually prevails, so that net investment demand is zero. Now assume a fall in the market rate of interest. It may be supposed that this raises the present value of the asset in question as well as reducing the supply price, and the new indicated optimal stock of the asset is accordingly $K^{*'}$. Thus the actual capital stock now lags behind the optimal or desired stock by the amount $K^* - K^{*'}$.

Is there any satisfactory way in which this discrepancy in the desired *stock* of capital can be translated into an investment *flow* demand? What is needed is a statement to explain the size of the investment flow demand by which the capital stock is enlarged or contracted. Without such a statement there can be no acceptable theory of investment as such but only a theory of optimum capital stocks. It is at this point that certain conceptual and empirical difficulties are encountered that are not readily resolved.

Until now it has been assumed, albeit tacitly, that the supply price of capital assets was given as a datum existing independently of the actual speed of the capital stock adjustment process. For any individual firm this is probably acceptable as it can purchase from existing inventories and stocks, but for the economy as a whole it is probably false. More reasonably, the supply price of capital assets will be positively related to the speed of adjustment.[5] This situation is illustrated in figure 3.5, where the capital goods industry is assumed to be geared to meeting normal replacement demands, $0R$, at a constant cost X. Beyond this point, however, positive net investment is assumed to encounter progressively rising marginal costs and hence a rising supply price positively related to the rate of investment.

The salient features of the analysis contained in figures 3.3 and 3.5 are now combined. In figure 3.6, where the actual capital stock is denoted by K^* whilst the optimal stock is $K^{*'}$, the demand price of an *incremental* unit of the asset is indicated by $v£$ whilst the supply price of the incremental unit is $x£$. This incremental unit will accordingly be produced within the current period. As the capital stock is adjusted, however, the demand price of successive incremental units will decline whilst, under present assumptions, the supply price will rise. Clearly the indicated equilibrium is at K^e where demand and supply prices are equated. Thus the optimal amount of investment during the current period is $K^e - K^*$, and similar reasoning will imply a determinate optimal investment strategy in succeeding periods with the positive portion of the curve now emanating from K^e. In this manner

5 Were it not, investors would seek to make indicated adjustments instantaneously, giving rise to infinite rates of investment and disinvestment demand. In such circumstances actual investment spending would be determined by the capacity of the capital goods industry on the one hand and by the rate of depreciation and obsolescence upon the other.

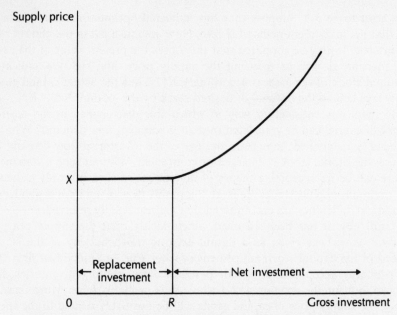

Figure 3.5   Supply price of capital in relation to the rate of investment

the gap between the initial actual and desired capital stock will be progress-ively eliminated over succeeding investment periods, with investment demand in the current period always being less than in the immediately preceding period.[6]

It is now a simple step to generate the investment demand curve. In the initial equilibrium situation the desired and actual capital stock were equated and consequently the level of investment demand was zero. With the decline in the interest rate a first-period investment demand equal to $K^* - K^e$ was generated. Thus a normal investment demand curve is obtained, inversely related to the rate of interest. In successive periods the level of investment progressively falls as the gap between actual and desired capital stocks is reduced. Ultimately, as a new equilibrium is regained the level of investment demand falls to zero. Thus a fall in the rate of interest will generate a positive and determinate investment demand curve which over succeeding periods is progressively shifted inwards until it ultimately coincides with the vertical axis at existing interest rates. This process of adjustment from one equilibrium to another is shown in figure 3.7.

---

6 Strictly, under present assumptions, the gap between K^* and $K^{*\prime}$ will tend to but never actually attain zero.

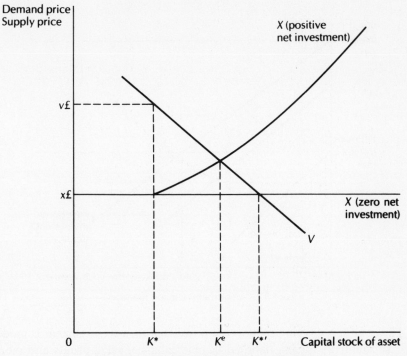

Figure 3.6   Determining the rate of investment

The foregoing analysis has indicated that investment involves two distinct issues; first the need to determine the desired capital stock, and second
the need to determine the pace at which any indicated adjustment to the
desired capital stock will occur. It follows, *inter alia*, that monetary policy
must be evaluated in terms of this dual context. Thus, for example, a given
interest rate change may have a profound impact upon the desired capital
stock but exert a minor influence upon the level of current investment
spending. It is the latter consideration which is paramount in short-term
stabilization policy.

Dynamic Theories of Investment Behaviour

Admittedly, the previous analysis has been static and has dealt with interest
rate changes under the assumption of *ceteris paribus*. This implies that once
an equilibrium has been attained net investment will return to zero and all
investment spending will be replacement investment only.

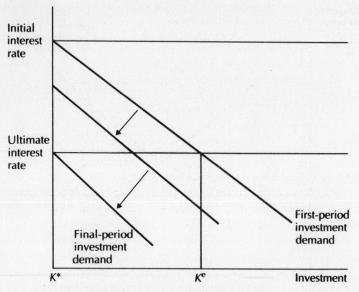

Figure 3.7   Investment demand function

However, if a growing economy is postulated then the argument is modi-fied substantially. Rising national income enhances sales, profits and more importantly expectations of future sales and profits. In the context of the former analysis this would imply a rising of discounted present values or the demand prices of capital assets and justify positive net investment. If the economy were growing in a steady state equilibrium this would generate a steady state growth of net investment spending. Although the existence of steady states cannot be assumed, it can none the less be asserted that investment will be positively related to movements in national income.

There are a number of theories which relate investment to income levels. By far the most well known, and certainly one of the oldest, is the so-called *accelerator theory* of investment.[7] This postulates a fixed technical relation-ship between capital and output. An increase in final demand justifies more output and hence calls forth more net investment. A simple example will illustrate the essence of the doctrine and also highlight its limiting assump-tions. Assume that the capital stock consists of 10 units, each with a life of five years and each producing ten units of final output per year. Then in a steady state situation final demand would be equal to 100 units of output, net investment would be zero and replacement investment would equal 2

---

7 The first attempts to formulate a coherent accelerator theory of investment appear to have been by Bickerdike (1914) and Clark (1917).

units per year. In such a situation, suppose final demand rises to 120 units. Given a fixed capital output ratio this would require 12 units of capital, implying net investment equal to 2 units. A 20 per cent increase in final demand, therefore, is responsible for generating a 100 per cent increase in total investment spending. Moreover, assume that in the following period final demand remains unchanged at its new level; there is no further justification for net investment, and in this example gross investment spending would now be halved although final demand has not fallen. Thus the accelerator theory relates the level of investment spending to *changes* in the rate at which output is changing, and in large measure goes a long way to explain the unstable nature of investment outlays.

The elementary model outlined above is altogether too mechanistic to furnish a precise insight into investment behaviour in the real world. It assumes away the existence of stocks and inventories and the possibility of excess capacity. It assumes that there are no constraints upon new investment activity, whether financial or otherwise, and further it postulates an automatic response to temporary fluctuations in consumer spending without any lags to establish the permanency of the demand change. None the less, it goes some way to explain the volatility of investment spending and the acceleration principle is an indispensable element (in some form or another) in almost any modern explanation of the business cycle. Its dynamic nature derives from the fact that investment in the current period depends upon the state of demand in the immediately preceding period. Formally, the elementary model outlined may be specified as

$$I_t = \alpha(S_t - S_{t-1}) \tag{3.5}$$

where I is net investment, S is final sales demand and the subscript denotes the period involved. If it is assumed that final sales demand is proportional to national income, the more usual formulation of the acceleration principle is obtained:

$$I_t = \beta(Y_t - Y_{t-1}) \tag{3.6}$$

In this formulation the accelerator coefficient (α or β) is taken to be a constant and the indicated investment spending is assumed to be completed within one period, permitting net investment to return to zero if there is no further change in demand.

Both of these are fundamental shortcomings of the naïve or simple accelerator model. A *constant accelerator coefficient* implicitly assumes that the firm is operating at full capacity and will respond to an increase in demand with new investment. It goes without saying that if a firm has spare capacity then this will be utilized prior to any new investment. In an economic climate with many firms operating at less than full capacity, one would imagine that as and when an upturn occurred it would be some time before investment responded as idle capacity was used up. Furthermore, even if the firm is operating at full capacity there are bound to be lags involved in the reaction to any perceived change in demand. New capacity is unlikely to be planned let alone investable funds committed until such time as the firm is confident that the change in demand is permanent rather than transient. Even when a decision to commit funds has been taken there are inevitably supply lags of the type mentioned in connection with the Keynesian marginal efficiency of capital approach.

These difficulties can be relatively easily accommodated. For example, one could allow for spare capacity by rewriting equation 3.6 as

$$I_t = \beta(Y_t - Y_{t-1}) - \delta K_t \tag{3.7}$$

where δK_t is the proportion of the capital stock which is currently idle. Likewise, lags can be accommodated by permitting adjustment to occur over a number of periods. This more realistic version of the acceleration principle is sometimes referred to as the *flexible accelerator model*.

According to this formulation, which enjoys a certain amount of empirical support, investment is geared to the difference between the actual and the optimal capital stock with the latter being linked to income growth. Thus

$$I_t = \alpha(K^* - K_{t-1}) \tag{3.8}$$

and $K^* = \gamma Y$. Rising income generates an increase in the optimal capital stock and thus raises net investment outlays. It will be noted that the adjustment to the optimal capital stock occurs with progressively declining magnitudes of net investment, in keeping with the static analysis of the capital stock adjustment process. The process is shown in figure 3.8. At time t the optimal capital stock K^* is assumed to be double the actual capital stock K. With an accelerator coefficient equal to 0.75, three-quarters of this deficiency will be made up over the succeeding period t_1, three-quarters of the remainder (that is, three-sixteenths) will be made up in period t_2, and so forth. As before, the actual capital stock asymptotically approaches but never actually attains the optimum.

Another conceptual problem with the fixed accelerator coefficient, which strictly speaking is not accommodated by the flexible accelerator in any systematic manner, is that it does not allow for changes in production technique due to variations in relative factor prices. In microeconomic terms it assumes in effect that movement from one isoquant to another takes place along a linear expansion path. Intuitively this is not an attractive or appealing proposition; it denies the possibility of adjustments towards the optimal capital stock being relatively labour saving or capital

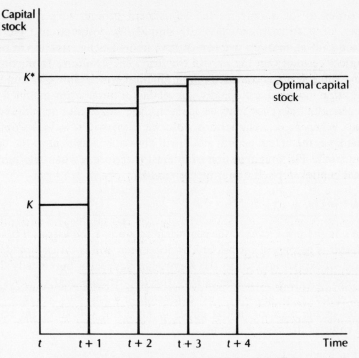

Figure 3.8   Investment with the flexible accelerator

saving, or more accurately it precludes switches from one to the other. It is the neglect of this aspect of investment behaviour which has encouraged the modern neo-classical approach.

The Neo-classical Analysis of Investment

The neo-classical approach is associated with the work of Jorgensen (1967). This approach is of interest for several reasons. First, like the Keynesian cost of capital approach it is firmly rooted in microeconomic foundations. Second, it focuses on the cost of capital but unlike the Keynesian analysis it emphasizes the cost of capital relative to other inputs rather than the cost of capital *per se*. Third, whereas the Keynesian and accelerator approaches have something to say about both the determination of the optimal capital stock and the factors which influence adjustment when the optimal and actual capital stocks diverge, the neo-classical approach concentrates only on the former.

In order to focus only on the adjustment process Jorgensen makes a number of (standard neo-classical) simplifying assumptions. Thus it is assumed that all markets are competitive and efficient, ensuring in particular perfect certainty on the part of the firm. The firm aims to maximize its present value subject to a production function which embodies continuous substitution possibilities. Finally, as all factor inputs are assumed to be homogeneous, reference may be made to 'the' wage rate and 'the' cost of capital. When these assumptions hold the firm will always be optimally adjusted, i.e. the actual capital stock will always be identical to the optimal capital stock. The only question of interest therefore is what determines the optimal capital stock. In the Jorgensen model

$$K^* = f(p, w, c) \qquad (3.9)$$

where p is the price level, w the real wage rate and c the *user cost of capital*. The latter is a concept introduced by Jorgensen and is rather broader than the cost of capital implicit in the Keynesian approach. Specifically the real user cost of capital is influenced by the opportunity cost of investing in capital goods r, an allowance for depreciation d and an allowance for any changes in the price of capital goods $\dot{q}$, since this will affect the resale or scrap value of the asset. Formally

$$\frac{c}{p} = \frac{r + d - \dot{q}}{p} \qquad (3.10)$$

From Jorgensen's standpoint the crucial variable in the determination of the optimal capital stock is the real user cost of capital relative to the real wage rate. Other things being equal, increases in the real wage rate relative to the real user cost of capital will result in a more capital intensive production technique, and therefore increases in the optimal capital stock. The approach is compelling in its simplicity and, at the very least, has helped redirect attention towards the role of relative factor prices.

The Importance of Profit and Retained Earnings

Implicit in the accelerator analysis is the notion that profits, or the expectation of profits, is an essential ingredient in the investment decision. Certain commentators have refined this notion to focus upon one element of profits, namely *retained earnings*, as being a crucial determinant in the volume of investment spending. The reason is that firms will have a strong preference to finance investment out of retained earnings as opposed to using debt finance or issuing new equity. The (imputed) cost of using retained earnings will be less, often substantially less, than the cost of borrowing in the capital market whilst the issue of new equity suggests a weakening of overall control by increasing the number of shareholder votes. Retained earnings are equal to net profits (after meeting provision for depreciation needs) less any tax payments to government or dividend payment to shareholders. One policy implication of the analysis is that any factor increasing the size of retained earnings, such as tax cuts or more generous depreciation allowances, may have a sizeable impact on investment outlays.

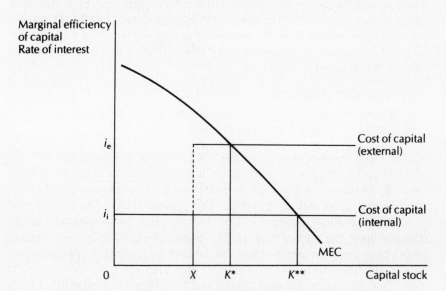

Figure 3.9   Internal and external funds and the optimal capital stock

This situation is illustrated in figure 3.9, which reverts to the Keynesian marginal efficiency of capital approach. Although it has previously been indicated that this approach is logically inferior to the discounted present value approach, it does possess one expositional virtue in *explicitly* including the current cost of funds in the determination of the optimal capital stock. In figure 3.9 the cost of using internal funds is i_i and the cost of employing external funds is i_e. If internal funds are limited to $0X$ the optimal capital stock is shown to be K^*; with unlimited internal funds the

optimal capital stock would be K^{**}. The size of retained earnings, therefore, may be an important determinant of the desired capital stock but of
itself it does not specifically indicate anything about the nature of investment demand – that is, the speed of adjustment to the desired capital stock.
For this some other hypothesis is needed, such as the flexible accelerator
model briefly outlined earlier.

Some Policy Implications

Various possible determinants of investment behaviour have been indicated,
and it is now possible to take stock and describe, if only briefly, the distinct
policy stances arising from the analysis. For this purpose, the classification
originally proposed by Jorgensen and Siebert (1968) is followed. Competing
theories are denoted as

(1) Neo-classical theories
(2) Keynesian oriented (accelerator/expected profit) theories
(3) Liquidity (retained earnings) theories.

Neo-classical theories are predictably marginalist in approach and view the
cost of capital, relative to other factor inputs, as crucial in the investment
decision. Markets are assumed to clear, and profit maximizing behaviour
requires that firms seek to maximize their present values. The fundamental
conclusion of these models is that the demand for investment goods
depends upon the cost of capital. The principal objection to neo-classical
theory rests upon the premise that the demand for investment goods cannot
be derived from the profit maximizing theory of the firm. Following the
stock/flow distinction between capital and investment first noted by Lerner
(1944), it is argued that finite variations in interest rates will *ceteris paribus*
generate finite variations in the desired capital stock which in turn will
imply either *infinite* rates of investment or disinvestment or zero investment
demand in the condition of equilibrium. There is accordingly only one rate
of interest consistent with a finite investment demand and that demand is
purely replacement demand. It is difficult to construct a worthwhile theory
of investment upon such a premise. Even if it is possible to derive a meaningful investment demand function from the conventional theory of the
firm, as Jorgensen (1967) insists, by adopting the thesis that the firm pursues
a continuous optimal path of capital accumulation, significant policy conclusions do not necessarily follow. The importance of changes in relative
prices, occasioned by monetary changes operating upon the rate of interest

or fiscal changes upon the user cost of capital, will depend upon the elasticity of substitution of the aggregate production function.[8] It is generally conceded that the value of this coefficient will lie between zero and one. A value close to one will imply that an interest rate change, for example, will exert a significant impact upon investment demand, whereas an elasticity of substitution coefficient close to zero will imply that comparative factor prices changes exert but minimal effect.

Keynesian oriented theories posit that interest rate changes and relative factor price changes have a minor effect in comparison with changing profit expectations associated with the uncertain level of future demand. This indeed appears to be Keynes's emphasis in his celebrated defence of the *General Theory* (Keynes, 1937a). To the extent that future profit expectations disproportionately reflect the current state of affairs, this contention would appear to lend support to the accelerator theory. The policy implication is that investment can be stimulated by suitable demand management policies.

The neo-classical thesis suggests that price flexibility, and especially comparative price flexibility, fulfils an important role in determining the investment decision. Policies which promote competition and allow free movement of labour and capital are thus important to the efficient allocation of investable funds. Keynesian oriented policies, on the other hand, tend to question the significance of comparative factor price flexibility on grounds of empirically observed price rigidities.

A compromise position which straddles these two opposing schools of thought suggests that interest rates and relative prices are important in determining the desired equilibrium capital stock, whereas the level of aggregate demand together with profit expectations remains a powerful tool

---

8 The elasticity of substitution measures the responsiveness of the change in factor combinations in response to the change in comparative factor prices. It can be represented as

$$E_s = \frac{d(L/K)}{d(r/w)} \frac{(r/w)}{(L/K)}$$

where L and K are the labour and capital inputs and w and r are their respective prices per unit of time. In the mathematically convenient (and hence frequently invoked) Cobb–Douglas constant returns production function

$$Q = AL^\alpha K^{1-\alpha}$$

the elasticity value is equal to one, so that as relative factor prices alter, exactly compensatory changes occur in factor proportions leaving respective income shares constant.

for influencing the actual rate of investment demand in the adjustment process – especially in non-market clearing situations which imply trading at disequilibrium prices.

Although empirical findings in support of differing interpretations have often been invoked, the evidence suffers from the difficulty of distinguishing between cause and effect with the result that controversy still remains. In particular, the failure thus far to obtain a strong clear cut relationship between investment spending and interest rates has been invoked to suggest a possible invalidation of the monetarist transmission mechanism between monetary and real economic variables. These findings have been reinforced by the results of admittedly deficient questionnaires which purport to deny any significant role to interest rates (see White, 1936). However, in opposition to this point of view it can be argued that monetary forces exert a *direct* and powerful impact upon the level of aggregate demand and output which in turn can stimulate investment outlays. Arguments along these lines are forcibly presented by Laidler (1971a). One conclusion which appears to emerge and enjoy a reasonable consensus in the empirical findings is the relative unimportance of liquidity theories (retained earnings) in determining the corporate investment decision. Whilst arguably important to small- and medium-sized firms this would not appear to be a major constraint for large organizations which collectively dominate aggregate business investment behaviour. Finally, it may be noted that the time lag involved in the investment response to changes in the fundamental variables governing investment are both long and variable. It would, therefore, appear unlikely that government attempts to manipulate investment spending would contribute significantly to meeting short-term stabilization goals.

Concluding Comments

In this chapter a variety of approaches to the determination of investment has been considered; these approaches emphasize in particular either the role of output changes (like the accelerator approach) or some aspect of the cost of capital. As was seen in the final section there is a certain amount of empirical support which can be advanced in support of both factors. This should not be read as evidence of inconclusiveness since both may have a role to play. Some notion of the cost of capital is clearly relevant to the determination of the optimal capital stock, with variations in output and profit being more relevant to the analysis of adjustments when there is some discrepancy between the actual and optimal capital stocks.

Further Reading

Keynes's (1936) analysis of the marginal efficiency of capital approach to investment remains one of the clearest outlines of the basic principles involved. Although the acceleration principle was first formally identified by Clark (1917), Eckaus (1953) is a neat statement of the theorem. Knox (1952) provided a lucid and thorough critique of the simple accelerator model. Flexible accelerator models have been developed and refined over the past fifteen years or so. Smyth (1964) provides an interesting example. Jorgensen (1967) is usually credited with the seminal contribution to the neo-classical approach to investment.

Surveys of empirical studies of investment behaviour are available in Jorgensen (1971) and Lund (1971). A concise (if inevitably terse) survey of theoretical and empirical studies of investment is given in Junankar (1972).

A useful collection of readings is provided by Helliwell (1976).

4

The Government Sector

Of all the sectors making up the macroeconomy, the government sector ranks as both the most important and in many respects the least susceptible to economic analysis. The importance of government in influencing the aggregate economy cannot be underestimated and it stems from a combination of the following factors.

Size. The sheer size of the government sector means that virtually any government decision will impinge upon the economy at large. The government is a substantial employer of labour and hence the adoption of a given stance upon public sector pay will have repercussions upon private sector pay bargaining. The government will also exercise considerable discretion in matters of timing when meeting backdated pay settlements, for example, and thus will be able to time such payments so as to exert their most favourable macroeconomic impact. Finally, the government is the prime example of a monopsonistic buyer and is able to command substantial discounts in its buying policies which inevitably impinge upon contracts in the private sector.

Production and Consumption. The government sector plays a major role in both producing and consuming national output. It is therefore of considerable importance not only as a constituent of aggregate demand but also in supplying resources to the private sector. In particular, its pricing policy for public sector services and the output of nationalized undertakings will have major implications for private sector profitability. In this connection, it may be noted that the price index for public sector output and services often deviates substantially from general price indices invoked to measure overall inflation.

Regulatory Powers. Third, the government exercises considerable regulatory powers which often imply substantial compliance costs for the private sector. Stipulations about safety procedures, pollution control, product liability legislation and so forth may exercise considerable influence especially upon exporters competing in international markets where such restrictions may not apply. Other legislation, such as employment protection legislation, termination agreements and legislation determining the rights and obligations of trade unions carry obvious implications for private sector employment costs.

Policy Control. Of principal importance is the fact that the government shapes and dictates the course of macroeconomic policy and is able to impose coercive penalties upon the other sectors in the form of tax and interest rate changes. Alternatively, of course, the government may choose to pursue a monetary and fiscal stance deemed favourable to the private sector. Of fundamental importance will be the government's strategy on regional policy, or upon the adoption of exchange controls, import controls and so forth. Above all, the government more than any other economic sector will exert a dominant influence upon the formation of expectations.

Debt Funding. Although any economic sector is able to enter into debt obligations, the government sector, at least at the central government level, is unique in being able to fund its debt obligations by measures which are tantamount to an increase in the supply of high-powered money.

Political Influences. Finally, the government sector may adopt a pattern of behaviour which departs from the strictly economic rationale which is assumed to underly behaviour in other sectors. This is not to deny the premise of maximizing behaviour *per se* upon the part of the government sector, but merely to assert that political considerations may take precedence over purely economic ones.

The Composition of Government Expenditure and Revenue

With reference to the size of the government sector, central and local government combined are responsible for expenditures totalling approximately 44 per cent of GNP (see Black, 1985). This figure, however, should not be taken to indicate the actual command of the government sector over resources since a substantial portion of government spending takes the form of *transfer payments* to the private sector. None the less, government transfer payments will influence the overall allocation of resources even though control of such expenditure remains with the private sector. This will be the case, for example, with taxes imposed upon the relatively well-to-do to finance unemployment benefit and supplementary benefits to the poor and unemployed.

Government expenditures can be conveniently subdivided into three groups. First of all, there is *current spending* upon goods and services such as in health, education and defence. Collectively, these will amount to approximately 21 per cent of GNP. Second, transfer payments in the form of pensions, unemployment benefits, students' grants and interest payments on national debt will account for some 13 per cent of GNP. Third, *real capital expenditure* upon social infrastructure such as roads, hospitals, schools and housing, together with grants and loans to nationalized undertakings and those undertakings partly government owned, will account for approximately a further 3 per cent of GNP. Additional minor items are accounted for by overseas grants and certain subsidies to the private sector.

With regard to government sector receipts, by far the most important source is direct income taxes, including National Insurance contributions, which collectively account for approximately 21 per cent of GNP. Sales taxes, expenditure excises and VAT will add a further 16 per cent in terms of GNP. Government income from property (including council house rents) is not an insignificant source of government revenue. Finally, any excess of expenditures over receipts will be met by government borrowing from the other sectors. The last item, which can loosely be identified with the *public sector borrowing requirement* (PSBR), grew sharply in the late 1970s and became prominent as the linchpin in the medium-term financial strategy announced by the Conservative administration returned in 1979. Detailed discussion of the PSBR and its importance to the money supply will be deferred until chapters 6 and 18.

The Changing Status of Fiscal Policy

The economic analysis which followed in the wake of the Keynesian revolution transformed the macroeconomic status of the government sector. Previously it had been assumed that the government sector was unable to appreciably influence the macroeconomy, since government outlays would have to be financed by drawing resources from the private sector.[1] The net impact upon the aggregate economy, therefore, was considered to be of minimal importance and from this chain of reasoning it was a relatively simple step to the proposition that 'good government is government which

---

1 This version of the 'crowding out' controversy was aptly summarized as 'What was gained on the swings of public investment was, therefore, liable to be lost in part on the roundabout of private investment.' (Middleton, 1982).

governs least'. The Keynesian revolution transformed this thesis and with it the entire nature of fiscal policy. Now it became understood that changes in government expenditures and taxes could become the primary determinants of the level of economic activity and the budgetary or financial implications could be conveniently ignored. Government tax and expenditure changes would directly contribute to or subtract from the level of aggregate demand, and moreover these initial impacts would be magnified in their influence upon the economy by virtue of the machinations of the Keynesian multiplier. It suggested, perhaps over-optimistically, that comparatively small changes in taxation or government expenditures would have a dramatic impact upon the economy. In the wake of these developments, considerable attention was accorded to a precise theoretical analysis of tax and expenditure changes. It was quickly concluded that changes in government expenditure were more high powered than equivalent costing changes in taxation, and from this developed the theorem of the balanced budget multiplier. Second, and along essentially similar lines, considerable attention was given to the comparative impact of direct and indirect tax changes from which it was concluded that indirect taxes were superior in their macroeconomic impact. Throughout these theoretical developments, which provided the analytical basis for the advocacy of fine tuning and demand management generally, comparatively scant attention was given to the monetary or financial implications of government fiscal measures. Monetary policy was relegated to a minor role and Keynesianism became equated with fiscalism – with or without Keynes's blessing. Although arguably the wheel has now turned full circle, with monetarism dominant in British policy statements, it is appropriate to examine the underlying reasons for this optimism in the use of fiscal instruments. In what follows, the theorem of the balanced budget multiplier and the composition of the tax mix will be examined in some detail. Consideration of the monetary and financial implications of government budgetary measures and their relation to the so-called crowding out controversy will be deferred until chapter 12.

The Balanced Budget Multiplier

An important theoretical implication of the Keynesian analysis which rapidly gained acceptance and influenced attitudes towards fiscal intervention lay in the formulation of the so-called *balanced-budget multiplier theorem*. The essence of this theorem is relatively simple. It lies in the assertion that marginal propensities to consume will differ throughout the economy and accordingly that transfers of income to those possessing high marginal propensities to consume, financed by tax levies upon those with lower marginal propensities, will raise the overall level of aggregate demand within the economy. The theorem has been developed primarily within the context of public versus private sector, with the public or government sector possessed of the higher marginal propensity (MPC = 1). This leads to the conclusion that an increase in government outlays upon goods and services, financed by additional taxation upon the private sector (so that the overall budget balance remains unchanged), will not be neutral with respect to the level of income. More specifically, the theory was developed to show that an increase in government outlays upon goods and services, financed by additional tax levies, would lead to a raising of the income level by an amount precisely equal to the increase in government spending. This precise formulation of the theorem was the consequence of the elementary economics involved and was illustrative only; it was not intended as a precise guideline for practical policy purposes. Indeed, to the extent that the precise formulation spelled out the restrictive assumptions under which its conclusions would hold, it emphasized that the actual outcome might be subject to a wide range of uncertainty. None the less, the concept was of importance to the development of fiscal policy and macroeconomic intervention generally, and paradoxically it carried implications which might appear anti-Keynesian.

First of all, the balanced budget theorem is of particular interest in the assessment of the efficacy of fiscal policy measures, for it is only here that resulting financial changes may legitimately be ignored. In the case of increased expenditures being financed by increases in the money stock or by the sale of bonds to the private sector, the total impact upon the economy is compounded by the monetary or interest rate/wealth changes. Accordingly, it becomes conceptually difficult to isolate the purely fiscal change from the other attendant influences, which creates problems in the assessment of the fiscal measure. With a balanced budget fiscal change, however, there is a 'pure' fiscal measure which in principle should permit its net impact to be adequately assessed. Although, as will be seen, some conceptual problems remain (with regard to the appropriate definition of a balanced budget change) when tax receipts are endogenous, none the less the underlying theory pointed to the conclusion that 'pure' fiscal policy could significantly affect income and employment levels. Indeed, the balanced budget multiplier theorem becomes a Keynesian justification for non-deficit finance. Budgetary deficits are not necessary for full employment to prevail, providing the authorities are willing to expand the public sector sufficiently. It is, of course, implicit in the theorem that £ for £ changes in government expenditure upon goods and services are more effective in their macroeconomic impact than equivalent change in tax revenues; indeed, it is upon this premise that the theorem rests. However, it does not follow that changes in government expenditure are necessarily more efficient as a means of macroeconomic control. Tax changes may be easier to enact and administer. They may possess a shorter lag in effect and have a wider regional impact than expenditure changes, which by their nature tend to have a regional concentration.

Now that these initial points have been made, a more rigorous formulation of the balanced budget multiplier is presented before discussing some of the more important reservations and qualifications to the theorem.

The Multiplier with Exogenous Taxes

For ease of exposition it will be assumed that private investment outlays are autonomous, and complications arising from consideration of the monetary sector will be dispensed with. In order to bring out some of the implications more clearly, explicit distinction will be made between government expenditures upon goods and services and government transfer payments, as well as between endogenous taxes and taxes which may be considered independent of income. Then, within the context of a closed economy,

$$Y = C + I + G \tag{4.1}$$

$$C = a + bY_d \tag{4.2}$$

$$Y_d = -n + Y(1 - t) + R \tag{4.3}$$

$$I = \bar{I} \tag{4.4}$$

$$G = \bar{G} \tag{4.5}$$

where Y, C, I and G are national income, consumption, investment and government expenditures upon goods and services respectivey, and Y_d is disposable income or income net of tax. t is the income tax rate, and n denotes autonomous taxes such as lump sum levies, licence fees and the like. R refers to transfer receipts accruing to the private sector from the government. Solving for the equilibrium level of income,

$$Y = \frac{a - nb + bR + I + G}{1 - b + bt} \tag{4.6}$$

Total taxes T are simply equal to income taxes plus non-income taxes. Thus

$$T = tY + n \tag{4.7}$$

For the moment, assume that the income tax rate is zero ($t = 0$) and thus that all tax receipts stem from the autonomous element n. Accordingly, the government expenditures multiplier is given by

$$\frac{dY}{dG} = \frac{1}{1 - b} \tag{4.8}$$

whilst the tax multiplier is

$$\frac{dY}{dn} = \frac{-b}{1 - b} \tag{4.9}$$

and the total change in income arising from a balanced budget fiscal change is simply

$$dY = \frac{\partial Y}{\partial G}\, dG + \frac{\partial Y}{\partial n}\, dn \qquad \text{where } dG = dn \tag{4.10}$$

$$= \left(\frac{1}{1 - b} + \frac{-b}{1 - b}\right) dG = dG \tag{4.11}$$

This result (that the increase in income is exactly equal to the increased government outlay upon goods and services) is the traditional conclusion of the balanced budget multiplier theorem. Although it rests upon a number of simplifying assumptions, and in particular ignores the monetary sector, it serves to emphasize a number of issues pertinent to the analysis.

First, *the income expansion so obtained is independent of the value taken by the marginal propensity to consume.* This follows because the increased expenditure is simply given by

$$\Delta G - \Delta T(MPC) = \Delta T - \Delta T(MPC) = \Delta T(1 - MPC) \tag{4.12}$$

The MPC refers here to the private sector since the MPC of the government is assumed to be unity. To this increase in expenditure a normal multiplier must be applied in order to determine the total impact upon the level of national income. But in this simple model the multiplier is given by

$$\frac{1}{1 - b} = \frac{1}{1 - MPC} \tag{4.13}$$

Consequently, the total expansion of income arising from the balanced budget change is simply

$$\Delta T(1 - MPC)\, \frac{1}{1 - MPC} = \Delta T = \Delta G \tag{4.14}$$

Second, and following on from the first point, the result of equation 4.11 implies that *extending the analysis to the open economy in no way modifies the analysis as long as the government expenditure falls solely upon domestic output which has no import content.* Allowing for imports by the private sector is simply akin to a decrease in the marginal propensity to consume.

What if the increased expenditure by government had not fallen upon goods and services but instead had taken the form of increased transfer payments? Then, as intuition would suggest, the income expansion is negated and the multiplier is zero. Transferring money from one sector of the economy to another via the tax transfer mechanism would leave the level of income unchanged provided marginal consumption propensities are equal in the two sectors. More formally,

$$dY = \frac{\partial Y}{\partial R} dR + \frac{\partial Y}{\partial n} dn \qquad \text{where } dR = dn$$

$$= \left(\frac{b}{1-b} + \frac{-b}{1-b} \right) dR = 0 \qquad (4.15)$$

The Multiplier with Non-zero Income Taxes

The assumption that income tax rates are zero is now dropped. Income tax receipts (and thus total tax receipts) are now endogenous upon the level of income. Does this affect the argument in any systematic way? The first difficulty which arises concerns the appropriate definition of a balanced budget fiscal change. If the increase in government expenditure upon goods and services is financed by an equal increase in autonomous taxes then there will be a balanced budget fiscal change in the short run; however, with income taxes endogenous the resulting income expansion will imply a movement towards fiscal surplus. The induced increase in fiscal receipts over and above the increased government expenditure will have reper-cussions upon money and bond markets and there will no longer be a 'pure' fiscal change in the long run. Alternatively, if a balanced budget change is defined to include the induced increase in direct taxes, then initially the tax proceeds will be insufficient to cover the increased government outlays. Monetary and/or bond market repercussions will thus arise in the short run and it will only be in the long run that fiscal receipts rise sufficiently to cover the increased expenditure. When taxes are endogenous upon income changes, therefore, the concept of a 'pure' fiscal change becomes exceedingly nebulous. Indeed, the ideal of a fiscal experiment which is not in some way contaminated by accompanying monetary, interest rate or wealth effect changes is shown to be an impossibility – a conclusion which carries impli-

cations for the assessment of the respective potencies of monetary and fiscal
policy.

None the less, each of these situations is now pursued in turn when the
income tax rate is positive. Consider first a balanced budget fiscal change
defined with respect to the short run. In the case of increased government
outlays on goods and services $dG = dn$, and in the case of increased government transfers payments $dR = dn$ as before. In the former case the total
change in income is given by

$$dY = \frac{\partial Y}{\partial G} dG + \frac{\partial Y}{\partial n} dn \qquad \text{where } dG = dn$$

$$= \left(\frac{1}{1-b+bt} + \frac{-b}{1-b+bt}\right) dG$$

$$= \left(\frac{1-b}{1-b+bt}\right) dG < dG \qquad\qquad (4.16)$$

The total multiplier is now *less than unity* in contrast to the conventional
conclusion. Moreover, the value of the multiplier is no longer independent
of the value taken by the marginal propensity to consume. Somewhat surprisingly, the multiplier as defined above is *less* the *greater* the marginal
propensity to consume, and vice versa. That is to say,

$$\frac{d\left(\dfrac{1-b}{1-b+bt}\right)}{db} = \frac{-(1-b+bt)-(t-1)(1-b)}{(1-b+bt)^2}$$

$$= \frac{-t}{(1-b+tb)^2} < 0 \qquad\qquad (4.17)$$

The intuitive explanation for this result is that the ultimate multiplier incorporates the additional deflationary consequences of the induced fiscal
receipts arising from the endogenous income tax. The greater the marginal
propensity to consume the greater will this additional deflationary impact
be for any given rate of income tax. Similar reasoning suggests that the
multiplier as defined above will be greater the smaller the rate of tax and
vice versa; thus

$$\frac{d\left(\dfrac{1-b}{1-b+bt}\right)}{dt} = \frac{-b(1-b)}{(1-b+bt)^2}$$

$$= \frac{-b+b^2}{(1-b+bt)^2} < 0 \qquad\qquad (4.18)$$

for all b less than 1, the normal case.

This suggests that the conventional conclusions of the balanced budget multiplier theorem are modified once income taxes are considered endogenous and the balanced budget multiplier is defined with respect to the short run. However, no such modification is implied with respect to the increase in government outlays being directed towards increased transfer payments. Then

$$dY = \frac{\partial Y}{\partial R} dR + \frac{\partial Y}{\partial n} dn \qquad \text{where } dR = dn$$

$$= \left(\frac{b}{1 - b + bt} + \frac{-b}{1 - b + bt} \right) dR$$

$$= 0 \qquad\qquad (4.19)$$

Thus, whether or not taxes are endogenous, the zero outcome of the balanced budget multiplier with transfer payments remains the same – again, in accordance with intuitive reasoning.

A balanced budget fiscal change is now defined to refer to the long term. In this case the increased government spending upon goods and services, or alternatively upon transfer payments, is just matched by increased taxes, including any endogenous increase in taxes arising from income expansion. This implies that the condition for a balanced budget change is given by either

$$dT = dn + dYt = dG \qquad \text{where } dG = dT \qquad (4.20)$$

or

$$dT = dn + dYt = dR \qquad \text{where } dR = dT \qquad (4.21)$$

Consider the former. This can be written

$$dn = dG - dYt \qquad\qquad (4.22)$$

Accordingly, the balanced budget fiscal change is derived from

$$dY = \frac{\partial Y}{\partial G} dG + \frac{\partial Y}{\partial n} dn \qquad \text{where } dn = dG - dYt$$

$$= \left(\frac{1}{1 - b + bt} \right) dG + \left(\frac{-b}{1 - b + bt} \right) (dG - dYt)$$

$$= \frac{dG - bdG + bdYt}{1 - b + bt} \qquad\qquad (4.23)$$

Hence

$$dY(1 - b + bt - bt) = dG(1 - b) \qquad\qquad (4.24)$$

and

$$dY = \frac{dG(1 - b)}{1 - b} = dG \qquad (4.25)$$

Thus, when the balanced budget multiplier is defined with respect to the long term, where the increased government outlays upon goods and services are covered by both autonomous and induced fiscal receipts, the traditional conclusion of the unity multiplier is restored. The long-term zero-transfers multiplier is also unaffected, as the reader will readily be able to verify for himself by similar reasoning. In the latter case the induced tax proceeds are, of course, also zero.

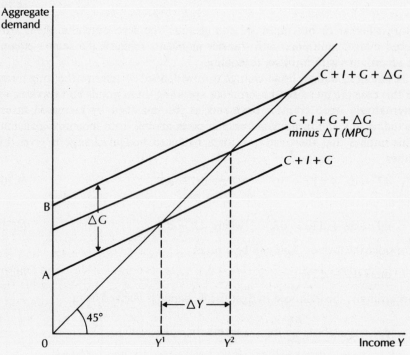

Figure 4.1   Logic of the balanced budget multiplier $\Delta G = \Delta T$

Figure 4.1 illustrates the logic of the unity balanced budget multiplier. In this figure, increased government expenditure raises aggregate demand by ΔG but the effect of taxation is to reduce it by $\Delta T(MPC)$. As long as the MPC is less than 1 the net effect is to raise aggregate demand, and income rises from $0Y^1$ to $0Y^2$ *equal to* 0A to 0B.

Table 4.1 summarizes the analysis to date.

TABLE 4.1
The Balanced Budget Multiplier Theorem

Equation $\quad Y = \dfrac{a - bn + bR + I + G}{1 - b + bt}$

Balanced budget change Pure fiscal measure $t = 0$	Short-run balanced budget change $t > 0$	Long-run balanced budget change $t > 0$
$dY = dG$ for $dn = dG$	$dY < dG$ for $dn = dG$	$dY = dG$ for $dn = dG - dYt$
$dY = 0$ for $dn = dR$	$dY = 0$ for $dn = dR$	$dY = 0$ for $dn = dR - dYt$

Transfer Payments in Kind

Thus far the balanced budget multiplier theorem has been analysed by invoking two polar cases, the one where the government raises expenditures upon goods and services and the other where it increases the existing level of transfer payments. There is, however, an intermediate situation, that of a combined policy whereby the government increases taxation to purchase additional goods and services which it then gives to recipients in the form of transfer payments in kind. This, of course, reflects the situation with respect to the provision of free school milk, certain maternity benefits and so forth. This form of benefit is often advocated upon the grounds that it enjoys the support of the taxpayer whereas untied cash payments might not. The issue of concern here, however, is the extent to which such provision influences the value of the balanced budget multiplier.

This question can perhaps most readily be approached in terms of conventional indifference analysis. Figure 4.2 shows savings on the vertical axis and the consumption of composite goods on the horizontal. Given the indifference curve the optimal combination of consumption and savings for some hypothetical individual is revealed to be at point E with consumption of goods equal to 0A and savings 0Y. Now assume that in this situation the individual concerned suddenly finds himself the recipient of a composite bundle of goods bestowed upon him by government and equal to the amount 0X. How will the individual respond? His initial reaction is to experience an income gain which allows him to raise both his level of consumption and his level of saving. In terms of the diagram, his budget line MN is altered to MPT by the free provision of goods 0X and his optimal consumption/savings combination is now indicated by E′. His savings have increased from 0Y to 0Q. However, except in very trivial cases, it is not possible to save out of payments in kind; consequently, the increased savings takes the form of saving out of alternative monetary income and this saving serves to offset the multiplier impact of the increased government outlays on goods and services. In the extreme case,

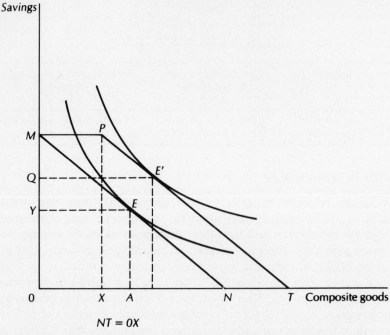

NT = OX

Figure 4.2   Transfer payments in kind and the balanced budget multiplier

where the recipient values the income gain experienced as equal to its cost and where he has the same marginal propensity to consume as the taxpayer, the entire impact of the multiplier is negated. This is because he increases his saving by the amount of the income gain experienced, ΔY, multiplied by his marginal propensity to save, whilst the taxpayer will reduce his saving by the amount of the tax to finance the provision of goods ΔT, multiplied by his marginal propensity to save. If the goods or services are valued at cost, ΔY equals ΔT and if marginal saving propensities are uniform there is no net change in the level of aggregate demand.

The Composition of the Tax Mix

Virtually every elementary treatment of Keynesian economics includes reference to the theory of the balanced budget multiplier. It is therefore somewhat surprising that elementary expositions of macroeconomics fail to make a similar and arguably more important distinction between the aggregate demand impact of a change in direct taxation and that of an *equal yield* change in indirect taxation. Just as a change in the composition of government outlays between goods and services and transfer payments may have a net demand impact, so too may a change in the composition of the tax mix exert inflationary or deflationary consequences.

The reasons for this comparative reticence are not hard to seek. Indirect taxes are notoriously difficult to incorporate into formal national income models because they imply price changes of unknown degree which cannot be readily accommodated by an analysis stated in real terms. Moreover, indirect taxes raise the possibility of *money illusion* upon the part of consumers which further complicates the analysis.[2] In consequence, many formal models of fiscal policy admit of the existence of lump sum taxes or primitive proportional income taxes whilst simultaneously denying the presence of sales or consumption taxes. A priori, such a procedure is difficult to justify when it is recalled that indirect taxes often account for 50 per cent or more of total tax proceeds. Arguably, such a departure from reality would be permissible if it could be shown that the nature of the tax source was of no consequence to the subsequent analysis and conclusions of the model. However, precisely the opposite situation prevails; it has long been argued, as part of the conventional wisdom of public finance, that indirect tax levies exert a greater deflationary impact upon the macroeconomy than do equal yielding direct taxes.

This argument may be traced back, at least implicitly, to Keynes who proposed a consumption function which was non-linear and which exhibited a declining marginal propensity to consume with rising income. If this is the case, and if direct taxes (income taxes) fall primarily upon the rich whilst exempting the poor, whereas sales taxes are more regressive and impinge upon the total population, it follows that £ for £ the sales tax will exert a greater impact upon the level of demand. Alternatively, the income tax exerts a greater impact upon saving than does a comparable sales tax. When compared upon an equal yield basis, therefore, the sales tax will exert the stronger impact upon the level of aggregate demand. Even if the differential impact upon demand is slight, it will be magnified in its income and employment impacts by the operation of the Keynesian multiplier.

The Keynesian demonstration of the superiority of indirect taxes was never particularly convincing, partly because consumption taxes need not be especially regressive. Such taxes include specific excises which can be (and often are) imposed at decidedly high rates upon luxury products con-

---

2 A commonly accepted definition of money illusion would contend that money illusion is present when a consumer continues to make the same nominal money outlay in the face of a tax-induced price rise. In contrast, if he takes the tax into account and raises his outlay in order to maintain, if only partially, his former real consumption standard, he is said to be free of money illusion.

sumed by the comparatively wealthy. In addition, however, the empirical evidence culled from studies of consumer behaviour indicated little difference in marginal consumption patterns of different income groups over a broad range of incomes. A linear consumption function destroys the entire basis of the Keynesian claim, whether sales taxes are regressive or not.

It is precisely for this reason that the contribution by Cary Brown (1950) takes on renewed significance. Adopting a simple Keynesian model for a closed economy, Cary Brown demonstrated that a sales tax would exert a greater macroeconomic impact than an equal yield income tax even under the assumption of a uniform marginal propensity to consume, and regardless of whether money illusion existed or not. This demonstration served to confirm the earlier Keynesian intuition in that the result derived from the greater propensity of the income tax to deplete savings.[3]

This analysis is subject to several qualifications, however. First, it rests upon the assumption that the sales tax is passed forward in its entirety in a tax-induced price rise. No further price changes are then permitted to occur.[4] Second, the comparative effectiveness of the two taxes is demonstrated solely with respect to comparative yields; the period of adjustment is not considered within the conventional comparative static framework. Finally, perhaps the most serious reservation noted by Peston (1971) stems from the unrealistic model analysis which posits the existence of an income tax, when sales taxes are absent, for purposes of comparison with a world characterized by sales taxes but possessed of no income taxes. In a real world situation, the two types of taxes would exist simultaneously and moreover their yields would be highly interdependent.

In attempting to deal with this additional complication Peston adopts the analytically convenient device of holding total tax proceeds constant whilst changing the ratio of direct to indirect taxes. In doing so, he is able to demonstrate unambiguously that an increase in the direct/indirect tax ratio with total tax proceeds held constant will be expansionary in its impact upon real output. Thus Peston's model reaffirms the conventional wisdom of the superiority of indirect taxes but this time within the context of a multitax world. Again, this conclusion rests upon the assumption of the full shifting of indirect taxes, but none the less it represents a considerable

---

3 Strictly, the result is demonstrated only for an economy with positive savings and the demonstration relied upon a rather complicated algebraic manipulation not reproduced here. A full treatment is presented in Shaw (1972).

4 This is the basis of a critique by Peacock and Williamson (1967) which formulated a wage response to the increased price level implicit in the case of a sales tax and assumed absent in the case of the income tax. With prices related to wage increases they then went on to develop a wage price spiral which showed that the sales tax could generate more inflationary consequences than the income tax.

advance upon the analysis of single-tax states.[5]

Quite apart from the conclusions of the formal model analysis, there are other reasons to suggest that indirect taxes will exert a greater deflationary impact. Thus, for example, indirect taxes will raise prices; to what degree will depend upon the actual patterns of incidence, but none the less it is reasonable to conclude that they will generate an increase in the aggregate price level. To this extent, they will imply an increased demand for transactions balances and, *ceteris paribus*, lead to an increase in interest rates. The latter may be expected to 'crowd out' a certain amount of private sector expenditure, both because of the presumed relationship between investment and interest rates and also because of negative wealth effects as the real value of bonds are reduced. To the extent that higher interest rates lead to a raising of the exchange rate, the demand for domestic output will fall as export demand contracts and imports become more price competitive. All things considered, therefore, there are convincing reasons for believing that indirect taxes have greater real effects. If this is the case then they should be fully allowed for in any reforms aimed at restructuring the overall tax burden. And the composition of the tax mix should be logically included in the armory of fiscal instruments.

A change in the composition of the tax mix leaves the budget surplus/deficit unchanged and hence involves no change in the money stock. How then are the expansionary real effects associated with a switch from indirect to direct taxation to be financed? Under the present assumptions of complete shifting, any change in the composition of tax receipts involves price effects. It is the change in the aggregate price index consequent upon the tax mix change which implies changes to the *real* money stock. Thus, in contrast to the theorem of the balanced budget multiplier, which abstracts from price changes, a change in the composition of the tax mix has dual consequences. It involves first of all an expenditure shift, along Brown–Pestonian lines, but equally it involves price changes which alter the real value of the money stock.

Concluding Comments

This chapter began by indicating the overriding importance of the government sector to the macroeconomy, and it has been demonstrated how government decision-making will exercise a pervasive influence upon

---

5 Peston's technique maintains tax proceeds constant in nominal terms. Thus, as the direct/indirect tax ratio is increased the shifting assumption implies falling prices. Total tax proceeds rise in real terms and yet the net effect on real output is expansionary.

private sector behaviour even whilst maintaining or adopting a strictly non-interventionist stance. Not only is the government of dominant importance in its expenditure and employment policies, but its policy announcements – or the lack of them – will condition expectations throughout the private sector. Indeed, from the standpoint of the rational expectations school, the conditioning of appropriate expectations is a valid function of government in conducting the adjustment to a preferred state of affairs – a lower inflation rate, for example.

Two theoretical analyses of the government sector which evolved from the Keynesian model analysis were examined in some detail. The first of these, the well-known balanced budget multiplier theorem, was analysed in regard to both income and non-income taxes, to demonstrate the proposition that a change in the level of government outlays, with no change in the position of the budget surplus or deficit, will not normally be neutral in its impact upon the equilibrium level of national income.

A very similar but comparatively little-known issue, namely the question of the composition of the tax mix, was then examined. Again the consequence of Keynesian model analysis, this thesis demonstrates that indirect taxes are usually more high powered in their macroeconomic impact than equivalent direct taxes. Thus, as in the case of the balanced budget theorem, government can influence the macroeconomy without necessarily disturbing its overall budgetary deficit/surplus position – in this case by changing the composition of its tax receipts. It should be emphasized that the formal analysis of this chapter is decidedly Keynesian oriented and that alternative statements, such as the monetarist contention of the importance of the budget constraint, are deferred until chapter 12.

Further Reading

An elementary guide to the significance of the government sector can be culled from Black (1985) and Peston (1982). For detailed analysis of government expenditure and receipts there is no substitute for the annual blue book on *National Income and Expenditure* (HMSO) together with the short guide published every ten years (HMSO, 1981). For an analysis of the elementary multiplier models stemming from government expenditures and taxation see Peacock and Shaw (1976). Significant articles on the balanced budget multiplier include Salant (1957) and Peacock (1972). With regard to the analysis of the tax mix the principal references are the ones already mentioned in the text, specifically Brown (1950) and Peston (1971). Other contributions include the Peacock and Williamson (1967) attempt (already mentioned) at extending the analysis to an inflationary setting, Forster and Shaw (1976) and subsequent critiques by McLean (1978) and Signer (1978).

5

The Demand for Money

Individuals demand goods and services because they yield utility. In the same way, they demand money because of the benefits yielded by the possession of money. In this respect, money may be deemed a 'good' on a par with any other commodity. It follows that the demand for money, like the demand for any other good, is a real demand; it is a demand for the actual services yielded by the possession of a *real* stock of money and not simply a demand for a nominal amount of cash denominated in sterling, dollars or any other currency unit.

Although money may be regarded as a good it is none the less the case that the services yielded by money are unique. It is owing to the unique role and functions performed by money that it takes on a dominant role in the functioning of the economy, and for this reason economists have given considerable time and effort to analysing the factors influencing the demand for money. It is difficult if not impossible to imagine a modern economy existing without money, and any factor substantially affecting the demand for money will have repercussions upon the economy generally.

The Functions of Money

The essential functions performed by money can be enumerated as follows:

The Medium of Exchange Function. Money acts as a medium of exchange and hence permits an interval of time to separate the act of buying and selling commodities. In the context of a barter economy the exchange of goods would imply the simultaneous occurrence of buying and selling commodities upon the part of each transactor to an exchange. Money eliminates this need for a 'double coincidence of wants'. It allows one to sell commodities or services without simultaneously purchasing. In this way it greatly facilitates exchange and thus widens the scope for profitable exchanges to take place. This medium of exchange function is undoubtedly the single most important function possessed by money and without it it is difficult to imagine how society could acquire the benefits stemming from specialization and the division of labour.

The Store of Value Function. A moment's reflection will indicate that money is able to perform its medium of exchange function primarily because it acts as a store of value. The reason why one is willing to sell commodities or services in exchange for money which will be used to make purchases at a later date is because of the fact that money retains its value over time. If this were not the case individuals would be unwilling to hold money and it would cease to perform its primary exchange function.

Money is not of course a perfect store of value since its real value is eroded at a rate equal to the rate of inflation. The greater the rate of inflation the less well will money perform its store of value function and the less readily will it serve as a medium of exchange. At the same time, other assets will serve as a store of value and some – antiques, old masters and so forth – may outperform money in this respect. Money, however, has one great advantage over such real assets, namely that in principle it is readily divisible.

The Standard of Deferred Payment Function. Closely related to the store of value function is the function of deferred payment performed by money. This means simply that loans and future payments are agreed and con- tracted in money terms, the monetary unit being accepted as the means of settling future accounts. Clearly, this function can only be adequately per- formed by money if it is sufficiently protected against inflation in being able to perform its store of value function.

The Unit of Account Function. It is convenient to adopt the monetary unit as the unit of account in which prices are quoted and accounting records kept, although it is by no means essential. Virtually any commodity with a reasonably stable value could serve as *numeraire* although here too the potential divisibility of money is an additional asset.

The unit of account function performed by money illustrates graphically the gains in efficiency, in the form of reduced transactions costs, obtained by the existence of money. In a pure barter economy, for example, with n commodities there will be $n(n-1)$ exchange ratios since every commodity would have an exchange ratio with every other (but not of course with itself, in which case the exchange ratio is automatically unity). Of these exchange ratios, however, only half are required since the rate of exchange between a table and a chair is precisely equal to the inverse of the rate of exchange between a chair and a table. Hence a total of $n(n-1)/2$ indepen- dent exchange ratios is obtained. With one commodity acting as a unit of account, however, only $n-1$ independent exchange ratios are needed, which implies a considerable reduction in the information needed for rational trading to take place.

The nature of the demand for money is of paramount importance to the entire question of the significance of the monetary variable and to the role of monetary control of the macroeconomy. Essentially the value of money, as indeed that of any other commodity, can be viewed as being determined by the forces of supply and demand. An explanation of the extent to which the authorities can in practice control the money stock is delayed until the next chapter; for present expositional purposes, the money supply will simply be assumed to be exogenously determined.

Classical Monetary Theory – the Traditional Quantity Theory

The Transactions Approach

Fisher's famous equation of exchange, $MV = PT$, where M is the total money stock, V its velocity of circulation or the average number of times that each monetary unit is utilized in a given accounting period, T the total number of all transactions and P the general price level, is justifiably one of the best-known tautologies in economics. It is a tautology in that it asserts merely that total monetary expenditure is equal to the monetary value of all goods traded. By invoking certain assumptions it is, however, possible to transform the identity into a theory. If velocity is determined by habit, institutional arrangements, banking practices and so forth, then it may be assumed constant in the short term, and if T is also rendered a constant, which is not so unreasonable if full employment output is posited, then the following well-known result is obtained:

$$M\bar{V} = P\bar{T} \quad \text{or} \quad P = \frac{M\bar{V}}{\bar{T}} \tag{5.1}$$

$$\therefore \quad \Delta M \Rightarrow \Delta P$$

Here the increase in the money stock is the causal agent in initiating the rise in prices, and the transactions demand for money then responds passively to this price increase. *Ceteris paribus*, the demand for money would be unit elastic.

The Cambridge Cash Balance Approach

An alternative formulation of the traditional quantity theory of money was propounded by the Cambridge school of economists, led by Marshall,

Pigou and Robertson. The general approach taken by the Cambridge cash balance equation is to express the demand for money as a percentage of the real income of society. Thus the real demand for money may be expressed as kY where Y is real income and k is the percentage of real income over which people collectively wish to maintain command in the form of cash holdings. If the nominal money stock is exogenously determined to be M, then the required equilibrium between supply and demand is brought about by the price mechanism. Then

$$M = pkY \tag{5.2}$$

where p is the price index of current output. Thus

$$p = \frac{M}{kY} \tag{5.3}$$

which can be compared to Fisher's equation

$$P = \frac{MV}{T} \tag{5.4}$$

Hence

$$\frac{M}{kY} = \frac{MV}{T} \tag{5.5}$$

or

$$\frac{1}{V} = \frac{kY}{T} \tag{5.6}$$

Providing the ratio of income to transactions, Y/T, remains constant, the Cambridge k is simply proportional to the reciprocal of V. An increase in k implies a decrease in V and vice versa, and both indicate a decrease in the velocity of circulation. The demonstration of the strict quantity theory of money requires constancy in both k and V. This is hardly surprising; the Cambridge k was purely a transactions demand for money and as such was implicit in Fisher's formulation.

The Keynesian Analysis of the Demand for Money

The demise of the traditional quantity theory of money was closely associated with the evolution of Keynes's thinking on monetary matters and culminated in the publication of the *General Theory*, which claimed that the money stock was important only to the extent that it influenced the rate of interest and set up repercussions stemming from the interest rate change.

Moreover the thesis was propounded, later to be eagerly seized upon by Keynesians if not by Keynes himself, that situations could exist whereby an increase in the money stock would have zero impact upon interest rates and hence zero effect on the economy *in toto*. What was involved in this proposition was the assertion that an increase in the money stock could generate countervailing changes in velocity so as to completely cancel and negate the impact of a changed money supply. In short, this thesis implied the extreme variant of the view that the demand for money is interdependent with its supply – completely contrary to the traditional formulation of the quantity theory of money. Fundamental to this assertion was the distinctly Keynesian emphasis upon the importance of expectations in influencing the demand for money balances. The so-called *speculative* motive of the demand for money was added to the traditional transactions demand. This is the distinguishing characteristic of the Keynesian contribution and it is this feature, or rather the significance of this feature, which the revised monetarist doctrine has sought to deny or play down in its empirical importance.

Keynesian Motives for Money Holding

In the *General Theory* Keynes divided the motivation for holding money balances into three component parts, namely

(1) The transactions motive
(2) The precautionary motive
(3) The speculative motive.

The Transactions Motive for maintaining cash balances is essentially akin to the classical thesis. Given institutional lags between the receipt of factor incomes and expenditure outlays, a certain amount of money will be required to permit normal day-to-day transactions within the economy and the real value of this transactions demand will be closely related to the real income of society. The assumption here is that the real volume of transactions will be closely related to the real income of the economy and this in turn will imply a nominal demand for transactions cash related to the monetary value of national income. Thus the transactions demand for cash can be indicated as

$$L_1 = kPY \tag{5.7}$$

The Precautionary Motive is very closely related to the transactions motive in that it may be considered as the amount of cash that one carries in excess of one's expected transactions needs owing to the existence of uncertainty.

Certain outlays, essentially of a transaction nature, may be unforeseen (as in the case of an unexpected medical bill, for example) and the rational individual will therefore demand a sum of money over and above his expected transactions needs to deal with such contingencies. This amount will be determined by the individual's subjective expectation or probability of finding himself in some unforeseen condition and will clearly differ between individuals, but in the aggregate it seems reasonable that it should be related to the level of real income and in nominal terms to the price level. Accordingly, there would appear to be very little justification for distinguishing between the transactions and precautionary motives.[1] Thus a generalized transactions demand for cash, L_1, can be considered which encompasses the precautionary element, and it can be posited that

$$\frac{dL_1}{dPY} > 0 \tag{5.8}$$

The Speculative Demand for money or alternatively the asset demand for money is the amount of money that the individual desires for speculative financial transactions when the conditions appear favourable. To simplify the analysis conceptually, Keynes assumed the existence of only two financial assets, non-interest-bearing cash and interest-bearing non-redeemable government bonds (consols). Now although such bonds are never redeemed by the government they are nevertheless exchanged in the capital market and their market value will fluctuate with changes in the market rate of interest.

To illustrate, suppose the government issues a non-redeemable bond for £100 which pays a yearly dividend of £5. The effective interest rate is accordingly 5 per cent. The fact that the government is able to sell such a bond at this price implies that the market rate of interest is in the order of 5 per cent. Now if some time later the market rate were to rise to 10 per cent, the holder of this bond would be able to obtain only £50 consequent upon its sale, since now £50 is all that is required to yield an interest income of £5. In a similar fashion, had the market rate of interest fallen to $2\frac{1}{2}$ per cent the bondholder might reasonably expect its market value to approximate £200. The example here is extremely simplified but the point being laboured is that bond prices are inversely related to market rates of interest. The reader will appreciate that what is involved is determining the present value of an interest-yielding asset as was demonstrated in chapter 3.

In deciding whether to keep a certain portion of his wealth in the form of money or bonds, therefore, the rational investor will consider not simply

---

1 For an opposite view see Whalen (1966).

the interest yield differential between the two assets but also his expectation of a possible change in the market value of government bonds. In short, a decision to purchase bonds involves not only the prospect of an interest income stream but also the prospect of a capital gain or loss.

It was Keynes' contention that the asset or speculative demand for money, L_2, would be inversely related to the rate of interest. Three arguments support this stance. First, the cost of keeping money idle in the form of speculative balances is of course the interest forgone. The cost is therefore higher when interest rates are high and on this ground alone one would be induced to economize on speculative cash holdings when interest rates are high.

Second and most important is the part played by the expectation of capital gains or losses. It is assumed that the rational individual entertains some expectation as to the future course of interest rates. He has some expectation of a *normal* rate of interest with which he expects the existing market rate ultimately to coincide. If this expected or normal interest rate is above (below) the current market rate, he is expecting the market rates to rise (fall) and therefore bond prices to fall (rise). In such a situation he will move out of bonds (cash) and hold cash (bonds) in order to avoid any capital loss (make a capital gain). In the intermediate case where the potential investor expects the interest rate to be unchanged he will, of course, hold bonds and no cash in order to take advantage of the interest yield. This analysis suggests that the investor maintains *either* cash *or* bonds but not both simultaneously. His situation is akin to that depicted in figure 5.1 where B represents the critical expected interest rate.

However, different individuals will entertain different ideas as to the probable future rate of interest, and in the aggregate will in all probability be holding a combination of both cash and bonds. At higher rates of interest, however, more and more individuals will, *ceteris paribus*, entertain the belief that interest rates must fall in the future. The aggregate demand for speculative cash balances will accordingly decline. Ultimately a rate of interest may be attained at which no one believes it can go higher and the expectation of a future fall in the market rate will become universal. At this point, the demand for idle cash balances will become zero as everybody will try to move into bonds in the certain expectation of making a capital gain. This situation is depicted at point A in figure 5.2. Conversely, the lower the interest rates the more general the belief that future rates must rise; the more general the belief that future bonds prices will decline the greater will be the movement into cash. Ultimately there will be some minimal rate of interest such that the universal expectation is for a future rise, and at this point there will be no call for bonds with the demand for idle balances becoming infinite up to total wealth. In figure 5.2 this situation is depicted at point B. This is

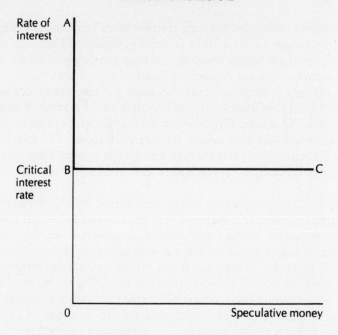

Figure 5.1   Individual's asset demand for money ABC

therefore the rationale for the general conclusion that the demand for speculative cash holdings will be inversely related to the rate of interest for the
aggregate economy.

A third and related argument reinforces this conclusion by comparing the
extent of any capital loss against interest yields at different rates of interest.
As might be expected, the extent of any given loss net of interest yield will
be greater at lower rates of interest for any given increase in the prevailing
market rate.[2] The force of this point stems from the fact that interest rate
changes on the part of the monetary authorities are of finite amounts, a
change of $\frac{1}{4}$ per cent being normally the smallest feasible.

Thus, whilst the transactions cum precautionary demand for money is
related to income levels directly, the asset demand for money is inversely

---

2 To illustrate, consider an investment of £1000 in consols at 5 per cent. This will
yield £50 per annum. If after three years the interest rate rises to 6 per cent the value
of the consol will fall to £833. The loss is £167 or, after consideration of the interest
yield, £17. The same example assuming an initial interest rate of 2 per cent rising to
3 per cent after three years provides a capital loss of £333 less the yield gain of £60 –
implying a net loss of £273. This example stems from Dillard (1948).

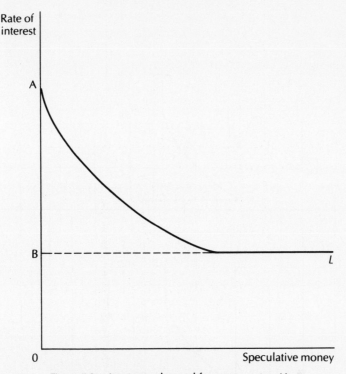

Figure 5.2   Aggregate demand for asset money AL

related to the rate of interest.

$$\frac{\mathrm{d}L_2}{\mathrm{d}i} < 0 \qquad\qquad\qquad (5.9)$$

Since the total demand for money is simply L_1 plus L_2, equal to L, it
follows that the total demand for money must also be inversely related to
interest rates. To illustrate, consider the composite figure 5.3. In part (a) is
depicted the transactions demand L_1 as invariant to the interest rate and in
part (b) the asset demand L_2 as a negative function of the interest rate. In
part (c) the total demand (or *liquidity preference* in Keynes's terminology) is
shown as a combination of (a) and (b) and must also therefore reveal some
interest elasticity. The issue which is crucial for policy purposes turns upon
the extent of this interest elasticity.

Money Market Equilibrium

The implication of figure 5.3(c) is that the demand for money will increase
as interest rates fall. The question remains, why do interest rates fall? The

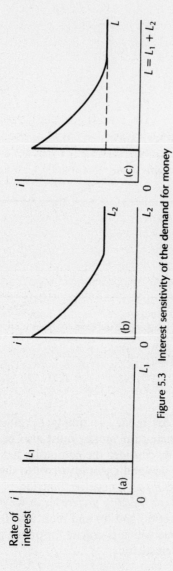

Figure 5.3 Interest sensitivity of the demand for money

Keynesian answer is simplicity itself; the rate of interest is determined by the supply and demand for money and hence a fall in the rate of interest is associated with an increase in the money stock. But since the interest rate fall increases the demand for money this implies that supply and demand are interdependent. The situation is therefore one in which an increase in the supply of money generates a complementary increase in the demand for money (akin to a decrease in velocity) so as to negate or minimize the impact of the monetary change. This situation is brought out with the aid of figure 5.4. The value of money, $1/P$, is shown to be determined by the demand for money and the money stock M. If the money stock is doubled to $2M$ but the demand for money is also doubled, then the value of money is left unchanged. This is the essence of the Keynesian denial of the traditional quantity theory of money. Even if the demand does not double, any increase in demand will offset in part the predictions of the traditional statement.

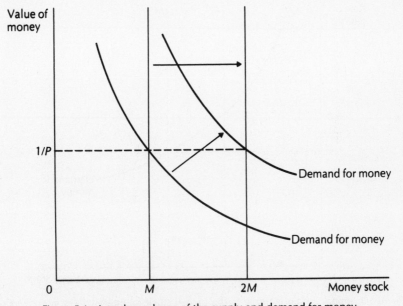

Figure 5.4   Interdependence of the supply and demand for money

The Keynesian doctrine of liquidity preference is thus fundamentally at odds with the traditional quantity theory. The latter had minimized the role of changes in the demand for money (velocity) and in particular had tended to exclude supply changes as a possible cause of changes in demand. None the less, it should be emphasized that Keynes was not seeking to minimize the role of money although this was the emphasis to be pursued by many of his later disciples. The emphasis that Keynes was insistent upon was that the impact of a money stock change would work through the associated change in the interest rate. In the normal course of events, an increased money supply would imply a fall in interest rates (see figure 5.5) which in turn would stimulate both investment and consumption outlays. These in turn would be magnified in their impact upon the economy by the normal operation of the multiplier and the result would be an expansion of money national income. Whether this increase occurs upon the side of output changes or price changes would depend largely upon whether there existed unemployed resources. If resources were fully employed then the impact of increased investment and consumption expenditure would necessarily be reflected in price increases and the quantity theory would be vindicated ·in principle – although with a distinctly different *transmission mechanism* than that employed in the traditional doctrine.

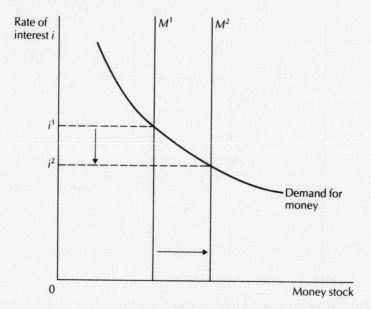

Figure 5.5   Impact of an increase in the money stock on interest rates in conventional Keynesian theory

However there remains one important theoretical exception to the sequence of events described, an exception that Keynesians tended to believe provided the *coup de grâce* to the quantity theory. This is the case where an increase in the money stock has no impact whatsoever upon interest rates and hence no impact at all upon the macroeconomy. Consider again point B in figure 5.2. At this point there exists the universal belief that interest rates must rise. Accordingly, no one is willing to buy more government bonds. In such a situation, if the government were to enlarge the money supply there would be no effect upon the interest rate. Since the money stock at any time must be held by somebody, the enlarged money supply would find its way into the hands of the public. But with no change in the income level there is no desire to add to transactions balances. With no desire to purchase government bonds on the understandable grounds that future bond prices must fall, the additional cash must be added to existing idle speculative money holdings. The asset demand for money is thus rendered infinite at this point, imposing a minimum constraint upon interest rates.

This is the situation which became referred to as the *liquidity trap* and implies the complete impotence of monetary policy. It will be illustrated by reference to figure 5.6. In such a situation any increase in the money stock is

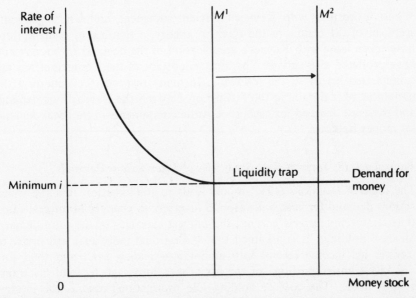

Figure 5.6   Liquidity trap – zero impact of an enlarged money supply upon the rate of interest

simply accumulated in the form of idle cash balances. Now clearly the velocity of an idle deposit is nil. Consequently, this process is accompanied by a general decrease in the average velocity of money. In terms of Fisher's equation, the increase in the money stock is exactly offset by a decrease in the average velocity of money so that no change takes place in total expenditures and no impact is transmitted to the remainder of the economy. The quantity theory is denied. It should be emphasized that Keynes did not appear to attach much importance to this situation, except as an interesting theoretical possibility, and generally held that an increase in the money stock would be accompanied by a decline in interest rates. None the less, the analysis indicated that the decline in interest rates could be substantially limited and small variations in the rate of interest might not be expected to exert much impact upon investment or consumption spending. Any generalized statement about the effect of a change in the volume of money upon the aggregate economy could not longer be maintained. The traditional quantity theory appeared to have been eclipsed in the upheaval of the Keynesian revolution.

Post-Keynesian Modifications to the Demand for Money

Whilst in keeping with Keynes's original statement, and whilst generally sceptical of the claims of the quantity theory, a number of contributions have taken issue with Keynes's specification of the demand for money and have proffered alternatives. The most important of these contributions are summarized briefly in the following. In many respects, they question the usefulness of maintaining the distinction between the transactions demand and the asset demand for cash as separate components in the total demand for money holdings.

Baumol and the Interest Rate Sensitivity of Transactions Demands

The logic of Baumol's (1952) model leads to the assertion that the transactions demand for cash will respond inversely to changes in interest rates, thus reinforcing, *ceteris paribus*, the interest elasticity of the total demand for cash holdings. It is assumed that the rational individual will prefer to transfer his income receipt into an interest-yielding asset and then successively transfer portions of the asset back into cash to fulfil his transactions needs. The cost of holding idle transactions cash is the interest forgone; this explains the incentive to minimize cash holding by increasing the frequency with which one turns assets into cash. However, there are costs associated with liquidation of the asset – not least the cost of inconvenience. Hence the dilemma confronting the rational maximizing individual – how to allocate one's assets between cash and interest-yielding bonds, given that there are costs in holding cash and costs associated with turning bonds into cash. More formally, if Y is the income receipt, i the rate of interest, b the cost of turning bonds into cash and K the value of the bonds turned into cash to meet successive transactions needs, the question confronting the utility maximizer is how to determine the size of K, the cash holding per transactions period. Since the average cash holding will be $K/2$, the interest forgone by holding cash will be $(K/2)i$. The cost of turning assets (bonds) into cash will be determined by the number of occasions liquidation is resorted to; thus the liquidation cost is $b(Y/K)$. Total costs are, accordingly,

$$TC = b(Y/K) + (K/2)i \qquad (5.10)$$

which will be minimized when

$$\frac{d(TC)}{dK} = 0 \quad \text{or} \quad -bY/K^2 + i/2 = 0 \qquad (5.11)$$

Solving for K yields

$$K = \sqrt{\frac{2bY}{i}} \qquad (5.12)$$

and the transactions demand for cash, the average cash holding, is

$$\frac{K}{2} = \tfrac{1}{2}\sqrt{\frac{2bY}{i}} \qquad (5.13)$$

The rational individual thus acts to minimize the total costs associated with meeting his transactions needs, and a raising of the rate of interest will decrease his demand for transactions cash and vice versa. It may also be noted that if the act of liquidation were costless there would be no demand for transactions balances – a conclusion intuitively appealing.[3]

Tobin and the Keynesian Asset Demand for Cash

The Keynesian asset demand for cash rests upon the assumption that individuals possess a concept of a normal or expected rate of interest. If the existing market rate of interest is in excess of the normal rate, then the expectation is that market rates will fall or alternatively that bond prices will rise. In such a situation, all asset cash would be turned into the purchase of bonds in the anticipation of making a capital gain and consequently the individual's asset demand for cash would be zero. Conversely, if

---

3 It will be appreciated that Baumol's specification modifies the Keynesian transaction demand in one further respect. Whereas the Keynesian demand for transaction balances was strictly proportional to the income level, Baumol's model implies possible economies of scale in cash holding by positing a non-proportional relationship.

existing market rates lie below that expected, the individual would possess a zero demand for bonds and his demand for asset cash would be infinite. The logic of the Keynesian position, therefore, is that the individual holds either asset cash or bonds but not both simultaneously; the conventional Keynesian aggregate demand curve for asset money holdings is accordingly derived from the assumption that different individuals possess different expectations about the normal rate. This dichotomy has been summarized with the aid of figures 5.1 and 5.2.

The difficulty with such a statement lies in the fact that it does not accord with the observation that individuals are inclined to hold both speculative balances and bonds simultaneously. To meet such an objection Tobin (1958) proposed a reformulation of the Keynesian demand for asset money which asserts that potential bondholders are uncertain about future interest rates. If uncertainty prevails, then investment in long-dated bonds involves the risk of a capital gain or loss. The potential investor therefore must weigh the element of risk against the expected return his investment will yield. Optimal decision-making requires resort to conventional indifference analysis and suggests that normally the individual will hold both bonds and speculative balances.

The argument is summarized with the aid of figure 5.7. The lower portion of the figure depicts the allocation of total assets between idle cash holdings and bonds, whilst the upper portion illustrates the trade-off between risk, measured on the horizontal axis, and expected return,[4] measured on the vertical. Assume the initial interest rate i_1. Then, as revealed by the indifference curves, the optimal combination will be OX of risk combined with an expected return OZ, implying an investment of OA in bonds and retention of YB in cash. Now consider the effect of an increase in the rate of interest. The interest line will be pivoted leftwards to i_2, raising the expected return associated with any degree of risk. How will the individual investor respond? A priori, it is not possible to provide a definitive answer to this question. The rise in interest rates will incorporate an *income effect*, permitting the investor the luxury of undertaking less risk, whilst also promoting a *substitution effect* in favour of more risk as the cost of maintaining idle balances is now increased. However, if as depicted in the diagram the substitution effect is the stronger, the investor will increase his risk-taking and deplete his holding of asset cash. In the figure, the degree of risk rises to OR, the expected yield becomes OE, investment in bonds is indicated as OC and speculative money balances fall to YS. All that is needed to obtain the

---

4 The expected return includes the expectation of a capital gain or loss possessing an expected mean value of zero.

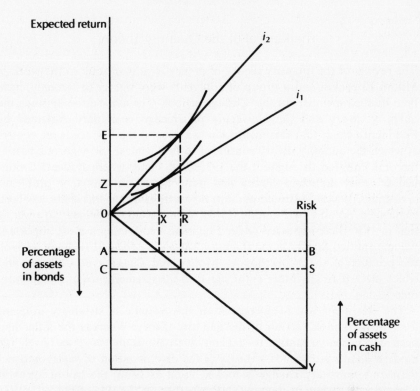

Figure 5.7   Risk and the simultaneous holding of cash and bonds

Keynesian result of an inverse relationship between the asset demand for money and the rate of interest is the assumption that the substitution effect outweighs the income effect in an analysis that reconciles the simultaneous holding of both cash and bonds.

Tobin's analysis must be considered an advance upon conventional Keynesian analysis primarily because it is consistent with the empirically observed fact that certain individuals do indeed hold both bonds and money for speculative purposes, which is implicitly denied in the Keynesian analysis. In so doing, it fully allows for differences in individual preferences and tastes towards risk and can, of course, be generalized to choices involving more than two assets. Together with Baumol's specification of an interest-sensitive transactions demand for money which is non-proportional to income, it serves to strengthen the case for the overall Keynesian approach to the demand for money.

The Revival of the Quantity Theory

The revival of the quantity theory of money is primary due to the work of Milton Friedman and a group of adherents who, rightly or wrongly, have been dubbed members of the 'Chicago school'. The association between the quantity theory and the University of Chicago is in part explained by Friedman's claim that this institution 'was one of the few academic centers at which the quantity theory continued to be a central and vigorous part of the oral tradition throughout the 1930s and 1940s, where students continued to study monetary theory and write theses on monetary problems' (Friedman, 1956a). It should perhaps be mentioned that this claim has been challenged, notably by Patinkin (1969). What cannot be denied, however, is that in 1956 there appeared under Friedman's editorship a most important volume entitled *Studies in the Quantity Theory of Money* (Friedman, 1956b), the product of the Workshop in Money and Banking at Chicago, and which more than any other event signalled the re-emergence of the quantity theory.

The statement which emerges from this volume is strikingly different from the orthodox version of the quantity theory. Whereas the latter had been concerned primarily to explain fluctuations in the price level, the modern quantity theory is a theory of the determination of *money national income*. A monetary change is looked upon as being the causal agent in generating a change in money GNP, whether on the side of output, prices or some combination of the two. In this respect, at least, it is similar to the conventional Keynesian theory which argues that a change in the money supply will normally generate a change in money GNP by working through interest rate changes. Indeed, one of the controversies between Keynesians and monetarists turns upon the most appropriate approach to national income determination. Keynesians emphasize income expenditure relationships and the stability of the multiplier (stable marginal propensity to consume), where monetarists point to the alleged stability of the velocity function.

If the quantity theory is a theory of the determination of money national income, it follows that the impact of a change in the money stock can be either upon physical output, or prices, or some combination of the two. In this respect, it is not unlike the modern Keynesian approach which argues that the impact of a change in the money stock will reveal itself either in output or in price changes, depending upon the extent of unemployed resources. However, in contrast to the Keynesian statement, the relationship between changes in the money stock and resulting changes in money national income is held to be much more predictable and the special case of the liquidity trap, whereby a change in the money stock exerts no effect, is explicitly denied. Further, the extent to which changes will occur upon the side of output or prices will depend in large measure upon the period employed. It is Friedman's assertion that whilst changes in the volume of money may influence short-term movements in output, employment and interest rates, in the long run these variables will approach their 'natural' levels which exist independently of the volume of money.

Of central importance to the revised quantity theory is the assertion that there exists a stable demand function for real money holdings. This of course is not to assert that the quantity of real money holdings remains unchanged but only that it varies in a reasonably predictable way in response to changes in a few key variables. For Friedman, the most important elements influencing the demand for money are the rates of return on money and other assets, both real and financial, the level of permanent income, and the ratio of non-human to total wealth. More specifically, the demand for real money holdings may be written as

$$\frac{M}{P} = f(r_m, r_b, r_e, P^e, Y, w, u) \tag{5.14}$$

r_m is the expected nominal rate of return on money; it will ordinarily be zero for money kept in the form of cash but may be either positive or negative with regard to money held in the form of bank deposits, according to whether such deposits yield net interest or are subject to net service charges. r_b is the expected nominal rate of return on bonds, including expected changes in their prices, and likewise r_e is the expected rate of return on equities, allowance again being made for expected price changes. P^e is the expected rate of change of prices, and hence the expected nominal rate of return on real assets if for simplicity their expected yield is ignored. Y is permanent income and hence an index of total wealth, and w that percentage of total wealth which is held in non-human form and thereby readily realizable – as for example property holdings. Finally, the variable u takes account of all other influences which may determine preference patterns generally. Thus, for example, an increase in the expectation of inflation would normally produce a decline in the demand for money holdings – that is, a rise in velocity. Far from velocity being constant, as was tacitly implied in many of the more naïve versions of the traditional approach, it will respond to significant changes in the above variables in a *predictable* and rational manner. But – and this seems to be the essence of the modern approach – the variables described are normally subject to only slow change over time whereas the supply of money may experience abrupt change. If this is the case, and velocity is subject only to gradual change

over time whilst the money stock may rise and fall rapidly, the clear implication is that the demand for money is independent of its supply.

If the demand for money does not show great variation by comparison
with the supply, which may experience considerable and rapid fluctuation,
then changes in the value of money – which as anything else are to be
explained in terms of supply and demand – are almost always supply determined.

To quote Friedman (1968):

> It is clear from this discussion that changes in prices and nominal
> income can be produced either by changes in the real balances that
> people wish to hold or by changes in the nominal balances available
> for them to hold. Indeed, it is a tautology, summarized in the famous
> quantity equation . . . . The quantity theorem is not, however, this
> tautology. It is, rather, the empirical generalization that changes in
> desired real balances (in the demand) tend to proceed slowly and
> gradually or to be the result of events set in train by prior changes in
> supply, whereas, in contrast, substantial changes in the supply of
> nominal balances can and frequently do occur independently of any
> changes in demand. The conclusion is that substantial changes in
> prices or nominal income are almost invariably the result of changes
> in the nominal supply of money.

This passage also makes it clear why the interest rate sensitivity of the
demand for money is such a vital issue. In the UK the attempt has been
made to control the money supply by controlling interest rates. Accordingly, it follows that if the demand for money was highly interest elastic,
supply and demand would be interdependent and no precise causal influence could be discerned.

The fundamental point of issue between the traditional quantity theory
and the Keynesian onslaught turns upon the crucial question of what constitutes an effective substitute for money balances. The Keynesian position
is to contend that the only close substitute for money is alternative financial
assets. It follows that if the monetary authorities increase the volume of
money excessively a purchase of financial assets will occur and interest rates
will fall. The reduction in interest rates renders money holding more attractive and other assets less attractive until eventually a new equilibrium is
restored between the actual money stock and desired holdings. The implication is that the demand for money would be unstable or – what is the same
thing – the velocity of money would be subject to considerable variation as
a consequence of changes in its supply. Irrespective of the extent of the
interest rate effect, the conventional Keynesian position is to postulate that

the induced consequences for investment and consumption spending would be limited. The limitation on investment spending derives from the assumption that investment demands are often interest inelastic whilst the limitation on induced consumption effects implies that the wealth effect of a fall in interest rates (applicable to the holders of government debt, for example) is a minor factor in the consumption function.

In contrast, the traditional quantity theory had maintained that the only possible substitute for excessive money balances was goods and services; the role of financial assets was virtually ignored. There followed the common conclusion that an enlargement of the total money stock would increase the monetary expenditure on commodities, thereby generating price increases. Implicit in this approach and essential to the validity of the doctrine was the assumption that the demand for money was comparatively stable – that is, the velocity was comparatively constant. This assumption was usually justified upon the grounds that the only demand for money was the normal transactions demand. Moreover, if the principal determinant of consumption expenditure is permanent income (as monetarists would contend) then it is likely that the demand for transactions balances will be stable and predictable.

The modern revival and reformulation of the quantity theory straddles both these viewpoints. Money is looked upon as a substitute for all assets whether real or financial. An increase in the quantity of money will accordingly generate a general increase in demand for commodities in addition to exerting an impact upon interest rates. Although the immediate impact may indeed be felt in financial markets, complete adjustment will involve the commodity markets as well.

Of fundamental importance to the modern quantity theory is the belief that the demand for money is generally insensitive to changes in the interest rate. If the demand for money were to reveal a substantial degree of interest elasticity it would imply that a change in the money stock should be accommodated by a comparatively small change in interest rates, inducing people to extend their demand for money to match the supply. Under these conditions little could follow from a change in the money stock; the impact upon commodity markets would be minimized and the enlarged money supply would simply be held at the lower interest rate, implying a significant decline in the average velocity of money. If, on the other hand, the demand for money were decidedly interest inelastic then the initial interest rate change would not satisfy those people holding excessive money balances; direct spending on goods and services would occur, influencing the level of money incomes within the economy. Implicit in this contention of interest rate insensitivity is the notion that the transactions motive dominates the asset motive in the total demand for money.

Some Empirical Evidence

The preceding theoretical arguments have suggested reasons why the demand for money might be expected to respond positively to real income changes on the one hand and negatively to interest rate changes upon the other. Before the empirical evidence is briefly reviewed it may be noted that the extent of this responsiveness is crucial for policy purposes and for the relative efficacy of monetary versus fiscal policy. In addition, the stability of any alleged relationship is fundamental to the monetarist inflationary mechanism and also carries implications for monetary control upon the part of the monetary authorities. Thus, for example, if the demand for money is a relatively stable function of income and the rate of interest, then it suggests that the monetary authorities may be able to control the supply of money by operating upon the demand for money by changes in the rate of interest. It is indeed the case in the UK that the authorities have relied upon the interest rate as a principal means of controlling and regulating the demand for money by the private sector. Finally, knowledge of the income elasticity of the demand for money is needed to establish money supply targets consistent with given rates of inflation, real gross domestic product (GDP) growth and interest rates. To illustrate, suppose the authorities are aiming at a 5 per cent increase in nominal GDP composed of a 2 per cent increase in real GDP and 3 per cent inflation, and that the income elasticity of the demand for money is estimated at 0.5. Then an increase in the nominal money supply equal to 4 per cent will be required in order to leave interest rates unchanged, since this is the amount by which the demand for nominal money is expected to increase.[5] Empirical findings concerning the determinants of the demand for money, therefore, are of interest in terms not only of the validation of theoretical standpoints but also of the formulation of the appropriate policy stance.

Virtually all the available evidence confirms the expected positive relationship between the demand for money and income on the one hand and the negative relationship between the demand for money and interest rates upon the other. However, considerable variation emerges in the values of the regression coefficients obtained. A good deal of this variation may be accounted for by pointing to differences in the definition of income, money and interest rates employed.

---

5 Since the demand for money is a real demand, a 3 per cent inflation rate will generate a 3 per cent increase in the demand for nominal money holdings, *ceteris paribus*. The additional 1 per cent then arises from the assumption of a 2 per cent growth in real income and the income elasticity of demand of 0.5.

Thus, for example, in the UK the demand for money exhibits greater interest elasticity when regressed against long-term rates of interest as opposed to short-term rates, and the interest elasticity is lower the broader the definition of money employed. However, some differences still remain, and in particular there is considerable controversy about the stability of the demand for money. In this respect, it is noteworthy that the evidence for the UK shows a marked difference from that obtained in the USA, especially in the period after 1971. In the USA a general consensus of opinion views the demand for money as relatively stable. An important study by Goldfield (1973) surveyed the empirical findings and concluded that long-run income elasticities were in the region of $+0.7$ and long-run interest elasticities averaged approximately -0.2.[6] Initially, it was widely believed that UK data and empirical findings, whilst less extensive than their American counterparts, would mirror these general findings. In an important and influential study Laidler (1971a) pointed to the similarity of British and American findings whilst at the same time noting that the UK results were much more sensitive to the definitions of money, income and interest rates employed and also more sensitive to changes in the length of lag structure assumed. In the period after 1971, however, the alleged stability appeared to break down and forecasts based upon previously estimated demand for money functions performed extremely badly. The date 1971 is significant since this marked the introduction in the UK of competition and credit control, which foreshadowed considerable aggressive competition between the banks and other financial institutions. This would suggest that the stability of the demand for money function would itself depend upon the nature of institutional changes.

Concluding Comments

This chapter has attempted to analyze the major influences governing the demand for money. This issue is of considerable importance owing to the unique role performed by money in the modern economy. Any significant change in the demand for money will have repercussions throughout the rest of the economy, with particular implications for interest rates and the price level. It has been seen that the evolution of ideas upon the demand for money has generated considerable controversy and has produced a conceptual revolution in the way economists view the macroeconomy. Today there

---

6 The regression coefficients pertaining to short-run data are much smaller, suggesting that the demand for money responds to real income changes and interest rate changes with a lag.

is a general consensus to the effect that two of the major influences on the demand of money are the rate of interest and the level of income, but differences still exist about the significance of the statistical relationships so obtained and indeed about the manner in which these variables are to be defined. Considerable dispute still remains in the area of policy implications. For example, if the demand for money is sensitive to a change in the rate of interest, however defined, it suggests that interest rate policy may be one means of controlling the supply of money by governing the demand. These issues, *inter alia*, will be taken up in the next chapter.

Further Reading

The best all round text on the demand for money remains Laidler (1985). This provides an overview of all the principal approaches as well as a concise and lucid review of empirical problems and empirical studies.

Chapters 13–15 of Keynes (1936) provide the original statement on the Keynesian transactions, precautionary and speculative motives for holding money. The seminal contributions on the post-Keynesian refinements of the transactions and speculative motives respectively are to be found in Baumol (1952) and Tobin (1958), and the seminal contribution on the modern monetarist approach in Friedman (1956a). Edited versions of the first two are to be found in Surrey (1975).

Empirical analyses of the demand for money now comprise an extensive literature. Surveys can be found in Laidler (1985, chapters 6 and 7), Bain (1976, chapter 5), Artis and Lewis (1981, chapter 2) and Dennis (1981, chapter 6). In addition, Goodhart and Crockett (1970) and Hacche (1974) are worthwhile references.

For a detailed analysis of the theoretical underpinnings of the demand for money, see especially Patinkin (1965) and Rousseas (1972).

6

The Supply of Money

In the analysis of the demand for money in chapter 5 it was assumed that the supply of money was exogenously determined and could be readily controlled by the monetary authorities. As we shall see later, control of the money supply is an important element in several strategies for economic management, in particular the several variants of 'monetarism'.

In this chapter we will examine the money supply process in somewhat greater detail. We will first of all attempt to establish whether in principle the money supply can be controlled, and the instruments which may be deployed in any attempts at monetary control. Following that, with particular reference to recent UK experience, we will consider whether in practice the money supply can be controlled. This issue has been the subject of heated debate in recent years and has exercised the minds of a great many academics, administrators and politicians.

The Money Supply Process

Before comment is made on the instruments which can be and have been employed to try and influence the money supply, the process by which the money supply expands or contracts in a modern developed market economy ought to be considered in more detail.

Money Multipliers

Most readers will be familiar with the proposition that if the central bank increases its liabilities and injects a volume of new notes and coins into the banking system, the commercial banks, in seeking profitable outlets for any addition to deposits, can expand the money stock by several times the original injection. The old adage 'every deposit creates a loan and every loan creates a deposit' concisely summarizes this process. Because the original increase in central bank liabilities results in a multiplied expansion of bank deposits, the original injection is referred to as *high-powered money*.

The extent to which any change in high-powered money is multiplied into a greater change in the money supply is dependent on the value of the *money multiplier*.

One of the most celebrated and frequently cited money multiplier models is that due to Friedman and Schwartz (1963). The details of this model can be elaborated quite easily. Assume that all banks in the system maintain a certain fraction r of their deposit liabilities D in the form of liquid assets to meet the needs of day-to-day demands for cash balances. These will be referred to as *bank reserves R*. Therefore

$$R = rD \qquad (6.1)$$

The *reserve ratio r* may be set by the authorities in a regulated system, or determined by prudential judgement in an unregulated system. *Deposit liabilities* are the assets of the general public. Not all of the public's financial assets will normally be deposited in the banking system, however. Ordinarily a certain fraction c of D will be held in the form of notes and coin C for day-to-day transactions and precautionary motives. Thus

$$C = cD \qquad (6.2)$$

Given equations 6.1 and 6.2, the stock of high-powered money can be defined as

$$H = C + R \qquad (6.3)$$

Variations in H result in multiplied variations in the money stock M, where this is defined as:

$$M = C + D \qquad (6.4)$$

The relationship between H and M can be easily ascertained. First, divide equation 6.4 by equation 6.3:

$$\frac{M}{H} = \frac{C + D}{C + R} \qquad (6.5)$$

Then divide the right-hand side of equation 6.5 through by D:

$$\frac{M}{H} = \frac{c + 1}{c + r} \qquad (6.6)$$

which can be rearranged to

$$M = \left(\frac{c + 1}{c + r}\right) H \qquad (6.7a)$$

According to equation 6.7a, the money stock and changes in the money supply are determined by the volume of high-powered money, the general public's currency/deposit ratio and the bank's reserve ratio. These factors are referred to as the *proximate determinants* of the money supply, and influence the money supply as follows:

$$\frac{\partial M}{\partial H} > 0 \qquad\qquad (6.7b)$$

$$\frac{\partial M}{\partial c} < 0 \qquad\qquad (6.7c)$$

$$\frac{\partial M}{\partial r} < 0 \qquad\qquad (6.7d)$$

The Relationships between M, H, c and r

The interrelationships between M, H, c and r can be illustrated diagrammatically. In figure 6.1 it is assumed for simplicity that the only source of reserves to the banks is currency, and that the volume of currency made available is determined by the public's currency/deposit ratio. If the central bank issues

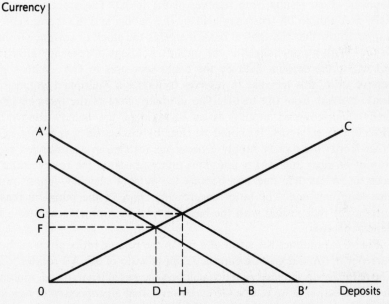

Figure 6.1   Effect of an increase in the volume of high-powered money on the money supply

0A of currency and the general public holds 0F, the remainder FA will be held by the banks. The extent to which the banks can use these reserves to create loans and further deposits is determined by their reserve ratio. If this were set at unity, then every deposit would have to be backed by currency and the slope of the line AB would have an absolute value of one. When the reserve ratio is less than one of course the banks need only hold a certain fraction of any deposit in currency and lend the remainder to deficit units, some of which will ultimately be redeposited. Thus, when the reserve ratio is less than unity, the slope of AB will have an absolute value of less than unity, reflecting the fact that the volume of bank deposits exceeds the volume of currency held by the banks. In figure 6.1, the position and slope of AB are determined by the stock of currency and the reserve ratio respectively, whilst the ray 0C is determined by the public's currency/deposit ratio. A higher value for this ratio would result in a steeper 0C, whilst a lower value would result in a shallower 0C.

This framework can be used to explore the impact of changes in H, c and r on M.

Assume initially that the stock of currency is given by 0A. Given an initial currency/deposit ratio of 0C, 0F is held by the public and FA deposited with the banks. Given a reserve ratio as reflected by the slope of AB, the banks use this currency to back loans, and the equilibrium volume of deposits which results from reserves of FA is 0D. The money supply initially amounts to 0F (currency held by the public) and 0D (bank deposits). Suppose now that the central bank increases the stock of currency from 0A to 0A'. With an unchanged c, the public's holdings of currency increase to 0G whilst the amount held by the banks increases to GA'. With a given reserve ratio, this increase in reserves facilitates a multiplied expansion of bank deposits from 0D to 0H. The ultimate effect of the increase in currency (high-powered money) is an increase in the money supply from 0F + 0D to 0G + 0H. It should be clear by inspection that DH > FG; in other words the money supply process has resulted in a multiplied expansion of M such that $\Delta M > \Delta H$. This follows because the reserve ratio has been set as less than one, and because the public's currency/deposit ratio is also less than one. The latter ensures that part of the initial increase in currency is redeposited with the banks, whilst the former generates a loan deposit process.

Figure 6.2 outlines the effect of a fall in the reserve ratio, given a stock of currency of 0A and given a currency/deposit ratio of 0C. AB rotates to AB'. The reduction in the reserve ratio facilitates increased lending and multiplied deposit creation of up to 0N. Given however that a proportion of new loans is held in currency and not redeposited, bank deposits increase from 0D to 0M, whilst currency held by the public increases from 0F to 0L, the overall impact being a rise in the money supply from 0D + 0F to 0L + 0M. The same analysis would apply, *mutatis mutandis,* to a rise in the reserve ratio.

Finally, in figure 6.3 the implications of a fall in the currency/deposit ratio are explored. Assume that this falls, and results in 0C rotating to 0C'.

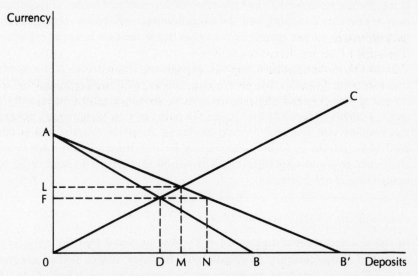

Figure 6.2   Effect of a change in the reserve asset ratio on the money supply

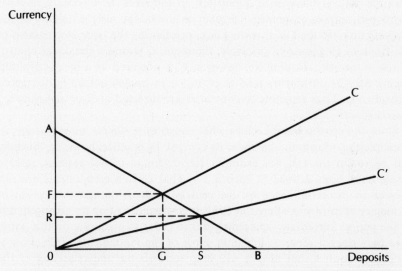

Figure 6.3   Effect of a change in the currency/deposit ratio on the money supply

With an unchanged reserve ratio, and a fixed stock of currency of 0A, the volume of currency held by the banks increases from FA to RA, which in turn facilitates a multiple expansion of deposits from 0G to 0S. Here one component of the money supply, currency held by the public, contracts whilst the other, bank deposits, expands. As long as the banks' reserve ratio is less than one, however, the expansion of deposits will exceed the contraction in currency holdings, and the overall impact will be an increase in the money supply. (It can readily be seen that this is the case in figure 6.3 where GS > FR.)

Thus the money multiplier model, or *monetary base* model as it is sometimes known, predicts that the money supply will be determined by *the volume of high-powered money* in the system, *the banks' reserve ratio*, and *the public's currency/deposit ratio*. From the point of view of monetary control this implies that if r and c could be taken as given, the authorities can control variations in M by manipulating H. If, however, c and r are essentially unstable and unpredictable, it could be that efforts to control M by controlling H are frustrated.

Controllability of High-powered Money

In the simple model of figures 6.1–6.3 it was assumed that the only component of H was currency. In equation 6.3, however, H was defined as equal to $C + R$, where the latter constitute non-currency reserves. If both C and R were liabilities of the central bank, then it would be reasonable to conclude that the central bank is in a position to influence H. Certainly in most developed market economies, currency in unambiguously a liability of the central bank. (In the UK this stock is controlled by the Issue Department of the Bank of England.) In principle, therefore, C is under the direct control of the authorities. In practice, however, C is not used as a means of influencing M. The authorities tend to permit C to be determined by the needs of exchange. Thus attempts to control H are directed at R or *non-currency reserve assets*.

Since the central bank decides what constitutes *eligible reserve assets*, in principle this too should be under its control. In practice, however, this may not be so. In the UK, for example, largely for historical reasons, reserve assets have been defined in such a way that certain components are not subject to direct influence by the central bank. Although the system of monetary control was altered in 1981, it is worth dwelling on arrangements in the period immediately preceding this in order to elaborate on this point. Not only does it serve to highlight some of the fundamental difficulties of monetary control, but also it will help towards an understanding of the rationale behind recent changes.

Between 1971 and 1981, reserve assets of the clearing banks in the UK were defined to include: the banks' balances with the Bank of England; UK Treasury bills; money at call in the London discount market; British Government stocks with up to one year to maturity; local authority bills eligible for rediscount at the Bank of England; and commercial bills. Table 6.1 gives details of the relative importance of each of these components for the period 1978–80. Clearly there are certain components over which the central bank can exercise direct influence, namely balances with the Bank of England, the total volume of Treasury bills and Government stocks though not the accounts actually held by the banks. In addition, in principle the issue of local authority bills can be controlled if central government imposes limits on the amount which local authorities can borrow using this source. In so far as these volumes are controllable, the stock of high-powered money can be controlled. There are two components, however, over which complete control cannot be exercised – namely commercial bills and money at call. The former is the less important of the two since an upper limit is placed on the amount of commercial bills which can actually be held.[1] It is worth noting however that this may still serve to complicate monetary control if the banking system were holding commercial bills at a very low level prior to a period of monetary restraint. As can be seen from table 6.1, money at call is a substantial fraction of total reserve assets. In principle the central bank has some control over this volume in that money at call with the discount houses has largely been made available for the purchase of Treasury bills. Other things being equal, therefore, a reduction in the number of Treasury bills released to the discount houses should result in a reduction in their demand for money at call from the clearing banks. A complication for monetary control could however arise if the discount houses place with the clearing banks reserve assets (like commercial bills) which are not included in the banks' own portfolio.

It might be argued that such complications are marginal and that the central bank can in practice exercise control over the bulk of high-powered money. Superficially there is some substance in such a view since, as table 6.1 indicates, notes and coin, balances with the Bank of England, Treasury bills and local authority bills constituted on average of around 80 per cent of high-powered money over the period 1978–80. To assume that because the central authorities are the source of most reserve assets they can therefore actually control the flow of such assets, is to oversimplify the process of monetary control in the extreme. To see why, consider further the source of variations in the supply of reserve assets.

The change in the volume of high-powered money over any given period

---

1 The clearing banks can hold up to 2 per cent of their total eligible liabilities in the form of commercial bills.

TABLE 6.1

Composition of Reserve Assets in UK Banks, 1978, 1979 and 1980

Year	Total	Balances with the Central Bank		Money at Call		UK and Northern Ireland Treasury Bills		Local Authority Bills		Commercial Bills		Government Stocks	
	£m	£m	% of total	£m	% of total	£m	% of total	£m	% of total	£m	% of total	£m	% of total
1978													
March	6,020	266	4.4	3,644	60.5	718	11.9	90	1.5	725	12.0	596	9.7
June	6,140	393	6.4	3,539	57.6	835	13.6	130	2.1	788	12.8	454	7.5
Sept.	5,827	363	6.2	3,219	55.2	944	16.2	133	2.3	782	13.4	387	6.7
Dec.	6,132	420	6.9	3,222	52.5	838	13.7	148	2.4	804	13.1	700	11.4
1979													
March	6,248	412	6.6	3,557	56.9	826	13.2	87	1.4	812	13.0	554	8.9
June	6,511	479	7.4	3,428	52.6	1,022	15.7	169	2.6	862	13.2	551	8.5
Sept.	6,645	490	7.4	3,867	58.2	858	12.9	172	2.6	915	13.8	344	12.5
Dec.	6,861	449	6.5	3,629	52.9	1,118	16.3	152	2.2	947	13.8	565	8.3
1980													
March	6,908	370	5.4	3,939	54.0	861	12.5	241	3.5	988	14.3	509	7.3
June	7,344	475	6.5	3,746	51.0	1,200	16.3	436	5.9	1,034	14.1	453	6.2
Sept.	8,478	664	7.8	4,555	53.7	1,090	12.9	412	4.9	1,168	13.8	588	6.9
Dec.	9,084	485	5.3	4,896	53.9	1,168	12.8	502	5.5	1,251	13.8	782	8.7

Source: Bank of England Quarterly Bulletin (various issues)

is determined by the amount which the authorities have to borrow over that time period, and the way in which this is borrowed. Specifically,

$$PSD + MAT = ECF + OMO_N + NMD + OMO_B + \Delta H \qquad (6.8)$$

where PSD is the public sector deficit, MAT are funds required for debt maturities, ECF is the change in foreign exchange assets, OMO_N are open market operations with the non-bank private sector, NMD are transactions in non-marketable debt (e.g. National Savings), OMO_B are sales of non-reserve asset debt to the banking system, and ΔH is the change in high-powered money (that is, the issue of currency and sales of securities to the clearing banks).

If equation 6.8 is rearranged, then

$$\Delta H = PSD + MAT - ECF - OMO_N - NMD - OMO_B \qquad (6.9)$$

The change in high-powered money is therefore determined by the extent to which the authorities can fund the *public sector deficit* without recourse to issuing notes and coin, and without recourse to selling government bonds to the clearing banks. Although the relationship between the public sector deficit and the volume of high-powered money will be examined in greater detail later, a number of observations should be made. First the change in the volume of high-powered money is dependent on non-bank demand for short-term government securities, bank demand for non-reserve asset (long-term) debt, the sale of non-marketable debt to the general public, and the magnitude of any balance of payments imbalance. The sale of non-reserve asset debt clearly depends on the yields offered on such securities relative to competing assets. The demand for such assets may not be easily predicted. This may be further complicated by the fact that the size of the deficit may turn out to be different from what is 'planned'. If, for example, interest rates are raised to restrict credit and to increase the attractiveness of government securities to the non-bank public, one outcome may be that output and employment are reduced. If this follows, the public sector deficit will automatically increase as tax receipts fall and social security transfers increase. The borrowing requirement is correspondingly increased and, *ceteris paribus*, so too is the extent to which this has to be funded by high-powered money.

The second complication which must be noted is the role played by the balance of payments. It can be seen from equations 6.8 and 6.9 that balance of payments surpluses and deficits (which for present purposes will be equated with ECF) will affect the borrowing requirement. If, for example, the UK runs an unanticipated balance of payments surplus, there would be net purchases (sales of) foreign exchange (sterling). To acquire the excess supply of foreign exchange the central bank would either have to issue more notes and coin, or have to sell some of its holdings of Treasury bills to obtain the necessary notes and coin. In the former case there would be a net increase in high-powered money. In the latter case there would also probably be an increase in high-powered money, since the existence of the surplus means that, other things being equal, more Treasury bills must be sold to the banks or the stock of notes and coin has to increase. The point is that the balance of payments is not an easily predictable magnitude, and in an open economy like the UK it may have important implications for monetary control. (This is something which will be returned to in chapters 14 and 15.)

Stability of the Reserve and Currency/Deposit Ratios

Even if the caveats which have been noted with respect to the controllability of H are inapplicable, it should be clear from equation 6.8 that for a systematic relationship to hold between H and M the money multiplier has to be stable. In other words the ratios r and c have to be taken as parameters. If they are variable rather than constant, then variations in r and c could offset variations in H.

There have been many occasions when a minimum value for r has been set in the UK by the central bank. The rationale behind such a requirement is that the clearing banks are forced to maintain a certain fraction of their assets in relatively liquid form in keeping with the tenets of financial prudence. Furthermore, by setting a reserve asset ratio the authorities are provided with a further control variable whereby they can influence the amount of credit creation which takes place. Clearly, however, even when a minimum reserve asset ratio is set, the clearing banks still have a certain amount of discretion over the actual reserve asset ratio maintained. When, for example, nominal and real interest rates are relatively high they may be expected to run down the ratio to its minimum (that is, become fully *loaned up*) compared with a situation of low interest rates and recessionary pressure. In such circumstances, a higher probability of default on loans might encourage them to permit the ratio to rise. (Interestingly, the UK experienced both high interest rates and recessionary pressures in the late 1970s and early 1980s. If anything the influence of high interest rates appears to have predominated, with banks tending to become fully loaned up.)

Table 6.2 reports the trend in the clearing banks' reserve asset ratios throughout the 1970s. Early in the decade the ratio declined quite significantly in response to a change in monetary arrangements in 1971 which had the effect of lowering the minimum r. Between 1976 and 1980 the ratio appeared to be relatively stable. In 1981 the ratios were abolished.

Much of the debate over whether the money supply is controllable or not centres on the stability of c, the public's currency/deposit ratio (or the

TABLE 6.2
Reserve Ratios of UK Banks, 1971–81

Year	Reserve Ratios (%)
1971	17.4
1972	15.7
1973	13.8
1974	13.4
1975	15.2
1976	13.8
1977	14.8
1978	13.6
1979	13.2
1980	13.5
1981	11.0

Source: Bank of England Quarterly Bulletin (various issues).
Notes: all figures apply to the fourth quarter of each year except for 1981 which applies to the second quarter.

general public's demand for cash balances). As has been seen in the previous chapter, those who argue that the demand for money is essentially a demand for a transactions asset would contend that c is both stable and predictable (and therefore so too is velocity). They would argue that c changes only slowly in response to technological change in the banking system. Thus for example over the long run c has tended to fall with increased use of credit cards.

It was noted in the last chapter, however, that the demand for money can be viewed as an exercise in portfolio selection and may therefore vary systematically with (for instance) changes in the rate of interest. Further-more, as Baumol's model demonstrated, this may be so not only in con-sidering a demand for speculative balances, but also in the case of transactions balances. If this is the case then this would comprise another potential source of variation in the money stock. Variations in H could be offset by variations in c. For example, a restriction of H which resulted in a rise in interest rates could stimulate a fall in c (and therefore an increase in velocity), which would serve to offset the effects of the initial contraction in the monetary base.[2]

Following from the simple multiplier approach, then, there are a number

---

2 Note that this depends on the definition of the money stock which we are working with. If this is a narrow definition (currency plus demand deposits), then the statement holds true. If, however, it is a broader definition (currency plus demand deposits plus interest bearing deposits, then it need not be true).

of question marks which can be placed against the controllability of the money supply. On the one hand those of a monetarist persuasion would tend to argue that r and c can both be regarded as stable, the former because it can be set by the authorities, the latter because the demand for money is stable, and therefore control of H is both necessary and sufficient for control of M. Those of a more Keynesian persuasion would question the stability of c and the controllability of H. Furthermore, they would in general be more sceptical of the presence of a clear break in the liquidity chain between money and near money which monetarists contend exists. This scepticism has tended to become more acute as the importance of non-bank financial intermediaries (NBFIs) has increased. Clearly if it is the case that money is readily substitutable for other financial assets, then the supply of money will be endogenous and less easily controlled by the monetary authorities. Monetary control requires the existence of a distinct group of assets for which the demand is stable and which are not readily substitutable for other financial assets.

Delineating the Money Stock

As was seen in chapter 5, the distinguishing characteristic of money is that it is an asset which can be used in the final settlement of a debt. In most societies, however, there may be more than one such asset in circulation at any time. Clearly therefore if one wishes to attempt to 'control' the size of the money stock, then one must delineate one group of assets which might be regarded as money from another group of assets regarded as non-money. The problem is of course that money is used not only for transactions purposes but also as a store of value. There may be certain highly liquid assets that are clearly and closely identified with the *transactions function*, such as notes and coin in circulation. Similarly, at the other end of the spectrum there exist certain highly illiquid assets which are clearly and closely identified with the *store of value function* such as long-term bonds. In between these extremes, however, there exists a range of assets of varying shades of liquidity, and it is far from obvious where the line should be drawn between money and non-money. In other words, there is no obvious break in the *liquidity chain*.

The point is easily illustrated by reference to the liquidity spectrum or chain in the UK. As has been noted, notes and coin in circulation are unambiguously 'money' used for transactions purposes; so too are demand deposits at commercial banks. If the authorities decide that notes and coin in circulation plus demand deposits are the relevant control variable, however, and pursue a policy of monetary contraction, one response on the part of economic agents might be to transfer cash balances from time deposit accounts to demand deposit accounts. Although time deposits are (in principle) less liquid than demand deposits,[3] in practice they are quickly realizable. One might therefore include deposit accounts in the definition of the money supply. If one does, however, are deposits in the home currency only included, or are domestic residents' deposits in other currencies also to be included? If there are no exchange controls, then clearly domestic residents' deposits in overseas currencies could have a marked influence on the domestic money stock. (One outstanding example of this is the 'repatriation' of Eurodollars which often accompanies monetary restraint in the USA.) Furthermore, if time deposits with commercial banks are included in the definition of the money stock, what about time deposits with non-bank financial intermediaries, such as building societies? After all, to many these are regarded as substitutes for commercial bank time deposits. If one is including time deposits because they can be realized relatively quickly, then what about other assets whose capital value can be realized almost as quickly – short-term securities like Treasury bills, for example? If short-term securities are included, what is the appropriate definition of the short term?

Clearly, as soon as a move is made away from assets whose capital value is immediately realizable (notes and coin) towards assets whose capital value it takes time to realize, the problem is faced of deciding where the line should be drawn. It could be argued that the issue is an empirical one, and the 'appropriate' definition of the money supply is dependent on the reason for control. Suppose, for example, one wishes to control the rate of growth in money supply because one is convinced that it is systematically related to the rate of change of prices. Careful perusal of time series data would perhaps reveal that one monetary aggregate bears a closer relationship to changes in the price level than others. If so then this is the aggregate to be controlled. This view too has been challenged, most notably by Goodhart (1975) who has argued that *any* measure of the money supply which is officially controlled loses its meaning because agents search for ways around the control in a relatively short space of time.[4]

---

3 In principle most clearing banks request five (working) days' notice prior to a withdrawal from a time deposit account. In practice this tends to be waived, certainly in the case of relatively small withdrawals.

4 This possibility is well illustrated by recent experience in the UK with the so-called 'corset', that is, the supplementary special deposit scheme, whereby if bank lending exceeded certain defined limits the banks were required to place supplementary special deposits with the Bank of England. One way in which the banking system responded to these controls was by devising new ways of creating credit by, for example, issuing acceptance credits whereby one company would hold a bank

Money Supply Definitions in the UK

This uncertainty over precisely what constitutes the money supply is evident in the UK where no less than seven different definitions of the money supply have been used in recent years. These are:

M0   notes and coin in circulation

M1   notes and coin in circulation plus sterling demand deposits held by the private sector

M2   notes and coin in circulation with the public plus sterling retail deposits held by the UK private sector with the UK monetary sector, building societies and National Saving Bank ordinary accounts

£M3   M1 plus sterling time deposits held by UK residents

M3   £M3 plus bank deposits in foreign currency held by UK residents

PSL1   private sector liquidity, that is, the private sector's share of £M3 plus private sector holdings of money market instruments (like treasury bills), and certificates of tax deposits

PSL2   PSL1 plus the private sector's savings and deposits with building societies and non-clearing banks

Clearly M0 is the narrowest definition of the money supply which is possible. Indeed, given almost perfect substitutability between cash and demand deposits, most analysts would regard M1 as a more satisfactory and meaningful measure of narrow money than M0. Notwithstanding this, M0 has recently found favour with the monetary authorities at the expense of M1. Both M0 and M1 concentrate on assets which do not have to be capitalized prior to being used for transactions purposes. The move through to the PSL definitions constitutes a move through the liquidity spectrum to include time deposits with non-clearing banks and short-term securities. Table 6.3 gives details of the order of magnitude of these aggregates for the 1976–85 period, whilst figure 6.4 charts their movement over the past few years. As can be seen from the latter, although all of the aggregates appear to be positively correlated over the period, for certain sub-periods there is less correlation between some.

The latter has been interpreted by some commentators as evidence of a high degree of substitutability between different assets. This view gains

---

guaranteed security and another company could obtain credit on the strength of it. This created considerable scope for circumventing central bank controls, and when the corset scheme was abandoned in the middle of 1980 the incorporation of transactions covered by such arrangements raised £M3 by about 6 per cent.

TABLE 6.3
Quarterly percentage in the UK Monetary Aggregates 1976–85

At end of period	M1 Amount outstanding*	M1 % change	£M3 Amount outstanding*	£M3 % change	PSL1 Amount outstanding*	PSL1 % change	PSL2 Amount outstanding*	PSL2 % change	Mo Amount outstanding*	Mo % change	M2 Amount outstanding*	M2 % change
1976 1	17,940	+5.4	37,960	+3.0	40,485	+2.8	69,397	+4.1				
2	18,530	+3.4	38,790	+2.2	41,246	+1.9	71,095	+2.5				
3	19,100	+3.1	40,300	+3.9	42,837	+3.9	73,256	+3.1				
4	18,980	−0.6	40,380	+0.2	43,030	+0.5	73,829	+0.8				
1977 1	19,540	+2.9	40,720	+0.9	43,284	+0.6	75,227	+1.9				
2	20,530	+5.0	41,740	+2.5	44,281	+2.3	77,181	+2.6				
3	22,020	+7.2	42,990	+2.9	45,510	+2.8	79,726	+3.3				
4	23,180	+5.3	44,540	+3.6	46,614	+2.5	82,420	+3.4				
1978 1	24,370	+4.9	46,880	+4.9	49,280	+5.5	86,913	+5.4				
2	25,010	+2.7	48,200	+2.8	50,130	+1.7	88,803	+2.2				
3	26,030	+4.1	49,400	+2.5	51,860	+3.5	91,570	+3.1				
4	27,070	+4.1	51,440	+5.2	53,943	+4.1	94,811	+3.6				
1979 1	27,620	+2.1	52,390	+1.8	56,148	+4.1	98,453	+3.8				
2	28,100	+1.7	54,310	+3.7	58,561	+4.3	101,957	+3.6				
3	28,970	+3.1	55,950	+3.1	60,660	+3.6	104,731	+2.7				
4	29,550	+2.0	58,030	+3.8	62,751	+3.5	107,730	+2.9				
1980 1	29,360	−0.6	59,570	+2.7	64,040	+2.2	110,415	+2.6				
2	29,950	+2.0	62,860	+5.5	67,634	+5.6	114,658	+3.8				
3	29,800	−0.5	65,790	+4.6	69,933	+3.4	118,015	+2.9				
4	30,730	+3.1	69,100	+5.0	72,893	+4.2	122,236	+3.6				
1981 1	31,880	+3.8	70,250	+1.6	73,233	+0.6	125,373	+2.5				
2	33,000	+3.5	73,310	+4.3	76,342	+4.2	130,148	+3.8				
3	33,410	+1.2	76,600	+4.5	79,793	+4.5	134,379	+3.3				
4	33,530	+0.4	78,350	+2.3	81,265	+1.9	136,090	+1.3				
1982 1	36,720	+9.5	87,860	+12.1	90,149	+10.4	141,187	+3.7				
2	37,590	+2.4	89,610	+2.0	91,553	+1.6	143,284	+1.5				
3	38,140	+1.5	90,870	+1.4	92,923	+1.6	145,222	+1.4	12,135	—	102,659	—
4	40,220	+5.4	93,850	+3.3	94,970	+2.2	148,536	+2.3	12,366	+1.9	109,316	+6.5
1983 1	41,090	+2.2	96,980	+3.3	99,006	+4.2	156,388	+5.3	12,313	−0.3	112,591	+3.0
2	42,980	+11.6	99,610	+2.7	101,173	+2.2	160,238	+2.5	12,625	+2.5	114,443	+1.6
3	—	—	99,250	−0.4	—	—	162,887	+1.7	12,905	+2.2	115,922	+1.3
4	—	—	101,840	+2.6	—	—	166,978	+2.5	13,219	+2.4	121,045	+4.4
1984 1	—	—	103,810	+1.9	—	—	194,731	+16.4	12,999	−1.7	125,255	+3.5
2	—	—	106,070	+2.2	—	—	200,961	+3.2	13,314	+2.4	129,007	+3.0
3	—	—	109,000	+2.8	—	—	202,678	+0.9	13,614	+2.2	131,289	+1.8
4	—	—	112,140	+2.9	—	—	213,509	+5.3	13,962	+2.6	135,053	+2.9
1985 1	—	—	116,190	+3.6	—	—	221,931	+3.9	13,704	−1.8	137,559	+1.9
2	—	—	118,450	+4.9	—	—	225,959	+1.8	14,041	+2.5	138,278	+0.5
3	—	—	124,140	+4.8	—	—	233,645	+3.4	14,212	+1.2	143,456	+3.5
4	—	—	127,190	+2.5	—	—	239,920	+2.7	14,425	+1.5	147,853	+3.1

Source: *Economic Trends* (seasonally adjusted) various issues.

* The definition of PSL2 has been widened to include the private sector holdings in terms of shares and SAYE deposits with building societies and sterling deposits (banks) over 2-year maturity. (This is a change in the definition as from 1983 onwards.)

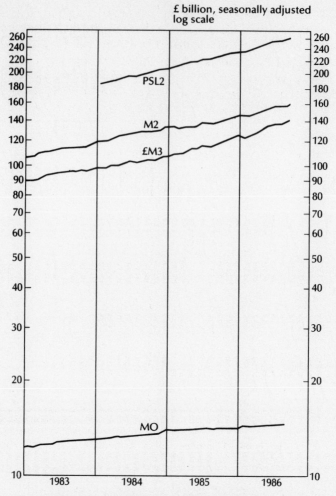

Figure 6.4   Trends in UK monetary aggregates 83–6
Source: *Economic Trends* Feb 1987, p. 53

further support if one examines the correlation between *changes* in various monetary aggregates rather than levels. Thus for example one finds that over the periods 1971–73 and 1979–81 the *changes* in M1 and £M3 were actually negatively correlated at times.

Monetary Control in the UK

Figure 6.5 presents a simple model of the complete money market, in which is assumed a stable money demand function M_d, inversely related to the rate of interest, and an exogenously given money supply function insensitive to interest rate changes. Suppose initially the money supply is M_1. If the authorities desire a money supply of M_2, it can be seen from the diagram that this can be attained through either a change in the quantity of money from M_{s1} to M_{s2} (which will raise its price), or a change in the price of money, that is an increase in the interest rate from r_1 to r_2 which results in a contraction of the demand for money. This might suggest that the

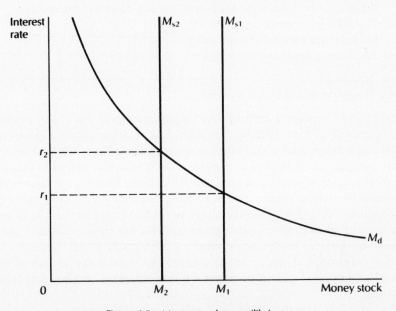

Figure 6.5   Money market equilibrium

choice of technique is simply a case of selecting between quantity controls or price controls. At the simplest level this is certainly so. When it is recalled, however, that any change in the money supply is itself the outcome of changes in a number of aggregates, it can be seen that the choice of technique is rather more complicated. Thus, quality controls could apply to bank deposits, or bank lending or private lending to the public sector, or changes in the reserve ratio; price controls could apply to bank deposits, bank lending, public borrowing from the private sector and so on. In fact, Gowland (1982) identifies no less than 17 methods of controlling M.

Constraints on space prevent the examination of the effects of all of these techniques in detail. Besides which, only a few have been relied on to any significant extent in the UK over the post-war period. These will be focused on with a view to commenting on some of the practical problems faced in controlling the money supply. The instruments which have been most widely applied in the UK are:

(1) *Quantity controls*
   (a) On bank lending to the non-bank private sector
   (b) On deposits through the supplementary special deposit scheme.
(2) *Price manipulations*
   (a) Sales of public sector debt to the non-bank private sector (open market operations)
   (b) Price effects on bank lending to the non-bank private sector.
(3) *Portfolio constraints*
   (a) Reliance on reserve asset ratios.
(4) *Monetary targets and the PSBR*

Before Competition and Credit Control

Prior to 1971 monetary control was largely attempted via *credit control*, that is, control of bank lending to the non-bank private sector. The central instruments deployed for this purpose were *credit ceilings*, imposed on the clearing banks, and *directives or moral suasion*. The former aimed to contain the total volume of credit creation, whilst the latter sought to influence the allocation of a given volume by for example directing the clearing banks to give priority to export oriented firms or public corporations. It is not unusual to find that, when quantitative controls are imposed on any commodity or service, inefficiencies arise as individuals invest resources in seeking ways around the controls; attempts to control the growth of the money supply via quantitative restrictions generated similar avoidance activities.

For example, because Bank of England controls applied only to the clearing banks there was a tremendous growth in *secondary banks* (merchant banks, savings banks, trade banks and so on), which were outside the London clearing system and were at the same time not subject to credit controls. Another by-product of using controls was the growth of so-called *disintermediation*, that is to say borrowing–lending agreements which bypass the banks completely. In some cases the process actually became institutionalized, as for example in the *intercorporate money market* where companies borrow and lend to each other directly without a bank acting as financial intermediary.

This growth of secondary activities is entirely predictable in some respects. The Bank of England exercised some discretion over the structure of interest rates via its control of bank rate, that is the rate at which it would lend money to the clearing banks. The fact that secondary banking and disintermediation became increasingly important in the 1960s is presumably indicative of an excess demand for credit at the administered price. Interest rate manipulations were on occasion used to try and influence credit demand through price; invariably, however, this instrument was only used when there was a balance of payments crisis. (As will be seen in chapter 20, since interest rate variations have a direct impact on the capital account of the balance of payments, they were frequently used in this period as an instrument for external balance.)

Note that although the potential usefulness of r (the reserve ratio) as a control variable was stressed earlier, it was simply not used over this period. Although a *cash ratio* (of 8 per cent of reserve assets) and a *liquidity ratio* (of 28 per cent of reserve assets) applied to the clearing banks, no systematic manipulation of these ratios for monetary control was practised. Monetary control via manipulation of r would amount to what is currently referred to as *monetary base control*; one feature of this is the market determination of interest rates, something which the UK authorities have been reluctant to accept.

One instrument which was used, however, and which has effects qualitatively similar to changes in r, was the use of *special deposits*. These were introduced in the UK in 1958. Their use entailed the placing of deposits by the clearing banks with the Bank of England, to be frozen at the latter's discretion, their objective being to reduce bank liquidity and reduce the ability of the banks to create credit. Special deposits were in fact employed quite frequently, and although Coghlan (1973) found some evidence to indicate that their use was effective, Crouch (1970) and Goodhart (1973) are sceptical of their impact.

Competition and Credit Control

In 1971 a new approach to monetary control was adopted with the introduction of *competition and credit control* (CCC), which seems to have been motivated by two objectives. On the one hand it was hoped that the new arrangements would stimulate greater competition between the clearing banks; on the other hand it was hoped that credit would be controlled more effectively than before 1971. The latter objective was born out of a dissatisfaction with the operation of direct controls, which not only were felt to have been ineffective but also made it difficult to measure changes in the volume of credit with any precision, since one could never be entirely clear on how much avoidance was actually taking place. Accordingly, reliance on quantitative controls was eschewed under CCC and instead greater emphasis placed on instruments which affected the money supply via price; in other words interest rate manipulations were thrust to the forefront. The target variable was seen as M3 and it was planned to control the change in this variable by operating on the demand for credit. (It might also be noted that CCC replaced the cash and liquidity ratio with a $12\frac{1}{2}$ per cent reserve asset ratio, although there was no intention to move to a system of monetary base control as a consequence of this.)

The CCC arrangements lasted until the end of 1973. In 1972 M3 grew by 22 per cent and in 1973 by 27 per cent. Since one of the principal objectives of the arrangements was to control credit in a more efficient way than previous arrangements, something clearly went badly wrong. The complete loss of control of the growth of the money supply can be traced to two factors. The first was the change in the reserve asset ratio. Gibson (1971) estimated that prior to the change, the clearing banks held around 20 per cent of reserve assets in the form of eligible liabilities. The reduction in the legal requirement to $12\frac{1}{2}$ per cent created considerable scope for a once and for all credit expansion. (Table 6.2 gives details of the changes in reserve ratios which occurred.) This could have been avoided if the cost of credit were permitted to rise sufficiently to choke off demand or if the authorities had used open market operations to counteract it.

The second factor was that, given the political sensitivity of interest rates, the authorities were apparently unwilling to permit nominal interest rates to rise to levels which would have allowed them to gain effective control over credit creation (see Gowland, 1982). As a result, real rates of interest were extremely low. In the end an attempt to regain monetary control was made via the reintroduction of quantitative controls in the form of the *supplementary special deposit* scheme. This effectively placed ceilings on the volume of deposits which banks could accept, and therefore the volume of lending in which they could engage. As was noted earlier, these controls (like credit controls in the 1960s) generated avoidance activity with the result that distortions were generated.

After Competition and Credit Control

Under the Conservative administration of 1979–87 eligible liabilities have continued to be specified. These comprise, for each of the clearing banks, their total sterling resources and determine each bank's 'cash ratio deposits'. Thus banks with eligible liabilities exceeding £10 million are required to deposit 0.5 per cent of eligible liabilities with the Bank of England. This is not a vehicle, however, for monetary base control, but rather a facility whereby the Bank of England is provided with liquid resources, for day-to-day purposes. In general, therefore, price has continued to be the main instrument of control. The mechanism of control was similar to the CCC experiment, namely the manipulation of interest rates to influence the demand for bank credit by the non-bank private sector. Thus if one wishes to contract credit demand, interest rates are raised, bank credit contracts, and ultimately bank deposits contract (to maintain equality of assets and liabilities). Thus from equation 6.4 the money supply is reduced. As in the earlier period, however, monetary control has proved to be far from easy. For example, the government set a target growth range of 7–11 per cent for £M3 for 1979–80, yet the actual out-turn was over 18 per cent. One might argue that this is simply a reflection of a reluctance to permit interest rates to rise to the requisite level. In principle the money supply can be controlled via controlling the demand for cerdit; in practice it may necessitate higher nominal interest rates than are regarded as politically feasible. Despite the fact that nominal interest rates were raised to historically high levels (17 per cent in autumn 1979) there may be something in this argument, especially bearing in mind that real interest rates remained low and probably negative.[5] If the demand for credit is a function of real interest rates rather than nominal rates, an expansion of credit demand is quite consistent with high nominal rates. It also seems the demand for credit schedule may actually have shifted. As a result of the lurch into recession and a consequent squeeze on profit margins, many firms were forced to borrow to meet wage demands and finance stockholding, and in some cases borrow further to service the initial loans. There is a good deal of qualitative evidence to indicate that the latter in particular took place via an extension of overdraft facilities (which directly inflates £M3).

This brief review of UK experience with quantitative controls and price manipulations serves to give some flavour of the practical difficulties of monetary control. In the case of the former, one inevitably has to make some judgement about what consistutes 'money'; if one makes an erroneous judgement then avoidance activity is inevitable. In the latter case some judgement has to be made about the interest elasticity of the demand for credit; if an erroneous judgement is made here, or if the political will is lacking to raise nominal interest rates to a sufficient extent, the growth of the money supply exceeds any targets laid down.

Public Sector Borrowing Requirement and the Money Supply

These difficulties are in part responsible for another approach to monetary control which has been applied in the UK possibly since 1974, certainly since 1979 namely manipulation of the public sector borrowing requirement (PSBR). As can be seen from equation 6.9, the magnitude of the public sector

---

5 The real interest rate is often measured as the nominal rate adjusted for *actual* inflation. In fact, to obtain a real rate the adjustment should be for *expected* inflation. Since it is impossible to directly observe expectations, it is often difficult to be precise about real rates.

deficit (which for simplicity will be equated with the PSBR) affects the change in high-powered money. Although there is some controversy over the precise relationship between the PSBR and the money supply (see Peacock and Shaw, 1981), basically the contribution which the PSBR makes to the change in high-powered money is equivalent to the PSBR minus that part of it which can be financed by sales of government bonds to the non-bank private sector. This relationship has been recognized for a very long time, but an erroneous belief in the independence of fiscal policy, combined with a reluctance to use the PSBR as an instrument of monetary control, precluded the use of this as a target. Since 1979 the recognition of a budget constraint and the inter-dependence of fiscal and monetary policy have resulted in the Conservative government using the PSBR as an instrument of monetary control, basically by setting targets for monetary growth then fixing targets for the growth of the PSBR. As will be seen in chapter 18, however, the PSBR has proved no more straightforward to control than a given money supply target. This is in part due to the presence of political constraints, which are (rightly or wrongly) frequently difficult to resist. Thus cash limits set for particular public corporations are relaxed. A more important problem however has been that the PSBR is itself endogenous. In recession, *ceteris paribus*, government revenues automatically fall as unemployment rises, and expenditure auto-matically increases as transfer payments increase. This was something which the Conservative administration made insufficient allowance for in 1979–81 and was the principal element in the PSBR overshoot (see table 18.6).

Thus in the UK most attempts at monetary control have revolved around attempting to control H in equation 6.4, either by quantitative controls directed at bank credit and from there bank deposits; or by manip-ulating price, again primarily by influencing bank credit, and by controlling the government budget. Many of the problems which were alluded to in the discussion of monetary multipliers have been shown to have been experi-enced in the UK; there is another, the influence of the overseas sector, discussion of which will be deferred until the analysis of the balance of payments. These difficulties have led some commentators to advocate an entirely different system of monetary control, namely manipulation of r. From equation 6.4 it should be clear that, *ceteris paribus*, systematic manip-ulation of the banks' reserve asset ratio results in systematic variations in the money supply. This of course requires that the central bank or govern-ment is sole supplier of reserve assets and that it polices the system care-fully, the result being a system which would operate in a fashion analogous to a commodity-based regime (that is, a currency issue backed by a precious metal). In principle such monetary base control[6] would give the authorities

---

6 Monetary base control is practised in a number of countries, for example the USA.

control of the money supply but at a cost, namely complete surrender over interest rates. Interest rates become endogenous under a system of monetary base control. In the UK this more than any other argument is likely to mean that manipulation of r is eschewed as the principal instrument of monetary policy.

Concluding Comments

In principle a small number of proximate determinants of the money supply can be identified which may give the central authorities a 'handle' to influence the amount of money in circulation. In practice, however, monetary control may present intractable problems. These are in part related to the difficulty of isolating an asset which can be called 'money' and for which the demand is stable, and in part due to the way in which the volume of high-powered money is determined. The issue of controllability has been widely debated in recent years, and it will be returned to in the examination of the determinants of inflation in chapter 18.

Appendix: The Aggregate Demand Curve

In chapters 2 to 4 were analysed the determinants of the principal components of aggregate expenditure, namely consumption, investment and government expenditure. All of these functions were derived and discussed in real terms for analytical convenience. For certain policy discussions it is however important to have an idea of the money value of aggregate expenditure, or *aggregate demand*. The means for establishing this are now available, the money market having been discussed in chapters 5 and 6. Specifically, the aggregate demand (AD) for a given money supply can be ascertained. Strictly speaking, however, some familiarity with the *interaction* of the goods and money market is required for a formal derivation of the AD schedule. Most texts derive AD from the IS/LM model, and indeed this is done in this book in chapter 11. Since, however, the aggregate supply curve will be derived in the next chapter, and since this will provide the opportunity to consider some interactions between aggregate demand and aggregate supply, the AD schedule will be derived in this appendix. (Anyone already familiar with the IS/LM framework may find the derivation of AD in chapter 11 more to their liking.)

Consider first the aggregate expenditure function, that is, the sum of consumption, investment and government expenditure. This is graphically represented in figure 6.6 by the vertical addition of an investment and government expenditure function to a Keynesian consumption function,

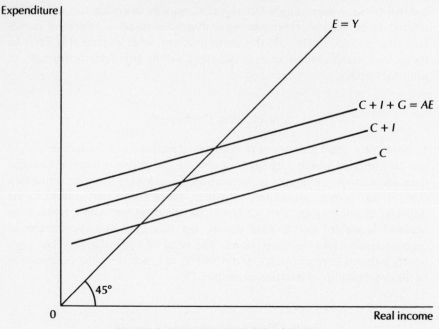

Figure 6.6   Aggregate expenditure function

within a familiar Keynesian cross diagram. For simplicity it is assumed that both investment and government expenditures are exogenously given. AE therefore represents intended or *ex ante* real expenditure. This schedule is, however, derived against the backcloth of a given real money stock. The nominal value of the intended expenditure will be referred to as aggregate demand.

Consider now figure 6.7. In the upper panel the intended (real) expenditure is E_1 which is consistent with a level of real income of Y_1. Given the nominal money supply this will also be consistent with a price level of P_1, giving a price income combination of $P_1 Y_1$ in the lower panel. Suppose now that intended expenditure increases, perhaps as a consequence of increased government expenditure, and that this shifts AE_1 to AE_2 in the upper panel. If the nominal money supply is held constant, the only way in which this increase in intended expenditure can be translated into monetary demand is if the price level falls. A price level fall would increase the real value of money balances and support the increase in real expenditure. Hence the higher real expenditure level E_2 and the higher level of real income Y_2 are associated with a lower price level P_2. Points a and b turn out to be two points on an aggregate demand curve AD_1. Further points could be generated by repeating this process, and it

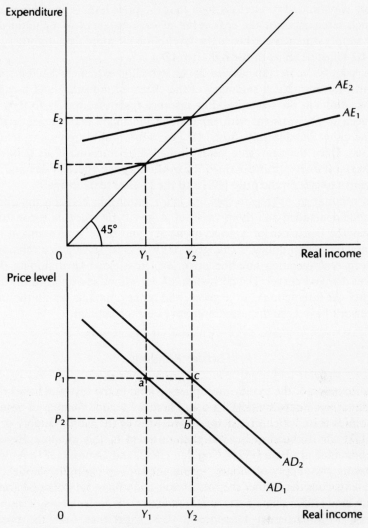

Figure 6.7   Aggregate expenditure and aggregate demand

would be found that aggregate demand is an inverse function of the price level. (Note that for expositional convenience we have drawn this schedule as linear – it may in fact be non-linear.)

Of course, the intended increase in government expenditure could have been accompanied by monetary relaxation. In other words the money supply could have been permitted to expand to accommodate the increased expenditure. In fact it is possible to conceive of a situation where the money supply is permitted to increase such that the price level is maintained at P_1. In such circumstances the real value of cash balances is maintained, but their supply is increased; hence the level of real income rises. In other words the AD schedule shifts to the right (to AD_2).

As will be seen, this device is analytically extremely useful since it permits, for example, a summary of the effects of monetary and fiscal policies via shifts in the schedules. For instance a shift from AD_1 to AD_2 is, as has been seen, consistent with expansionary demand management policies; on the other hand a shift from AD_2 to AD_1 would imply contractionary policies. Once the aggregate supply schedule is introduced, as in the next chapter, a framework is obtained for evaluating the effect of demand management policies on the price level and the level of real income.

To summarize, aggregate demand is a relationship between the quantity of goods demanded and the price level. A given AD schedule is constructed against the backcloth of a given monetary and fiscal stance and, if either monetary or fiscal policy is changed, AD will shift. Since it is a relationship between real spending and the price level it is downward sloping (like a market demand curve). The derivation of AD will be re-examined in chapter 11, after the interactions of the goods and money markets within the IS/LM framework have been discussed and have become familiar.

Further Reading

The discussion of the money multiplier process in the text was based on the Friedman and Schwartz (1963) work. There are a good number of monetary economics texts which give detailed accounts of the money supply process and take the discussion beyond that outlined in this chapter. Especially recommended are Bain (1976), Coghlan (1980) and Dennis (1981). As well as discussing the supply of money within the money multiplier model, all of these texts consider further the role of non-bank financial intermediaries.

Gowland (1982) offers a thorough review of the instruments of monetary control, with particular reference to UK experience over the post-war period. This is well supplemented by Artis and Lewis (1981). Dennis (1980) focuses on UK monetary experience in the 1970s in particular. A comprehensive analysis of money and prices in the USA and the UK over the period 1867–1975 can be found in Friedman and Schwartz (1982).

The medium-term financial strategy has stimulated a great deal of interest in the precise relationship between the PSBR and the money supply; Peacock and Shaw (1981) focus on this relationship.

7

The Labour Market

The analyses of aggregate consumption, aggregate investment and government expenditure permitted an examination of the components of aggregate demand. As was seen at the end of chapter 6, these various functions can be aggregated in order to derive an aggregate demand function for the closed economy as a whole.

The analysis of aggregate demand has, however, been conducted without reference to aggregate supply. This is analytically useful, since it permits a focus on each sector or aggregate individually; however, in order to comment on how the system as a whole may function under alternative scenarios, something must be said about the determinants of aggregate supply. Clearly the supply of goods and services in an economy, at a particular period in time, will depend upon the relationship between inputs and outputs. It will depend in other words on the economy's production function. The simplest representation of the production function we can take is:

$$Y = f(N, \bar{K}) \tag{7.1}$$

where N refers to the level of employment and K to the capital stock. If we assume the latter to be exogenously determined and fixed then variations in the supply of real output can be attributed solely to variations in the level of employment. The benefit of holding the capital stock constant, and essentially focusing on the short-run production function is that we can concentrate our analysis exclusively on the operation of the labour market. Later, in chapter 23 we shall evaluate how changes in the quality and quantity of the capital stock impact upon changes in the supply of real output through time. For the moment we will review the operation of the labour market as follows. First, we shall examine ther determinants of the supply of labour and demand for labour. Having done this we will identify the relationship between aggregate supply and the labour market, under alternative assumptions regarding the competitiveness of the labour market. Third, we will review the role of expectations in market clearing, and finally evaluate the impact of various institutional arrangements on market clearing. The reader might note that some of the major issues in this chapter are developed further in chapters 13 and 19.

The Supply of Labour

Microeconomic Foundations

Traditionally the analysis of the supply of labour is conducted within a choice-theoretic framework whereby the individual is presented with the choice between using his time for work or leisure. His allocation of time between work and leisure is then determined by his tastes and preferences for the two activities and by the opportunity cost of leisure.

Consider figure 7.1. In the upper panel, 0S denotes the maximum number of hours in a day whilst 0T indicates the minimum number of hours which will have to be reserved for 'leisure' purposes (that is, the minimum number of hours necessary for sleep, eating, and so on). The individual therefore has TS hours which he can allocate between leisure and work. The two activities are mutually exclusive; the former is unpaid, whilst the latter is rewarded by income. If the individual is free to choose the number of hours in a day which he will work, and he decides to use all of his time for leisure purposes, real earnings would clearly be zero.[1] If on the other hand all available time were spent working, real earnings would be maximized. If some intermediate position were chosen then real earnings would lie somewhere between their minimum and maximum.

If the real wage rate per hour is known, and it is assumed that this wage rate is invariant to number of hours worked (overtime payments are therefore ignored), an *earnings–leisure trade-off* can be traced out. Thus, with a real wage rate of W_1, working maximum hours would yield real earnings of $E_1(=R_1)$. For every hour less than the maximum which is used for leisure purposes, earnings are sacrificed, until with 0S hours allocated to leisure, real earnings are zero. The line R_1S is therefore the earnings–leisure trade-off (or budget constraint), the slope of which is determined by the wage rate.

The precise allocation of hours between work and leisure will be determined by the individual's tastes and preferences. These can be depicted by an indifference map. Indifference curves are ranked from south-west to north-

---

1 This is not the same as saying that his income will be zero. Given the existence of income support schemes, transfer payments like child benefit, family income supplement and social security benefits will ensure that a certain minimum income is guaranteed.

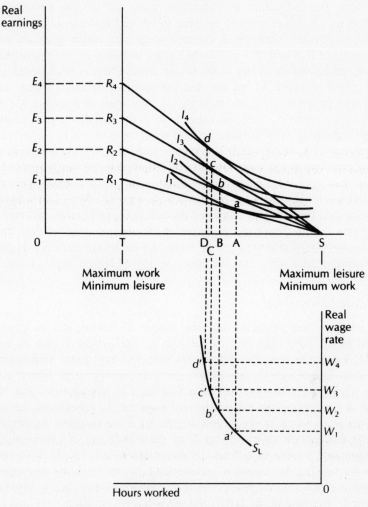

Figure 7.1   Derivation of the labour supply curve

east (indicating that both real earnings and leisure are 'goods' in the sense that more is preferred to less). Given the indifference map superimposed in figure 7.1, individual utility will clearly be maximized with TA hours devoted to leisure and AS hours worked. The real earnings associated with this choice are Aa (less than the maximum $0E_1$).

If the hourly wage rate were to increase, the slope of the earnings–leisure trade-off would become *steeper*, indicating that the opportunity cost of leisure had increased. Given the configuration of his indifference map, this will cause the individual to substitute work for leisure. Leisure hours decrease to TB, hours worked increase to BS and real earnings increase to $Bb(>Aa)$. Further increases in the real wage rate which generate budget constraints of R_3S and R_4S stimulate further increases in hours worked and further reductions in leisure time. If this information is transposed to the lower panel of figure 7.1 we see that the points generate a labour supply curve with points a', b', c' and d' being the analogues of points a, b, c and d in the upper segment. Over the range a' to d' the supply curve is positively sloped, indicating that increases in real wage rates result in an increase in the number of hours worked. It is conceivable that beyond a certain point further increases in the wage rate do not stimulate further increases in hours worked but may even result in a reduction in hours worked. This could occur at relatively high wage rates when the *income* effect of an increase in the wage rate (resulting in increased consumption of leisure) outweighs the *substitution* effect (resulting in decreased consumption of leisure). In this case the supply of labour curve S_L would be backward bending. However, concentration here will be on the positively sloped labour supply curve.

Aggregate Labour Supply

This analysis then suggests that the supply of labour will be positively related to the real wage rate or, for brevity, real wages. It can be argued that if this is the case for individuals then the horizontal summation of individual labour supply curves will generate an aggregate labour supply curve. Clearly this analysis has some relevance to aggregate labour supply in that it emphasizes the role of the real wage rate in influencing the choice of whether to work more or less hours. In some respects, however, the analysis has certain shortcomings from the standpoint of commenting on the aggregate supply of labour. In many cases, individuals have limited scope for varying the length of the working day or week. In this sense the analysis is clearly more appropriate to the self-employed than to most wage earners. In the case of the latter, the work–leisure choice is very much one of deciding whether to work say 40 hours per week or not to work at all. In other words, the decision for many on whether or not to join the labour force is very much a non-marginal decision. (It might be noted, however, that with the increase in female participation and the growth of part-time employment, this is no longer as true as it once was.)

This does not invalidate the above framework of analysis entirely, since clearly the decision of whether or not to join the labour force will be influenced by the going real wage rate. In the case of such a 'lumpy' decision, however, the opportunity cost of leisure will be determined not by the real wage rate *per se* but by the real wage per period, less an allowance for the use to which one's time could otherwise be put. In this respect Sapsford (1981) emphasizes that the relevant unit for decision-taking about labour force participation ought to be the household rather than the individual. Where the two are not synonymous, the decision about which member(s) of the household joins the labour force will be influenced not only by 'expected market earnings' *per se* (which is clearly dependent on the going real wage rate), but also by the availability of income transfers like unemployment benefits and the comparative advantages of members of the household as between market and non-market activities. The latter will include not simply leisure, as figure 7.1 implies, but also domestic pursuits such as child-minding and home maintenance. The structure of real wages, the real value of unemployment benefit (and of course the demand for labour) will determine the opportunity cost of having one member of the household refrain from becoming part of the labour force, but the decision will also be affected by tastes and preferences. In other words, given the structure of real wages, some households may have one member refrain from becoming part of the labour force owing to an unwillingness to employ a child-minder, or an unwillingness to live off convenience foods. Other households may be happy to employ child-minders, consume convenience foods, employ a housemaid and so on. Thus although it probably remains true to say that an increase in real wages will result in increased labour force participation (given the demand for labour), the extent of any response will depend on tastes and preferences.

The Demand for Labour

Microeconomic Foundations

The basic analysis of the demand for labour is also rooted in microeconomic analysis and, as with labour supply, it is possible to derive an aggregate curve from individual demand curves.

The short-run firm demand for labour can be easily derived. Take the case of a firm which sells its output and purchases inputs in perfectly competitive markets. As both buyer and seller, the firm is therefore a price taker. If it is assumed that capital costs are given and labour is the only variable input, the price of this input which the firm faces is the real wage rate. When faced with a given real wage rate, say $(W/P)_1$ how many labour inputs will be purchased? From the firm's viewpoint the relevant calculation is the value of output produced by an additional unit of labour, relative to the cost of employing that unit. The value of an additional unit produced can be referred to as the *value of marginal product* (**VMP**), where

$$VMP = MPP \times P \tag{7.2}$$

That is, the value of marginal product is equal to the *marginal physical product* (the increment to total product) times the price at which the increment will sell. In the case of a perfectly competitive firm, price will be fixed. MPP will, however, vary as employment of labour varies in accordance with the principle of *diminishing marginal productivity*. Thus with a fixed price of output and diminishing marginal productivity of labour, the VMP curve will take a negative slope as in figure 7.2. Furthermore, since in

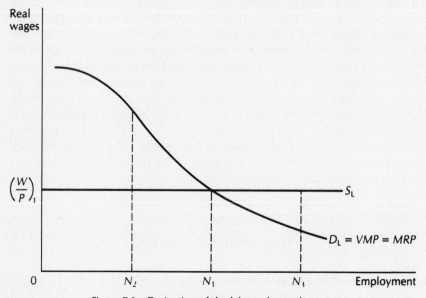

Figure 7.2   Derivation of the labour demand curve

perfectly competitive product markets price is equal to marginal revenue, this curve can also be labelled as the *marginal revenue product* curve (**MRP**), where

$$MRP = MPP \times MR \tag{7.3}$$

This is the increment to total revenue associated with the employment of an additional unit of labour, and it is this which determines the firm's demand for labour.

To ascertain how much labour will actually be employed, the real wage rate is introduced. If the firm is a price taker, labour supply S_L will be perfectly elastic at the going real wage rate of $(W/P)_1$. Given $(W/P)_1$ the firm will employ N_1. Expansion (contraction) of employment from levels below (above) N_1 would always result in total profit increasing. For example, if the firm employed N_2 units, increases in employment would add more to total revenue than to total cost for all increments up to N_1. Further expansion of employment beyond N_1, however, say to N_3 would add more to total cost than total revenue (since $(W/P)_1 > MRP$) and total profit would decline. Clearly with a given MRP schedule a rise (fall) in the real wage rate would result in a contraction (expansion) of labour demand.

Aggregate Labour Demand

Given therefore a diminishing marginal product of labour, the demand for labour would be expected to be inversely related to the real wage rate. However, one cannot simply horizontally sum labour demand curves to derive an aggregate demand curve without acknowledging at least three complications.

1. The foregoing analysis assumes that the firm concerned is a perfect competitor in its product markets. This assumption ensured an equality between VMP and MRP. Were an allowance to be made for monopoly or imperfectly competitive conditions in product markets then clearly an allowance would have to be made for the fact that the firm's average and marginal revenue curves will diverge. Although MRP will still be downward sloping (as therefore will be demand for labour) it will lie below VMP, and therefore employment under monopoly or imperfect competition will be less than that associated with perfect competition (on *ceteris paribus* assumptions).

2. Short-run conditions have been explicitly assumed. In the long run, when the firm is free to vary its inputs of both factors an allowance would have to be made for substitution between factor inputs as relative factor prices altered. In fact the application of this analysis to a long-run perspective still results in the conclusion that the firm's demand for labour will be inversely related to the real wage rate, but the long-run labour demand curve will be more elastic (over the relevant range) than any given short-run curve. The reason for this is that variations in labour inputs will affect the marginal productivity of other factors. Thus, given a fall in the real wage rate, employment will increase. This will tend to raise the MRP of capital; more capital will be employed which will tend to shift the MRP of labour out to the right, which in turn will tend to increase employment further. Thus the long-run change in employment in response to a change in the real wage rate will be greater (other things being equal) than the short-run change.

Once the industry demand curve is identified the aggregate labour demand curve can be derived by horizontally summing industry demands. In the aggregate the demand for labour will therefore be inversely related to the real wage rate, but without very detailed knowledge about industry demand curves it is not possible to be more specific about its precise configuration.

Employment and Aggregate Supply

Now that labour supply and labour demand have been discussed, labour market equilibrium and its relationship to aggregate supply can be considered. To simplify matters the short-run situation given by the production function of equation 7.1 is taken where labour is the only variable factor of production.

Labour market equilibrium occurs when a real wage rate is established which equates aggregate labour demand with aggregate labour supply. In figure 7.3 this occurs with a real wage rate of $(W/P)_e$ and N_e. In a competitive system where both labour demand and labour supply are a function of the real wage, the equilibrium established at e would be stable in the sense that any deviation away from $(W/P)_e$ will set in motion forces which will push the real wage rate back to its equilibrium level. If for example a real

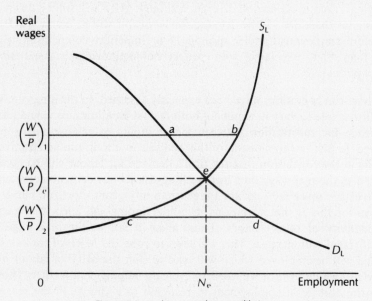

Figure 7.3   Labour market equilibrium

wage of $(W/P)_1$ were established, excess supply of *ab* would result. Competition between labour for the relatively scarce jobs would tend to depress money wages (and therefore real wages) and push the system back towards $(W/P)_e$. The same would apply *mutatis mutandis* to the excess demand of *cd* which is associated with a real wage of $(W/P)_2$.

Aggregate Supply with a Perfectly Competitive Labour Market

The derivation of the aggregate supply function under competitive conditions can be demonstrated by reference to figure 7.4. In quadrant (a) labour market equilibrium is established with a market clearing real wage of $(W/P)_1$. It will be assumed that this is consistent with full employment

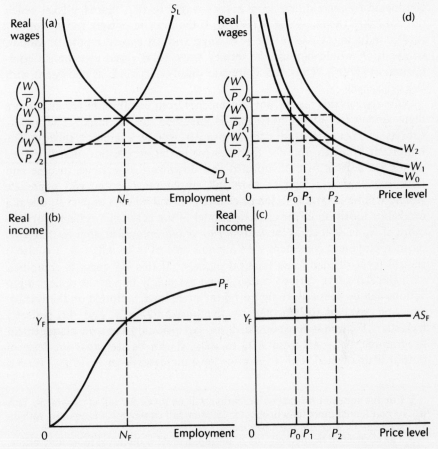

Figure 7.4   Derivation of the aggregate supply curve with a competitive labour market

(N_F).[2] Given the aggregate production function in quadrant (b) this is consistent with a level of national income of Y_F. Quadrant (c) traces out the *aggregate supply* curve, that is, the relationship between the level of income and the price level. With full employment income of Y_F, an aggregate supply curve AS_F is found which is completely inelastic with respect to the price level and is dependent only on real variables, namely the productivity of labour and the real wage rate. The only function of the price level in this model is to determine the nominal wage rate consistent with the equilibrium real wage rate of $(W/P)_1$. This can be demonstrated by reference to quadrant (d). W_1 denotes a given nominal wage, its inverse slope indicating that as the price level rises the real wage will fall. A rise in the price level from P_1 to P_2 would therefore tend to reduce the real wage towards $(W/P)_2$, stimulating an excess demand for labour. This excess demand would be eliminated by the bidding up of money wages to W_2, that is, a level which re-establishes the real wage of $(W/P)_1$. If the price level were to fall from P_1 to P_0, inducing a rise in the real wage and an excess supply of labour, competition would depress the money wage to W_0 and re-establish equilibrium at $(W/P)_1$. Thus, the aggregate supply curve AS_F is consistent with *any* price level.

Note that in this model, any movements from equilibrium are little more than tendencies, and adjustment is assumed to be rapid. The implications of lags in the adjustment process will be examined shortly. The important point to note for the moment is the proposition that if money wages are flexible in both upward and downward directions, income and output will always tend to their full employment levels, and aggregate supply will be invariant to the price level. As will be seen in part II, this is a central proposition in the classical model of the economic system. Furthermore, if N_F is defined as the *natural rate of unemployment*, that is, that level of unemployment consistent with a stable rate of price inflation, it is also a central tenet of many neo-classical models.[3] If this AS curve is combined with the AD curve derived earlier, some extremely important policy implications can be deduced. In figure 7.5 the price level is plotted on the vertical axis and level of real income on the horizontal axis, and the perfectly inelastic AS curve is reproduced. If an expansionary demand management programme shifts AD from AD_1 to AD_2, it can be seen that the level of output is unaffected, whilst the price level increases from P_1 to P_2. *With a*

---

2 For the moment no precise definition will be given for full employment. This will be considered more fully in chapter 19. Here full employment is equated with an absence of all involuntary unemployment.

3 The concept of the natural rate of unemployment is discussed more fully below, and in chapter 13.

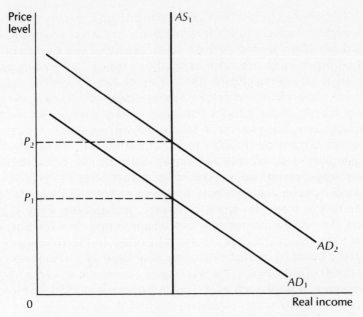

Figure 7.5   Effect of a shift in AD with a perfectly inelastic AS

vertical aggregate supply curve, demand management policies have no impact whatsoever on the level of employment and real output. Put another way, nominal policies only affect nominal variables. Because a frictionless labour market has been assumed, variations in prices quickly feed through to variations in money wages leaving real wages unaltered. Consequently, the labour market always clears. In a 'typical' classical model, the market clearing level of employment would coincide with full employment. In a 'typical' neo-classical model, it would coincide with the natural rate of unemployment. If the latter happens to be consistent with a socially undesirable level of unemployment, it cannot be altered by fiscal and monetary policies. In the same way as nominal instruments affect only nominal variables, real instruments must be used to influence real variables (like employment). Thus AS can only be shifted through policies designed to influence the way in which the labour market operates.

Aggregate Supply with Labour Market Imperfections

As will be seen in the next chapter, the proposition that the real economy would be unresponsive to changes in nominal demand (as reasoned via the vertical aggregate supply curve) was a central feature of the classical paradigm. The kind of institutional arrangements and market imperfections which might mitigate against a frictionless labour market and invalidate the classical paradigm formed part of the substance of the Keynesian revolution (although they were also explicitly recognized by leading classical theorists, most notably Pigou, 1944). Keynes focused on two factors in particular – imperfectly competitive labour supply as a result of the importance of labour unions, and the possibility of *money illusion* on the part of wage bargainers. The presence of labour unions could mean that there are adjustment asymmetries to shifts in *AD*. If *AD* shifts to the right such that the price level is raised and 'the' actual real wage lies below the market clearing wage, upward adjustment of the money wage could follow quite quickly. If however contractionary fiscal and monetary policies shift *AD* to the left, money wage cuts might be resisted, perhaps as a result of money illusion, that is, the proposition that labour supply is a function of the money wage rate rather than the real wage rate. In this case money wage reductions would be resisted even when price level reductions are occurring concurrently. Consequently, the real wage is maintained at a level above the equilibrium real wage (such as $(W/P)_1$ in figure 7.3) and the labour market fails to clear. Excess supply (unemployment) of *ab* ensues.

In figure 7.6 is outlined the implications of downward inflexibility of money wages for aggregate supply. Commencing from a price level of P_1 and a market clearing real wage of $(W/P)_1$, which is consistent with full employment, assume that the price level falls from P_1 to P_2. To maintain the full employment level of output, money wages should fall to W_2. If money wage reductions are resisted such that nominal wages remain at W_1, real wages rise to $(W/P)_2$ and the level of employment becomes demand determined. It can be seen from quadrant (a) that with a real wage of $(W/P)_2$ employment would contract to N_2. Given the production function *PF* in quadrant (b) this results in a reduction in output to Y_2. If this is taken across to quadrant (c) it is clear that *AS* is positively sloped over the range $Y_2 Y_F$. If the assumption is made of a further fall in the price level to P_3 with the maintenance of money wages at W_1, the consequent increase in the real wage to $(W/P)_3$ further reduces employment to N_3 and output to Y_3, indicating that *AS* is also positively sloped in the range $Y_3 Y_2$.

Contrast this with the situation where, again commencing from equilibrium, the price level rises to P_4. In the strict case of money illusion no change in labour supply would occur, and aggregate supply would remain unaffected. In the case where labour unions are active full compensation for the rise in the price level may be sought, the outcome being that the real wage is maintained at $(W/P)_1$ and aggregate supply is again unaffected.

The model of figure 7.6 therefore suggests that aggregate supply will be positively sloped below the full employment level of output. That is to say

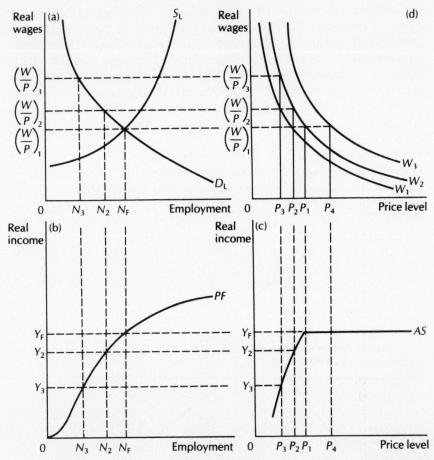

Figure 7.6 Derivation of the aggregate supply curve with an imperfectly competitive labour market

there may exist a direct relationship between price level changes and changes in output up to full employment.[4]

It has already been seen in figure 7.5 that, when AS is inelastic, policy-induced shifts in aggregate demand can have no effect on the level of output

---

4 It ought to be noted that given the assumptions of this analysis, there is likely to be a ratchet effect present. Thus, when the price level rises to P_4 and the money wage to W_3, the latter would be viewed as the minimum wage reductions in which are unacceptable. The positively sloped section of AS would then emanate from point 2. Further increases in the full employment price level would shift the elastic section of the curve further up the vertical section.

but only alter the price level. By contrast, when *AS* is positively sloped as in
figure 7.7 the same policy-induced shift would result in both the price level
and the level of output being affected with the relative impact on prices and
output being determined by the slope of the *AS* schedule over the relevant
range. As can be seen from figure 7.7 the shift in *AD* has a relatively greater
impact on output relative to prices in the case of AS_2 compared with AS_1.

Clearly, therefore, if the policy-maker believes that labour market forces
operate in such a way as to generate a vertical (or steeply sloped) *AS* curve

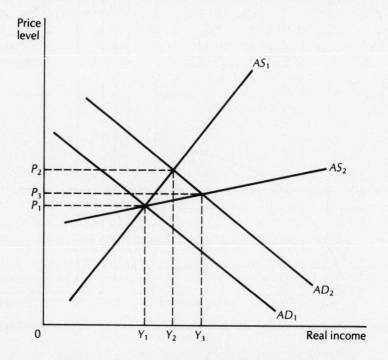

Figure 7.7   Effect of a shift in *AD* with elastic *AS* curves

he is likely to see the role of demand management policies as being one of
changing the price level. If on the other hand he is convinced that behavioural relations in the labour market generate an *AS* schedule which is
relatively flat, he would take the view that active demand management
policies can effect changes in output and employment. This is an issue
which has received a great deal of academic attention recently, and as will
be seen it is at the heart of much macroeconomic controversy of recent
years.

Expectations Formation and Market Clearing

Adaptive Expectations and the Labour Market

In order to elaborate further, the assumption is retained that both labour supply and labour demand are a function of the real wage rate. In a situation where the price level is changing, however, it may not be a straightforward matter for agents in the labour market to evaluate how the real wage is changing. In order to evaluate a given money wage rate, agents need to make a forecast of how the price level will change over the period to which the given money wage applies. In other words they need to form expectations of price level changes, and the manner in which those expectations are formed has a crucial bearing on market clearing in the labour market.

The way in which agents form their expectations depends on the quantity and quality of information which they have at their disposal. Other things being equal, the better informed agents are about the way in which economic processes operate, and the better the quality of their information, the less likely they are to make errors in forecasting. Initially, consider a situation where labour demand is a function of the money wage rate deflated by the *actual* price level, whilst labour supply is a function of the money wage deflated by the price level *expected* when a wage agreement is struck. One could rationalize this by arguing that since employers are involved in price setting they have good quality information on how prices are changing and forecast accurately. Employees on the other hand do not have such ready access to information on price changes and have to make a guess at how prices will change. Thus,

$$D_L = f(W/P^a) \tag{7.4}$$

$$S_L = f(W/P^e) \tag{7.5}$$

Clearly if any divergence between P^a and P^e occurs between one wage agreement and the next, there is scope for divergence between D_L and S_L and disequilibrium in the labour market which could be influenced by variations in fiscal and monetary policy. Such a divergence could occur if employees formed their expectations about changes in the price level *adaptively*, that is to say they used past experience as a guide to forecasting changes in the price level. A simple adaptive process would be the one described by equation 13.12, namely

$$P_t^e = \lambda P_{t-1} + (1 - \lambda)P_{t-1}^e \tag{7.6}$$

This implies that agents *forecast* the price level on the basis of the price level in

148   MACROECONOMIC SECTORS

the previous period (P_{t-1}) and the extent to which their forecast of the price
level in the previous period (P_{t-1}^e) was wrong. The adjustment coefficient λ lies
between zero and one. This system of expectations formation will be discussed
more fully in chapter 13. The important characteristic to note for the present
is that if expectations are formed adaptively, they can lag behind reality, and
P^e and P^a can diverge.

Take a specific example. Suppose a wage agreement is reached in time t on
the basis of $P^e = \varepsilon$, where ε is some positive price level. Between t and $t+1$ an
unexpected price change occurs such that $P^a > \varepsilon$. Employers take as their
reference point actual prices and would therefore correctly perceive any
increase in the price level as being associated with a fall in the real wage and
labour demand expands. Employees, on the other hand, whose expectations
lag behind reality, fail to perceive that the real wage has changed, and
employment and output increase. This describes a world with a positively
sloped AS curve. Thus in figure 7.8 the shift in AD from AD_1 to AD_2 raises the
price level from P_1 to P_2, and increases real output from Y_1 to Y_2.

The objection has been made that this type of mechanism relies on
money illusion in some form on the part of employees. This may be a
reasonable postulate in the short run. In the long run, however, the gap

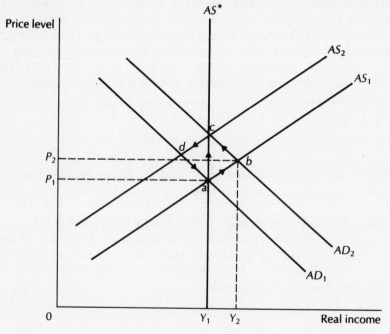

Figure 7.8   Short-run and long-run AS curves and adjustment to a shift in AD

between actual and expected price level changes will be perceived and adjustments made accordingly. In other words, once it is realized that the real wage has fallen in the move from a to b in figure 7.8, employment (and output) will contract along AD_2. This contraction will cease when actual and expected price levels are equal, that is to say when D_L and S_L are equated. This in fact occurs at the initial level of output Y_1. Note now, however, that the price level has been raised. The only *long-run* consequence of the expansionary demand management policy is to increase the price level but leave the level of employment and output at their 'natural' levels, that is, those levels consistent with a stable price level.

The process would be exactly reversed for a leftward shift in aggregate demand stimulated by contractionary fiscal and monetary policies. If AD_2 is shifted to AD_1, the actual price level falls and initially expected prices lag behind. Real wages are increasing as a consequence. The increase in real wages is however perceived first by employers (since $P^a < P^e$) and labour demand contracts. There is a movement from point c to point d on AS_2. Gradually as expectations catch up with reality and the real wage returns to its equilibrium level, there is a shift from d to a and equilibrium is re-established at the natural level of output and employment.

These ideas were originally enunciated by Friedman (1968) and Phelps (1968) and refined in the 1970s. This line of analysis suggests that in fact both positively sloped and vertical AS curves coexist. In the short run the AS schedule is positively sloped because those agents supplying labour services adjust gradually to changes in nominal demand, rather than instantaneously as the competitive model requires. In the short run, then, shifts in AD can affect output and employment as well as prices. The process of adjustment is gradual rather than partial, and ultimately expectations catch up with reality and full adjustment takes place. This occurs when actual changes in the price level are the same as expected changes, that is, at the natural rate of output and employment. In the long run, therefore, output and employment are completely insensitive to changes in nominal demand, and this is described by the vertical aggregate supply curve AS^* in figure 7.8.

From the standpoint of demand management policy, this view of the way in which adjustments to disequilibrium in the labour market occur has two crucially important implications:

(1) It unequivocally suggests that in the long run the government cannot systematically influence the level of output and employment through manipulations in monetary and fiscal policy.
(2) It implies that deviations in the level of employment from its natural level are a consequence of mistaken expectations. In the event that

unemployment rises in the adjustment $c \to d \to a$ in figure 7.8, it is as a consequence of individuals temporarily withdrawing from the labour market in the belief that the real wage has fallen.

Rational Expectations and the Labour Market

As a result of the importance of these propositions this line of analysis has been exhaustively examined and re-examined over the last decade. One line of development has been to question the expectations mechanism in such a way as to conclude that changes in *AD* may not even influence output and employment in the short run. This is one of the central propositions of the *rational expectations* (RE) school of thought.

The RE school dates back to two papers by Muth (1960, 1961) but owes much to the work of Lucas (1973, 1975) and Sargent and Wallace (1975) among others. This line of analysis contends that the expectations mechanism implied by equation 7.6 is fundamentally unsound because it suggests that, when forecasting the rate of inflation for the purposes of concluding a wage agreement, employees take account only of past events and not of current and future possible events. To dramatize this, it implies that if OPEC raises the price of oil by x per cent on the day a wage deal is concluded it will be ignored. Furthermore, as will be seen in chapter 13, the mechanism in equation 7.6 means that the rate of inflation may be *systematically* underpredicted from one period to the next. Both of these propositions, it is argued, are inconsistent with rational optimizing behaviour. If instead individuals formed their expectation of price level changes rationally rather than adaptively, the adjustment to a change in nominal demand is rather different.

If an agent forecasts the expected price level rationally, P^e would be

$$P_t^e = E(P_t | I_{t-1}) \qquad (7.7)$$

In other words, the expected price level would be equal to a forecast which is made on the basis of *all* relevant information available at the time of the forecast. This relevant information would include current information on, for example, government intentions about fiscal and monetary policy. We are in effect assuming that employees are as well informed as employers. Thus, in the event that it was known that the government intended to shift AD_1 to AD_2 in figure 7.8, the effects of this expansionary demand management intervention would be anticipated. In other words, *expected prices would not lag behind actual prices but would move along with them* and adjustment would take place directly from a to c. (The same applies *mutatis mutandis* for s shift from AD_2 to AD_1). Therefore, agents in the labour market adjust quickly to changes in nominal demand and, consequently, nominal changes do not influence real magnitudes *even in the short run* – the short-run *AS* curve is also vertical. In fact, the only circumstances under which employment and output can deviate from their natural levels is if a mistake is made when forecasting price changes. This could occur if some completely unexpected event occurs (like an OPEC price hike) or if the authorities say they are going to shift AD_2 to AD_1 but instead shift AD_2 to AD_3 as in figure 7.9. Because agents are taken by surprise in both these circumstances there may be some real effects in the short run. Thus in figure 7.9 the announcement of an intention to shift AD_2 to AD_1 by contractionary fiscal and monetary policies would lead to adjustment from *a* to *b*. Instead, however, the authorities shift AD_2 to AD_3. Agents in the labour market are initially taken by surprise and output and employment temporarily rise above Y_1. Once however it is realized what the authorities have actually done, output and employment would return to their natural levels, the adjustment path being $b \rightarrow c \rightarrow d$. The locus *bc* would be referred to as the *surprise supply function*. If the policy intention of shifting AD_2 to AD_3 had been preannounced, adjustment would have taken place from *a* to *d*. The implications of the analysis are therefore that as long as policy intentions are preannounced and are stuck to, real output and employment will be un-affected by changes in demand management policies even in the short run.

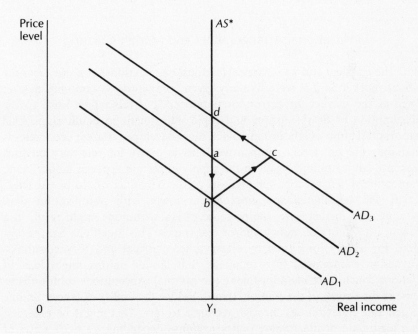

Figure 7.9   Surprise supply function

The rational expectations paradigm has generated a great deal of controversy and it will be examined more critically in chapter 13. For the moment the interest is simply in the implication that the labour market can clear in a reasonably frictionless manner, and in the implication that because the labour market is self-equilibrating, all unemployment is essentially voluntary. Thus a glance forward to table 19.1 and figure 19.1 shows that a dramatic increase in unemployment has taken place in the UK in recent years. The labour market has manifestly failed to clear, despite preannouncement of policy intent on *AD*. This would be explained by the rational expectations school as the outcome of a combination of unanticipated shocks (like the 1979 oil price hike), and an increase in voluntary unemployment as a result of rising real unemployment benefits and falling real wages. In terms of the analysis earlier in this chapter, it is claimed that households are taking a rational intertemporal decision to take leisure time now (for home maintenance and so on) and work later when real wages rise. For many commentators, the very idea that so many should 'choose' leisure is inherently implausible as is the entire notion of zero involuntary unemployment. The dissatisfaction has resulted in a re-evaluation of the way in which labour markets operate and a closer examination of the kind of institutional arrangements which exist and which may make the labour market less than perfectly frictionless.

Institutional Arrangements and Market Clearing

Both the classical and neo-classical (rational expectations) analyses treat the labour market as if it were like any given competitive commodity market (such as the market for carrots or potatoes). It is this which leads to the presumption of flexible prices and rapid adjustment to equilibrium. One important feature of labour markets in most developed market economies is that they are not freely competitive. This is partly for one very obvious reason – labour unions result in the supply of certain types of labour being monopolized. Microeconomic analysis predicts that, as would be expected, wages will be higher and employment lower with unionization than without; and furthermore, the presence of labour unions might result in a downward rigidity of money and/or real wages. This much has been recognized for a very long time by classical/neo-classical and Keynesian/neo-Keynesian economists. In recognizing that labour unions might lead to frictions which frustrate adjustment, the rational expectations solution is to remove the source of the friction, that is, reduce the ability of labour unions to generate inflexibilities through recourse to law. This might be regarded as a legitimate or illegitimate policy response depending on one's views of the role which labour unions play in a modern society. Even if one were to endorse such a policy, however, a further question is begged: would the labour market suddenly become frictionless and adjust quickly to changes in aggregate demand, or are there other imperfections which contribute to relatively slow adjustment?

Labour Market Segmentation

One important characteristic of the labour market which will limit flexibility by restricting mobility is that it is *segmented*, both geographically and occupationally. There are sociocultural ties which tend to restrict geographical mobility, and there are acquired skills which tend to restrict occupational mobility. As a result of this segmentation one might find a mismatch of labour demand and supply by geographical region and/or occupational category. The excess supply which emerges as a consequence of the labour market failing to clear owing to this segmentation is frequently referred to as *structural unemployment* and, as will be seen in chapter 19, this is viewed by many as being at the heart of the UK regional problem.

One might object that labour market segmentation is a necessary but not a sufficient condition for a non-clearing labour market since, if there were free and unfettered competition, there would still be a tendency to equilibrium as a result of wage flexibility within and between (geographical and occupational) segments. Thus wage differentials between occupational groups would emerge, reflecting relative scarcities, and different prices for the same occupational group across regions would emerge, again reflecting relative scarcities. This may very well be true. It does not, however, invalidate the fact that attachment to a particular locality may generate inflexibility.

Search Costs

Many classical and neo-classical models implicitly assume that search costs are zero. In effect, every worker has full information on the structure of wages, and the distribution of wage offers available to employed workers who are thinking of quitting, or unemployed workers who have actually quit. In reality, of course, job search is not costless. An unemployed individual can be expected to have in mind a reservation wage, that is, a minimum wage which is required to induce him to sacrifice leisure for work. In order to establish whether to accept employment, the individual needs to search firms to obtain information on wage offers. This process clearly takes time, especially since empirical evidence suggests that unemployed individuals search for permanent rather than temporary jobs. Moreover, the reservation wage may itself change during search in a way that prolongs the period of unemployment. For example, other things being equal, an increase in the ratio of vacancies to unemployment should increase the probability of a job offer, which in turn will tend to increase the reservation wage. In addition, an increase in the distribution of wage offers raises the expected returns to search and in turn the reservation wage. In both cases the individual would be willing to search for longer.

Social Convention

Consider further the question of wage flexibility. It is often argued that wages are inflexible (especially in a downward direction) simply as a consequence of the activities of labour unions and that free competition is frustrated only by such institutions. This *simpliste* view has been challenged recently. Akerlof (1979) has pointed to the role of such intangible forces as notions of 'fairness' and good behaviour, bolstered by social pressure, as being important forces mitigating against free competition. Thus even in a situation where close to 3 million people are recorded as unemployed in the UK, one finds few (if any) examples of individuals offering their services to a given employer at a wage of less than he is paying existing employees. As Solow (1980, p. 8) remarks:

> Obviously there are no Emily Post manuals to consult as regards the behaviour of laid off workers, but you would certainly not be astonished to learn that self-esteem and the folkways discourage laid off workers from undercutting the wages of their employed colleagues in an effort to displace them from jobs.

The neo-classical (rational expectations) paradigm suggests that as an unemployed worker spends a longer time unemployed, he will engage in search activity and ultimately realize that real wages are falling, which will cause him to reduce his reservation wage. In response to this, Solow continues (p. 8)

> Reservation wages presumably fall as the duration of unemployment lengthens but my casual reading suggests that this shows up more in a willingness to accept lower paid sorts of jobs than in thorough going competition for the standard job.

Unemployment Benefits

Solow goes on to note that this sort of behaviour is accommodated by the availability of unemployment benefit, and indeed this is another institutional feature of the labour market which may help slow down the adjustment process. In terms of the simple model discussed in figure 7.1, the provision of unemployment benefit would mean that the budget lines do not converge at point S but at some point vertically above S, indicating that real earnings (or strictly speaking income) are positive with maximum leisure time. Furthermore, since the provision of unemployment benefit reduces the relative price of leisure, the individual may substitute leisure for work as in figure 7.10. In a situation where no benefits are provided the budget line is Y^*RS,

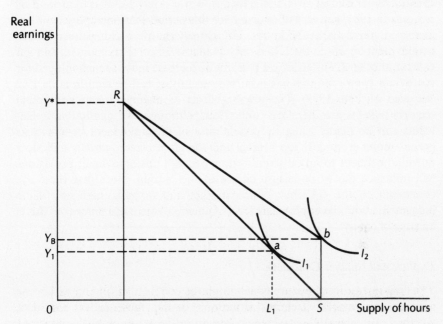

Figure 7.10   Disincentive effect of unemployment benefit

the relative price of leisure being given by the slope of RS. The utility maximizing individual settles at a on I_1 working L_1S hours and taking $0L_1$ for leisure, thereby earning income of Y_1. Once benefits are introduced the individual can have an income of Y_B, with maximum leisure (and zero work). In effect the relative price of leisure is reduced as shown by the budget line Y^*R_b. The individual could reach a higher indifference curve without working any hours at all. In simple terms this is the analysis which underlies the disincentive argument about benefits.

Since, as was noted earlier in this chapter, the work–leisure decision is a 'lumpy' one – one either works or does not (for the majority of wage earners anyway) – the availability of unemployment benefits might lead some individuals voluntarily to leave the labour market to engage in non-market activities either of a legal (DIY) or illegal (working for cash in hand) variety.

Some argue that this is an increasingly important consideration. Indeed Minford and Peel (1981) have argued that the real value of social security benefits should be cut in order to increase the attractiveness of work at the margin. There may appear to be some substance in this argument since the ratio of unemployment benefit to average post-tax income (for a married man with two children) increased quite dramatically in the UK from 45 per cent in 1964 to 78 per cent in 1971. Since then however it has declined to around 60 per cent in 1981, and it is of course over this period that unemployment has increased most markedly in the UK. Furthermore, earnings related unemployment benefit in the UK is only available for up to six months, and flat rate for another six months, yet a dramatic increase in those unemployed for more than twelve months has occurred recently as can be seen in table 19.2 (see also Nickell, 1979). The precise effects of unemployment and social security benefits are therefore contentious, although two qualitative judgements can be made. First, the availability of unemployment benefit does permit more prolonged job search and therefore *ceteris paribus* will slow down adjustment to any disequilibrium. Second, unemployment provisions will influence the work–leisure choice at the margin. Note that these are comments on the efficiency of the market and do not entail any value judgement about the appropriate level of unemployment benefit *per se*. This is an issue of equity.

Explicit and Implicit Contracts

The final institutional feature which might be commented on and which can generate non-market clearing situations is the presence of contracts, whether of the legal variety (as is common in the USA) or of the informal, implicit variety (as is more common in the UK). In a flexible competitive market, prices would be changed regularly. In an ideal labour market money wages would adjust quickly to productivity changes and changes in the price level. In most developed market economies one observes, however, the agreement of contracts between employer and employee which deliberately fixes the wage for a specified period of time. In the UK this is usually a year; in the USA it can be as much as three years. Once a contract is agreed it is unusual to have it altered before its expiry date. Thus the individual is committed to a given money wage for a specified period of time. This can certainly explain stickiness or inflexibility of money wages which frustrates market clearing. Furthermore, it may also provide a basis for justifying an upward sloping *AS* curve even in a rational expectations model (albeit as a short-run phenomenon). If all contracts expire simultaneously (as in the Japanese system) there may be a fairly well-defined short-run AS curve. If, however, contracts are overlapping the possibility of leapfrogging is introduced, reducing further the probability of a market clearing equilibrium. (Gordon, 1982, invokes this feature of the Japanese wage bargaining system as being a contributory factor to macroeconomic stability in that country compared with the UK and the USA).

The response of some new-classical economists to the role of long-term contracts is similar to their response to labour unions or unemployment benefit, namely if the institutions impede market clearing, and if there is no foundation for the institutions in rational optimizing behaviour, then they should be removed or reformed. This is certainly the case where contracts are concerned which, it is argued, engender macroeconomic instability and are inefficient from the individual's viewpoint (see Barro, 1977). A good deal of recent research suggests, however, that although wage contracts may very well prevent a tendency to continuous market clearing they may be rational from the point of view of employer and employee. Hahn (1980), for example, emphasizes the role of transactions costs. Changing wages is not a costless activity, especially since the probability of disagreement between employers and employees is high. Employers wish to avoid continuous conflict over wages (the cost of which may be high in lost output) whilst employees also have an incentive to avoid continuous conflict, again because it is costly (in terms of income forgone). A satisfactory way of minimizing conflict may be to negotiate contracts, even though there may be a trade-off with macroeconomic efficiency. (Gordon, 1982, argues that the single most important factor in explaining the three-year contract system in the United States is conflict avoidance.)

Employers may have other incentives for negotiating contracts. If wages are changed on a continuous basis then so too must be prices. This may be appropriate in auction markets, but may be less practical in other commodity markets. The administered price controversy of the 1930s generated many insights into the transactions costs of changing prices, and a recent paper by Gordon (1981) has documented reasons why price adjustment may be gradual.

The work of Azariadis (1975) on *implicit contracts* documents how risk-averse workers may enter into a contract to ensure a stable rather than fluctuating wage over a given period. From the firm's standpoint, there is an additional incentive provided by the firm's investment in specific skill development. A longer-term contract ensures that the firm reaps some benefit from such investment. It may also provide employers with the incentive to hoard labour during the downswing of a business cycle to save on recruitment costs in the upswing. Given the easier access to funds on the capital market which firms enjoy, such arrangements may be more efficient than the alternative of fluctuating wages with consumers/households using the capital market to smooth earnings themselves.

Thus all these institutional factors might result in the AS curve being positively sloped, at least in the short run. Furthermore, they may also help explain why the slope of the AS curve may appear to differ from country to country. For example, Gordon (1982, p. 41) concludes a cross-country comparison of the role of institutional factors by contending that as a result of institutional differences, '. . . of any given fluctuation in aggregate nominal demand, a larger fraction takes the form of a change in real output and employment in the United States than in the United Kingdom or Japan'. In other words, the UK and Japanese AS curve might be described by AS_1 in figure 7.7, whilst the USA curve is described by AS_2.

Concluding Comments

Some time has been spent studying the labour market, and many of these issues will be returned to in chapter 13 and chapter 19. The way in which the labour market adjusts to changes in nominal demand is at the heart of most macroeconomic controversy. This follows because labour supply is integrally linked to the shape of the aggregate supply curve, and this in turn determines whether there is any scope for demand management policies to influence real output and employment. In a smoothly operating, frictionless labour market, money wages would adjust quickly to changes in prices in order to ensure continuous adjustment to the market clearing real wage. In such circumstances policy-induced variations can have no effect on real output and employment. It has been seen, however, that there are many institutional features of labour markets which might result in a tendency to sticky rather than smooth adjustment, and perhaps also non-market clearing.

Further Reading

The traditional microeconomic anlaysis of labour demand and labour supply is outlined in most specialist texts on labour economics; a useful text to consult is Sapsford (1981).

Macroeconomic controversies over the efficacy of stabilization policy has resulted in a blossoming of the literature on the microfoundations of the labour market and the way in which it responds to demand stimuli. Expectations formation will be examined in a great deal more detail in chapter 13. For the moment, however, two useful introductory overview articles are noted which will provide an extremely good foundation to chapter 13, namely Maddock and Carter (1982) and Mayes (1981). More advanced literature on expectations will be discussed at the end of chapter 13.

An excellent treatise on the role of labour market institutions is Okun (1981), whilst Hall (1980) provides a survey of recent work on contracts. A useful empirical assessment of the effects of labour market institutions on aggregate supply is Gordon (1982). Pissarides (1985) provides a survey paper of recent work on search theory and several of the papers in Sapsford and Tzannatos (1988) relate to labour market institutions.

Nickell (1979) provides an analysis of the effect of a rising replacement ratio on unemployment levels in the UK, and Nickell (1980) an analysis of the pattern of unemployment in the UK. The recent volume edited by Creedy (1981) contains a number of useful essays, especially the one by Casson on recent developments in macroeconomics and the labour market. A comprehensive series of papers relating to the nature and causes of unemployment in a number of industralized economies is to be found in *Economica* (1986). The paper on the UK in this volume by Layard and Nickell is an excellent piece of applied economics.

PART II

Macroeconomic Systems

The number of rational hypotheses
that can explain any given phenome-
non is infinite
    Robert M. Pirsig

In this part of the book will be examined competing theories of the relationships underlying broad economic aggregates and of the behaviour of the macroeconomy. A largely historical or evolutionary approach will be adopted, even though this implies the examination of theories now defunct or which have been effectively refuted and falsified if only in part. The justification for adopting this procedure springs from a conviction that to understand fully the significance of intellectual endeavour, in whatever field of study, requires a knowledge of what has gone before. Is it really possible to comprehend the revolutionary nature of Einstein's theory of relativity, for example, without a knowledge of Newtonian mechanics? Such examples could be repeated endlessly and in whatever field of study one would care to select. And the same is no less true of economics. Such has been the remarkable development of economics over the past thirty years, reflected in an enormous growth of specialized academic journals on both sides of the Atlantic, that the amount of time formally devoted to the history of economic thought and economic history, once commonplace in undergraduate economic courses has been placed at a premium. Now, even at a fairly early stage of one's economic training, specialized courses abound in quantitative techniques, statistics, linear programming, econometrics, operations research and mathematics for economists of differing degrees of sophistication. Such developments are obviously inevitable and doubtless desirable; after all, the changing composition of undergraduate degree courses merely reflects efficient resource allocation in response to the changing composition of demand. None the less there is a cost, and the cost is a diminished awareness of past intellectual developments in one's chosen field of study. And, to repeat, an understanding of the past is imperative to a full appreciation of the present.

First, therefore, an examination is made of a stylized version of classical economics and of the reasons why the logic of the theory suggests that the system will attain a state of full employment as the normal state of affairs. Lapses from full employment could occur but they would be but temporary disturbances from the long-term equilibrium state. Next are discussed the possible grounds upon which Keynes attempted to challenge and deny the classical thesis, and then the various interpretations that have been made of the *General Theory* in an attempt to decipher its true message. Considerable attention is then devoted to the Hicksian *IS/LM* framework since this structure, more than any other, has been employed to encapsulate the essence of 'Keynesian' economics and of the ensuing controversy of the 'Keynes versus the classics' debate and of the relative efficacy of monetary versus fiscal interventionist policies. For all its shortcomings, the *IS/LM* framework is capable of considerable modification and extension, and by introducing the concept of the budget constraint it is possible to explore a good many of the tenets of modern monetarism and of the debate over 'crowding out'.

With this broad theoretical framework as a background, specific theoretical issues such as conflicting theories of output and inflation can be examined. Once again an evolutionary approach is adopted so that, for example, the modern theory of rational expectations is seen in part to be a reaction against the earlier ascendency of adaptive expectations. Once the leading schools of thought have been examined and compared a major step forward is undertaken by extending the analysis to the open economy and by examining the implications of alternative economic theories operating under different exchange rate regimes. This permits account to be taken of the constraints generated by the existence of the external account in the formulation of macroeconomic policies.

8

The Classical Economic System

The body of macroeconomic thought existing prior to the publication of Keynes' *General Theory of Employment Interest and Money* in 1936 has become known as the *classical macroeconomics* and culminates in a particular view of employment creation, the so-called classical theory of employment. This classical period allegedly stems from the time of Adam Smith, Say and Ricardo through J. S. Mill, Marshall and ultimately to the work of A. C. Pigou. To suggest that there was a unified theory of employment spanning such an interval of time is to perpetrate a gross distortion; the suggestion is primarily Keynes's and must be included amongst his lesser achievements. Not only did the so-called classical economists exhibit substantial differences of opinion over many fundamental issues, but even when there appeared to be agreement there were often major differences in interpretation.[1] For the most part, Keynes equated classical employment theory with the work of A. C. Pigou, which he regarded as the most complete exposition of the classical viewpoint.[2] It is in fact the case that one can identify certain elements or strands of thought in the earlier classical writers, which when combined permit a certain caricature of an employment theory which would not be widely at variance with the underlying thesis propounded in Pigou's influential work (Pigou, 1933). It is in this sense that it becomes tenable to depict a certain 'classical' macrostructure. Whilst there would be no unanimity amongst the classical scholars with regard to the individual building blocks, and whilst different classical

---

1 This was particularly true with reference to the interpretation accorded to Say's Law of Markets (see Schumpeter, 1961, pp. 619–25). The belief that there was a unified body of mainstream macroeconomic thought was probably reinforced by Keynes's favourable references to Malthus, Gesell, Marx and other heretical dissenters to economic orthodoxy.

2 'I have criticized at length Professor Pigou's theory of unemployment not because he seems to me to be more open to criticism than other economists of the classical school; but because his is the only attempt with which I am acquainted to write down the classical theory of unemployment precisely.' (Keynes, 1936, p. 279)

writers might choose to emphasize different aspects of the foundations, there would in all probability be a general consensus with regard to the desirability of the edifice as a whole.

The Essential Features of Classical Macroeconomic Systems

It is in this sense that reference may be made to the 'classical macro-economics'. What are its essential features? First of all, and largely under the influence of Benthamite or utilitarian philosophy, the classical economists postulated an economic system which assumed rational maximizing behaviour upon the part of all classes and agents in society. Capitalists would seek maximum profits whilst wage earners would seek to maximize the difference between the utility of income earned and the disutility of work effort. Moreover, this maximizing behaviour would be played out against a background of competition and within a time horizon which, whilst generally unspecified, implied a term sufficiently long and flexible to permit any indicated adjustment. Expectations were generally stable, the role of uncertainty being minimized, and knowledge was a relatively inexpensive good. *False trading*, that is, trading at non-equilibrium prices, accordingly, did not arise.

The analysis was couched in flows rather than stocks and the governing influence upon relative flows was relative prices. Money, whilst important to the absolute price level à la quantity theory, was accorded very little influence upon the real forces and magnitudes of the economy. It facilitated exchange by acting as a medium of exchange and avoiding the need for a double coincidence of wants, but beyond this obvious gain in efficiency it was immaterial to the real welfare of the economy. Indeed, it is probably correct to say that the classical economists held a conceptual view of the economy which would correspond to the economics of barter; money, in Pigou's words, was a 'veil' beyond which it was necessary to trespass in order to understand the real forces governing the economy.[3] These comments provide a basic framework of the classical model; they suggest the following tenets, which will be identified with classical employment theory.

1. Unemployment, often on a sizeable scale, can and does occur and for a variety of reasons. The peace of 1815, and the too sudden substitution of machinery for labour-intensive activity, provide graphic examples.

---

3 This distinction was subsequently to become known as 'the classical dichotomy'.

2. In the event of such unemployment there would be set in force automatic tendencies which ultimately would serve to restore full employment equilibrium providing free competition were permitted.

3. Finally, there is little or nothing that the government can do to hasten the process of adjustment other than to ensure that the forces of competition are allowed to reign. In particular, government spending upon public works programmes would merely drain employment-creating resources from the private sector and would have no net impact upon the volume of employment *per se*. This thesis, which became known as the 'Treasury view', provided the cornerstone for the advocacy of non-interventionist policies, and also provides the classical precursor to the present-day 'crowding out' controversy, to which frequent reference will be made.

As has been indicated, to encapsulate the classical employment model in this way is altogether too *simpliste* and arguably does less than justice to the main protagonists in the evolution of macroeconomic thinking prior to Keynes. None the less, it is this framework which Keynes set himself to deny and under Keynes's persuasive influence it is this framework which has survived the Keynes versus the classics controversy and the appraisal and reappraisal of Keynesian economics. Regardless of its historical accuracy, therefore, it behoves us to examine its theoretical underpinnings in more detail.

The Classical Model

Classical writers tended to divide the economy into its real and monetary sectors and generally assumed that the two were essentially independent of each other.

Fundamentally, the real sector of the economy is determined solely by two behavioural equations concerning the supply and demand for labour in the labour market and a technical relationship specifying the relationship between the volume of labour employed and the level of national output.

To consider the latter first, with the capital stock assumed constant in the short run, output Y is positively related to labour input N. Thus

$$Y = Y(N) \tag{8.1}$$

and $dY/dN > 0$, which implies that the marginal product of labour is always positive, but $d^2Y/dN^2 < 0$, which reiterates the classical belief in the Law of Diminishing Returns.

The demand for labour is negatively related to the real wage, which in turn is equated with the marginal product of labour. Hence

$$N_d = N_d\left(\frac{W}{P}\right) = \frac{dY}{dN} \tag{8.2}$$

where W is the money wage and P a representative price index.

The supply of labour is likewise treated as a function of the real wage, so that

$$N_s = N_s\left(\frac{W}{P}\right) \tag{8.3}$$

and it is assumed that $dN_s/d(W/P) > 0$. Thus it is assumed that higher real wages will always call forth more labour effort – substitution effects always predominate over income effects in modern terminology – and problems arising from the possibilities of backward bending supply curves are neatly side-stepped. Thus both demand and supply curves of labour will be normally sloped and, given the existence of competition, a determinate market clearing solution is indicated, providing both the equilibrium real wage and the amount of labour actually employed. To this given volume of employment there will correspond, given the state of technology, a determinate amount of real output. This composite solution is depicted in figure 8.1. Conceptually, and in keeping with Ricardian tractability, one can think in terms of a one-commodity economy, corn, with wage labour being paid in kind. Labour receives the amount (W/P)EQ0 whilst the employing classes retain SE(W/P). Such an analysis neatly avoids any difficulties arising from the 'sale' of national output. Not only is money not a determinant of the system but it is not even necessary; in such an economy money does not matter.

A number of comments appear pertinent to the analysis. First of all, the employment level so determined represents full employment and consequently the level of output is the full employment level of output. This is because at the going rate of real wages no labour is unemployed which wishes to work for that wage; in this sense, there is no *involuntary* unemployment. Providing competition is allowed free reign, whatever disturbance arises within the labour market (as for example a sudden increase in the desire for leisure reflected in an upward shift of the supply curve) there will always be some equilibrating adjustment to the real wage rate that is able to clear the market and maintain full employment. Second, *ceteris paribus*, any increase in the level of employment is only accommodated by a decrease in the real wage; employment levels and real wages are inversely related in terms of this analysis. (In terms of the analysis of chapter 7, the world is the one of the vertical AS curve).

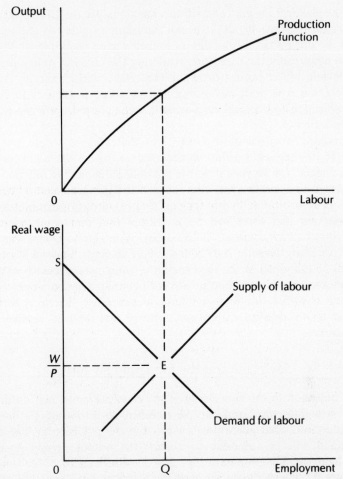

Figure 8.1   Classical determination of output, employment and the real wage

Given the logic of the model, it follows that involuntary unemployment equilibrium is only possible in the long run if artificial restrictions are placed upon the equilibrating role of real wages. These restrictions may arise on the supply side in the form of trade union intervention. Unemployment will occur if real wages are maintained above that level which equates supply and demand. Sustained unemployment, therefore, is the consequence of monopoly trade union power overriding the forces of competition. The policy implication is clear; employment can be increased by decreasing the real wage and for the classical economist the real wage can be reduced by cutting the money wage. It is for this reason that any attempt to deny the classical *theoretical* tradition must analyze the effects of cutting money wages in some detail. It is not sufficient to sidestep the issue by asserting the downward inflexibility of money wages. Such inflexibility may indeed be empirically the case, thus rendering the classical policy prescription irrelevant, but it cannot deny the theoretical underpinnings. It is for this reason that it is both misleading and belittling to Keynes to suggest that his objection to classical employment theory rested upon the premise of wage inflexibility.

It is perhaps worth while pointing out that Keynes would not have objected to the classical solution depicted in figure 8.1 as a possible outcome. Indeed, for Keynes it was a possible outcome but one he would have regarded as a *special* case – the case where aggregate demand was just sufficient to absorb the full employment level of output.[4] His objection lay in the assertion that there was no guarantee that the requisite demand would always be forthcoming. The classicists were able to ignore this complication primarily because they found refuge in Say's Law of Markets – which will be examined in the next section – which was generally taken to imply that whatever level of output was forthcoming demand would always be sufficient to absorb it.[5] In a very fundamental sense, therefore, Keynes's real objection to classical employment theory was directed against Say's Law of Markets.

Say's Law and the Monetary Sector

Keynes's objection to the conclusion of the classical model just outlined is relatively straightforward and may be summed up in one simple but penetrating question: what guarantee is there that the requisite level of aggregate demand will be sufficient to absorb the output arising from the classical analysis? Diagrammatically, this question can be posed with the aid of figure 8.2, which simply appends the conventional Keynesian 45° line diagram to the previous figure. In part (a) of the figure the level of aggregate demand indicates the sustainable level of real output at Y_1. Part (b) of the figure translates this output level into the required number of labourers via the production function (employment function) and in part (c) of the figure the resulting degree of unemployment is indicated by the distance U.

---

4 Significantly, the title of Keynes's book is *The General Theory* . . . .

5 Say's Law of itself guarantees not full employment but merely that whatever level of output is forthcoming will be fully taken up. Thus Say's Law is equally applicable to the depressed levels of output which characterized the 1930s as it is to full employment. The classical argument for full employment is accordingly based upon other considerations, of which, as has been indicated, the assumption of competition is vital.

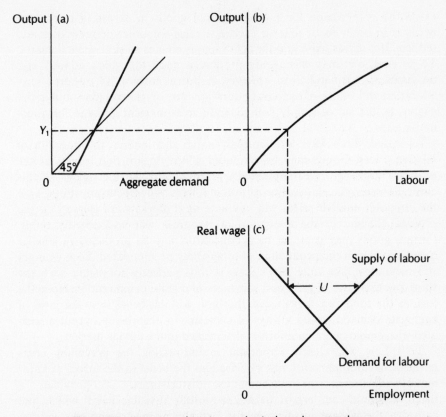

Figure 8.2   Keynesian objection to classical employment theory

Keynes's elementary model, therefore, is a demand determined model with the direction of causation being clearly (a) to (c). Moreover, for Keynes there can be no assurance that cutting money wages – the classical prescription for unemployment – will provide the appropriate remedy, for in this case there may well be feedback effects upon the level of aggregate demand, especially if money wage cuts generate expectations of future price declines.

The essential issue raised here is, why did the classical economists believe that they could dispense with the demand element? The answer stated simply is that they took refuge in Say's Law of Markets which appeared to affirm that in the *aggregate* a deficiency of demand is a logical impossibility. Say's Law has been subject of considerable interpretation of varying degrees of sophistication. However, the simplest view, namely that 'supply creates its own demand', comes closest to Say's original intention of explaining the nature of exchange in a specialized economy. Where the division of labour exists the only reason for producing final goods in excess of one's own needs is in order to be able to exchange them for other commodities and services. It is in this sense that the act of supply creates an equivalent demand. To be sure, one may mistakenly produce a good for which nobody else possesses any demand; this, however, is but a problem of resource mis-allocation and will be of temporary duration only. In general then, and in the aggregate, the act of supply will generate an equivalent demand for alter-native goods.

As stated, Say's Law is admittedly naïve and ignores the question of relative prices. Goods may be produced which do not find buyers at the prices or exchange rates stipulated and anticipated by the sellers. In this event, however, the classical belief in the powers of competition will provide the antidote; relative prices will fluctuate until markets are cleared. In the process, changes in the allocation of resources will undoubtedly occur. Certain goods may cease to be produced or may be produced in smaller quantities, whilst the production of others may be stimulated. Such changes will inevitably take time. Say's Law is thus perfectly consistent with the short-run existence of gluts and shortages of certain commodities. None the less, in the long run it provided the basis for the belief that the level of aggregate demand would always be sufficient to absorb the output associ-ated with employment equilibrium determined in the labour market.

Say's Law was clearly important in buttressing the prevailing com-mitment to non-interventionist policies and the belief in the forces of auto-matic   adjustment   to   autonomous   disturbances.   It   provided   a macroeconomic counterpart to Adam Smith's 'invisible hand' which had provided the welfare justification for virtually unconstrained competition on a microeconomic basis. For Ricardo, it led directly to the notion that there could not be an excess of capital accumulation and thus to a denial of Malthusian notions that saving propensities could be excessive. It was ideally suited to the prevailing philosophy of the time and widely endorsed and invoked. In one form or another it became the unifying strand in the classical macroeconomics.

The question remains as to whether it is valid. In the context of a barter economy, in which the law was initially invoked, and allowing for a time horizon long enough to permit the required adjustment in barter exchange ratios, the law becomes almost tautological. But does the law hold for a monetary economy, where workers do not produce final goods for direct barter but instead sell their labour services for money income?[6] In this case, the act of supply creates not an equivalent demand but rather an associated

---

6 This distinction is sometimes referred to in terms of Say's Identity and Say's Equality (see Becker and Baumol, 1952).

monetary income. In order for the law to hold the monetary income so created must generate a demand equal to the monetary value of the act of supply. Symbolically it is required that

$$\varphi \Rightarrow Y \Rightarrow D = \varphi \tag{8.4}$$

where φ is the value of goods produced Y is the monetary income and D is the aggregate level of monetary demand. It is reasonable to postulate an equality between φ and Y since one acceptable method of estimating national income is simply to sum all the attendant production costs. Thus the condition for Say's Law to remain valid reduces to the proposition that $Y = D$ – that is, that all monetary income is translated into monetary demands. For the classical economist this proposition appeared almost self-evident, and indeed had been explicitly stated by Adam Smith in his famous assertion 'that what is annually saved is as regularly consumed as what is annually spent, and nearly in the same time too; but it is consumed by a different set of people'. Clearly, what is required is the condition that saving be equated with investment in the *ex ante* sense. Since monetary income is either consumed or saved, and demand is for either investment goods or consumption goods,

$$Y = C + S \tag{8.5}$$

$$D = D_c + D_i \tag{8.6}$$

and since D_c is by definition equal to C, the condition $Y = D$ requires $S = D_i$.

For the classical economist this equality is a logical consequence of classical interest rate theory. According to this doctrine the fundamental determinants of the rate of interest are the twin forces of productivity and thrift. The former provides a demand for capital (supply of bonds) determined by the marginal productivity of capital, whilst the latter provides a supply of saving. More formally, saving is related to the rate of interest, so that

$$S = S(i) \tag{8.7}$$

and $dS/di > 0$ where i denotes the interest rate. Investment demand is equally geared to the rate of interest, so that

$$I = I(i) \tag{8.8}$$

and $I/di < 0$.

Thus the supply and demand curves for capital are normally sloped, and appending the equilibrium market clearing condition that

$$S = I \tag{8.9}$$

permits the determination of saving, investment and the rate of interest.

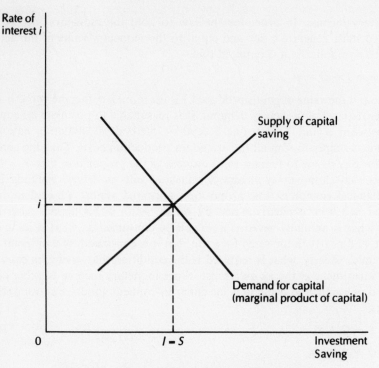

Figure 8.3   Classical theory of interest determination

The classical theory of interest determination is illustrated in figure 8.3. The rate of interest becomes the equilibrating force which maintains equality between saving and investment and thus maintains the level of aggregate demand. An increase in the desire to save, for example, implies an outward shift in the supply curve of capital, an immediate fall in the rate of interest and an extension of investment spending equal to the cutback in consumption demand. The classical theory of interest rate determination, and in particular the belief that interest rates revealed great flexibility in response to any change in underlying market conditions, thus becomes the cornerstone of classical macrotheory by underpinning the validity of Say's Law within the context of a monetary economy.

The rate of interest which equated savings and investment was to become known as the 'natural rate of interest', following Wicksell in his *Lectures on Political Economy* (Wicksell, 1934) and Keynes in his *Treatise on Money* (Keynes, 1930). The classical model implicitly assumed that the market rate of interest would always correspond to the so-called natural rate. But both Wicksell and Keynes were to explore conditions under which the market rate of interest might deviate from the natural rate and thus destroy the

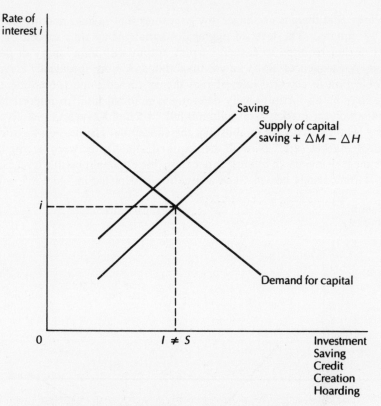

Figure 8.4 Loanable funds theory of interest rate determination

equality between saving and investment required for Say's Law.

Why should such a divergence occur? A number of possibilities present themselves. On the one hand, not all savings may be placed on the market in the form of demand for bonds. People may find themselves with a demand for cash and thus decide to hoard out of their savings. This is one consequence of permitting money to possess a store of value function in addition to the conventional transactions demand function assumed in classical economics. On the other hand, the supply of capital placed on the market may exceed the supply of savings if the banking sector is engaged in credit creation. This more sophisticated formulation of interest rate theory, which was to become known as the *loanable funds theory*, is illustrated by reference to figure 8.4. The demand for loanable funds is equated with the demand for productive capital assets (supply of bonds) as before, but now the supply of loanable funds is equal to saving plus the flow of new money originating from the banking sector (ΔM) less any hoarding element (ΔH).

It follows that there is no longer any guarantee that savings and investment will be equated. The level of aggregate demand may thus exceed or fall short of that required to sustain current output with inflationary or deflationary consequences; Say's Law is invalidated. A more specifically Keynesian objection to classical interest rate theory turned upon the notion that there may be an institutionally determined minimal limit to interest rates below which the market rate could not fall. Much of Keynesian interest rate theory is concerned with establishing the conceptual justification for such a minimal market rate.[7] Now if the required equality between saving and investment demands an interest rate below this minimal possible level, Say's Law is immediately denied. Such a situation is depicted in figure 8.5, where

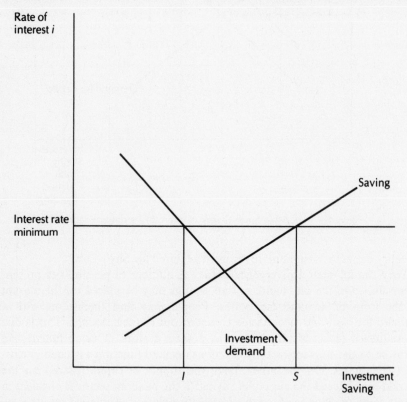

Figure 8.5   Keynesian denial of classical interest rate theory – an institutional floor to interest rates

7 Prior to Keynes, all excessive saving doctrines had foundered upon this very point. Malthus, for example, had been unable to explain why the excessive accumulation of capital did not lead to a zero rate of interest.

at the institutionally determined minimal interest rate *ex ante* saving exceeds *ex ante* investment by the amount *IS* with predictable deflationary consequences.[8]

The following is a summary of the argument so far. The classical system had posited that full employment would be the normal outcome of the bargaining process in the labour market if the natural play of competition was allowed. Moreover, whatever the output level corresponding to this full employment equilibrium, the level of aggregate demand would be sufficient to absorb it. The latter assurance derived from Say's Law of Markets which in turn depended upon the classical formulation of interest rate determination. Thus, to a large extent, Keynes's attack upon the classical structure was an assault upon their formulation of the theory of interest. The alternative formulation proposed by Keynes does not guarantee the *ex ante* equation of savings and investment; nor does it guarantee that current output levels are sustainable. It can hardly be considered surprising therefore that much of the immediate post-Keynesian controversy should focus so heavily upon the question of interest rate determination.

The Role of Money

The classical model just outlined is a model stated in real terms, with the nominal money stock exercising no influence upon the real sector of the economy. In such a model, the role of money is significant solely for nominal values. With a given money stock and a constant velocity, money national income is given as

$$\bar{M}\bar{V} = Y_m \tag{8.10}$$

Since real income is already determined, the equation

$$Y_m = PY \tag{8.11}$$

permits the determination of the price level and hence the determination of the nominal wage

$$W_m = \frac{W}{P} P \tag{8.12}$$

---

8 As will be seen (chapter 11), it was left to Pigou to salvage the classical system from the force of this attack. The celebrated Pigou Effect would show that in such an event automatic tendencies would arise to arrest the rate of saving. The saving schedule would be progressively shifted inwards until it intersected the investment demand curve at the minimal interest rate level.

It follows that a doubling of the money stock, from whatever cause, with a constant velocity will merely double prices, nominal income and nominal wages whilst leaving real variables unchanged. This is the nature of the *classical dichotomy* between the real and monetary sectors as well as an affirmation of the quantity theory of money. For the classical writers the quantity theory of money was an integral element in the dichotomy and in the alleged neutrality of money.

Concluding Comments

In this chapter an attempt has been made, albeit far too briefly, to outline the essential features of the classical system and the reasons for the classical belief that the natural long-run equilibrium condition for the macro-economy implied a state of zero involuntary unemployment. It has been shown that the classical conclusion rested upon certain postulates and conditions including Say's Law of Markets, whose validity, in turn, is seen to depend crucially upon the classical theory of interest determination. If this interpretation is correct, it would suggest that Keynes's assault upon the classical model was in large part an attack upon classical interest theory. Finally, an outline was given of the nature of the classical dichotomy and the reasons for the belief that money stock changes would influence only nominal magnitudes – a conclusion, as will be seen, remarkably similar to certain modern-day monetarist contentions.

Further Reading

Any genuine understanding of classical economics and the classical theory of employment demands a reading of the original source material. Reliance upon secondary sources, no matter how perceptive or authoritative, always encounters the danger of caricaturing the classical writers. In particular, the writings of Smith (1904), Ricardo (1951–5), Mill (1966) and Say (1964), together with Ricardo's correspondence with Malthus, provide valuable insight into issues where the classical economists differed with regard to their views on the macroeconomy; such differences are invariably obscured by attempts to survey the content of classical economics.

With regard to the secondary sources, however, Schumpeter's monumental work (1954) is especially rewarding, and particularly incisive with respect to Say's Law. A detailed analysis of Ricardo's macroeconomics is provided by Shoup (1960). A carefully researched study of the classical economists is that by O'Brien (1975), whilst Corry (1962) provides an analysis which emphasizes the homogeneity of classical thinking with respect to macro-economic issues. On policy issues generally, Robbins (1952) and Samuels (1966) deserve particular mention whilst Presley (1979) provides a recent re-evaluation of the contribution of Robertson. Cochrane (1970) provides an exhaustive attempt to summarize pre-Keynesian macrotheory. Interesting shorter expositional pieces on classical macrotheory are to be found in Hagen (1966) and Ackley (1961) and (1978).

9

The Economics of Keynes

The previous chapter has sketched, albeit in a somewhat *simpliste* fashion, the essence of classical employment theory with which Keynes was to take issue. That Keynes was seeking to deny the classical thesis is beyond doubt; the question which remains, however, and which is still unresolved, is the precise nature of Keynes's attempted denial. That this question should remain in contention some forty-five years after the publication of the *General Theory* is in itself remarkable particularly in view of the detailed analysis to which the latter has been subject. None the less this is in fact the case, and it is possible to identify three distinct and opposing interpretations of Keynes which command respect. These might be characterized as the unstable expectations thesis, the general equilibrium model and the Hicksian income–expenditure approach.

The Context and Scope of the General Theory

Before turning to these three opposing viewpoints of the message of the *General Theory*, it is perhaps necessary to point out what that volume was *not* concerned with. Keynes was not attempting to argue that unemployment was the consequence of a lack of flexibility in money wages. Indeed, had he done so he would have been postulating the classical theory of unemployment, as he fully recognized.

> For the Classical Theory has been accustomed to rest the supposedly self-adjusting character of the economic system on the assumed fluidity of money wages; and, when there is rigidity, to lay on this rigidity the blame of maladjustment. (Keynes, 1936, p. 257)

Keynes was not merely attempting to deny one of the assumptions underlying the classical model on the grounds of its being at variance with the real world. The *General Theory* occupied Keynes for fully five years;[1] had

---

1 See his letter to Florence Keynes (Moggridge, 1973, vol. XIII, p. 653).

he merely been refuting the plausibility of downward wage flexibility it would scarcely have taken half an hour. Keynes was not simply questioning the assumptions of classical theory but attempting to deny the theoretical model given its assumptions. He believed himself to be writing a major work in economic theory, and as he made clear in a letter to George Bernard Shaw he had no doubts that he was involved in his *magnum opus*.

> I believe myself to be writing a book on economic theory which will largely revolutionise – not, I suppose, at once but in the course of the next ten years – the way the world thinks about economic problems. . . .
>
> I can't expect you, or anyone else, to believe this at the present stage. But for myself I don't merely hope what I say, in my own mind I'm quite sure. (Moggridge, 1973, vol. XIII, p. 492)

Whether Keynes succeeded in denying the classical theory is a matter of dispute depending upon the interpretation to be accorded to Keynes. The conventional wisdom would tend to the view that Keynes failed in his theoretical objective but none the less succeeded in revolutionizing the policy climate in sanctioning a far greater degree of policy intervention.[2] This issue will be returned to later; first, however, the question why these difficulties of interpretation should arise, and persist for so long, must be confronted.

First and foremost, the *General Theory* is an extremely difficult book. It is difficult to read and all the evidence suggests that Keynes found it difficult to write. At times the syntax becomes extremely tortuous and unclear; at others the tone is almost flippant and suspiciously tongue in cheek. It was written over a considerable time and doubtless Keynes's own perception of the issues altered over the years. Inconsistencies arise and accordingly it is possible by careful selection to derive opposing viewpoints. The difficulties are compounded by the introduction of new terminology for established economic concepts.[3] Moreover, it is arguable whether the definition of income adopted or the emphasis upon user costs, supplementary costs, windfall losses, wage units and so forth are appropriate to the methodology adopted; certainly, these terms have disappeared from elementary

---

2 Long before Keynes, other economists in both the UK and the USA had advocated public works programmes and similar measures to alleviate unemployment. Keynes, however, particularly with the multiplier concept borrowed from Kahn, provided the required theoretical rationale.

3 Thus, for example, the marginal efficiency of capital replaced the Marshallian marginal productivity concept, whilst the doctrine of liquidity preference substituted *inter alia* for the Cambridge k of earlier analysis.

'Keynesian' textbook expositions. More than one eminent scholar has suggested that Keynes was not fully aware of what he was writing or where it was to lead him.[4] Many of the difficulties might have been resolved had Keynes revised the work in the light of subsequent criticism and commentary. But this was not to be. The nearest that Keynes came to a restatement was in a defence to the critics[5] in his famous *Quarterly Journal of Economics* article (Keynes, 1937a). Here Keynes emphasized the importance of the state of long-term expectations, or rather the unstable nature and uncertainty surrounding long-term expectations, as a pivotal point of departure from classical theory.

One notable feature of the *General Theory*, which is in part responsible for a certain lack of precision to the arguments proffered, is that Keynes avoided any attempt at a formal mathematical model. Indeed, he specifically warned against the employment of mathematics on the grounds that it would cloak interdependencies between variables. Thus

It is a great fault of symbolic pseudo-mathematical methods of formalising a system of economic analysis . . . that they expressly assume strict independence between the factors involved and lose all their cogency and authority if this hypothesis is disallowed. . . . Too large a proportion of recent 'mathematical' economics are mere concoctions, as imprecise as the initial assumptions they rest on, which allow the author to lose sight of the complexities and interdependencies of the real world in a maze of pretentious and unhelpful symbols. (Keynes, 1936, pp. 297–8)

None the less, despite this stricture, Keynes was to endorse the simultaneous equation model presented by Hicks in his famous 'Mr Keynes and the Classics' (Hicks, 1937). Keynes 'found it very interesting and really had next to nothing to say by way of criticism' (Moggridge, 1973, vol. XIV, p. 79).

---

4 'Thus, Keynes became "the greatest economist of our time" (meaning that his contribution was so indisputable that no one need concern himself over precisely what it was) and the *General Theory* an "acknowledged classic" (meaning that no active economist reads it, for fear of discovering that the master was himself confused about the message he had to impart to posterity).' (Johnson, 1970, and, 'There were moments when we had some trouble in getting Maynard to see what the point of his revolution really was, but when he came to sum it up after the book was published he got it into focus.' (Robinson, 1973)

5 The critics were formidable, being Leontief, Robertson, Taussig and Viner and published in the November 1936 edition of the *Journal*.

One fundamental difficulty in the interpretation to be accorded to the *General Theory* rests upon its presumed relationship with the *Treatise on Money*. That the former derived in part from the discussions and controversies surrounding the latter is beyond dispute. Whether the *General Theory* should be looked upon as replacing the *Treatise* or merely extending and building upon its foundations is altogether a more difficult issue to resolve. If the *General Theory* is regarded as a distinct break from its predecessor, presumably now discarded by its author, a more radical interpretation is suggested. In contrast, if the *General Theory* is looked upon as a continuation and evolution of the *Treatise* upon which Keynes sought to improve by adding a theory of output changes to the theory of prices changes already contained therein, then arguably the break with tradition is less sharp and revolutionary. This issue is of importance to the subsequent interpretation to be accorded to 'Keynesian' positions upon the relative potency of monetary versus fiscal actions.

In the *General Theory* Keynes makes frequent reference to the *Treatise* partly to clarify changes in terminology. More specifically, however, he writes:

> The relation between this book and my *Treatise on Money*, which I published five years ago, is probably clearer to myself than it will be to others; and what in my own mind is a natural evolution in a line of thought which I have been pursuing for several years, may sometimes strike the reader as a confusing change of view. (Keynes, 1936, p. vi)

None the less, the evolutionary process is dramatic involving the transition from a static to a dynamic view of the economy. Thus

> my lack of emancipation from preconceived ideas showed itself in what now seems to be the outstanding fault of the theoretical parts of that work (namely, Books III and IV), that I failed to deal thoroughly with the effects of *changes* in the level of output.... The dynamic development as distinct from the instantaneous picture, was left incomplete and extremely confused. (Keynes, 1936, pp. vi–vii)

The foregoing discussion has suggested reasons why there may exist legitimate differences over the question of Keynes's fundamental message and his assault upon classical employment theory. One's perception of Keynes's views cannot be divorced from their period, and this is as true of Keynes's fellow disciples as it is of latter-day commentators. In the last resort, the question of what Keynes really meant (or arguably, what he should have meant) turns upon a view as to what is central and what is merely peripheral, what is essential and what is merely incidental, in his writings; in this way apparent inconsistencies and obscurities may readily be resolved, at least to the satisfaction of those adhering to that interpretation. (Coddington, 1976)

In what follows, three opposing interpretations of the *General Theory* are outlined.

The Unstable Expectations Thesis

Classical economics viewed the world as consisting of individual economic agents, motivated by the desire to maximize their own individual welfare, subconsciously promoting the aggregate good whilst simultaneously generating market clearing situations. Such was the power of the 'invisible hand' and the force of competition. Implicit in the classical approach is the belief in the existence and attainment of a market equilibrium and more importantly that individual maximizing behaviour will promote such an equilibrium. Such a solution requires certain constraining conditions, the presumption of reasonable knowledge about markets and market behaviour, and the existence of stable expectations about the future.

If these conditions are not satisfied, and in particular if expectations about the future are continually changing in the light of events, then there can be no guarantee that the indicated equilibrium will be attained. Moreover, if there exists interdependence between expectations so that one person's beliefs influence another's, divergent movements away from the indicated equilibrium may be experienced.

According to one influential interpretation of Keynes, this was precisely his belief with respect to investment demands. The state of long-term expectations, or the state of confidence, has a profound impact upon the marginal efficiency of investment schedule. But the state of long-term expectation would be an extremely unstable and precarious thing; it will be unduly influenced by the facts of the current situation which will be subject to sudden change. Ignorance is the dominant characteristic in estimates about future prospective yields of capital assets, and accordingly such estimates will be held in little confidence. Moreover, the valuation of future capital assets will be greatly influenced by current evaluation of existing assets upon the stock exchange. But the stock exchange evaluation may have little relevance to the true value of the asset. The increasing ownership of equity by persons having no involvement in day-to-day management of the business in question accentuates possible divergencies of stock market valuations from true valuations of the asset. Moreover, professional investors are not concerned with the true valuation of an asset as such; rather their concern is with what the market evaluation will be over the next few months no matter how irrational or divorced from true values that may be. In these circumstances there can be no guarantee that the volume of investment will conform to the needs of society, or that it will generate a situation whereby capital markets are cleared. Thus

> There is no clear evidence from experience that the investment policy which is socially advantageous coincides with that which is more profitable.

and

> When the capital development of a country becomes a by-product of the activities of a casino, the job is likely to be ill-done. (Keynes, 1936, pp. 157 and 159)

In addition, however, there is another consequence of the existence of uncertainty and ignorance surrounding future values of capital assets. Given the existence of a liquid asset, namely money, in a world of uncertainty and erratic capital valuations, it becomes open to the individual to opt out of investment in real assets altogether and in so doing to opt out of any accompanying employment creation. Hoarding is a logical counterpart to uncertainty and ignorance.

This interpretation of the essence of Keynes culls support principally from the 1937 *Quarterly Journal of Economics* article and chapter 12 of the *General Theory*. In essence, it throws doubt upon the private enterprise system's ability to generate the required amount of investment; moreover, it suggests that monetary policy directed merely towards controlling the rate of interest may be inadequate to provide the corrective. Keynes did not shrink from the obvious conclusion:

> I expect to see the State, which is in a position to calculate the marginal efficiency of capital goods on long views and on the basis of the general social advantage, taking an ever greater responsibility for directly organising investment; since it seems likely that the fluctuations in the market estimation of the marginal efficiency of different types of capital, calculated on the principles I have described above, will be too great to be offset by any practicable changes in the rate of interest. (Keynes, 1936, p. 164)

The revolutionary nature of this interpretation of Keynes should not be overlooked. In this view, Keynes was not merely suggesting that the classical macroeconomic model of the economy was at fault; rather he was stating that no such complete model of the economy was possible if it were to do justice to the state of long-term expectations. In short, orthodox economics was adrift and there was nothing that could be put in its place. As will be seen in chapter 13, it is ironic that recent work on generating theories of endogenous expectations formation has largely been formulated within a neo-classical framework.

The General Equilibrium Model

The Marshallian theory of value is essentially partial equilibrium analysis; it studies individual market situations under the assumption of *ceteris paribus*. That is to say, it assumed that it is feasible to analyse changes in individual market supply and demand curves in isolation from what is happening in other markets. This assumption is, of course, strictly untenable as Marshall was fully aware.[6] The real world is characterized by interdependence; changes in any one market will exert feedback influences upon markets elsewhere which in turn will rebound once more upon the market initiating the change.

General equilibrium theory expressly allows for such interdependence. It views the economy as a series of mutually interdependent markets for each and every good in the economy. It thus attempts to analyse the economy from a microeconomic viewpoint by focusing upon individual markets, but since it examines all markets simultaneously, allowing for interdependencies, it is equally macroeconomic in character. An alternative way of approaching this distinction is to say that whereas in partial equilibrium analysis the prices of all goods other than the one under observation are exogenous, in general equilibrium analysis all prices are endogenous.

Now whilst the Marshallian approach is obviously the pragmatic way to analyse any given market structure, and whilst it has great expositional value, its very incompleteness renders it conceptually unsatisfactory. In con-

---

6 Marshall was extremely careful in his choice of market examples in an attempt to minimize the obvious difficulties. Thus, for example, the *ceteris paribus* assumption encompasses real income despite the fact that any price change occurring in the market in question must affect real income. Marshall thus chose commodities such as tea which occupied a minor fraction of consumers' budgets and thus minimized attendant income effects (see Marshall, 1920, p. 92ff.)

trast, the Walrasian[7] general equilibrium model is intellectually appealing if at the same time mathematically demanding. It conceives the world in terms of a series of complex simultaneous equations, and the intriguing question which then arises for mathematicians is whether or not a solution will exist; that is to say, will there be a price vector which is able to equate supply and demand in all markets simultaneously? The answer to this question raises all sorts of difficult problems which have only recently produced satisfactory answers.[8]

The economist, however, is concerned not just with the possible existence of a solution to a set of simultaneous equations. He insists that the indicated solution possess possible economic significance; that is to say, negative values must not enter the price vector. Moreover, the question which intrigues him is whether the market system, assuming competitive maximizing behaviour, is capable of attaining any indicated solution? This is the question which is neatly sidestepped in Walrasian economics by the adoption of the mathematically convenient but artificial device known as *tâtonnement*. This takes the form of assuming the existence of an auctioneer (presumably possessed of a minicomputer) who calls out prices for each and every good. Prospective buyers and vendors then respond to these prices by tendering 'fictive tickets' indicating the quantities they wish to buy and sell. If the price vector so established does not clear all markets simultaneously no exchange is permitted to take place. The auctioneer will revise his prices and the whole process will recommence. In this way, the market gropes towards the equilibrium price vector and no false trading – that is, trading at non-equilibrium prices – is allowed to interfere with the indicated adjustment process.

Now it is precisely this fiction of the auctioneer which renders general equilibrium theory largely irrelevant to the problems which concerned Keynes. For if false trading is ruled out so too is any analysis of disequilibrium sequences by which the economy might move from one equilibrium

---

7 Leon Walras is generally regarded as the founder of modern general equilibrium theory in that he first posited, if he did not entirely answer, the fundamental issues of whether in such a system there would exist a competitive equilibrium; would it be unique and would it be stable? For a penetrating insight into Walras's *Elements d'Economie Politique Pure ou Theorie de la Richesse Sociale,* see especially Schumpeter (1961, pp. 998–1026).

8 Walras's approach to this question was in terms of equating the number of equations with unknowns given certain restrictions upon the nature of permissible equations, but it was not until the development of fixed point theorems in mathematics in the 1950s that a general proof was finally possible. The major innovators in the development of the Walrasian tradition have included Hicks, Arrow, Hahn, Debreu and Malinvaud.

to another. Moreover, such an assumption eliminates any uncertainty about the future – the future is always a market clearing one. Restricting oneself solely to equilibrium conditions permits the absence of time; the world is one of timeless truths. In contrast, Keynes was attempting to confront the problems of a modern capitalist economy in which production involved *time* and hence involved expectations about the future which might be held with differing degrees of confidence and certainty. The issues with which Keynes grappled have all been neatly put aside by the benevolent role of the omnipotent auctioneer. What then is the relevance of general equilibrium theory to the message of the *General Theory*?

It is at this point that a neo-Walrasian interpretation of Keynes is encountered which is intimately linked with the names of Clower and Leijonhufvud (see Clower and Leijonhufvud, 1975; Leijonhufvud, 1968). What is suggested here is that Keynes moved away from the partial equilibrium analysis of the Cambridge Marshallian world towards a general equilibrium approach along Walrasian lines but characterized by its extremely aggregative nature. Thus Keynes viewed the economy in terms of four all-inclusive and interdependent markets – the markets for commodities, money, bonds and labour. In addition, Keynes readily conceded that within this aggregative system a set of prices could exist so as to clear all markets simultaneously including the market for labour. But in the absence of the calculating auctioneer the stability of such a price vector cannot be guaranteed. Prices may be established in the various aggregated markets which do not equate supply and demand and yet a certain amount of trading will take place. Moreover, the existence of such false trading may aggravate the disequilibrium situation.

If this interpretation is correct then Keynes made a fundamental break from the Marshallian tradition. For in the Marshallian theory, if prices do not equate supply and demand then a fairly immediate price change is indicated. The adjustment towards equilibrium is thrown upon the side of prices. In contrast in a false trading situation the disequilibrium price is maintained with the adjustment process being thrown upon the side of quantity changes. Moreover, such quantity changes imply further income changes which may exert disequilibrating feedback impacts upon other markets. To illustrate the argument advanced here, consider figure 9.1. Two markets are illustrated – the market for commodities and the labour market. Assume initially that full employment prevails but that prices are too high to clear the commodity market. If traders attempt to maintain existing prices then the adjustment process is thrown upon the side of quantity changes. A situation of excess supply develops with stocks and inventories increased as effective demand falls short of supply at existing prices. The decision to maintain existing prices, it may be noted, is perfectly

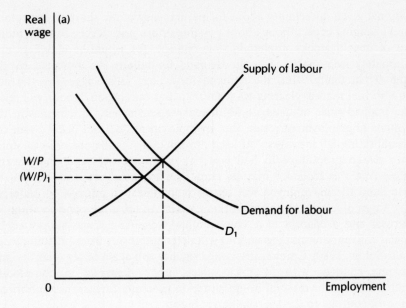

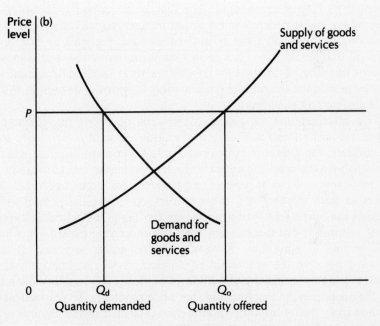

Figure 9.1 False trading and market interdependence (a) labour market (b) commodity
market

rational given uncertainty about the permanency of the shortfall in demand and changing expectations about possible future price levels. But the build-up of unsold stocks implies income changes for would-be suppliers and ultimately feeds back upon the demand for labour. As indicated by the line D_1 in figure 9.1(a) the demand for labour falls, suggesting the new equilibrium market clearing wage $(W/P)_1$. But once again, labour will resist the implied price adjustment. With real wages unchanged, changes in the volume of employment result. But unemployment does not bring about the equilibrating fall in wages – at least not initially – as the unemployed enter into search procedures to find work at the previously experienced wage. Moreover, this tendency may be reinforced by social conventions. On the one hand the unemployed will regard it unethical to attempt to undercut the wages of fellow employed workers, whilst on the other considerations of fairness and a concept of a 'conventional' wage (sometimes supported by social conventions and legislation) will deter employers from pursuing wage cuts (Solow, 1980). Comparative wage rigidity will again imply quantity and income changes with feedback effects upon demands in commodity markets. Thus the disequilibrium situation generates further disequilibrium, in stark contrast to the Marshallian solution.

This sequence demonstrates two concepts which may be considered essential to Keynesian thought. The first is the notion that the *effective demand* for goods depends upon actual income received (the consumption function) and may fall short of *notional demand*, regarded as that level of demand that would have been forthcoming had labour been able to sell its desired quantity of labour time at existing wage levels. The second is the pivotal position of the multiplier in possibly magnifying deviations from the indicated market equilibria.

This interpretation of Keynes differs sharply from the conventional, which views the *General Theory* primarily in terms of comparative statics. In contrast, the attention is pivoted firmly upon disequilibrium situations and analyses the resulting adjustments in dynamic terms. Ultimately, even in the absence of the auctioneer, adjustments will occur upon the side of prices as both workers and entrepreneurs experience the painful learning process that their reservation prices are too high. A classical full employment solution is not inconsistent with the underlying model, yet none the less, in this interpretation, Keynes's achievement is very real. It lies in pointing out that the automatic adjustment of the classical analysis rests upon the highly artificial assumption of perfect price flexibility guaranteed by the auctioneer; in emphasizing that price rigidity is the consequence not of monopoly but of imperfect information, and that in the absence of such *tâtonnement* the disequilibrium adjustment process could be extremely long; and further in stressing that initial reactions to disequilibrium situations are more likely to widen the discrepancy between actual and equilibrium prices/quantity relationships. Keynes thus emerges as a major theorist of macroeconomic disequilibrium.

This interpretation of Keynes does not necessarily imply that Keynes believed himself to be working in a Walrasian framework or that he concerned himself unduly with the Walrasian issues of the existence of a competitive equilibrium. Indeed, as Joan Robinson (1969) has commented, Keynes started from a Marshallian short-period situation in which *money* prices are linked to the state of effective demand. In contrast, the Walrasian approach effectively dispenses with money to the extent that all transactions are conducted in kind. Indeed, according to Clower (1975)

> Keynes must rather have intended to offer the world an analytically manageable aggregative version of the kind of *general process analysis* that Marshall himself might have formulated had he ever felt the need explicitly to model the working of the economic system as a whole.

None the less, it does suggest that Keynes was indeed a major theoretical innovator whose main achievement lay in breaking away from equilibrium theorizing which had dominated economics for more than a century. It is not so much that Keynes provided the answers but rather that he groped towards a methodological procedure which in the last analysis represented a truly revolutionary break from established tradition.

The Hicksian Income–Expenditure Approach

The foregoing interpretations of the *General Theory* have viewed that work as a major and radical departure from prevailing classical orthodoxy and suggested that Keynes made a revolutionary breakthrough in theoretical economics. In contrast, the more modest and widely accepted view, which perhaps can be termed the conventional wisdom, springs from the interpretation of Hicks (1937) and suggests not so much a revolution in economic thinking but rather a far-ranging reformation of classical ideas. In this view, Keynes accepted much of classical thought with his major innovation being the emphasis upon a monetary theory of interest. Moreover, this interpretation of Keynes leads essentially to the judgement that Keynes failed to overthrow the theoretical framework of classical economics in that his demonstration of unemployment equilibria is shown to depend upon very restrictive assumptions such as wage rigidity. Keynesian unemployment theory is thus shown to be a special case of the classical system and one fully allowed for by the classical writers. In short, on a *theoretical level* the 'Keynes versus the classics' controversy is shown to be essentially bogus or else relatively trivial and concerned with minor issues such as the comparative influence of money and saving upon interest rates.

None the less, it is this interpretation that 'Keynesian disciples' have seized upon to proclaim their version of the Keynesian message. For they argue that the Keynesian special case is the only relevant one for modern-day economies. Money wage rigidities preclude dependence upon automatic adjustment mechanisms. Moreover, the beauty of the Keynesian formulation lies in the fact that it clearly indicates the manner in which the authorities can rectify the deficiency of the market system. The Hicksian income–expenditure model suggests that stable relationships exist between aggregate flows of income, expenditure and output and thus provide the basis for the claim that by controlling income flows the government can control the level of aggregate demand, output and employment. The Hicksian interpretation of the *General Theory* heralds the changed status of fiscal and budgetary control and the belief that the authorities can so 'fine tune' the economy that unemployment is eliminated as a major scourge of modern society. Thus, in these terms, Keynes's achievement lies not on the purely theoretical level but rather in the realm of economic policy. Keynes is credited with underpinning the rationale for interventionist policies at the aggregative level, whilst leaving individual decision-making largely unconstrained; he is responsible for the changed status of fiscal policy and indeed for exercising a humanizing influence upon the cold logic of the dismal science.

It is this interpretation which has dominated macroeconomic thinking in the post-war period and the policy discussions and controversies surrounding the relative potency of monetary versus fiscal action. Whether it is the economics of Keynes or not, it is none the less the content of modern macroeconomics, and it is this interpretation which will be explored in detail in this book. For present purposes, however, merely the essential characteristics of the so-called *IS/LM* model will be indicated. The model contains two fundamental and *independent* equations; one relating the level of real income and rate of interest consistent with equilibrium between the supply and demand for goods and services (the goods market equation); and the second relating the level of real income and rate of interest consistent with equilibrium between the supply and demand for money (the money market equation). These two simultaneous equations can then be combined to provide a solution for the level of real income, and hence output and employment and also the rate of interest. The original Keynesian assertion was that the employment level so obtained need not comply with the full employment level, and moreover that in such an event there need be no automatic adjustment towards full employment income. The resulting debate followed two distinct paths – a theoretically oriented argument which led to a general consensus denying the latter proposition or granting that it was tenable only if money wages revealed rigid downward inflexibility, and a policy oriented argument focused upon the relative potency of monetary versus fiscal policy. Keynesian oriented economists directed their attention primarily towards the policy implications, with a marked tendency to downgrade the efficacy of monetary changes upon the grounds that both investment and consumption expenditures were in practice relatively insensitive to interest rate changes. A feature of Keynesian policy oriented economics, therefore, has been a tendency to place emphasis upon fiscal or budgetary means of controlling the level of aggregate demand with scant attention given to the financing implications of any resulting budgetary deficits.

In recent years the Hicksian income–expenditure model has been subject to a two-sided assault. Upon the one hand, the monetarist/neo-classical revival has been accompanied by the assertion that the goods and money markets are not formally independent as represented in the elementary model but are intimately linked, so that any change in the money stock exerts fairly predictable impacts upon spending flows in commodity markets. This criticism has been reinforced by recent analysis of the government budget constraint and the monetary implications of fiscal deficits. This has called into question the efficacy of fiscal policy by suggesting that fiscal measures could be being offset or 'crowded out' by accompanying monetary or wealth changes.

On the other hand, the Hicksian *IS/LM* model has been portrayed as a complete distortion of the economics of Keynes, most particularly by Leijonhufvud who draws a distinction between Keynesian economics – meaning the *IS/LM* model interpretation of the *General Theory*, with its emphasis upon comparative static equilibria – and Keynes's economics – by which Leijonhufvud means the disequilibrium economics derived from a neo-Walrasian view of the *General Theory* and the *Treatise on Money* combined.

Concluding Comments

This chapter has grappled with the thorny question of the real nature of Keynes's attempt to deny the classical thesis. That this issue should persist and still arouse major controversy almost fifty years later is in itself remarkable. As has been seen, the major interpretations can be reduced to the following:

(1) That Keynes was emphasizing the unstable, erratic and unpredictable state of long-term expectations in contrast to classical assumptions of relative certainty and predictability.
(2) That Keynes was presenting a highly aggregative general equilibrium approach to macroeconomic problems in place of the partial equilibrium analysis which dominated classical thinking.
(3) That Keynes was attempting to integrate real and monetary forces in the determination of output and employment in contrast to the prevailing classical dichotomy between real and monetary sectors.

Whatever the truth there is no doubt that, as far as the conventional wisdom is concerned, victory belonged to the third interpretation; Keynesian economics has largely been identified with the Hicksian framework, which has dominated macroeconomic theorizing. The subsequent analysis, therefore, will concentrate upon this framework and the later modifications to it.

Further Reading

Needless to say, in order to try and understand the true meaning of Keynes there can be no substitute for the original sources – although this does not constitute any guarantee of success! Certainly both Keynes (1936) and Keynes (1937a) must be regarded as essential reading, and it is interesting to relate both to the content of at least volume one of Keynes (1930). Since Keynes directed his attack upon classical employment economics primarily at Pigou's (1933) interpretation, it is instructive to read the latter and obtain a 'feel' for the structure which Keynes sought to deny in addition to his critique of Pigou in (Keynes, 1937b). The magnificent edition of Keynes's collected writings, produced for the Royal Economic Society, permit one to glimpse the intellectual excitement created by the Keynesian revolution, and the correspondence between Keynes and both his disciples and critics makes for fascinating reading. In this respect volumes XIII and XIV edited by Moggridge (1973) are certainly worth perusing.

Such has been the overwhelming influence of Hicks's (1937) seminal paper reprinted in both Mueller (1966) and Lindauer (1968) that it is wise to include it amongst one's primary sources of reading. At the same time, however, it is instructive to relate it to Hicks's changing view of Keynes and his increasing sense of dissatisfaction with the *IS/LM* framework. In this connection one should look to Hicks (1973, 1974 and 1980).

In addition to Leijonhufvud's influential work referred to in the text, a much simpler introduction to the essence of his interpretation can be culled from Leijonhufvud (1969) or alternatively Hines (1971). Additional commentary is to be found in Brothwell (1975), Jackman (1974) and Shaw (1976), whilst Cross (1982a) provides an introduction to the policy implications. In addition to the other references mentioned in the text, Harcourt (1977) and Loasby (1976) are particularly useful. Finally, a highly readable and magnanimous retrospective view of Keynes is provided by Pigou (1952), and an interesting question is posed by Grossman (1972). Recent reinterpretations of the General Theory include Fender (1981), Chick (1983), Coddington (1983) and Kohn (1986), whilst a stimulating, if perhaps a little one-sided reassessment is that by Burton (1986).

10

The Hicksian *IS/LM* Analysis

Regardless of the interpretation to be accorded to the economics of Keynes, there can be no doubt that within a very short space of time of the appearance of *The General Theory* there evolved a body of thought labelled Keynesian which was to be contrasted with the classical economics. This doctrine was essentially the economics of the simultaneous equation model derived by Hicks in his famous 'Mr Keynes and the classics' (1937), and it is this model which has dominated the development of macroeconomic thinking to the present day.

Essential Features of the *IS/LM* Framework

The essence of this Keynesian framework can be summarized very simply. Full equilibrium requires equilibrium in the commodity market and equilibrium in the money market. Only then will the economy experience a stable volume of real output and employment.

Commodity market equilibrium is summarized in the *IS* equation or the *IS* curve, which expresses a relationship between real output and real interest rates such that the aggregate demand for goods and services is just equated with their supply in the *ex ante* sense. That is to say, it summarizes all possible combinations of income and interest rate consistent with the *ex ante* equality of supply and demand in the goods market.

With regard to money market equilibrium, stability requires that the total demand for money in the economy be equated with the money stock. The demand for money, as was seen in chapter 5, will depend upon the level of income and the rate of interest. The money stock, on the other hand, is assumed to be determined by the monetary authorities working through the banking system. The *LM* equation or *LM* curve summarizes such equilibrium positions. More specifically it summarizes the relationship between real output and real interest rates such that the aggregate demand for money is just equated with the money stock.

Derivation of the *IS* Curve

In the simplest Keynesian model, national income is given by consumption plus investment demand, and both the government sector and international trade are dispensed with.[1] The national income equation is then

$$Y = C + I \tag{10.1a}$$

Assume that consumption is a linear function of the level of income and that investment demand is a linear (negative) function of the rate of interest. Thus

$$C = a + bY \tag{10.2}$$

where a is consumption at zero income and b is the marginal propensity to consume, and

$$I = d - fi \tag{10.3}$$

where d is the autonomous component in investment demand and f indicates the interest rate sensitivity of investment spending.

Combining equations 10.1a, 10.2 and 10.3,

$$Y = a + bY + d - fi \tag{10.4}$$

which yields

$$Y = \frac{a + d - fi}{1 - b} \tag{10.5}$$

Equation 10.5 is essentially a representation of the *IS* or goods market equation. It specifies firstly that the income level cannot be determined without reference to the rate of interest. Second, it highlights that for any given consumption function and any given investment demand curve there will be a rate of interest consistent with any predetermined income level. Alternatively, it may be said that the *IS* equation summarizes all possible combinations of interest rate and level of income which satisfy equality between savings and investment in the *ex ante* sense.

---

1 This is indeed the model used by Keynes and by Hicks in his famous article. Conceptually, it is perhaps worth while to note that the absence of a government sector or international trade raises no real problems. Government expenditures can be decomposed into consumption and investment outlays respectively, and for purposes of analysis the absence of international trade can be assumed away by tacitly adopting the vantage point of the world economy.

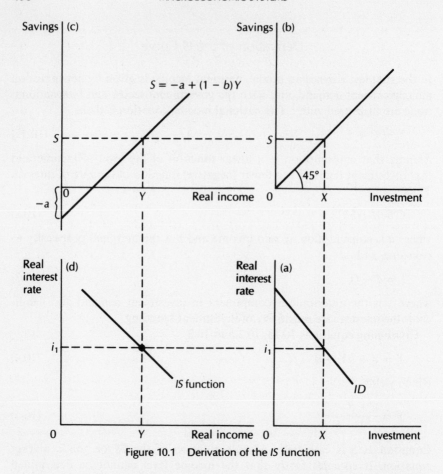

Figure 10.1   Derivation of the *IS* function

These relationships are perhaps made clearer if they are derived geo-metrically. In the composite figure 10.1 part (a) depicts the investment demand schedule as a negative linear function of the rate of interest. Again, it should be emphasized that this demand schedule, as any demand sched-ule, is an *ex ante* concept displaying a set of intentions indicating what the level of investment spending would be at any given interest rate. Since, in the context of the present model, savings and investment are equated *ex post*, part (b) of the figure invokes a 45° construct to depict this *ex post* equality. In part (c) the Keynesian consumption function shows the level of income necessary to generate any required degree of savings *ex ante*. Thus, for example, assume the interest rate i_1. Given the investment demand schedule this implies the *ex ante* investment demand $0X$. If this investment demand is ultimately realized it implies an equivalent amount of *ex post* saving, $0S$, as shown in part (b) of the composite figure. The generation of this amount of saving *ex ante* would require an income level $0Y$. One combination of interest rate i_1 and income level $0Y$ is thus obtained consistent with the *ex ante* equation of savings and investment, and this combination plotted in part (d) of the figure provides one point on the *IS* curve. Proceeding in this manner by selecting alternative initial interest rates, the *IS* curve is generated and depicts all feasible combinations of income and interest rate providing equilibrium in the goods market.

Derivation of the IS Curve with a Government Sector

It is now a simple matter to extend the analysis to take specific account of a government sector financed by a proportional income tax. Such a modification is useful because it allows consideration of fiscal policy specifically within the model analysis. The national income equation will now be represented by

$$Y = C + I + G \tag{10.1b}$$

Consumption will now be a linear function of disposable income so that

$$C = a + bY(1 - t) \tag{10.6}$$

where t is the proportional rate of income tax. As before, investment is given by equation 10.3 and it is assumed that government spending upon goods and services is autonomously determined, so that

$$G = \bar{G} \tag{10.7}$$

Solving for Y provides a new *IS* equation, namely

$$Y = \frac{a + d - fi + \bar{G}}{1 - b + bt} \tag{10.8a}$$

Equation 10.8a conveys essentially the same information as equation 10.5, namely that the income level cannot be determined without reference to the rate of interest and that, for any given income level, there will be an interest rate consistent with the *ex ante* level of aggregate demand being equal to the supply of output.

As before, the *IS* relationship can be represented graphically. Essentially, the procedure adopted in the construction of figure 10.1 is repeated but part (a) of the composite figure is modified to allow for the element of government expenditure and part (c) to allow for the influence of the proportional income tax. Thus in figure 10.2 part (a) shows the level of investment demand *ID* pertaining to any given interest rate together with the autonomously determined volume of government expenditure. Hence the *ID + G*

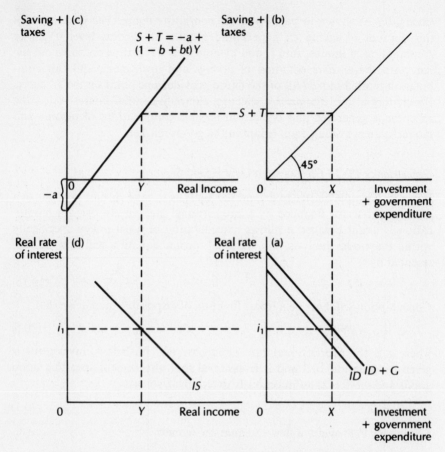

Figure 10.2   Derivation of the *IS* curve with a government sector and taxation

curve is obtained. Thus, for any given rate of interest i_1 there will be a determinate volume of investment demand plus government expenditure, $0X$. Part (b) of the figure now invokes the 45° line to translate this into an equivalent amount of saving plus taxes, since *ex post* the two must be equal within the confines of the present model. With a determinate consumption function and known rate of taxation, part (c) then determines the income level needed to generate this amount of savings plus taxes *ex ante*.[2] As

---

2 The $S + T$ schedule falls, of course, to the left of the original savings schedule. This is because the tax reduces saving by the amount $T(1 - b)$ where T is the tax yield, whilst adding to the savings plus taxes curve by the amount T. The net increase is thus $T - T(1 - b) = Tb = bYt$. The intercept of the two curves is of course the same and equal to $-a$.

before, therefore, a given point on the *IS* curve is obtained corresponding to the initial interest rate i_1, and proceeding in this manner, taking alternative initial rates of interest, the required *IS* curve incorporating a government sector is generated.

Derivation of the *LM* Curve

As long as investment demand (or indeed, consumption demand in more sophisticated models) is functionally related to the rate of interest, it is not possible to determine the equilibrium level of income without appealing to the money market. The *IS/LM* analysis possesses the great virtue of taking the money market into account and giving it equal weight in the joint determination of national income and the rate of interest. This emphasis is very much in keeping with Keynes's own views upon the importance of money, and marks a departure from the classical dichotomy between the real and the monetary sectors.[3]

For purposes of exposition in the present chapter it will be assumed that the monetary authorities can effectively control the money supply, and hence this will be treated as an exogenously determined variable.[4] This permits a focus solely upon the demand for money, and in keeping with the analysis of chapter 5 the demand for money will be taken to be determined by the level of income and the rate of interest. More specifically, the demand for money is considered to be positively related to the income level and negatively related to the rate of interest, as depicted by the following linear equations:

$$L = \theta + vY - qi \qquad (10.9)$$

where L is the total demand for money, and θ is the demand for money regardless of the income level or rate of interest and reflects a precautionary demand. Assuming the money stock M is exogenously determined, money

---

3 This is in stark contrast to the elementary 45° line portrayal of Keynesian economics which, by treating investment demand as either autonomous or functionally related to the income level via the accelerator, effectively dismisses the role of the money market entirely. Paradoxically, it was the 45° line model which captured the spirit of Keynesianism in later controversies and which highlighted the claims of fiscal policy intervention and minimized the importance of monetary variables.

4 As was seen in chapter 6, this issue of effective control over the money supply is one which often divides monetarists from Keynesians even when there is broad general agreement concerning the importance of money. Monetarists tend to favour exogenous relationships (subject to policy control) whilst Keynesians lean more to endogenous relationships.

market equilibrium requires $L = M$ or alternatively

$$M = \theta + vY - qi \qquad (10.10)$$

which gives

$$i = \frac{vY - M + \theta}{q} \qquad (10.11)$$

as the solution for the rate of interest. Equation 10.11 may be regarded as the LM equation, which argues that the level of income enters as a determinant of the rate of interest. In addition, the LM equation specifies that for any given demand for money function and exogenously determined money stock there will be a combination of interest rate and income level consistent with equality between the supply and demand for money.

In order to derive the LM function graphically it is necessary to break down the demand for money into its two component parts, the income component and the interest rate component. Thus

$$L = L_t + L_a \qquad (10.12)$$

$$L_t = \theta_1 + vY \qquad (10.13)$$

$$L_a = \theta_2 - qi \qquad (10.14)$$

where L_t is the transactions demand for money, L_a the asset demand for money and θ_1 and θ_2 sum to θ. Figure 10.3 part (a) depicts the asset demand for money as a negative function of the rate of interest. In part (b) of the figure the exogenously determined money stock may be divided between transactions needs M_1 and asset needs M_2. Thus, with the interest rate i_1 the asset demand will be $0A$. Given the exogenously determined money stock $\bar{M}$ this implies that the amount remaining to fulfil transactions purposes will be $0T$, since the distance $\bar{M}T$ on the vertical axis is equal to the distance $0A$ upon the horizontal axis. This follows from the fact that the money stock can be used to meet either asset demands or transactions needs, the relationship between the two being given by the invariant 135° line.

With a given amount of money $0T$ allocated to transactions purposes, and with a given velocity of circulation of the money stock, indicated by the slope of the ray in part (c) of the composite figure, the determinate income level $0Y$ will be obtained. Thus, given the asset demand for money, the exogenously determined money stock and the velocity of circulation, the income level $0Y$ which in conjunction with the interest rate i_1 equates the total supply and demand for money. Proceeding in this way, by selecting alternative initial rates of interest, the LM curve is derived in part (d), and shows all feasible combinations of income level and interest rate consistent with equilibrium in the money market.

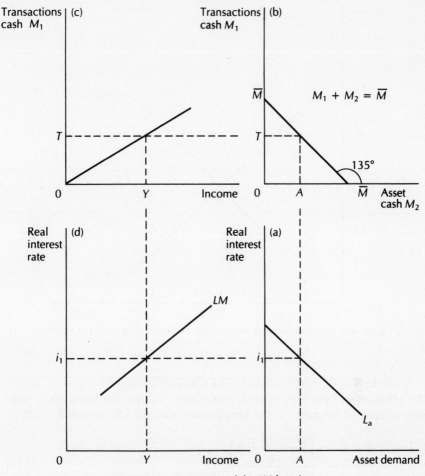

Figure 10.3   Derivation of the *LM* function

Equilibrium

The *IS* function summarizes all combinations of interest rate and income level consistent with equilibrium in the goods market; the *LM* function provides identical information consistent with equilibrium in the money market. By combining the two a unique combination of interest rate and income level can be achieved which reconciles equilibrium in both markets simultaneously. This is the situation portrayed in figure 10.4, where Y^* and i^* denote the equilibrium values of income and interest respectively.

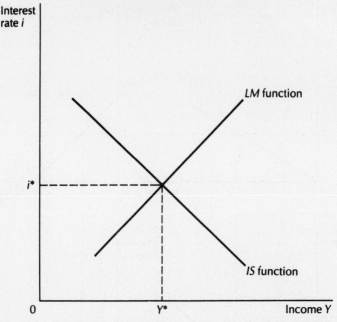

Figure 10.4   Determination of equilibrium income level and rate of interest

Mathematically, what is implied by the equilibrium condition is simply the solution of two simultaneous equations. Taking the elementary non-government *IS* equation 10.5 in conjunction with the *LM* equation 10.11,

$$Y = \frac{a + d - f\left(\dfrac{vY - M + \theta}{q}\right)}{1 - b} \qquad (10.15)$$

and

$$i = \frac{v\left(\dfrac{a + d - fi}{1 - b}\right) + \theta - M}{q} \qquad (10.16)$$

from which the equilibrium values of *Y* and *i* can be derived:

$$Y = \frac{a + d + f\left(\dfrac{M - \theta}{q}\right)}{1 - b + \dfrac{fv}{q}} \qquad (10.17)$$

and

$$i = \frac{\theta + v\left(\dfrac{a+d}{1-b}\right) - M}{q + \dfrac{vf}{1-b}} \tag{10.18}$$

Alternatively, taking the government sector *IS* equation 10.8a in conjunction with the *LM* equation 10.11,

$$Y = \frac{a + d + \bar{G} - f\left(\dfrac{vY - M + \theta}{q}\right)}{1 - b + bt} \tag{10.19}$$

and

$$i = \frac{\theta - M + v\left(\dfrac{a + d - fi + \bar{G}}{1 - b + bt}\right)}{q} \tag{10.20}$$

from which the equilibrium levels of income and rates of interest can be derived:

$$Y = \frac{a + d + \bar{G} + f\left(\dfrac{M - \theta}{q}\right)}{1 - b + bt + \dfrac{fv}{q}} \tag{10.21}$$

and

$$i = \frac{\theta - M + \left(\dfrac{va + vd + \bar{G}}{1 - b + bt}\right)}{q + \dfrac{vf}{1 - b + bt}} \tag{10.22}$$

The foregoing analysis is essentially the Hicksian interpretation of the *General Theory* which sees the equilibrium level of income being determined by both classical and 'Keynesian' influences. The equilibrium so determined may be considered a stable one in that with supply and demand being equated in both commodity and money markets simultaneously and in the *ex ante* sense there is no tendency for any change. Moreover, there is no guarantee that the equilibrium so obtained will correspond to the full employment equilibria in terms of the *IS/LM* context. In the Hicksian interpretation this is what Keynes was attempting to demonstrate, against the logic of the classical analysis. Subsequent analysis was to question the permanency of the Hicksian unemployment equilibria in the absence of extremely restrictive and unrealistic assumptions; none the less, this was the framework which was eagerly accepted by fiscally oriented 'Keynesians' and endorsed by Keynes himself.

Characteristics of the *IS/LM* Analysis

In order to bring out some of the implications of the analysis it is useful to examine the characteristics of the model in more detail. In particular, it is crucial to an understanding of the subsequent 'Keynes versus the classics' controversy to know how the position and slopes of the respective *IS* and *LM* curves are determined.

The IS Curve

First consider the *IS* curve. Any increase in autonomous expenditure, whether investment, consumption or government expenditure, will have the effect of shifting the *IS* curve outwards to the right. *Ceteris paribus* therefore, and assuming the *LM* curve is positively sloped, the net effect would be to secure a raising of national income and the rate of interest – the latter arising from the increased transactions demand for cash consequent upon the higher level of national income. This situation is depicted with the aid of figure 10.5.

Returning to the quadrant diagram of figure 10.2, an autonomous increase in either investment expenditure or government expenditure would generate an outward shift of the combined $ID + G$ curve in part (a) of the figure, whereas an autonomous increase in consumption spending is revealed as a downward shift of the combined $S + T$ curve in quadrant (c).[5] Both serve to occasion an outward shift of the *IS* curve in part (d) of the figure. It is perhaps of greater interest to enquire as to the extent of the outward shift of the *IS* curve arising from the autonomous expenditure increase. To pursue this point, from figure 10.6 will be derived two distinct *IS* curves corresponding to differing assumptions made with respect to the savings plus taxes curve of part (c) of the composite figure. In part (a) there is a given $ID + G$ curve from which the required *IS* curve can be derived by selecting appropriate initial interest rates. However, if the savings plus taxes curve $S + T_1$ is assumed, the *IS* curve IS_1 is obtained, whereas if the savings plus taxes curve $S + T_2$ is invoked the *IS* curve IS_2 is obtained. Note that the *IS* curves differ not only with respect to position but also with respect

---

5 As the consumption function $C = a + bY(1 - t)$ now becomes $C = a + \Delta a + bY(1 - t)$.

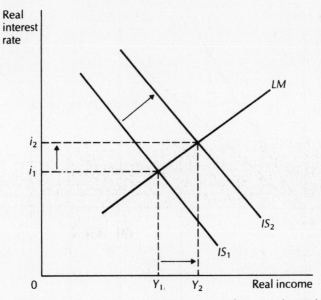

Figure 10.5 Effect of an increase in autonomous expenditure in the Hicksian *IS/LM* model

to slope, the IS_1 being possessed of a flatter slope than IS_2. Note also that the autonomous spending components are identical in the two cases; investment, government expenditure and the autonomous consumption element a are the same in both derivations. The only difference, responsible for generating a new *IS* curve distinct in *both position and slope*, is the difference in *slope* of the $S + T$ curves. The slope of the $S + T$ curve is of course determined solely by the marginal propensity to consume upon the one hand and the rate of income taxation upon the other – precisely the variables entering into the multiplier equation for a change in autonomous expenditures. To see this, refer back to the *IS* equation 10.8a for a government sector and write A for the sum of autonomous components a, d and $\bar{G}$. Then

$$Y = \frac{A - fi}{1 - b + bt} \tag{10.8b}$$

and

$$\frac{dY}{dA} = \frac{1}{1 - b + bt} \tag{10.8c}$$

represents the autonomous expenditures multiplier.

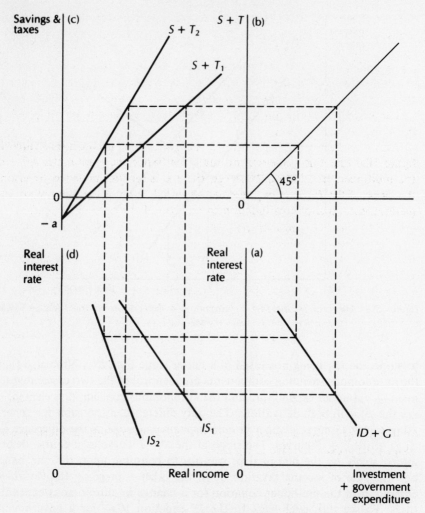

Figure 10.6 *IS* curve derived under alternative multiplier assumptions

The following is a summary of the argument thus far. For any given level of autonomous expenditure, the *IS* curve will fall farther to the right the flatter the slope of the combined savings plus taxes curve. Moreover, for any given increase in autonomous expenditure the outward shift of the *IS* curve will be greater the flatter the combined slope of the savings plus taxes curve. In turn, the savings plus taxes curve will be flatter the greater the marginal propensity to consume *b* and the lower the rate of income taxation *t*. As inspection of equation 10.8c demonstrates, the greater the marginal propensity to consume and the lower the rate of income taxation the greater will be the autonomous expenditures multiplier. The conclusions are, first, that for any given level of autonomous spending the position of the *IS* curve will lie further to the right the greater the value of the multiplier; and second, for any given increase in autonomous spending the induced outward shift of the *IS* curve will be greater the greater the value of the multiplier. Indeed, it may be demonstrated that the outward shift of the *IS* curve is equal to the increase in autonomous expenditure multiplied by the value of the multiplier.[6]

With regard to the slope of the *IS* schedule, it has been demonstrated in figure 10.6 that this slope will normally be flatter the greater the value of the multiplier. In addition, however, there is a second influence governing the slope of the *IS* function, namely the initial slope of the investment and government expenditures function in part (a) of the composite figure. The greater the interest rate sensitivity of investment demand, the flatter will be the slope of the combined investment and government expenditures schedule and the flatter the resultant *IS* curve. The less interest elastic is investment the steeper will be the resultant *IS* curve. In the extreme case, that of a perfectly inelastic investment demand function, the $ID + G$ schedule will be vertical and so too will the resulting *IS* function. In this case, the value of the multiplier has no influence upon the shape of the *IS* curve.

From the above analysis, it should be clear that the effect of an increase in the rate of taxation is to shift the *IS* curve inwards,[7] with the extent of the inward shift being governed by the income tax multiplier, given by

$$\frac{\mathrm{d}Y}{\mathrm{d}t} = \frac{-b(A - fi)}{(1 - b + bt)^2} < 0 \tag{10.8d}$$

It follows also, *ceteris paribus*, that the *IS* function will be more steeply sloped the greater the rate of taxation.

The LM Curve

The determinants of the position and slope of the *LM* curve are now considered. First of all, it is clear that with a given money stock and a given

---

6 It will be noted that as long as the *LM* curve is positively sloped the outward shift of the *IS* curve will always be greater than the increase in national income. This is because the autonomous expenditures multiplier referred to here does not take into account the repercussion of higher income levels on the rate of interest – and hence upon the volume of private sector investment spending.

7 The qualification referred to in footnote 6 of this chapter is equally applicable here. The inward shift of the *IS* curve derived from the *IS* equation will be greater than the decline in income because now as income falls, so too will the transactions demand for cash and the rate of interest – giving some positive stimulus to private investment spending.

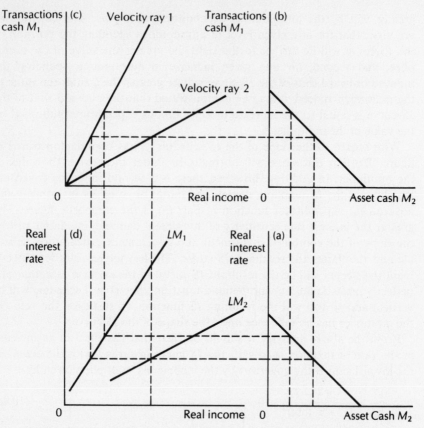

Figure 10.7   Importance of velocity to the position of the *LM* function

asset demand for cash, the initial position of the *LM* curve will be determined by the income velocity of money. This is demonstrated in figure 10.7,
where two distinct *LM* curves are derived by invoking differing assumptions with regard to the velocity relationship. The greater the velocity of
circulation of money, revealed by the lesser slope of the ray in part (c) of the
figure, the more the *LM* curve will lie to the right. Increasing the velocity of
circulation rotates the velocity relation in a clockwise direction, and as it
rotates so too will the *LM* relation. Second, an increase in the money stock,
ceteris paribus, will imply an outward shift of the *LM* curve. In the context
of figure 10.3 the extent of the outward shift of the *LM* curve due to any
given increase in the money stock, depicted in the outward movement of the
135° line of quadrant (b), will be determined by the velocity of circulation.
Other things being equal, the outward shift of the *LM* curve will be greater

the higher the degree of income velocity and *vice versa*. Essentially, there-fore, an increase in the money stock and an increase in the velocity of circulation of the money stock have virtually identical effects in moving the *LM* relation outwards,[8] and normally, assuming a negatively sloped *IS* curve, will have the effect of raising income and lowering the equilibrium rate of interest. This situation is portrayed in figure 10.8.

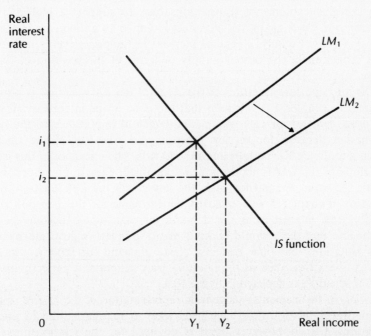

Figure 10.8   Similar effects of a money stock increase and velocity increase on income and the rate of interest

Other influences may effect a shift of the *LM* function. A change in the expectations of the holders of speculative asset cash, for example, will change the position of the asset demand for money curve in quadrant (a) of figure 10.3. Thus, if asset cash holders become more convinced that lower interest rates are here to stay they will have less fear of investing in govern-ment bonds and therefore will reduce their demands for idle money. The net

---

8 Strictly speaking, a velocity increase and a money stock increase are not for-mally identical in terms of the *LM* construct, since the former pivots the *LM* function in a clockwise direction whilst the latter generates a positive outward shift of the curve. To all intents and purposes, however, the two are very similar in the expansionary effects they imply for income and employment.

effect is to release more cash to meet transactions needs, with the result that the *LM* curve is again shifted outwards. Such a change in expectations as described here is essentially equivalent to an increase in the total money stock with regard to the position of the *LM* schedule. By very similar reasoning, account may be taken of the impact of a change in the general level of prices upon the position of the *LM* function. If prices fall, *ceteris paribus*, there will be a reduced demand for transactions balances permitting the given volume of transactions cash to support a higher level of transactions. Once again, the net effect is similar to an increase in the total money supply. Equally, a general increase in the price level is tantamount to a reduction in the money supply in terms of the position of the *LM* curve.

The all-important question of the slope of the *LM* function is now considered. In chapter 5 it was seen that the issue of the interest sensitivity of the asset demand for cash was of fundamental importance to the overall Keynesian demand for money function and was one of the questions tending to divide Keynesians and monetarists. The relevance of this issue to the slope of the *LM* function is now examined. Clearly, the more interest elastic the asset demand for cash, the flatter will the *LM* function tend to be. Also in chapter 5 was explored the rationale for the assertion that at suitably low interest rates the demand for cash would become perfectly elastic and that there would be no demand to invest in government bonds. This situation, that of a perfectly elastic demand for money, which has hitherto been described as the liquidity trap, generates a perfectly horizontal *LM* schedule as depicted in figure 10.9.

So far, in the elementary algebraic representation of the *IS/LM* analysis, simple linear relationships have been used to summarize the *IS* and *LM* equations. Clearly however there is no need for the relationships to be linear. Indeed, the arguments advanced in chapter 5 would suggest that the interest sensitivity of the asset demand for cash would increase progressively with the fall in interest rates until the region of the liquidity trap was reached. Invoking such a non-linear asset demand for cash in the quadrant diagrams would understandably generate an equally non-linear *LM* schedule. Figure 10.10 shows the typical Keynesian asset demand for cash as described in chapter 5 together with the corresponding *LM* function. In the region of the liquidity trap when the asset demand for money becomes perfectly interest elastic, the *LM* function is horizontal. Conversely, at sufficiently high rates of interest the asset demand for cash is reduced to zero and the *LM* function is correspondingly vertical. In between these two regions the *LM* function is positively sloped with the degree of curvature increasing as interest rates rise and presenting a mirror image of the asset demand for money function.

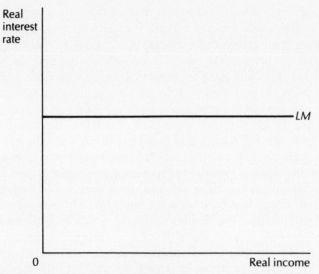

Figure 10.9   Horizontal *LM* curve stemming from the perfectly interest elastic asset demand for cash

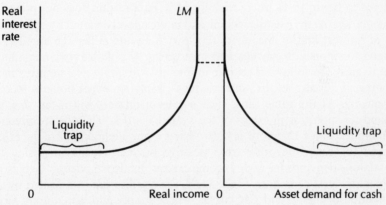

Figure 10.10   Relationship between the asset demand for cash and the *LM* function

The Meaning of Equilibrium

The meaning of the Hicksian *IS/LM* equilibrium can now be examined more closely. As has been seen, any position upon the *IS* curve implies that savings and investment are equated *ex ante* so that the demand for goods and services is precisely matched by the forthcoming supply. There is thus no tendency towards unintended investment or disinvestment in stocks and inventories; realized sales are equated with planned sales and expectations are fulfilled. The goods market displays no justification for any change.

Similar reasoning applies to the money market. A position on the *LM* curve implies that the *ex ante* demand for cash is exactly matched by the available supply. There is no unintended accumulation of money or running down of money balances below that which is considered optimal. In short, the authorities are supplying just the amount of money – no more and no less – that the private sector wishes to hold. In such a situation there can be no reason for any change to occur *unless there are forces set in motion to alter the underlying IS/LM functions themselves.* The initial Keynesian postulate was to suggest that full equilibrium could prevail in a situation of less than full employment without any tendency for such equilibrium to be disturbed. In contrast, the classical rebuttal to this Keynesian model argued that if less than full employment equilibria prevailed then there would be forces set in motion which would feed back upon the basic *IS/LM* functions and disturb the initial equilibrium. The conditions under which such forces would or would not prevail became the crux of the theoretical dispute between Keynes and the classics, as will be examined in some detail in the next chapter. For present purposes, it is perhaps useful to fix the concept of equilibrium in mind by examining the situation where it does not prevail, in *either* the commodity market or the money market. Consider the situation depicted in figure 10.11 where initially, at X, equilibrium does not prevail in either market. At the existing income and interest level denoted by point X the rate of interest and/or income is too low to equate either the supply and demand for money or savings and investment. A possible dynamic adjustment to this is as follows. This rate of interest will imply *ex ante* investment spending in excess of *ex ante* savings, implying expansionary income movements. At the same time, such a rate of interest will mean that the demand for money is in excess of the available stock. The upward pressure upon interest rates, therefore, is in two parts – one stemming from the excess demand for cash, the other from positive income expansion raising the transactions demands for cash. Income expansion also implies an increase in the planned level of savings. Once again, full equilibrium is indicated by the intersection of the *IS* and *LM* curves, where supply and demand are again equated simultaneously in all markets. Whatever the initial situation, the existence of a negatively sloped *IS* curve in conjunction with a positively sloped *LM* curve implies negative feedback and strongly suggests that the indicated equilibrium will be attained.

It is for this reason that the Hicksian interpretation of Keynes focuses attention firmly upon conditions of equilibrium. It is the prime example of the comparative static methodology. Any autonomous disturbance, such as an increase in the money supply, can be superimposed on a given equilibrium and the resultant new equilibrium immediately identified. Time is eliminated from the adjustment process. Moreover, the adjustment process

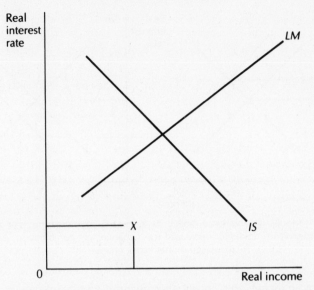

Figure 10.11   Complete disequilibrium in the Hicksian *IS/LM* model

is always one of convergence to the new equilibrium. It is for these reasons that critics of the *IS/LM* apparatus, in particular Leijonhufvud, maintain that the *IS/LM* model involves a fundamental distortion of Keynes's position; on their reading. Keynes was primarily concerned with disequilibrium uncertainties arising from the time paths of adjustment and the possibility of false trading generating increasingly divergent movements from the indicated solution.

The Policy Framework

One reason for the undoubted success of the Hicksian *IS/LM* analysis was that it literally bristled with policy implications at a time when policy prescription was at a premium. Moreover, although the formal framework became identified with the 'Keynesian school' of economics there was nothing explicit in the underlying theory to suggest a predilection for fiscal as opposed to monetary policy. The 'Keynesian' orientation toward fiscal as opposed to monetary policy, therefore, does not derive from the basic model *per se* but rather from specific Keynesian assumptions that were to be incorporated into the model. Whether Keynes himself would have approved of these later 'Keynesian' mutations is perhaps open to dispute. Certainly the basic model gives equal weighting to monetary and to fiscal

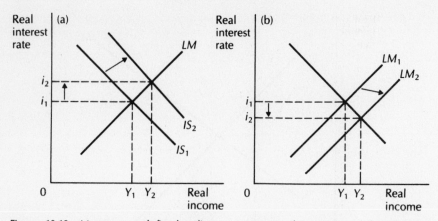

Figure 10.12 Monetary and fiscal policy as a means of increasing real income (a) increased expenditure change, decreased tax change or combination of both (b) increased money stock change

intervention in being able to enhance income and employment, as illustrated in figure 10.12. Part (a) of the figure illustrates fiscal intervention, either in the form of increased government expenditures or reduced taxation (or indeed some combination of both), whereas part (b) illustrates the effect of an enlarged money stock. Indeed, a priori, one might expect a monetary change to exert a greater impact upon the economy than a fiscal oriented change, to the extent that in the former case the interest rate falls whilst in the latter it rises. With a given money stock any attempt at expansionary fiscal policy whether by increasing government expenditure or reducing taxes must imply some increase in the rate of interest, which in turn will choke off a certain amount of investment spending in the private sector. This offset to expansionary fiscal policy provides an example of automatic stabilization; here the fixed money stock is acting as an automatic stabilizer which 'crowds out' a certain portion of the fiscal impact. The extent to which fiscal policy is *crowded out* will depend upon two influences; first, the impact of the fiscal change upon the rate of interest, and second the interest sensitivity of private sector investment demand to the interest rate change. Zero crowding out will occur if the fiscal change exerts no interest rate impact (the case of a horizontal *LM* curve) or if the investment demand function is perfectly inelastic with respect to interest rate changes (the case of a vertical *IS* curve). These cases are illustrated by figures 10.13 and 10.14. Complete crowding out occurs if the rise in the interest rate is sufficient to curtail private sector investment by the amount of the fiscal stimulus. This is the case of the vertical *LM* curve illustrated in figure 10.15. The 'normal' situation, presumably, would be that of partial crowding out where both *IS* and *LM* functions are normally sloped. This

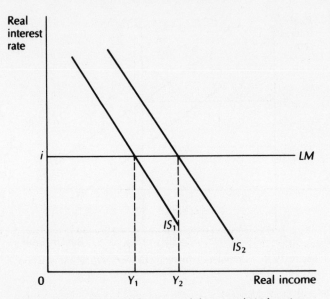

Figure 10.13   Zero crowding out with horizontal *LM* function

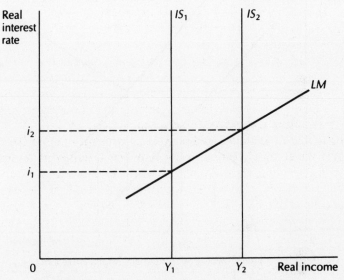

Figure 10.14   Zero crowding out with vertical *IS* function

situation is described in figure 10.16. Here fiscal intervention raises the income level from Y_1 to Y_2. In the absence of crowding out, which arises in consequence of the interest rate rise and the negative slope of the *IS* curve, income would have risen to Y_3. The extent of crowding out is accordingly given by $Y_3 - Y_2$.

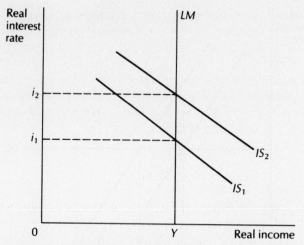

Figure 10.15   Complete crowding out with vertical *LM* function

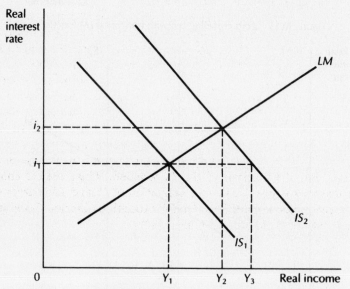

Figure 10.16   Partial crowding out – normally sloped *IS/LM* functions

Concluding Comments

In this chapter the derivation of the *IS* and *LM* functions has been considered in detail, and the determinants of their positions and slopes have
been examined. The meaning of equilibrium has been emphasized, and the

obvious policy implications of the analysis have been indicated. As a pedagogical device, the *IS/LM* construct has no equal in the sphere of economics, unless it be the concept of supply and demand itself. The reader
will, however, appreciate that it is a highly mechanistic construct, and the
results deriving from it and the policy controversies to which it gives rise
depend ultimately upon the underlying assumptions incorporated into the
model analysis. Their relevance to reality will be crucial in determining the
appropriateness and utility of the framework.

Further Reading

As mentioned in chapter 9, any introduction to *IS/LM* analysis must logically begin with Hicks's seminal paper (1937). An important elaboration of
the Hicksian framework was made by Modigliani (1944). That Keynes
appeared to be essentially in sympathy with Hicks's interpretation is fully
brought out in Hicks (1973). Also, the fact that Hicks's attempt to *interpret*
Keynes did not necessarily constitute his own view of the working of the
macroeconomy is made clear in Hicks (1980) and in Brunner and Meltzer
(1973). The latter make the point that the conventional treatment of *IS/LM*
obscures the role of relative price changes which was an important part of
the classical system, which Hicks was attempting to incorporate into a
classical–Keynesian synthesis. Also of interest from a retrospective viewpoint are chapters 8 and 9 of Hicks (1967). The former of these, 'The classics
again', appeared initially as a critical review of Patinkin (1955) in the *Economic Journal*. It brought forth a spirited reply (Patinkin, 1959) in which
Patinkin argues the case for interdependence between a change in the
money stock and the position of the *IS* function. There are, of course,
numerous textbook expositions of the derivation of *IS* and *LM* curves and
their attendant policy implications. Useful expositions include Dornbusch
and Fischer (1981) and Parkin and Bade (1982).

11

Comparative Statics of Classical,
Keynesian and Monetarist Models

The Hicksian *IS/LM* framework was readily accepted as being the appropriate model for macroeconomic analysis by both Keynesians and classicists. Its ready adoption was partly to be explained by Keynes's own endorsement, but in addition it provided a firm and logical foundation to which the participants in macroeconomic controversies could refer. In brief, something concrete was provided in place of the rather implicit structure which had gone before. Moreover, the *IS/LM* analysis was appealing in its own right. It was consistent with orthodox maximizing behaviour and it took full account of the importance of monetary influences upon the rate of interest. Rooted in elementary simultaneous equations, it was easily and readily grasped and lent itself to mechanical manipulations with engaging simplicity whilst at the same time suggesting a pseudoscientific basis to economic enquiry. Whatever the reasons, the framework itself was never a major source of contention; rather it was the assumptions underlying the framework and the use to which it could be put which divided economists into their Keynesian, classical and monetarist camps.

The Policy Dispute

As was demonstrated in chapter 10, there is theoretical justification for believing that the *LM* curve will exhibit variations in slope going from horizontal to vertical. For purposes of exposition, three regions of the *LM* curve are distinguished in the stylized figure 11.1 (For expositional convenience we have drawn these as linear segments. It may be that the functions are curvilinear.)

If the *IS* curve intersects the *LM* curve in region 1, then monetary policy exerts no influence upon the level of income, only fiscal policy being able to raise income and employment. If the intersection occurs in region 2, then both monetary and fiscal policy are able to generate increased income and employment levels. Finally, if the intersection occurs in region 3 then monetary policy alone is effective in generating expansionary forces. Fiscal policy

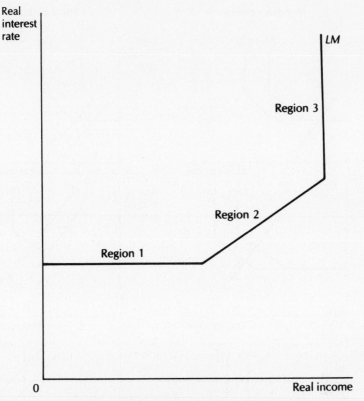

Figure 11.1   Stylized representation of the *LM* curve

is revealed to be completely ineffective as the accompanying rise in interest rates chokes off an equivalent amount of spending from the private sector. These relationships, admittedly mechanical and *simpliste*, are illustrated in figure 11.2.

The Keynesian Scepticism

The viewpoint that became readily identified with Keynesian economics (though not necessarily with Keynes himself), namely that in conditions of severe unemployment monetary policy was likely to be largely ineffective, can now be analysed. Two distinct lines of thought leading to this position can be identified. On the one hand, there was the view buttressed by considerable empirical evidence (Wilson and Andrews, 1951; White, 1956) to the effect that the rate of interest was of but minor influence upon the volume of investment spending. In the extreme case of a completely interest

Monetary policy   **Fiscal policy**

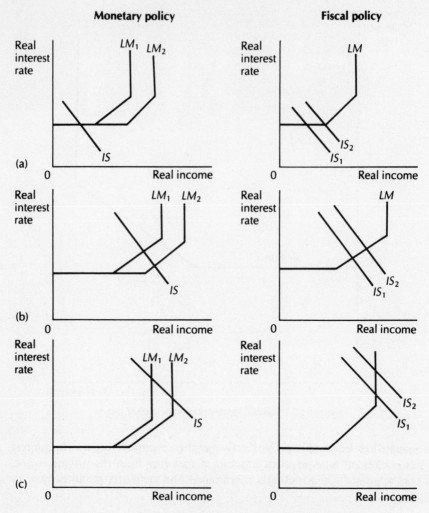

Figure 11.2   Comparative efficacy of monetary and fiscal policy

inelastic investment schedule, the *IS* curve would be vertical and increases in the money stock would exert no impact whatsoever upon the level of income and employment. This extreme situation is depicted in figure 11.3. On the other hand there was the Keynesian assertion which suggested that the supply and demand for money were interdependent. That is to say that an increase in the money stock would lower the rate of interest and the resulting fall in the interest rate would extend the speculative demand for money. The increase in the holdings of speculative idle balances, with

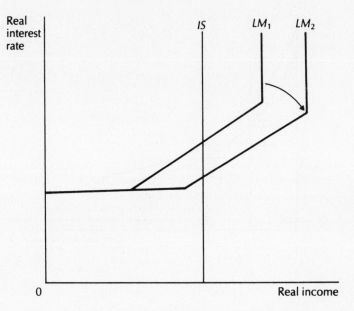

Figure 11.3   Interest inelastic investment demand and the ineffectiveness of monetary policy

a zero velocity, implies a decline in the average velocity of money generally. In terms of the simple quantity theory equation, $MV = Y_m$, the increase in M is being countered by the induced fall in V. In the limiting case, the entire increase in the money stock is being absorbed into idle balances so that the fall in the average velocity of money exactly offsets the increased monetary stock with no change in the level of money national income. This is the situation implicit in figure 11.2(a) but it is perhaps useful to spell out the argument in greater detail with reference to figure 11.4. In part (a) of the figure is shown the situation consistent with the general tenor of Keynes's argument whereby the rate of interest i_1 is the consequence of the demand for money L_{y1} and the initial money stock M_1. Now assume an increase in the money stock to M_2. The immediate consequence is a reduction in the rate of interest to i_2, which extends the total demand for money from $0L_1$ to $0L_2$. This extension in money demand implies a decline in velocity which offsets in part the monetary increase. However, this is not the end of the story, for the fall in interest rates under normal Keynesian conditions will stimulate investment spending. The increase in investment spending implies an increase in the level of income (equal to the increased expenditure multiplied by the multiplier) which in turn serves to raise the transactions demand for cash. The increase transactions demand raises the

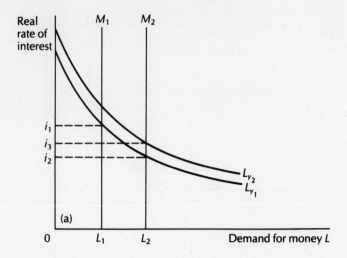

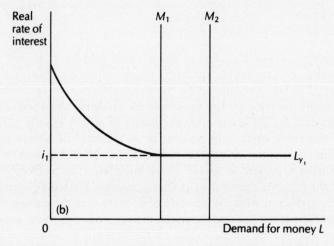

Figure 11.4 Monetary expansion under (a) 'normal Keynesian' and (b) liquidity trap
conditions

total demand for money to L_{y2} and the interest rate to i_3. Although monetary expansion has been countered in part by the induced velocity change
there is none the less a positive expansion of income. This is the normal
Keynesian sequence which Keynes made explicit in the *General Theory* and

which may be summarized notationally as

$$\Delta M \Rightarrow -\Delta i \Rightarrow \Delta I \Rightarrow \Delta Y = \Delta Ik$$

where k is the multiplier.[1]

In contrast to this normal sequence of events, however, there is the special case, eagerly seized upon by Keynesians, whereby the increased demand for cash negates the entire impact of monetary expansion and prevents any fall in the rate of interest. This situation, usually referred to as the liquidity trap, is depicted in figure 11.4(b), where the increased money stock M_2 leaves the interest rate unchanged; this is the case where the decline in velocity exactly offsets or crowds out the impact of monetary expansion. There is no doubt that Keynes considered this a distinct possibility although he gave it no more than passing mention in one paragraph of the *General Theory* (Keynes, 1936, p. 172). None the less, in 'Keynesian' hands not only was it the ultimate sanction of fiscal policy but equally it became the kingpin in the attempt to deny the classical theory of self-adjustment to full employment equilibrium. This topic is now discussed.

The Theoretical Controversy

As has been seen, the classical economists assumed that unemployment would be self-eliminating given conditions of competition in the labour market which would ultimately lead to a decline in money wage rates. If Keynes was to deny the classical self-adjustment process to full employment equilibrium upon a theoretical level he obviously had to examine the consequence of declining money wages in some detail regardless of the practi-

---

1 Although Keynes is explicit about this sequence it is perhaps of interest to note that he was guilty of the age-old confusion between a shift of the curve and a movement along it. Thus he assumes that the total demand for money schedule (liquidity preference) is negatively related to the rate of interest because of both the transactions motive and the asset motive. Thus

As a rule, we can suppose that the schedule of liquidity-preference relating the quantity of money to the rate of interest is given by a smooth curve which shows the rate of interest falling as the quantity of money is increased. For there are several different causes all leading towards this result.

In the first place, as the rate of interest falls, it is likely, *ceteris paribus*, that more money will be absorbed by liquidity-preferences due to the transactions motive. For if the fall in the rate of interest increases the national income, the amount of money which it is convenient to keep for transactions will be increased more or less proportionately.... In the second place, every fall in the rate of interest may, as we have just seen, increase the quantity of cash which certain individuals will wish to hold because their views as to the future of the rate of interest differ from the market views. (Keynes, 1936, pp. 171–2)

cality of pursuing such a policy. And indeed, Keynes paid considerable attention to this question.[2]

In general, it would be fair to conclude that Keynes was generally agnostic with respect to the outcome of wage cuts upon employment. He conceded that there were circumstances in which the net effect would be beneficial. Thus, for example, he allowed that in the context of an open economy wage cuts leading to lower prices would be beneficial to employment in the export sector which would exert multiplier impacts elsewhere in the economy. The entire issue is bedevilled by expectations as to possible further cuts but in the main Keynes concluded that the principal beneficial impact would be upon the rate of interest. For if wage reductions generate falling prices there will be a reduction in the transactions demand for cash conducive to a fall in the rate of interest. The fall in the rate of interest would stimulate investment and thus raise income and employment. This effect, *the Keynes effect* of a decrease in money wages, is identical to an increase in the quantity of money, as Keynes fully recognized:

> We can, therefore, theoretically at least, produce precisely the same effects on the rate of interest by reducing wages, whilst leaving the quantity of money unchanged, that we can produce by increasing the quantity of money whilst leaving the level of wages unchanged. (Keynes, 1936, p. 268)

Two conclusions automatically follow. If money wage cuts and increasing the money stock are alternative policies then there is no question as to which is the preferred option. The government can readily influence the volume of money through open market operations. In contrast, attempts to cut money wages will be long drawn out, will be socially divisive and will involve distributional changes generally to the disadvantage of the weaker classes of society.[3] It is not so much that Keynes denied the efficacy of money wage cuts under certain conditions; rather, his opposition rests upon there being a much simpler, easier and fairer alternative.

The second conclusion, however, is the one that Keynesians depended upon to deny the automatic self-adjustment of the classical system. If money wage cuts are formally identical to increases in the money stock then

---

2 Apart from the somewhat meandering excursion into the history of economic thought in chapter 23, where Keynes deals with mercantilism, the usury laws, stamped money and theories of underconsumption, chapter 19 on changes in money-wages, with an appendix on Pigou's theory of unemployment, is the longest chapter of the *General Theory*.

3 Wage cuts also face the drawback of increasing the real burden of the national debt and hence taxation and through it the state of business confidence (see Keynes, 1936, p. 264).

it follows that in those circumstances where the money stock is impotent to influence income and employment, then policies of money wage cuts are equally impotent. Clearly, this is the situation of the liquidity trap already depicted in figure 11.2(a). Keynes is explicit upon this point:

> It follows that wage reductions, as a means of securing full employment, are also subject to the same limitations as the method of increasing the quantity of money. . . . Just as a moderate increase in the quantity of money may exert an inadequate influence over the long-term rate of interest, whilst an immoderate increase may offset its other advantages by its disturbing effect on confidence; so a moderate reduction in money-wages may prove inadequate, whilst an immoderate reduction might shatter confidence even if it were practicable.
>
> There is, therefore, no ground for the belief that a flexible wage policy is capable of maintaining a state of continuous full employment. . . . The economic system cannot be made self-adjusting along these lines. (Keynes, 1936, pp. 266–7)

The Vindication of Classical Employment Theory

Keynes has argued that the beneficial effect of a cut in money wages would be akin to an increase in the money stock and thus in the context of the *IS/LM* framework would be represented by an outward shift of the *LM* curve. Moreover, in the case of the liquidity trap, such a policy would be completely ineffectual in raising income and employment. Such was the denial of the automatic adjustment mechanism of classical employment theory. Clearly, in such a situation the classical theory could only be salvaged if it could be shown that there existed automatic tendencies to effect an outward shift of the *IS* function. It was this task which A. C. Pigou was to set himself when he came to compose his study *Employment and Equilibrium (1941)* to be published some five years following the *General Theory*. In a very real sense, therefore, the evolution of a consistent, coherent and logical classical theory of employment was a post-Keynesian phenomenon and one for which the credit must very largely belong to Keynes.

Pigou's thesis, stated simply, was that a cut in money wages would raise the level of aggregate demand quite independently of any interest rate effect. Assuming that prices fall proportionately to the fall in money wages, aggregate monetary demand will be reduced in line with the price level leaving real aggregate demand unaffected. But in addition, the decline in the price level will raise the real value of all money cash balances and other forms of private sector wealth which have a fixed monetary value – such as redeemable national debt. This increase in private sector wealth will stimulate consumption spending by reducing the need to save out of any given

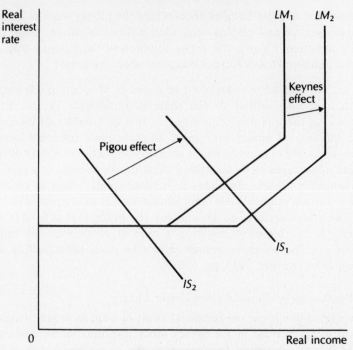

Figure 11.5   Effects of cutting money wages

income level. The celebrated *Pigou effect* thus reveals itself in an outward
shift of the *IS* curve. Providing both wages and prices exhibit unlimited
downward flexibility the outward shift of the *IS* curve will be made continuous, generating an expansion of income and employment. Ultimately, even
if the initial intersection of *LM* and *IS* occurs in the region of the liquidity
trap, the outward shift of the *IS* curve will be such as to allow the Keynes
effect to come into operation. This is the situation summarized in figure
11.5.

It should be strongly emphasized that Pigou was concerned only with a
theoretical nicety to demonstrate the impossibility of permanent unemployment equilibria given the assumption of unlimited wage and price flexibility. He was concerned to vindicate the classical belief that the economy
would tend towards full employment equilibrium on purely theoretical
grounds. He was not advocating that reliance be placed upon the automatic
adjustment mechanism or that policies advocating wage cuts should be
adopted on practical grounds. Indeed, Pigou endorsed many of the policy
implications of the Keynesian model.

Reliance upon the Pigou effect as a practical policy measure must be
ruled out on a number of grounds. All the evidence would indicate that the

empirical significance of the Pigou effect is limited, thus requiring an inordinate degree of wage and price flexibility (Mayer, 1959). In turn, the required degree of flexibility would demand an extremely lengthy period in order to be effected. Meanwhile it would be socially divisive and involve income distribution changes determined solely by the respective bargaining strengths of the various classes involved and being difficult to reconcile with accepted notions of fairness and equity. Thus the conventional wisdom became one in which Keynes had lost the theoretical fight but had won the policy war and in particular had provided a theoretical framework to which positive fiscal and monetary policy could be related.

The mystery which remains is, why did Keynes ignore the Pigou effect? He was clearly aware of the importance of wealth in influencing spending patterns and included unforeseen changes in the money value of wealth as a major factor in causing short-run changes in the propensity to consume (Keynes, 1936, pp. 92–3). It is arguable that Keynes discounted the Pigou effect on the grounds of its minor empirical significance, but this would be inconsistent with his avowed *theoretical* aim. After all, he had paid great attention to the effect of wage cuts even though the practicality of such cuts was of necessity limited. Nor does it seem realistic to propose that Keynes was dealing with a model which admitted only inside money, for he was always, even as a theoretician, concerned with the relevance of economics to practical policy-making and the affairs of the real world. It is inconceivable that he would have formulated a model which did not treat of outside money.[4] The simplest answer to the riddle is that the Pigou effect was something that Keynes overlooked when developing the implications of his theory. Nor would such an oversight be exceptional; Pigou himself was to make no mention of it in his controversial attack dealing with wage cuts in the *Economic Journal* (Pigou, 1937).[5]

---

4 The distinction between inside and outside money is a simple one. Inside money refers to monetary creation by the private banking sector in the process of creating bank deposits. Outside money is the fiat money issued by the government authorities through the central bank. The Pigou effect does not arise in the case of a pure inside money economy because although price falls will increase the net worth of creditors this effect will be offset by the increased real indebtedness of debtors. The Pigou effect arises in the case of outside money because the issue of such money by the government ensures that the private sector is on balance a net creditor.

5 Keynes considered this 'the work of a sick man, which no one would print who was in his right mind'. Joan Robinson concurred, adding 'he is so far gone that you have to rationalise him to find a coherent error'. According to Kahn, 'Gerald Shove says that without exception this is the worst article he has ever read', a verdict with which Piero Sraffa was to concur (see Moggridge, 1973, vol. XIV, p. 234f). Yet within a matter of a few years Pigou was to provide the theoretical foundation that classical employment theory had hitherto lacked.

An alternative and extremely ingenious explanation has been put forward by Leijonhufvud. In his view Keynes ignored the Pigou effect because it was irrelevant to the central issue of unemployment. In this interpretation unemployment is the consequence of relative prices being out of line and in particular the demand price of capital assets being too low relative to the price of labour. If this is the case then all-round deflation as implied by the Pigou effect becomes an irrelevancy since it leaves relative prices unchanged. In sharp contrast, the Keynes effect is relevant because it leads to a decrease in the rate of interest and hence to an increase in the demand price of capital assets relative to the wage cost of labour. Thus Keynes was being perfectly logical in pursuing the claims of wage cuts via the interest rate effect whilst simultaneously ignoring the Pigou effect. The *IS/LM* analysis only serves to cloud the argument since, encompassing solely a one-product economy, it is unable to deal with relative prices upon which employment ultimately depends. The Leijonhufvud interpretation, it should be noted, represents an attempt to re-establish Keynes's reputation as major theoretical innovator as opposed to the conventional wisdom which sees his achievement to lie primarily in the policy field.

Extending the Hicksian Framework

Consumption and the Rate of Interest

Thus far, consumption demand has been assumed to be a linear function of the level of income. In addition, however, it has been argued that consumption will depend upon prevailing rates of interest. Indeed, this was part and parcel of classical interest rate theory, which assumed that a greater volume of saving would be forthcoming at higher rates of interest. As has been seen, the classical postulate of a positive association between the rate of interest and the flow of savings is open to dispute. Both income and substitution effects are involved. A rise in the rate of interest makes saving more attractive at the margin (the substitution effect) but equally it implies a real income gain which permits the greater consumption of goods. A priori, therefore, it is not possible to provide a determinate conclusion to the issue of how an interest rate change will affect the choice between consumption and saving out of a given income *flow*.

There is, however, another reason to suggest that a decline in interest rates may stimulate consumption spending, and this refers to the relationship between the rate of interest and the net value of the *stock* of existing assets including government bonds and securities. Keynes did not attach much importance to the influence of the interest rate upon consumption out of a given income flow, but he clearly thought the influence of the interest rate upon capital values an important factor. Thus

There are not many people who will alter their way of living because the rate of interest has fallen from 5 to 4 per cent, if their aggregate income is the same as before.

but

The consumption of the wealth-owning classes may be extremely susceptible to unforeseen changes in the money-value of its wealth. This should be classified amongst the major factors capable of causing short-period changes in the propensity to consume.

and

Perhaps the most important influence, operating through changes in the rate of interest, on the readiness to spend out of a given income, depends on the effect of these changes on the appreciation or depreciation in the price of securities and other assets. (Keynes, 1936, pp. 92–4)

There would thus appear some justification for making consumption not just a positive function of the level of income but also a negative function of the rate of interest. Such a modification is easily accommodated in the *IS/LM* framework and reveals itself in a decrease in slope of the *IS* curve.

Investment and the Level of Income

Hitherto, investment demand has been regarded solely as a function of the rate of interest. However, as suggested by the well-known accelerator concept of investment behaviour, examined in chapter 3, investment may also be related to the level of final sales demand and hence to the level of income. The inclusion of income as an argument in the investment decision carries far-reaching implications for the *IS/LM* framework which threatens the entire stability of the model's analysis.

The analysis of chapter 10 depicted investment spending as a simple function of the rate of interest. From equation 10.3,

$$I = d - fi$$

If this investment schedule is modified to allow for the influence of income changes,

$$I = d - fi + jY \tag{11.1}$$

where j is the marginal propensity to invest. This equation may be combined with the elementary framework developed in chapter 10, equations

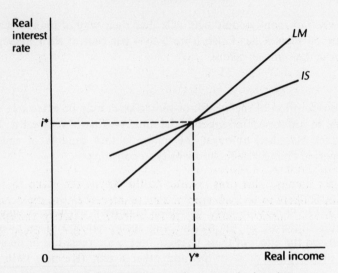

Figure 11.6   Stable equilibrium with a positively sloped *IS* curve

10.1a and 10.2, to yield

$$Y = a + bY + d - fi + jY \qquad (11.2)$$

This gives

$$Y = \frac{a + d - fi}{1 - b - j} \qquad (11.3a)$$

as the solution for the *IS* equation. It will be noted that the *IS* equation can be rewritten as

$$Y = \frac{a + d}{1 - b - j} + \frac{-f}{1 - b - j} i \qquad (11.3b)$$

where $(a + d)/(1 - b - j)$ is the intercept and $-f/(1 - b - j)$ the slope of the *IS* curve. It follows that it is possible for the *IS* curve to possess a positive slope if, and only if, the term in the denominator is negative. But such an outcome is perfectly plausible; the condition for a positively sloped *IS* curve is simply the condition that the marginal propensity to invest exceeds the marginal propensity to save.

The possibility of an upward sloping *IS* curve, which characteristically was anticipated by Hicks in his seminal article (Hicks, 1937), raises many intriguing issues and carries important implications for policy. First of all, a stable solution for the level of income now requires that the slope of the *IS* curve be less steep than the slope of the *LM* curve. This situation of stable equilibrium is illustrated by figure 11.6. Second, an increase in the quantity of money now implies an *increase* in the rate of interest. This is pertinent to much of the controversy between Keynesians and monetarists. The former tend to look upon movements in the rate of interest as being indicative of monetary stringency or monetary ease, whilst the latter tend to disregard interest rate movements *per se*, preferring to focus their attention upon the volume of money. The existence of an upward sloping *IS* curve would tend to substantiate the monetarists' position and suggest that the rate of interest is a poor indicator of expansionary or contractionary policies. Finally, if the *IS* curve is upward sloping, then the impact of an increase in the money stock upon the level of income will be greater the more *interest elastic* the demand for money. This runs counter to the Keynesian claim that monetary policy is likely to be ineffectual the more interest elastic the demand for money, since it implies greater scope for offsetting velocity changes. This counter-argument based upon the positive sloped *IS* curve is given in figure 11.7.

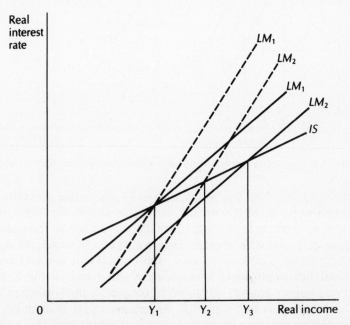

Figure 11.7   Monetary expansion with (a) interest elastic money demand $\Delta Y = Y_1 - Y_3$ (solid *LM* lines) (b) interest inelastic money demand $\Delta Y = Y_1 - Y_2$ (dashed *LM* lines)

The Flex Price Model

The foregoing analysis has been implicitly stated in real terms with prices assumed constant. In terms of the depressed conditions of the 1930s from

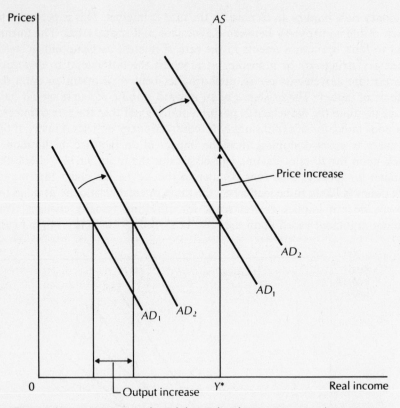

Figure 11.8   Aggregate supply and demand and Keynesian price determination

which the model evolved this seems a perfectly reasonable postulate. With both surplus supplies of labour and capital in abundance, there was no reason why an increase in aggregate demand should not be translated into an increase in output with prices holding constant. In essence, the Keynesian model is demand determined with supply conditions assumed perfectly elastic until full employment is approached. In terms of the aggregate demand and supply analysis advanced in chapter 7, the Keynesian model can be caricatured as in figure 11.8. Aggregate supply is assumed to be perfectly elastic until capacity income, Y^*, is attained; until this point any increase in aggregate expenditure translates into output increases; beyond this point, any increase in aggregate demand implies increased prices.

It is a simple matter to link this aggregate demand and supply model with the Hicksian IS/LM model in a world of constant prices. This is done with the aid of figure 11.9. The upper part of the figure shows the IS/LM determination of income and interest at Y_1 where capacity income is

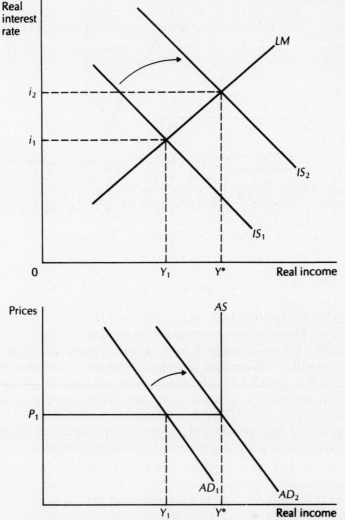

Figure 11.9 Linking *IS/LM* analysis and aggregate supply and demand analysis with constant prices

assumed to be Y^*. The lower portion depicts the aggregate supply and demand equation giving price–income combination P_1Y_1. If government policy now effects a shift of the *IS* curve to achieve the full employment income level (indicated by the IS_2 line) this will be matched by the outward shift of the aggregate demand curve in the lower part of the figure. Capacity income Y^* prevails in both cases, and there is no change in the

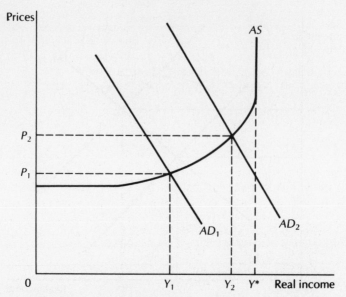

Figure 11.10   Simultaneous increases in prices and real output

price level although an increase in the real rate of interest occurs in consequence of the higher demand for transactions balances.

However, once the assumption of a perfectly elastic aggregate supply curve at less than full capacity income is dropped, the analysis becomes considerably more complex.[6] Increases in aggregate demand will then have the effect of generating simultaneous increases in both prices and output as indicated in figure 11.10. Once it is attempted to incorporate a variable price level into the basic *IS/LM* framework, a conceptual difficulty is encountered. The *IS* curve, being a *real* expenditure demand, is drawn as a function of the *real* rate of interest and is invariant with respect to price

---

6 Keynes fully recognized that prices would in fact increase before full employment was reached. Thus

> The increase in effective demand will, generally speaking, spend itself partly in increasing the quantity of employment and partly in raising the level of prices. Thus instead of constant prices in conditions of unemployment, ... we have in fact a condition of prices rising gradually as employment increases. (Keynes, 1936, p. 296)

and

> As output increases, a series of 'bottle-necks' will be successively reached, where the supply of particular commodities ceases to be elastic and their prices have to rise to whatever level is necessary to divert demand into other directions. (Keynes, 1936, p. 300)

changes. The LM curve, however, as has previously been seen is not invariant with respect to price level changes. An increase in prices will shift the curve inwards as the real value of the stock of money is decreased and vice versa.

To consider the link between the Hicksian framework and aggregate supply and demand analysis, consider figure 11.11. In the upper portion of the figure the IS and LM schedules determine an initial interest–income combination given by $i_1 Y_1$. The LM schedule is drawn for a specific price level, P_1, and hence is indicated as LM_1. In the lower portion of the figure is the aggregate supply and demand analysis. At the price level indicated by P_1 it is known that demand is equal to Y_1 (as determined above) and consequently the point $P_1 Y_1$ is one point on the aggregate demand schedule. Suppose, however, that this point does not fall upon the aggregate supply curve. With the aggregate supply curve as shown in the lower figure there is excess aggregate demand at the price P_1. *Ceteris paribus* the price level will rise, and as it increases it will generate an upward shift in the LM function in the upper figure. As the price level increases to P_2, the applicable LM curve becomes LM_2 and in conjunction with the invariant IS curve will imply the interest–income combination $i_2 Y_2$. Thus at the price level P_2 aggregate demand is equivalent to Y_2, providing a second point upon the aggregate demand curve. Here again demand exceeds supply, generating further price increases, and this process will continue until generation of the equilibrium denoted by the combination $P_3 Y_3$ in the lower figure and the combination $i_3 Y_3$ given by IS/LM_3 in the upper figure.

Does such an equilibrium as indicated by the combined $P_3 Y_3$ and $i_3 Y_3$ situation imply full equilibrium for the macroeconomy? To return to the classical emphasis, the answer to this question depends upon whether full employment prevails within the labour market and whether, if full employment does not prevail, the force of competition will drive real wages down. If unemployment and flexible wages coexist, the decline in real wages will extend the volume of aggregate output; aggregate supply will now exceed demand and prices will fall, with feedback effects upon the Hicksian IS/LM framework. Ultimate equilibrium will require the simultaneous equation of IS/LM curves, aggregate supply and demand curves and labour supply and demand curves in the labour market. For the sake of completeness, these conditions are illustrated in the composite figure 11.12.

In part (c) equilibrium is assumed to prevail between aggregate supply and aggregate demand at the price level P_1 and income level Y_1. It is also assumed that this combination is consistent with equilibrium in both commodity and money markets as depicted in part (b) of the figure with the interest rate i_1. Part (a) of the figure merely invokes a 45° line to translate

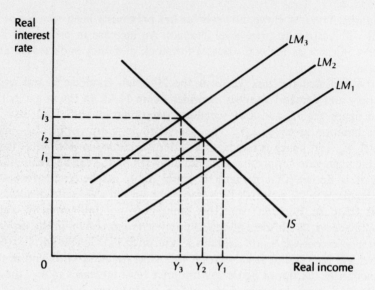

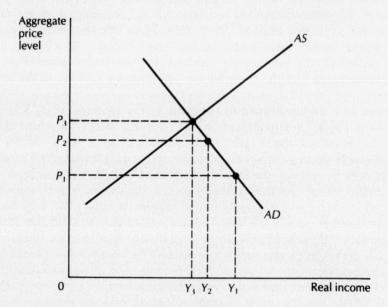

Figure 11.11 Linking *IS/LM* analysis and aggregate supply and demand analysis with variable prices

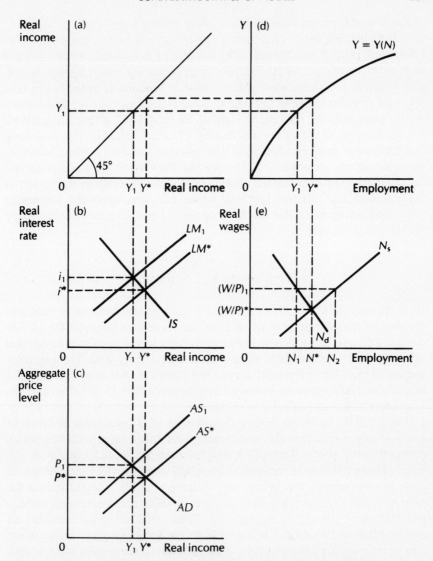

Figure 11.12 Linking *IS/LM* analysis, aggregate supply and demand analysis with the production function, employment and real wages

the income level Y_1 to the production function quadrant of part (d). From the production function can be derived the amount of labour N_1 needed to produce the output Y_1, and in turn this will imply a real wage equal to $(W/P)_1$ in part (e). However, at this real wage the amount of labour on offer is indicated as N_2. Unemployment prevails to the extent $N_1 - N_2$. In the classical world, competition will then cause money wages and real wages to fall; as wages fall, profit maximizing behaviour will extend the demand for labour and output will increase. The increase in output implies an outward shift of the aggregate supply function of quadrant (c), causing prices to fall, and as prices fall an outward shift of the *LM* function is generated in part (b) of the composite figure. Linking all these arguments together and following through with the underlying logic of the model will ultimately generate full equilibrium at the values denoted by Y^*, i^*, N^* and $(W/P)^*$. Assuming complete wage and price flexibility and ignoring the time horizon involved, there is a strong disposition in the present framework for a complete and full equilibrium to be attained.[7] This is indeed the generalized conclusion of the so-called *neo-classical synthesis* which followed upon the Keynesian revolution giving particular emphasis to the equilibrating role performed by relative price changes.

The Monetarist Contention

As previously indicated, much of the early controversy between Keynes and the classics turned upon the question of the respective slopes of the *IS/LM* curves; Keynesians emphasized those situations where monetary policy was relatively ineffective, whilst classicists took the contrary view. The appropriateness of the *IS/LM* formulation was not itself a matter of contention, and in particular the assumed independence between the *IS* function and the *LM* function was not called into question.

It is precisely upon the latter question, that of independence between *IS* and *LM* equations, that the monetarists have taken issue with Keynesian interpretations. Both Keynesians and monetarists would concur in the belief that an increase in the money stock will exert expansionary influences upon the macroeconomy. Where they differ is over the *transmission mechanism* by which the monetary change exerts its influence. Keynesians emphasize that any change in expenditure flows, whether upon the side of consumption or investment, will stem from the accompanying change in the rate of interest. The direct impact of an increase in the money stock is seen to fall upon interest rates as the excess money is channelled into financial assets. The indirect impact then follows from the influence exerted by lower interest rates upon consumption and investment spending – an influence which may be weak and uncertain depending upon the circumstances of the

---

7 The adjustment implied here could be hindered by the existence of a horizontal *LM* function. Then, has been seen, other aids would have to be invoked such as a wealth effect in the consumption function.

particular case. The underlying assumption in this analysis is that the only meaningful substitute for money is alternative financial assets. In contrast, monetarists are disposed to argue that an increase in the money stock will impinge upon expenditure flows irrespective of any change in the rate of interest. The increase in the money stock disturbs the equilibrium between actual money balances and desired money balances and, in the attempt to eliminate the excess supply, increased expenditure is generated over a wide range of goods and services as well as financial assets. It may well be the case that some reduction in interest rates occurs, stimulating additional spending, but quite apart from any interest rate induced effect there will be increased demands for national output. If unemployed resources exist this increase in the money stock will generate additional output; if resources are fully employed the outcome will be inflation and a higher level of imports. The underlying assumption here is that there are far wider substitutes for money than merely financial assets.

Essentially, the monetarist argument suggests that IS and LM functions are interdependent; an increase in the money stock implies not only an outward shift of the LM curve but also an outward shift of the IS curve and not merely a movement along it as Keynesians are wont to believe. This issue of interdependent IS/LM functions has considerable relevance to the potency of monetary and fiscal policy and in particular to the controversy over the crowding out debate. Recognition of possible interdependence between IS and LM functions has increased, with the greater awareness now being given to the financial implications of budgetary policies and in particular of the need to take account of the government budget constraint. This will be the subject matter of the next chapter.

Concluding Comments

This chapter has utilized the Hicksian IS/LM analysis to survey a considerable amount of ground. First, the conditions under which fiscal or monetary policy would exercise the greater potency were examined, and a possible source of dispute between Keynesians and the classics was indicated. Second, a framework was adopted to explore the possibility of stable unemployment equilibria given wage and price flexibility, and it was concluded that the combined workings of the Pigou effect and the Keynes effect would render this a logical impossibility in the long term. Several extensions of the IS/LM analysis were then explored, including the implications of a positively sloped IS function, and the link between the basic analysis, aggregate supply and demand and the labour market was examined. At each step the versatility of the analysis was extended without detracting from its relative simplicity and easy manipulation. Finally, the existence of possible interdependence between *IS* and *LM* functions was considered; this leads into the subject matter of the next chapter.

Further Reading

The classic article on the Pigou effect is by Patinkin and it appears in two distinct versions (Patinkin, 1948, 1951), the latter being reprinted in both Mueller (1966) and Lindauer (1968). A critical empirical study of the significance of the Pigou effect is provided by Mayer (1959). Additional useful comments are to be found in Stein (1949) and Tobin (1947), also reprinted in Mueller (1966). A detailed and controversial distinction between the Keynes effect and the Pigou effect is made by Leijonhufvud (1968, part VX).

Finally, the possibility of a positively sloped *IS* function with its implications for policy is analysed by Burrows (1974).

12

The Government Sector, the Budget Constraint and the Crowding Out Controversy

Hitherto the manner in which government expenditure is to be financed has been played down. It is, however, necessary to examine this question in some detail. Much of the earlier Keynesian analysis had been negligent in dealing with this issue, and this neglect ultimately led to the monetarist charge of naïvety in the formulation of policy measures and in particular to the charge that Keynesian measures fail to take into account the inflationary implications of deficit finance.

The Government Budget Constraint in the *IS/LM* Model

As has been seen in chapter 10, the *IS/LM* framework can be readily adapted to incorporate the government sector. In figure 12.1 the *IS/LM* construct is reproduced, but now the implications for the government budget constraint are considered. This is depicted in the lower portion of the composite figure, where it has been assumed that whilst government outlays are constant, tax revenues are endogenous upon income.[1] The significance of the intersection at point X is that here government outlays upon goods and services[2] are exactly offset by taxes, so that the government deficit is zero; the government has no need to recourse to issue of national debt or to the creation of new money. If this is not the case, then the government budget surplus or deficit will exert feedback effects upon the *IS* and *LM* curves, thus generating a new equilibrium.

If government tax receipts fall short of government outlays then the deficit must be financed either by additional bond sales, or by the creation

---

1 This is not to imply that all taxes are income taxes. Sales taxes, licence fees, and so on, will also normally display a positive relationship with income.

2 Perhaps it should be pointed out that government outlays in the form of transfer payments are being ignored, since conceptually these are negative taxes. The tax schedule drawn, therefore, is to be interpreted as taxes net of transfer payments.

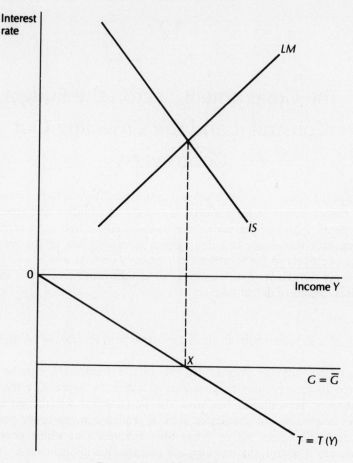

Figure 12.1   Stable equilibrium

of new money, or by some combination of the two. Thus

$$G - T = \Delta H + \Delta B \qquad\qquad (12.1)$$

where G is government outlays upon goods and services, T is net fiscal revenue, transfer payments having been treated as negative taxes, ΔH is the increase in the high-powered money stock and ΔB is the monetary value of new bonds issued to the private sector.[3]

---

3 Thus ΔB is the money obtained by the government upon the sale of additional bonds and not the par value of the bonds themselves. If all bonds are consols then ΔB is equal to PV/i, where PV is the par value of the bonds and i is the long-term rate of interest.

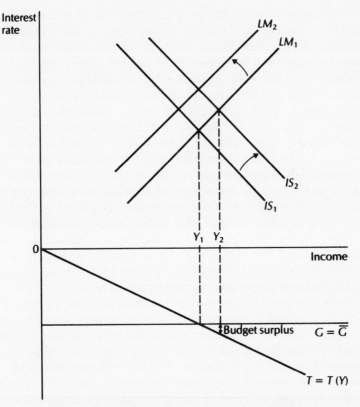

Figure 12.2 Budget constraint and the zero multiplier

By way of illustration, consider the analysis depicted in figure 12.2. Assume the initial situation at income level Y_1 with government outlays exactly offset by fiscal receipts. Accordingly, in this situation it is assumed that there is no change in the high-powered money stock or in the holding of bonds to disturb the indicated equilibrium. Now assume an autonomous increase in spending, say in investment spending, owing to a change in the prevailing state of expectations. Such a change will be reflected in an outward shift of the *IS* curve generating the income level Y_2, in keeping with standard Keynesian analysis, and the relationship between the change in income and the change in investment provides a measure of the Keynesian multiplier. At the income level Y_2, the *ex ante* levels of savings and taxes are again equated with the *ex ante* level of investment demand plus government spending, implying an equation between actual and intended consumption. Now, however, this is no longer the end of the story, in contrast with the earlier exposition. At the income level Y_2 the government budget is

now in a surplus position; the increase in the level of national income has
generated an increase in fiscal receipts in excess of the constant level of
government expenditure. Given the logic of the budget constraint, this
increase in receipts will be applied either to a reduction in the money stock,
or to some retirement of the national debt, or possibly some combination of
the two. Assume initially that it is utilized to cut back the supply of high-
powered money, which shifts the LM curve inward thus disturbing the
indicated equilibrium. The relationship between the reduction in the high-
powered money supply and the induced shift of the LM curve will be
determined by the extent of credit creation by the banking sector.[4] Regardless of this relationship, the inward shift of the LM curve will be known
precisely, and it will be made continuous until once again the original
income level Y_1 is regained. Only at this level of income will government
outlays be once again equated with fiscal receipts. Consideration of the
government budget constraint not only implies interdependence between IS
and LM functions, but also in this case completely negates the Keynesian
multiplier. In the present example the autonomous increase in investment
spending generates a long-run multiplier equal to zero.

Suppose, however, that the induced tax receipts caused by income expansion are now utilized to retire part of the national debt. This is the situation
examined in figure 12.3. As before, assume the initial increase in investment
demand will raise the income level to Y_2 and generate a budget surplus. As
the government now retires national debt, interest payments to the private
sector will fall, reducing disposable incomes. In turn, this promotes an
inward shift of the IS curve offsetting the previous expansionary income
movement. However, in the present case, this offset influence will not come
to an end when the original income level Y_1 is regained, because now, at
this previous equilibrium point, the budget will still be in an overall surplus.
This follows from the fact that retirement of the debt reduces government
transfer payments (negative taxes), thus generating an increase in slope of
the endogenous tax schedule. The ultimate equilibrium is accordingly indicated as being at Y_3, implying that the long-run Keynesian multiplier is
actually *negative* in the present case.

The Nature of the Budget Constraint

In the preceding analysis it was seen that whatever the original position of
IS and LM curves the ultimate equilibrium must coincide with the intersection of the government tax and outlay curves – the position of a balanced

---

4 With a 100 per cent required cash deposit ratio the two are rendered identical.

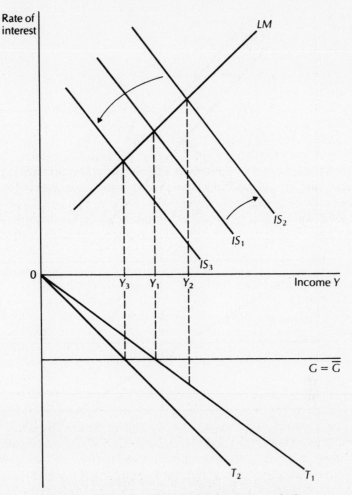

Figure 12.3   Budget constraint and the negative multiplier

budget. It is now posited that such an equilibrium exists; consider then the consequences of expansionary fiscal policy occasioned by an increase in government expenditure. This is the situation summarized with the aid of figure 12.4. Y_1 represent the initial stable equilibrium level of income consistent with a balanced budget. An increase in government expenditure will now alter this equilibrium, reflected in an outward shift of the IS curve and a downward shift of the government outlay curve. The short-run Keynesian equilibrium is denoted by the income level Y_2, and this outcome provides the justification for Keynesian oriented fiscal policy in periods of recession and unemployment. However, at the income level Y_2 a budget deficit of BD

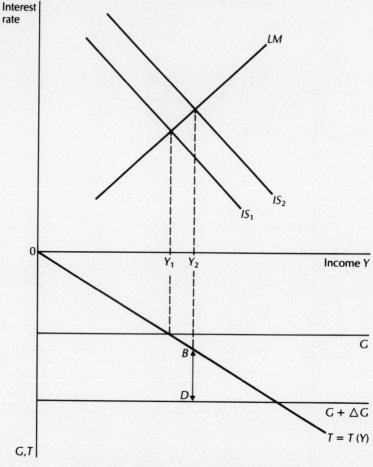

Figure 12.4   Budget constraint and fiscal policy

is incurred. The logic of the budget constraint insists that this deficit must be financed, and financed at all points in time. The question which remains is the nature of this financing.

A budget deficit can be financed in one of three ways – first by an equivalent increase in tax revenues, second by an equivalent increase in the high-powered money supply, and thirdly by an equivalent increase in proceeds obtained by bonds sales to the private sector.[5] Each situation is

_____

5 Or alternatively by some combination of these methods. For expositional purposes, they will be treated as being mutually exclusive, although the reader can readily analyse combined solutions should he/she so wish.

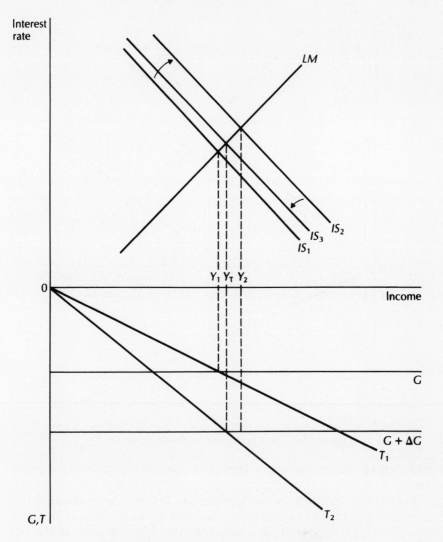

Figure 12.5   Fiscal policy: the tax financed deficit

examined in turn. In the case of tax increases, the slope of the endogenous tax function is raised, the *IS* curve is shifted inward and an eventual stable equilibrium is indicated at Y_T in figure 12.5. The tax-financed increase in government expenditure raises the income level above the original level Y_1 but below the short-term Keynesian equilibrium Y_2. The tax increase par-

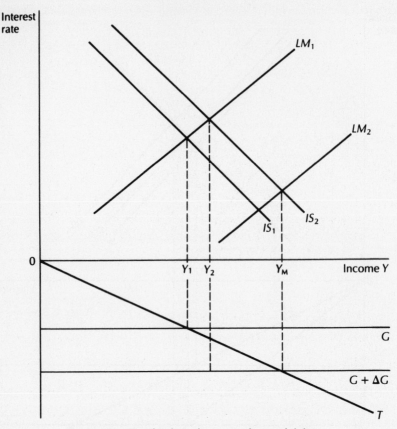

Figure 12.6   Fiscal policy: the money financed deficit

tially offsets the expansionary impact of increased government expenditure.[6]

Figure 12.6 analyses the same situation, but this time assuming the increased government expenditure is financed by an increase in the high-powered money supply. This is reflected in an outward shift of the *LM* curve with no change in the slope of the endogenous tax function, so that the ultimate equilibrium is indicated at the income level Y_M. The monetary financed deficit thus reinforces the expansionary effects of increased government expenditure and leads to an income level in excess of the short-term

6 The increase in government expenditure adds directly to demand an amount equal to the government outlay. The increase in taxes depletes demand by an amount equal to the tax increase multiplied by the marginal propensity to consume. If the latter is less than one, some net expansionary impact will remain. The balanced budget multiplier theorem was analysed in detail in chapter 4.

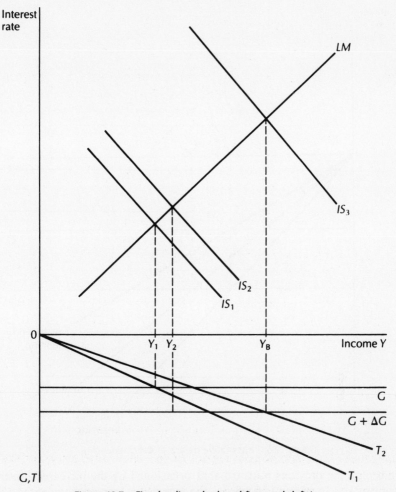

Figure 12.7   Fiscal policy: the bond financed deficit

Keynesian equilibrium level Y_2. It is partly this conclusion which forms the basis of the monetarists' claim that fiscally oriented policies will exert a minor impact unless they are accompanied by accommodating changes in the money supply.

Finally, figure 12.7 which analyses the case where the increase in government outlays is financed by the sale of additional bonds to the private sector – the case of debt finance. Here the increase in bond sales implies additional interest payments to service the enlarged debt. Such payments raise disposable income and hence consumption demands. Diagrammatically, this change implied an induced outward shift of the *IS* curve,

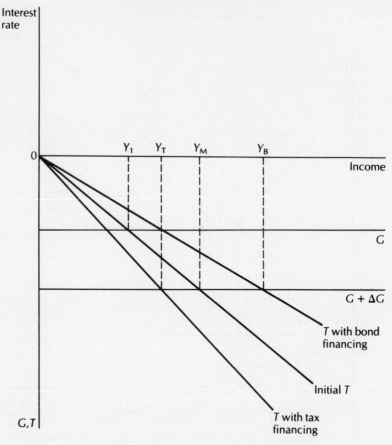

Figure 12.8   Alternative means of deficit financing

reinforcing the previous outward shift occasioned by the increased government outlays. In addition, however, the increase in transfer payments to the private sector implies, in terms of the analysis which treats transfer payments as negative taxes, a decrease in the slope of the endogenous tax function. Full stable equilibrium is accordingly achieved at the income level Y_B which not only exceeds the short-run Keynesian solution Y_2 but also is in excess of the monetary financed deficit Y_M. Figure 12.8 summarizes these various respective final solutions.

Clearly, the least expansionary type of policy is the tax-financed increase in government outlays – the so-called 'pure fiscal policy' which leaves the budget surplus or deficit unchanged. The monetary-financed increase in government expenditure has a much greater impact upon the level of income, partly because the increase in the money stock exerts downward pressure upon interest rates. Both Keynesians and monetarists would agree with these results. However, the most successful policy is shown to be the bond-financed expenditure measure, and implicitly, it is upon this case that Keynesians have rested their advocacy of the potency of fiscal policy. This position rests fundamentally upon two assumptions which are seldom explicitly specified – first that there is no limit to the extent to which the authorities can sell government bonds, and second that the resultant bond sales do not generate wealth effects which might disturb equilibrium. The first assumption clearly does not have universal application. In many of the less advanced economies, for example, the absence of confidence in the government of the day virtually prohibits this method of finance.[7] Whether bonds issued by the central government constitute net wealth from the viewpoint of the private sector is altogether a different issue and one which has generated considerable controversy.

Deficit Financing and Private Sector Wealth

At any time, private sector wealth can be thought of as comprising the holding of real capital assets (including equity holdings) and the holding of debt, both monetary and non-monetary, issued by the government. The nominal value of the latter varies inversely with movements in the interest rate. If it is assumed, for simplicity, that all government bonds are consols, then private sector real wealth may be represented as

$$W = K + \frac{M}{P} + \frac{N/i}{P} \qquad (12.2)$$

where W is private sector real wealth, K the holding of real capital assets and claims to such assets, M the money stock in circulation, N the par or nominal value of government bonds, i the long-term rate of interest and P an aggregate price index. How is private sector wealth influenced by the issue of new bonds? Clearly, the short-run value of real capital assets is unaffected by the manner in which the authorities choose to finance new expenditures.[8] Equally, the total private holding of money balances will also remain unchanged when the government receives money balances from the public in exchange for bonds which it then puts back into circulation

---

7 Suggesting that the nature of the budget constraint may differ significantly for less advanced economies. On this point and some of the inflationary implications, see Shaw (1981).

8 Strictly speaking this is incorrect since relative capital values may be influenced by resulting interest rate movements, especially if the time profiles of future income streams differ.

when it spends the proceeds. The total of privately held money balances is unaltered, in the aggregate, by the transaction, as long as the price level remains unchanged. The only change, therefore, is the increase in privately held government bonds, and it is this increase which constitutes the perceived increase in private sector wealth.

In the context of figure 12.7, this increase in private net wealth effects an outward shift of the *IS* curve, rendering the required amount of bond sales less than that previously required for equilibrium. However, at the same time the wealth effect raises the demand for money and effects an inward shift of the *LM* function, thus raising the amount of bond sales associated with the income level Y_B. The greater the wealth sensitivity and the demand for money, the greater the required amount of bond sales and the greater the rate of interest associated with their sale. The Keynesian analysis implicitly assumes that there is no limit to the amount of bonds that the government can sell. However, this may not be the case; confidence in the ability of the government to be able to redeem and service a given debt may well depend upon its extent in relation to GNP. Moreover, the interest rate required may be politically unacceptable. If wealth effects do significantly influence the demand for money then the induced rise in the required interest rate may force abandonment of the policy of finance through debt, forcing reliance upon relatively ineffective pure fiscal measures, or upon accommodating increases in the money supply. Such is the monetarists' contention.

Keynesians, quite predictably, tend to dismiss the alleged wealth effect as fallacious or to concede its existence but query its significance. That the wealth effect is essentially fallacious and illusory is indeed *logically* correct. The fact that the government opts to issue additional paper liabilities, whether money or bonds, cannot of itself raise the aggregate wealth of society. However, this is hardly the point at issue. Provided the private sector perceives its wealth as increasing and modifies its behaviour accordingly, a wealth effect is apparent whether or not the perception is justified. A more significant counter-argument turns upon the rise in the interest rate. In order to induce the private sector to purchase additional bonds the government will be compelled to make the terms sufficiently attractive by raising the existing rate of interest. This, in turn, will reduce the nominal value of existing bonds. In addition, it may be argued that the enlarged national debt occasioned by the increased issue of government bonds raises the prospect of future taxes to service and retire the debt. This depletion of future permanent income will offset, if only partially, the extent of any wealth effect. To attach a wealth perception to additional bondholding but not to future tax burdens is to take a peculiarly myopic view of one's assets and liabilities. Finally, the raising of the rate of return upon government bonds will render them comparatively more attractive *vis-à-vis* private sector equities, and the resultant portfolio adjustments will imply a decline in the capital value of the latter. All these influences, it may be contended, will combine to limit the empirical significance of the wealth effect stemming from the issue of government bonds.

The following is an attempt to summarize the argument so far. Once the government budget constraint is permitted to enter the analysis the elementary Keynesian mechanics of the original *IS/LM* construct are revealed to be too *simpliste*. In particular, short-run multiplier values which ignore the financing constraint are blatantly incorrect. Once this is admitted, fiscal policy must be appraised in the light of its financing. Tax-financed expansionary government spending is seen to exert a comparatively minor impact, as one might intuitively expect. Money-financed expansionary government spending is in contrast decidedly effective in raising the level of income, but the consequences of the enlarged money supply may carry inflationary implications for the aggregate economy. Depending upon one's view of the inflationary process this may impose a political constraint upon the extent to which one may resort to this method of finance. Finally there is the option of bond-financed expansionary government spending which, theoretically, is even more effective in exerting stimulating impacts upon real output. However, here too the implications of the required bond sales may be an interest rate which is politically unacceptable even assuming that it is always possible to float more debt at a price.

The Crowding Out Controversy

It is now possible to examine the claim, associated largely with the monetarist revival and in particular with the Federal Reserve Bank of St Louis (see Andersen and Jordan 1968) that expansionary fiscal policy may be largely ineffective in that it may be offset or crowded out by compensatory action occurring within the private sector.

Four distinct types of crowding out can be identified. First, there is *direct crowding out*, whereby an increased government outlay in real terms generates a fall in private sector real outlays; this may be either because the government provision is regarded as a substitute for a service hitherto provided by the private sector, or alternatively, if full employment prevails, because the increased government share of GNP must claw resources away from the private sector. In the first case, the provision of the government service induces a rise in saving and the increase in the overall savings propensity will counter, if only partially, the effects of the increased government outlay. Thus, for example, provision of free medical services will reduce the demand for private sector health care. The net effect is akin to a transfer payment in kind which generates an income gain and permits additional saving out of alternative income (a case that was considered in connection with the balanced budget multiplier theorem in chapter 4). In the second case, which implicitly assumes a fixity of resources, the increased government outlays are obtained only at the expense of the private sector, the resources being induced to transfer from private to public employment by the prospect of higher nominal earnings. In general, therefore, the latter type of crowding out will be accompanied by inflationary tendencies.

Second, there is *indirect crowding out*, whereby the fiscal change exerts side-effects quite apart from any financing considerations which may run counter to the direction of the fiscal thrust. The obvious example, to which reference has already been made, is the automatic stabilizing influence exerted by the existence of a fixed money stock. The increase in government spending, for example, generates a rise in income which increases the trans-actions demand for cash and *ceteris paribus* raises the rate of interest. As long as private sector investment spending is sensitive to interest rate changes some offsetting decline in investment demand will occur. In addi-tion, the induced rise in the rate of interest will decrease the value of existing bondholdings, implying a negative wealth effect which will impinge upon consumption spending. The sensitivity of both investment and con-sumption spending to interest rate changes is summarized in the slope of the *IS* curve. The flatter the slope of the *IS* function the greater will be the interest-induced offset to expansionary fiscal policy. At the same time, however, the slope of the *LM* curve will impinge upon the extent of the interest rate change associated with any given increase in government expenditure. The flatter the slope of the *LM* curve the less will be the interest rate change. This argument is summarized with the aid of figure 12.9. Here are displayed two *IS* functions, one relatively interest elastic and the other interest inelastic. Equally there are two *LM* schedules, again being relatively interest elastic and interest inelastic respectively. Assume the initial income level Y_1. An increase in government expenditure will raise the income level to Y_2 if no change in the interest rate is permitted to occur – that is, if monetary policy is accommodating. However, assuming the money supply remains fixed and acts out its permitted role as automatic stabilizer, the income level will fall below Y_2 and will be either Y_3, Y_4, Y_5, or Y_6 depending upon which of the *IS* and *LM* schedules is invoked. The least expansionary outcome will be the income level Y_6 obtained by the assumption of interest elastic *IS* schedules and interest inelastic *LM* sched-ules. In the extreme case, that of a vertical *LM* curve, the degree of crow-ding out is complete – irrespective of the shape of the *IS* schedule.

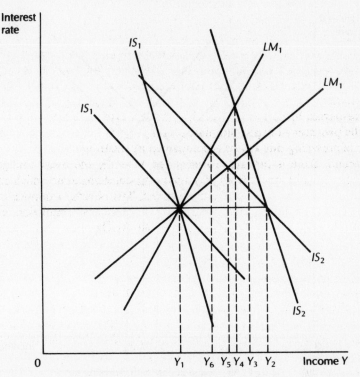

Figure 12.9   Interest elasticity of *IS* and *LM* functions and the degree of crowding out

A second case of indirect crowding out arises from consideration of tax changes upon the demand for money. Keynes, in the *General Theory*, had related both consumption spending and the demand for money to the level of income. Later commentators were to specifically take account of the government sector, and in so doing they made consumption depend more correctly upon the level of *disposable* income. However, they failed to apply this modification to the demand for money, thus perpetuating an inconsistency; if consumption demand is related to disposable income then logically so too will the transactions demand for money. Once this modification is allowed the possibility of indirect crowding out is again raised.[9] This situation is illustrated with the aid of figure 12.10. Assume an initial equilibrium at the income level Y_1, determined by the intersection of the IS_1 and

---

9 The first recognition of this possibility appears to have been by Holmes and Smyth (1972).

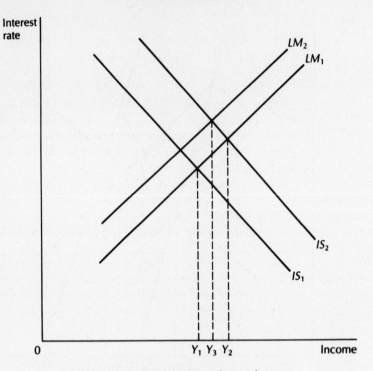

Figure 12.10   Tax multiplier with crowding out

LM_1 schedules. Now assume an attempt to impart an expansionary fiscal stimulus by cutting taxes. The increase in disposable income will generate an increased consumption demand, thus effecting an outward shift of the IS curve. At the same time, however, the increase in disposable income will generate an increased demand for transactions cash and thus imply an offsetting inward shift of the LM curve. Theoretically, depending upon the sensitivity of the transactions demand for money, the tax multiplier could be positive. In the present case this extreme assumption has not been made. None the less a considerable degree of crowding out is depicted; instead of the income level Y_2 implied by conventional Keynesian models, the income level Y_3 is obtained. This situation, it will be appreciated, does not arise from an assumed interdependence between IS and LM; rather it stems from the assumption that both IS and LM functions respond to the same fiscal stimuli – an assumption which is diametrically opposed to the conventional Keynesian wisdom.

Cases of direct and indirect crowding out are the ones which have figured relatively prominently in macroeconomic literature in one form or another. In contrast, the third classification of crowding out, *financial crowding out*, is relatively new and stems directly from consideration of the government budget constraint, which implied that a fiscal deficit could be financed in one of three ways. If the deficit is tax financed then there is substantial crowding out (figure 12.5). In contrast, if the deficit is financed by an increase in high-powered money no crowding out occurs, and indeed the expansionary impact of the fiscal measure is reinforced by the expansionary impact of the enlarged money stock (figure 12.6). It is also possible to finance accompanying deficits by bond finance. Here, the expansionary impact of fiscal policy combined with debt finance exceeds even the monetary-financed case; once again crowding out is absent provided the government can always sell additional national debt (figure 12.7). In turn, this requires confidence in the ability of the government authorities in being able to service and redeem the debt and also requires that there be no permissible limit, political or otherwise, to interest rates. The monetarist claim that fiscal policy is largely ineffective, unless accompanied by expansionary monetary policy, therefore rests upon a dual belief – namely, that, tax-financed deficits are ineffectual and that limits exist to permissible bond financing. Finally, it should be noted that the logic of the budget constraint overrides all other forms of crowding out. In particular, indirect crowding out is of a temporary duration only, given that in the last resort full equilibrium requires that the budget be finally balanced.

The Budget Constraint and Inflation

Hitherto, the financial implications of the government budget constraint have been examined with respect to movements in real output and employment but under the tacit assumption that prices are held constant. However, much of the interest in the government budget constraint springs from the belief that a deficit and the manner of its financing will be of considerable importance for the rate of inflation, and indeed much of the monetarist critique of Keynesian oriented policy measures springs from a feeling that the inflationary consequences have been inadequately analyzed.

From this perspective, ideally, government spending would be matched by taxes and the deficit would be zero. If a deficit does prevail, then it is preferable, given the overriding commitment to curb inflation, that it should be financed by the sale of bonds to the private sector rather than by increasing the high-powered money supply.[10] However, even if the budget deficit implies an increase in the money stock the consequences may still be deflationary within an inflationary setting if the increase in the money stock falls short of the rate of inflation. To pursue this argument further, a simple numerical example is given. Suppose the total money supply is £100m, whilst government outlays total £10m and endogenous taxes equal £9m. The current budget deficit is accordingly £1m. If this deficit is financed by an increase in high-powered money it may lead to a total increase in the money supply by, say, £5m. The net impact of financing the deficit, therefore, is an increase in the total money stock of 5 per cent per annum. Now if the rate of inflation were also equal to 5 per cent, this situation would tend to *continue indefinitely*. At least, this conclusion follows from invoking assumptions which do not stretch realism unduly. If government outlays are maintained in real terms and if endogenous taxes respond *pari passu* with nominal income levels so that the deficit is maintained at 10 per cent of government outlays, and if the relationship between the total money supply and the high-powered money supply remains a constant, then the increase in the money supply will be exactly equal to the inflation rate. In this situation there will be no increase in the *real* money supply arising from the financing of the deficit to disturb the existing situation. Thus, although the money supply will be increasing at an annual rate of 5 per cent this will be absorbed into monetary holdings since the demand for money, being a real demand, will also be increasing at a 5 per cent annual rate. That is to say, both the asset and transactions demand for cash will tend to rise in line with the increase in the nominal money supply; there will be no change in the position of the *LM* curve and no change in the real level of income.

This example is now repeated but under the assumption that inflation is initially running at an annual figure of 10 per cent. In these conditions, the annual increase in the money supply will be insufficient to meet the annual increase in the nominal demand for money balances. In effect, the real money stock will decline and the *LM* function will gradually be shifted inwards with deflationary consequences for the real economy. Under existing assumptions (that government outlays are maintained in real terms whilst tax receipts are effectively indexed to nominal income movements), the budget deficit will increase in both absolute and percentage terms. Thus the situation occurs, contrary to the earlier analysis, of a budgetary deficit being financed by an increasing money supply with deflationary reper-

---

10 It should not be assumed that deficit financing by bond sales has no impact upon inflation. If the money transferred into bonds had constituted 'idle' balances, its activization upon being spent by the government is in reality an increase in velocity, similar in its effects to an increase in the money supply.

cussions upon the real economy reinforced by a rising interest rate. This scenario is precisely that of the monetarist contention that unemployment and a loss of output is the price to be paid for the elimination of inflation. For with the rate of monetary increase well below that of inflation, the rate of price increases will ultimately fall; there will be insufficient means of finance to transact the turnover of GNP at the constantly rising price level.[11] The rising deficit in real terms will necessitate a further increase in the money supply in excess of its annual 5 per cent rate. At the same time, as the rate of inflation falls the two rates will eventually coincide. Stability will be regained when the annual increase in monetary growth is again equated with the rate of inflation, in the present case within the range 5–10 per cent.[12]

According to this analysis, the rate of inflation will continue to fall as long as the rate of monetary growth lies below the annual rate of inflation. It follows that the way to reduce and eventually eliminate inflation is to reduce progressively the growth of the money supply, despite the deflationary impacts this will exert upon the real sectors of the economy. In return this necessitates reducing the fiscal deficit by reducing government expenditure and raising taxes upon the one hand and by financing any deficit that remains by bond sales to the private sector on the other hand, even though this may necessitate extremely high rates of interest.

Once inflation has been eliminated the logic of the budget constraint will again reassert itself, with the consequences of the deficit revealing itself in expansionary real movements in the economy, assuming perfectly elastic supply conditions. If supply constraints exist, part of the impetus will be dissipated into price rises and may once again initiate an inflationary spiral.

In conclusion, consideration of the budget constraint generates two opposing eventual outcomes. In the absence of inflation, full equilibrium necessitates equality between government outlays and government taxes with zero change in the money supply and the volume of bonds issued. Policy multipliers should reflect this eventual outcome. If inflation exists, then a stable solution to the model no longer requires equality between government outlays and government receipts to the extent that the financial implications of any deficit (surplus) are just sufficient to accommodate the ongoing rate of inflation (deflation).

---

11 This conclusion makes clear two underlying assumptions which are fundamental to the monetarists' belief in the efficacy of money supply control – first that velocity increases are limited, and second and more important that the relationship between the high-powered monetary base and the total money stock is relatively constant. On the latter point see Chick (1977).

12 The inflationary effects of monetary growth will be reinforced by the decline in real output.

Concluding Comments

The previous discussion of the government sector has not specifically dealt with methods of finance (other than when dealing with the balanced budget multiplier theorem, when it was assumed that all outlays were tax financed). Now, however, the method of finance has been made explicit, and as a result many important conclusions have been reached:

(1) That *IS* and *LM* curves are interdependent and linked through the budget constraint.
(2) That monetary-financed expenditure policy is inevitably more high powered than equivalent tax-financed expenditures.
(3) That Keynesian belief in the long-term efficacy of fiscal policy rests upon the assumption of unlimited debt finance.
(4) That various possibilities exist for the short-term crowding out of fiscal policy measures.

Finally, it can be observed that the stability conditions for the extended *IS/LM* framework with a government budget constraint differ under inflation, in that monetary creation will not be disequilibrating if it is just sufficient to match the inflation rate.

Further Reading

The literature on the government budget constraint and the crowding out controversy is now extensive. Useful surveys are to be found in Artis, Burrows and Taylor, all published in Cook and Jackson (1979) with extensive references. Likewise, Currie (1978) and (1981) is recommended for providing a comprehensive summary of the leading issues. An elementary introduction to the crowding out controversy is presented in Shaw (1977) and Peacock and Shaw (1978). Amongst the seminal and influential papers, reference must be made to Blinder and Solow (1973) and Hansen (1973). A useful paper presented in terms of the *IS/LM* analysis is that of Silber (1970). Other interesting articles making specific reference to fiscal policy effectiveness include Buiter (1977), Scarth (1975) and Turnovsky (1977). Extensions to the basic analysis presented here include Alpine (1985) and Shaw (1987c), whilst a disturbing scenario outlining the possible consequences of runaway government debt is presented by Tobin (1986).

13

Output, Employment, Expectations and the Price Level

Chapters 8 to 12 contrasted the Keynesian and classical models within a conventional *IS/LM* framework. This framework has been used as an expository device for many years and is useful for bringing out the principal contrasts between the two systems. There are however certain fundamental shortcomings inherent in this methodology. First, it is basically a static framework which, although useful for comparative static analysis, is of rather limited value for analyzing the dynamics of each system. In other words, the framework is helpful in comparing equilibria but has little to contribute to the analysis of movements from one equilibrium to another. Second, the methodology implicitly assumes that monetary and fiscal policy are independent instruments. Increasingly the interdependence of the two instruments is being appreciated, as has already been noted in the analysis of the government budget constraint and the crowding out controversy in chapter 12. Third, and related to the above, the analysis is essentially conducted against the backcloth of a stable price level. Thus it is assumed that as *IS* and *LM* shift around up to the full employment level of output, the price level remains stable. Although it is implicit that increases in output beyond the full employment level may be inflationary, it is also implicit that such increases are easily reversible.

It has become increasingly obvious over the past twenty years or so that such behavioural assumptions about what are essentially the dynamic characteristics of the system are not entirely plausible, and that the relationship between output and changes in the price level may be rather more complicated than that portrayed by the mechanics of the simple model.

This chapter will consider explicitly the causes of variations in the aggregate price level, and in particular the manner in which variations in the price level might be affected by variations in output. Such an analysis goes to the very heart of recent work in macroeconomic theory and policy, and serves to highlight the important role which expectations may play.

Inflation and its Causes

Inflation is a *sustained* upward rise in the *general* price level. By empha-sizing 'sustained' this definition clearly excludes temporary jumps or falls in prices related perhaps to specific events. The 'general' price level refers to some representative price level which affects the majority of individuals. Thus the *retail price index*, which is the most frequently referred to indica-tor of inflation in the UK, is a weighted average of prices of a standard basket of goods and services. Variations in this index indicate how varia-tions in prices are affecting economic agents 'on average'.

As will be seen in chapter 18, governments are concerned with inflation because it tends to generate certain distortions in the economic system; that is, it can redistribute income in a capricious manner, it can raise the average costs of transactions, and it can result in relative prices being distorted. These issues will be considered more fully later. For the moment it will be taken as given that the authorities have an interest in controlling inflation, and first the causes of inflation and its relationship to output variations will be explored.

From elementary microeconomics, it is clear that an increase in the price of a given commodity can result from a shift in demand and/or supply. An analogous distinction can be made with respect to the macroeconomy. Thus, from the aggregate demand and aggregate supply curves which were derived in chapters 6 and 7, it can be seen that it is possible for price level changes to occur as a consequence of shifts in AD and/or AS.

It will be recalled that a given AD curve is derived on the assumption of money market equilibrium. Therefore as the price level falls (increases) the real value of a given stock of money balances increases (falls), real expendi-ture increases (falls) and real income increases (falls). In other words the AD schedule has a negative slope. Given the implicit assumption of money market equilibrium which underpins AD, any increases (decreases) in the money supply would shift AD to the right (left).

In chapter 7 was introduced the AS schedule. The slope of this was determined by the manner in which agents in the labour market responded to changes in the price level. It was seen that if labour supply was a function of the real wage, and the labour market cleared quickly, AS would be vertical. In other words, employment and real income would be insensitive to variations in the price level (and perforce to policies which changed the price level). If, on the other hand, labour supply were a function of the money wage rate, then AS could be positively sloped, at least up to the full employment level of real income. The latter possibility really relied on some market imperfection being present, such as money illusion, or contracts which fixed the price of labour for a given period. This in turn introduced a third possibility, namely that positively sloped and vertical AS curves could coexist – the former being short-run functions, the latter the long-run AS when full adjustment has taken place.

Demand Pull Inflation

Figure 13.1 outlines in stylized terms the simple mechanics of demand pull inflation. Assume the initial output level is Y_1 and price level P_1 (point a),

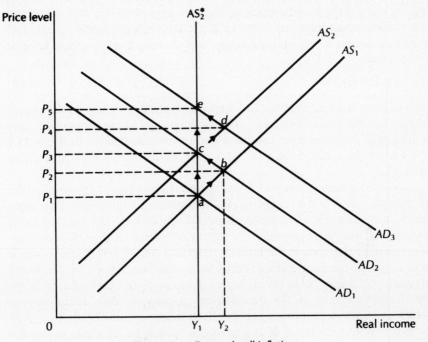

Figure 13.1   Demand pull inflation

and this equilibrium is disturbed by an increase in the money supply. This increases aggregate expenditure and shifts AD to the right, from AD_1 to AD_2. If aggregate supply is depicted by AS_1 then real output increases to Y_2 and the price level rises to P_2 (point b). If the AS curve is vertical, the shift in AD results in an increase in the price level from P_1 to P_3 (point c). Further shifts might take the equilibrium to d or e.

The manner in which any increase in the nominal money supply affects prices and output, and the extent to which any increase is divided between increases in output and increases in prices, has been the subject of some controversy. The latter question has been especially topical in recent years, and it will be examined in detail later in the chapter. For the moment concentration will be on the former.

Chapter 5 set out the simplest possible statement of the monetarist position on inflation in the form of the simple quantity theory equation

$$M\bar{V} = P\bar{Y} \tag{13.1}$$

This encapsulates two central propositions of the classical quantity theory position; first, the demand for money is a stable function of a small number of variables, and therefore the velocity of circulation V can be taken as stable; second, the factors which affect the supply of money M are separate from those which influence demand. If the classical assumption is invoked that real output Y will automatically tend to its full employment level, it follows that

$$\Delta M\bar{V} \rightarrow \Delta P\bar{Y} \tag{13.2}$$

that is, there is a deterministic link between the rate of change in the money supply and the price level, and furthermore changes in the supply of money will change the price level and leave real income unaffected. In figure 13.1 there would be a shift from a to c as a result of the shift in AD from AD_1 to AD_2.

As was also seen in chapter 5, the Keynesian analysis of the demand for money suggested that V could in fact be unstable and unpredictable, especially in conditions of underemployment equilibrium, the most graphic example of this being provided by the liquidity trap. Although most neo-Keynesian analysis views the liquidity trap as a purely pathological case, it was seen that the Keynesian demand for money was refined by, *inter alia*, Baumol (1952) and Tobin (1958), and it is this analysis which underpins the neo-Keynesian view of the *transmissions mechanism*, that is, the way in which a change in the money supply affects money income (PY). According to this view an increase in M causes wealth holders to substitute money for bonds and other financial assets in their portfolios. The more closely substitutable a given asset for money, the bigger the change that occurs, and there is a 'ripple' effect throughout the liquidity spectrum. Changes in the money supply do not therefore affect final expenditure directly but rather indirectly through its influence on real investment. When the money supply is increased, this could be stimulated directly through a reduction in the interest rate (as in the simple Keynesian analysis of investment of chapter 3), and/or through increases in the price of equities stimulating further equity issues. In this schema, then, changes in M can affect Y and can affect P (through the subsequent pressure of demand). The precise relationships are, however, essentially unpredictable, and depend on the sensitivity of investment to monetary policy and the extent to which V changes if M changes.

Friedman's (1956a) reformulation and refinement of the simple quantity theory analysis accepted the basic principle that changes in the supply of nominal money balances would result in adjustments in individual portfolios, but contended that the links between monetary expansion and final expenditure were altogether more direct than those posited by the neo-Keynesian approach.

This followed from Friedman's inclusion of real and financial assets in the demand for money function, such that when portfolio adjustment occurred it was associated not only with the substitution of one financial asset for another but also with substitution of money balances for real assets like consumer durables, housing and so on. In crude terms, although the demand for money was viewed as being a function of a larger range of variables than envisaged by the simple quantity theory approach, it was nevertheless a *stable* function, ensuring relative stability of V. In the event therefore that the authorities increase the money supply, stock disequilibrium is created in the money market. Individuals hold excess money balances in their portfolios and, in order to clear this excess supply, expenditure increases. Thus the link between monetary expansion and expenditure is direct. With respect to the division of a change in M between P and Y, subsequent work by Friedman suggested that in the short run both would be affected, whilst in the long run the full impact of any monetary expansion would be felt on prices. This will shortly be examined more closely. For the moment it might simply be noted that the essence of demand pull inflation is that an outward shift in the AD function raises the price level. The monetarist position is that monetary expansion is both necessary and sufficient to facilitate this process. Whilst not denying that this may be so, the neo-Keynesian position can be interpreted as one consistent with the view that monetary expansion is sufficient but not necessary. The additional pressure of demand could emanate from an autonomous increase in investment expenditure or from an increase in real investment stimulated by monetary expansion. In so far as both must ultimately be accommodated by an increased supply of money balances, both stands can be interpreted as being consistent with Friedman's assertion that 'inflation is always and everywhere a monetary phenomenon' (which as will be seen in chapter 18 is not the same as saying that control of the money supply is both necessary and sufficient to control inflation).

Cost Push Inflation

Whereas demand pull inflation originates in a shift in the AD curve with a given AS curve, cost push inflation originates with an autonomous shift in

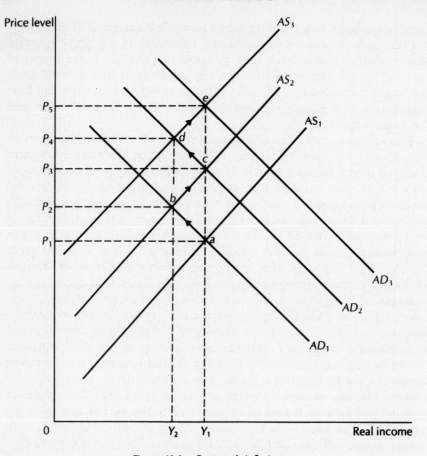

Figure 13.2　Cost push inflation

the *AS* curve. In figure 13.2 the leftward shift in *AS* with a given *AD* raises
the supply prices of factors of production such that less is supplied at any
given price level. With a given aggregate demand curve of AD_1, aggregate
output would fall to Y_2 and the price level would rise to P_2. Thus the shift
in supply has resulted in a price level change which is independent of the
level of demand. The resultant inflation is associated with a fall in output
(and employment). Such inflationary pressures which originate on the
supply side could emanate from any of the following three channels:

(1) increased raw material prices
(2) profit push
(3) wage push.

There are occasions when the prices of raw materials are administered upwards, as for example in the OPEC price hike of 1973–4 which quadrupled the posted price of crude oil between October 1973 and January 1974. In the event that the commodity concerned has relatively few substitutes, and demand is therefore relatively price inelastic, this feeds straight through into the prices of inputs and finished goods. Given a downward sloping AD schedule, a higher price level reduces the real value of money balances, and real expenditure and income are decreased.

Profit push inflation occurs when product prices are administered upwards in an attempt to increase profit margins. Such a mechanism of course relies on the exploitation of (product) market power, and there have been occasions when commentators have felt that profit push has been an important source of inflationary pressure, for example in the United States during the 1950s. Like imported inflation, however, profit push is only really useful in explaining once and for all changes in the price level, since there are limits to the extent to which prices are raised even if these are only the limits set by profit maximization. The phenomenon is not helpful in explaining the dynamics of an inflationary process once it is under way.

Wage push is the most widely discussed source of cost push inflation. This too relies on the use of market power to attempt to alter the distribution of income. In this case, however, it is factor rather than product market power which is relevant. Here the mechanism which applies is that labour unions push for increases in wages in excess of productivity growth. This is conceded by firms anxious to avoid the costs of a protracted dispute, and passed on in the form of higher prices. Again, referring to figure 13.2, the outcome is a leftward shift in AS, a rise in the price level and a fall in output and employment. The notion of wage push inflation commands wide popular appeal and, despite the difficulties of finding a proxy for union power, there is some empirical evidence to suggest that the presence of labour unions can induce an inflationary bias in the labour market, especially when they are active in industries where they face employers with some degree of product market power (see Trevethick and Mulvey, 1975, chapter 6). Like the profit push explanation of inflation, wage push is useful for explaining specific inflationary impulses (as in the UK in 1968–9 or 1978–9), but, also in common with profit push, it is fundamentally lacking as an explanation of sustained inflation, and for similar reasons. Since the underlying model is based on market power it is consistent with a once and for all wage push. In the case of a sustained inflation, where does the increased market power come from? Given a downward sloping labour demand curve, increased real wages will be associated with a lower level of employment. As unemployment increases it seems reasonable to suppose that union membership falls, and with it market power.

In a strict sense then wage push *per se* is not a *generally applicable* explanation for inflation. This is not however to do justice to more sophisticated approaches to wage push inflation which recognize this and which, while continuing to ascribe trade unions a central role in the inflationary process, recognize the importance of monetary accommodation. Thus in figure 13.2 a wage push shifts AS_1 to AS_2, raises prices from P_1 to P_2 and reduces output from Y_1 to Y_2. The authorities could respond to this by permitting monetary expansion to take place in order to reduce unemployment and re-establish an output level of Y_1. AD_1 therefore shifts to AD_2 and the price level rises from P_2 to P_3. The latter change could provide the stimulus for another wage push, again raising prices (to P_4) and lowering output (to Y_2 again). Monetary accommodation raises prices further and so the process repeats itself with an adjustment pattern of $a \rightarrow b \rightarrow c \rightarrow d \rightarrow e$. This view of inflation would see it as the outcome of a struggle between unions to alter the distribution of income, against the backcloth of a government aiming to hit a particular employment target. It must be noted, however, that even though a central role is given to the activities of labour unions, these activities still have to be 'validated' by monetary accommodation.

This type of mechanism is a far cry from the naïve view that cost push inflation is simply the outcome of the abuse of union power *per se*, and all that is necessary to control inflation is some form of wage control. Indeed this view, although it may claim to be cost push in spirit, is nevertheless consistent with Friedman's assertion that 'inflation is always and everywhere a monetary phenomenon'.

The acceleration of inflation which has taken place over the last fifteen years or so in most developed market economies has stimulated a great deal of research effort directed at establishing whether inflation is principally cost push or demand pull. Although none of this evidence can be recounted here, one thing which has been consistently reported for a great many countries is the close *association between monetary expansion and changes in prices*. This is not to argue that any link between money and prices is mechanistic and straightforward, such that causality is always unambiguous; as has been seen, one could argue the case for money being active or passive. Nor is it to argue that control of the money supply is both necessary and sufficient to control inflation in the short run. Rather it is to argue that, once an inflationary process is under way, the distinction between demand pull and cost push is not very important. The problems of inflationary control will be returned to in chapter 18. For the moment, however, it will be accepted that a long-run relationship between the money supply and inflation exists; attention will be focused on other significant issues from a policy standpoint, such as the precise relationship between inflation and employment, and how this relationship is affected by inflationary expectations. This permits a comment on an issue alluded to earlier in the chapter, namely what, for a given monetary expansion which serves to shift *AD* to the right, determines the distribution of the change in expenditure between prices and real income.

The Phillips Curve Relation

For many years it was felt that a systematic trade-off existed between the rate of inflation and the level of unemployment. The basis of this belief was the publication of a celebrated paper by Phillips (1958) which provided statistical support for the existence of a stable trade-off between the rate of change of money wages and the level of unemployment. According to Phillips this association held in the UK for long periods during the period 1861–1957. The so-called Phillips curve took the general form outlined in figure 13.3.

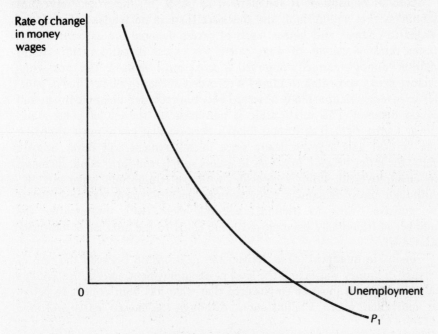

Figure 13.3   Phillips curve

The theoretical underpinnings to the Phillips curve were subsequently developed by Lipsey (1961), who focused on the level of excess demand in the labour market at any particular time, and on the implications which this has for the speed of adjustment of money wages. Specifically Lipsey assumed that

$$\dot{W} = f[(D_L - S_L)/S_L] \tag{13.3}$$

where D_L and S_L refer to the demand for and supply of labour respectively, and $\dot{W}$ refers to the rate of change of money wages.

If a linear functional form is imposed, as by Lipsey, equation 13.3 can be rewritten as

$$\dot{W} = \alpha[(D_L - S_L)/S_L] \tag{13.4}$$

Lipsey therefore takes the relatively uncontroversial proposition, portrayed in panel (a) of figure 13.4, that in the event of excess supply (demand) in the labour market the wage rate will fall (rise), and extends it by arguing that the *speed* at which wage rates rise or fall will be related to the *extent* of excess demand/supply. In the case of an excess demand, therefore, wage rates will rise more quickly from W_2 than W_1 in panel (a).

Speed of adjustment is summarized in panel (b); the origin represents labour market equilibrium, and therefore there is no tendency for money wages to change, and higher levels of excess demand are associated with faster rates of change of wage rates.[1] As excess demand in the labour market cannot be directly observed, a proxy must be used. The most satisfactory proxy according to Lipsey is recorded unemployment. Thus in panel (c) an inverse relationship is observed between recorded unemployment and excess demand. This relationship is non-linear to the left of point z and linear to the right. The former follows because that curve must approach the vertical axis asymptotically since unemployment will never become zero; the latter because increases in excess supply call forth equal increases in unemployment. Point z coincides with the equilibrium wage rate W_e. Although excess demand is zero, recorded unemployment will nevertheless be positive owing to frictional unemployment (with, presumably, the number of frictionally unemployed being equal to the number of vacancies available).

Finally, in quadrant (d) is derived the relationship between the rate of change of money wages and the level of unemployment, that is, the Phillips curve relation. It must be emphasized that what has been done is to derive an individual 'micro' Phillips curve. Although the 'macro' curve will take

---

1 The function could be extended to the south-west quadrant to relate wage change and negative excess demand. Presumably, however, an asymmetry would be observed, that is, higher levels of excess supply result in slower reductions in wage rates. This would be explained by reference to institutional arrangements which result in a downward inflexibility of money wages.

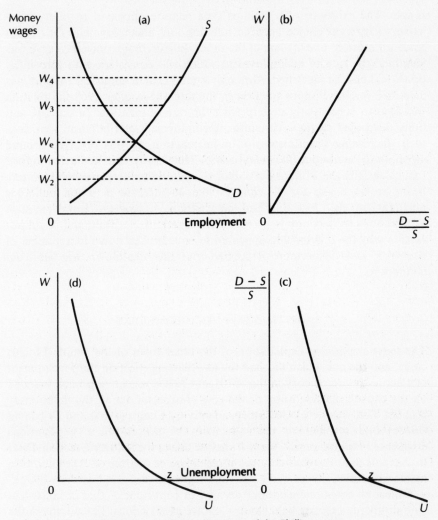

Figure 13.4   Lipsey's derivation of the Phillips curve

the same general configuration, it is derived from observations (that is individual points) on micro curves.

As Laidler (1971b) subsequently remarked, 'The simple theory of the Phillips curve ... was absorbed with remarkable speed into the generally accepted corpus of macro-economics.' Furthermore, it must be said that the acceptance was largely uncritical, with most emphasis being placed on testing for the presence of Phillips curves in a variety of countries and circumstances. The reason behind such an open-armed welcome is quite simple. The existence of a Phillips type relation appeared to offer policy makers a straight choice between inflation and unemployment. One could trade off more of one for less of the other. Furthermore, once the curve was identified the rate of unemployment which was consistent with zero inflation could also be identified. Although a good deal of empirical support was identified for the Phillips relation in the mid-1960s, after 1968 the relation was seen to consistently underpredict the rate of inflation. In the UK and other developed market economies, unemployment and inflation were seen to be increasing simultaneously. Initial reactions to this revolved around attempts to resuscitate the relationship. Thus many commentators argued that essentially the Phillips curve had shifted and/or its shape had changed, owing to once and for all changes like an increase in union militancy pursuant on pay restraint and devaluation. Ultimately, however, such explanations were country-specific rationalizations of a shift, and could not explain why the relationship appeared to have broken down in a number of countries, and furthermore it seemed that the breakdown was far from temporary.

Expectations in Macroeconomics

The most convincing explanation of the breakdown of the simple Phillips curve, and the one which has had the most lasting effect on the development of macroeconomic theory in the 1970s and 1980s, was an approach founded on the explicit consideration of the role of expectations in the inflationary process. This was developed independently by Phelps (1968) and Friedman (1968a) and resulted in the refinement of the so-called 'expectations augmented Phillips curve'. We will analyse this in the following section. Prior to that it is useful to outline some simple ideas of the role of expectations in macroeconomics.

Almost all economic decisions deemed to be rational – that is, consistent with utility maximizing behaviour – involve expectations. The purchase of a candy bar or a theatre ticket for example is undertaken in the light of a given expectation of the pleasure that consumption of the candy bar or visit to the theatre is going to provide. One expectation may be held with greater certainty than the other; candy bars (at least of the same variety) being more homogeneous than theatre plays or performances, but the principle is the same. The difference, in more formal terms, is simply that in the case of the visit to the theatre the variance around the expected mean value is likely to be greater than that associated with the consumption of the candy bar.

This difference, however, is not without significance. Two goods may possess the same expected mean value of marginal utility but one may have a far greater variance around the mean and therefore may involve – for the risk-averse individual – the prospect of an unacceptable outcome. Without pursuing such complications any further at this point it is sufficient to observe that utility maximization involves individual economic agents forming expectations – if only implicitly or intuitively – both about the expected mean outcome upon the one hand and the degree of variance around the expected outcome upon the other. It is in this sense that virtually all economic decisions involve expectations. Yet expectations have, until comparatively recently, been given scant attention in economic reasoning mainly owing to the difficulties of incorporating them adequately into the main body of economic theory. In recent years two methods of making expectations endogenous have been defined: namely, adaptive expectations and rational expectations.

Adaptive Expectations

Adaptive expectations are precisely that; they adapt in the light of past experience. We will formally analyse the adaptive mechanism later in the chapter. For the moment the essence of the adjustment process can be summed up with the aid of a simple and rather mechanical equation. Suppose an individual is forecasting the interest rate. Let us write i^e to represent the *expected* rate in any given time period, whilst i refers to the *actual* rate which did in fact prevail. Then we may express the expectation of the interest rate next period in the following way:

$$i^e_{t+1} = i^e_t + \lambda(i_t - i^e_t), (0 < \lambda < 1) \qquad (13.5)$$

where t denotes the time period and λ is an adjustment coefficient which lies between the values 0 and 1. That is to say our expectation of the rate of interest for the next period is equal to the expectation that we held with respect to the current period plus some fraction of the extent to which our expectation was shown to be incorrect. For purposes of illustration let us assume the adjustment coefficient takes the value 0.5 whilst the market rate of interest is 5 per cent and our expected rate or 'normal' rate is 10 per cent. Then in the next time period, in the light of our expectation being proved incorrect we would have

$$i^e_{t+1} = 10 + 0.5(5 - 10)\% = 7.5\%$$

In the following period, should the market remain stubbornly at 5 per cent we would have

$$i^e_{t+1} = 7.5 + 0.5(5 - 7.5)\% = 6.25\%$$

and subsequently,

$$i^e_{t+1} = 6.25 + 0.5(5 - 6.25)\% = 5.625\%$$

Thus, over time, and confronted by the fact that our expectation has persistently overestimated the actual rate of interest, we would gradually adjust our expected rate downwards until we attain a coincidence between our expectations and reality.

The speed of adjustment, depends, of course, upon the value of the coefficient lambda. In the limiting case where lambda takes the value 1, the adjustment process is complete within one period. This is a special case of the adaptive expectations thesis which underlies the Cobweb theorem of price determination. In this model, sellers assume that whatever price prevails in the market today, in the current period, will continue to prevail in future periods.

The adaptive expectations thesis was introduced into economics by Cagan (1956) to deal with the formation of inflationary expectations in conditions of hyperinflation and in many respects it has great appeal. It is simple to model, involving only a linear first-order difference equation and econometrically it is not difficult to obtain estimates of the adjustment coefficient. Moreover it has the appealing property that in the case of a once and for all change – say a price increase occasioned by a raising of indirect taxes – then sooner or later economic agents' expectations will come to coincide with reality. None the less, as we shall see later in the chapter, as a means of expectations formation it is not without its drawbacks.

Rational Expectations

An alternative view of the way in which expectations are formed is the rational expectations view. The rational expectations hypothesis possesses immediate appeal to the conventionally trained economist embodying as it does the assumption of utility maximizing behaviour. Specifically, it assumes that individual economic agents do not refer solely to past experience in forming expectations but also take account of current available information should they find it worthwhile. In addition, it is assumed that they process this information in an efficient manner to arrive at an expectation or forecast of the values to be taken by economic variables. So far, so good; few economists would be disposed to deny the foregoing mode of behaviour which conforms very neatly with the predilections of *homo economicus*.

The rational expectations hypothesis, however, comes in weak and strong versions. Loosely speaking, it is the weak version which is epitomized in the preceding paragraph. It implies little more than an assertion that individuals carry out a simple cost-benefit exercise to determine whether it is worthwhile to seek out available information (which oftentimes may be freely available) which they incorporate into their expectations formation process. The strong version of the thesis, however, which derives from Muth's seminal paper (Muth, 1961), is vastly different from the above, is far more stringent in its assumptions, and generates quite remarkable and startling conclusions which carry far-reaching implications for macroeconomics and macroeconomic policy.

The essence of the strict version of the rational expectations thesis can be summarized relatively simply. If economic variables are determined by a relatively easily identifiable process, which recurs, then sooner or later intelligent economic agents will learn to recognize the process and will begin to form their expectations in the light of knowledge of that process. The recognition and identification of the process implies that they possess, implicitly at least, a formal model of the economy. Moreover, ultimately, the model which agents possess will coincide with the *true* model which governs the economy, for if the model which agents use is incorrect they will learn of its falsity – their expectations will be proved wrong and they will modify the model in the light of that proof. Adoption of the correct model analysis to process current information means that the subjective expectations so formed are essentially informed predictions of future events and as such are essentially the same as the predictions of the relevant economic theory. In other words the expected value of an economic variable coincides with the true mathematical expectations to be taken by that variable. A simple example may make this clear.

Consider the tossing of an unbiased six-sided die. The expected value from the toss of the die is simply

$$EV = \frac{1}{6.1} + \frac{1}{6.2} + \frac{1}{6.3} + \frac{1}{6.4} + \frac{1}{6.5} + \frac{1}{6.6} = 3.5$$

Suppose the die were to be tossed a hundred times and an economic agent asked to predict the eventual score. An agent familiar with probability theory (knowing the true model) would opt for 350. Moreover, an agent lacking a knowledge of probability theory would also learn from experience to predict something in the region of 350 if the experiment were to be repeated again and again. In particular, he would soon learn that an expectation of, say, 500 was incorrect and in addition was *systematically* overly high. Sooner or later agents will learn to recognize the process and their expectation will eventually coincide with the true mathematically expected value. Now, of course, the expectation may prove to be incorrect in the sense that the value 350 may never actually occur; none the less this mode of expectations formation is efficient in the sense that over time it will minimize the extent of any error (minimize the variance around the mean value) and moreover the expected value of any forecast error will itself be zero. It is in this sense that rational expectations formation is deemed to be the optimal mode of expectational behaviour.

A number of implications follow. First, any forecast error will be completely uncorrelated with any available information which the economic agent finds worthwhile to analyse since if this were not the case – if any correlation existed – then the rational agent should logically use it in deriving his initial expectation. Secondly, it is implicit in this process that whilst an agent may make forecast errors – his expectation proves incorrect – he will not make systematic expectational errors. Thus forecast errors which remain are essentially random, that is, they possess a mean value of zero and reveal no discernible pattern.

Few people would be inclined to object to the sense of rational expectations in the case of our simple die experiment discussed above. However, the major implications derived from the hypothesis assume similar behaviour upon the part of economic agents with respect to the progress of the macroeconomy as a whole. That is to say, it is assumed that economic agents – and especially agents in labour markets – ultimately learn the true model of the economy and form expectations of interest rate movements, price movements and so on in the light of changes in aggregate demand which influence real wages – and hence their own behaviour. Moreover, in the case of changes in the level of aggregate demand arising from government macroeconomic policy the modification of agents' behaviour in the light of their expectations is such as to negate the impact of government policy. Stabilization policy is rendered impotent. This is what is referred to as the policy ineffectiveness proposition arising out of rational expectations theorizing.

As we shall see below, the assumption of rational expectations, and its implications for macroeconomic policy are not without their critics. For the moment let us explicitly incorporate expectations into our Phillips curve model.

The Role of Inflationary Expectations

At the heart of the *expectations augmented Phillips curve* were three assumptions, one of which was consistent with the original Phillips/Lipsey formulation, two of which questioned fundamental tenets of the Phillips/Lipsey versions. These assumptions were:

1. At the market clearing wage there will always be a certain amount of recorded unemployment which is voluntary and/or frictional in type. This level of unemployment has come to be known as the *natural rate of unem-*

ployment. Since it is determined by institutional factors such as the presence (or absence) of minimum wage legislation, institutional barriers to factor mobility, social security arrangements and so on, it can be shifted in the longer run by labour market policies.

2. The Phillips/Lipsey model generally emphasized money wages as being the target variable for agents in the labour market. Friedman/Phelps argued that this was an unreasonable proposition. Workers would bargain in real rather than money terms. To assume that they bargained in money terms is tantamount to arguing that money illusion is a persistent feature of the labour market.

3. The Phillips/Lipsey formulation had the rate of change of money wages as dependent on the level of unemployment. The Friedman/Phelps approach was a case of mistaken causality – the level of unemployment is dependent on the real wage rate rather than vice versa.

The reformulation of the Phillips curve once these criticisms are taken into account can alter the basic relationship fundamentally. If for the moment it is assumed that prices are set as a mark-up on wages and, further, that productivity change is zero, then

$$\dot{P}_t = \dot{W}_t \tag{13.6}$$

The obvious question now is, what determines $\dot{W}_t$? Because workers are assumed to bargain in real terms, they must make some allowance in their bargain for any changes in prices which they expect to occur over the contract period. Thus, if they agree on a wage deal to last for a twelve-month period, some allowance will be made for price changes which are expected to occur during the coming year ($\dot{P}_t^e$) as well as excess demand in the labour market (as proxied by U), that is

$$\dot{W}_t = f(U_t, \dot{P}_t^e) \tag{13.7}$$

or taking a more formal specification, and substituting $\dot{P}_t$ for $\dot{W}_t$,

$$\dot{P}_t = \alpha \dot{P}_t^e - \beta(U_t - U_{Nt}) \tag{13.8}$$

where $\dot{P}_t$ is the actual rate of change of prices, $\dot{P}_t^e$ the expected rate of change of prices, U_t the actual level of unemployment and U_{Nt} the 'natural' rate of unemployment. If for the moment it is assumed that $\alpha = 1$, and therefore that expected inflation is fully incorporated into actual price (and wage) changes, then the important result which follows is:

$$\dot{P}_t - \dot{P}_t^e = -\beta(U_t - U_{Nt}) \tag{13.9}$$

or

$$U_t - U_{Nt} = -\frac{1}{\beta}(\dot{P}_t - \dot{P}_t^e) \qquad (13.10)$$

In other words, *unemployment will only diverge from its natural rate if there exists a discrepancy between actual and anticipated inflation rates.* When actual inflation is equal to expected inflation, unemployment will be steady at its natural rate. When, however, *unanticipated* inflation is present in the system, (i.e. P_t and $\dot{P}_t^e$ differ) unemployment can diverge from its natural rate.

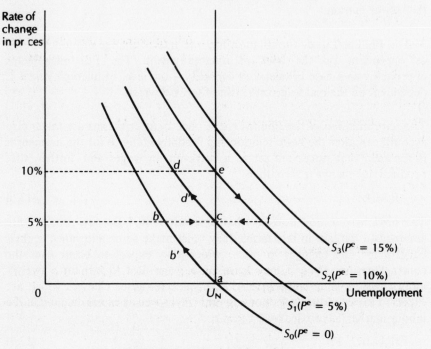

Figure 13.5   Natural rate hypothesis

This natural rate hypothesis can be explained more intuitively by reference to figure 13.5. If the movement begins at point *a* with a zero rate of price inflation which is *fully anticipated*, then unemployment would by definition be at its *natural rate* U_N. Suppose now that the authorities decide to expand aggregate demand by inducing a rightward shift in *IS* and/or *LM* which pushes *AD* to the right. The outcome of this will be assumed to be a 5 per cent expansion of the money supply. If the basic quantity theory identity is accepted then actual prices will rise in proportion to the expansion of the money supply as long as velocity remains constant. What will happen to real output and employment? According to the Phillips/Lipsey analysis, *real* output will rise, unemployment will fall, and movement will take place along the Phillips curve S_0, with equilibrium being established at b. For this to be a stable equilibrium, however, money illusion must be present, since what is implied is that labour supply has increased in response to a rise in money wages whilst real wages remain unchanged. In the Friedman model, however, workers bargain in real terms and set money wage demands according to the expected rate of inflation. Thus, assume

$$\dot{P}^e_t = \alpha \dot{P}_{t-1} \tag{13.11}$$

If the assumption is retained that $\alpha = 1$, full adjustment takes place in the period following any inflation. In terms of figure 13.5, wage bargains are struck in $t - 1$ on the basis of an expected inflation rate of zero. Thus, as money wages rise this is initially perceived as an increase in real wages (since it is deflated by $\dot{P}^e = 0$) and labour supply increases. Once it becomes obvious, however, that prices are increasing at the same rate as wages, and that the real wage is in fact unchanged, the additional labour is withdrawn and unemployment returns to U_N. If nothing else changes, inflation will remain stable at 5 per cent. If, however, the authorities attempt to raise real output again by monetary expansion the process is repeated with an initial shift from c to d on the short-run Phillips curve S_2, and ultimately a return to point e.

As originally formulated, this natural rate hypothesis suggests the following fundamental conclusions:

(1) There is no long-run trade-off between inflation and unemployment.
(2) Any trade-off which exists is entirely transient.
(3) It follows therefore that demand management policies can have no long-run effect on real output and employment, but instead only influence monetary variables (prices, wage rates and interest rates).
(4) The natural rate of unemployment can only be changed in the longer run by supply side policies designed to improve the flexibility and efficiency of labour markets.
(5) Any attempt to use demand management policy to maintain unemployment permanently below (above) the natural rate will simply result in explosive inflation (deflation). This follows from the configuration of the Phillips curves, that is, the asymptotic approach to the vertical axis.

Since the natural rate hypothesis can explain the coincidence of rising inflation and unemployment, and the apparent shifting of the Phillips curve,[2] many commentators have accepted the fundamentals of the analysis (although there might be disagreement over what the natural rate of unemployment is for any given economy). Clearly however much depends on the role of expectations. The absence of a long-run trade-off rests upon full adjustment being made for any discrepancy between actual and anticipated inflation, and the duration of any disequilibrium is determined by the length of time it takes for expectations to catch up with reality. These are issues which will now be investigated further. First, however, the attention of the reader is drawn to the similarity of this analysis with that revolving around figure 13.1, where it was discussed whether AS would be positively sloped or vertical. One important reason for a positively sloped AS was in a situation where expectations of inflation lagged behind reality. This is the analogue of the Phillips relation discussed here.

Output, Inflation and Adaptive Expectations

In developing the natural rate hypothesis above, it was assumed in equation 13.11 that expectations lagged behind reality by one period; since it was assumed that $\alpha = 1$, any past changes in inflation are fully adjusted for within one period. A more sophisticated formulation would permit agents to make mistakes in forecasting inflation and to learn from those mistakes. If therefore individuals made an error in forecasting the price level in the previous period, they would learn from that error in preparing their current forecast of inflation. This is the simple *error learning process* of expectations formation, which postulates that agents form their expectations *adaptively*. Thus, if the following formula was chosen

$$P_t^e - P_{t-1}^e = \lambda(P_{t-1} - P_{t-1}^e) \tag{13.12}$$

the individual would be allowed to revise his forecast of the price level (P_t^e) by some fraction of the error which he made in forecasting the price level in $t-1$. The adjustment which he would make is determined by the coefficient λ, where $0 < \lambda < 1$. Equation 13.12 can be arranged to:

$$P_t^e = \lambda P_{t-1} + (1 - \lambda)P_{t-1}^e \tag{13.13}$$

Since analogously,

$$P_{t-1}^e = \lambda P_{t-2} + (1 - \lambda)P_{t-2}^e \tag{13.14}$$

---

2 As figure 13.5 is constructed, adjustments take place in the manner $a \rightarrow b \rightarrow c \rightarrow d \rightarrow e$. In practice, one is however likely to observe something consistent with $a \rightarrow b' \rightarrow c \rightarrow d' \rightarrow e$ (and vice versa for reductions) such that any combination of inflation and unemployment could be observed.

$$P^e_{t-n} = \lambda P_{t-n-1} + (1 - \lambda)P^e_{t-n-1} \tag{13.15}$$

then backward substitution to eliminate $P^e_{t-1}, P^e_{t-2}, P^e_{t-3}, \ldots, P^e_{t-n}$ yields

$$P^e_t = \lambda P_{t-1} + \lambda(1 - \lambda)P_{t-2} + \lambda(1 - \lambda)^2 P_{t-3}$$
$$+ \cdots + \lambda(1 - \lambda)^n P^e_{t-n-1} \tag{13.16}$$

Clearly, since $0 < \lambda < 1$, the further one goes back into the past the smaller is $(1 - \lambda)^n$ and the less important is P_{t-n} in determining the forecast of P^e_t; that is, the weights decline geometrically. The general form for this system of expectations formation could be written as:

$$P^e_t = \lambda \sum_{i=0}^{n} (1 - \lambda)^i P_{t-n-1} \tag{13.17}$$

Substitution of 13.13 and 13.8 yields an adaptive expectations augmented Phillips curve of

$$P_t = \alpha\lambda P_{t-1} + \alpha(1 - \lambda)P^e_{t-1} + \beta(U_t - U_{Nt}) \tag{13.18}$$

If expectations are formed in this fashion they will always lag behind reality and a short-run trade-off between inflation and unemployment will exist. Furthermore if $\alpha = 1$ full adjustment will take place and the long-run Phillips curve will be vertical. The possibility exists however of $0 < \alpha < 1$, in which case the long-run Phillips curve will have a negative slope and a trade-off could exist, even in the long run. If $\alpha = 0$ then the short-run and long-run Phillips curves coincide. These possibilities are outlined in figure 13.6.

The issue of which of these curves is the actual long-run Phillips curve is far from being an academic question, since alternative configurations are consistent with alternative configurations of the aggregate supply curve. It seems quite implausible to contend that $\alpha = 0$ since this means that money illusion persists in the long run, a proposition which would find few adherents. More plausibly one might argue that $0 < \alpha < 1$ such that incomplete adjustment takes place, permitting some degree of long-run trade-off.

What we have provided is a more rigorous formulation of the adaptive expectations mechanism introduced in the previous section. One might, however, enquire as to why expectations of price level changes should lag behind reality. Why should adjustment fail to take place quickly? If expectations lag behind reality does it not imply money illusion? There may in fact be very good reasons why expectations lag behind reality thereby slowing up the process of adjustment to price level changes. As we saw in chapter 7, there may be a variety of institutional arrangements which protract adjustment, for instance the presence of implicit or explicit contracts. Moreover, agents in the labour market may have incomplete/imperfect information about what is

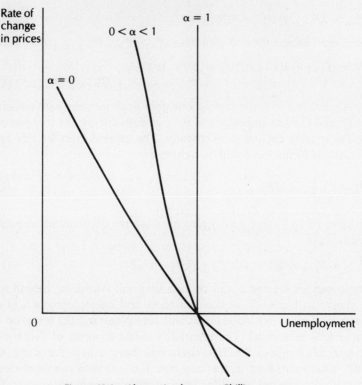

Figure 13.6   Alternative long-run Phillips curves

actually happening. In a regime of relatively low and slowly changing inflation it may be felt that the costs of acquiring full information are not justified by the benefits of a marginally better inflation forecast. In a high-inflation environment this calculus will of course change since the benefits of better forecasts are higher, making the probability of full adjustment higher.

The adaptive expectations hypothesis therefore provides a view of expectations formation which has a certain plausibility. It argues that agents adapt to past mistakes in making forecasts of price level changes. If individuals do behave in this way then the Phillips curve trade-off between inflation and unemployment is preserved. This, however, is only so in the short run. In the long run expectations catch up with reality and the trade-off disappears.

Output, Inflation and Rational Expectations

Despite its inherent plausibility the view that expectations are formed adaptively has been subject to a radical and fundamental attack over the last few years. This attack has been based on a number of objections to the concept.

1. The most compelling criticism perhaps is that if expectations are formed adaptively the individual agent in the labour market (or his representative, the trade union) only takes account of present and past price changes and takes no account of current events. Thus it implies that, for example, a devaluation or an incomes policy will not affect the formation of price expectations. Clearly this is consistent with non-rational behaviour.

2. If expectations are formed adaptively, and if the rate of inflation is increasing, then expectations will always lag behind the inflation rate. Thus no allowance is made for the individual agents adjusting fully for past mistakes. Again, it might be objected that it is essentially non-rational behaviour which would lead an agent to *systematically* make errors in his forecasts of inflation.

3. No explanation is given of how the value of λ is set, that is, what determines the fraction of past forecast error which influences current forecasts. Fleming (1976) has suggested that this might be directly related to the size of previous errors – large errors leading to a large λ, low errors leading to a low λ. With adaptive expectations the individual uses information in a mechanistic fashion. There is no attempt to use information efficiently.

These criticisms, in particular the assertion that agents will not in general systematically make mistakes since this is inconsistent with optimizing behaviour, led to the refinement of the idea of *rational expectations*. Basically the rational expectations doctrine asserts that agents have an incentive to acquire, and use efficiently, information about the variables which they are forecasting. In the case of a labour union preparing for wage negotiations, account would be taken not only of current price changes but also of the authorities' current posture on fiscal and monetary policy, the probability of an incomes policy being imposed, and so on. Moreover, this information will be used in a very deliberate way since the individual is assumed to have invested resources in learning about the way in which the economy functions. If expectations are formed in this manner, the implications for stabilization policy differ radically from those associated with adaptive expectations. With rational expectations not even a short-run trade-off is possible unless agents are taken by surprise when some policy action results in an unexpected change in prices.

Credit for the refinement of the concept of rational expectations and its implications for economic policy is most usually ascribed to Lucas (1972,

1973 and 1975), Sargent and Wallace (1975) and Barro (1976), although the concept (and some of its implications for policy), was originally introduced by Muth (1960, 1961).

Muth (1961, p. 316) summarized rational expectations as follows:

> Expectations of firms (or more generally the subjective probability distribution of outcomes) tend to be distributed for the same information set, about the prediction of the theory (or the 'objective' probability distributions of outcomes).

In other words, the rational agent will obtain information about the 'objective' probability distributions of outcomes associated with particular policy actions based on the relevant economic theory, and he will use this information to generate expectations about the variables in which he is interested. If the information is used efficiently, the individual's predictions or expectations will turn out to be the same as the relevant theories.

Thus, rather than taking information on past values of a particular variable and using this mechanistically to predict future values (as the adaptive expectations hypothesis implies), the agent uses past information to discern regularities in the pattern of economic activity, such that he can make efficient use of current information. Suppose again that an agent is forecasting inflation. His expectation of the price level can be written as:

$$P_t^e = E(P_t \mid I_{t-1}) \tag{13.19}$$

that is, the expected price level will be equal to his forecast of the actual price level which is conditional on all relevant information available at the time the forecast is made. Given this formulation, the difference between actual and expected price levels turns out to be:

$$P_t - P_t^e = P_t - E(P_t \mid I_{t-1}) = \varepsilon_t \tag{13.20}$$

where ε_t is some random forecast error. The important point to note about ε_t is that it is random. As such it is unpredictable. When making his forecast of the price level, the best guess that the individual can make about ε_t is that it will turn out to be zero.

Thus, if an agent is aware that there exists a systematic relationship between the rate of growth of the money supply in the past and the current price level of the form:

$$P_t = M_{t-1} + \sigma_t \tag{13.21}$$

where σ_t is some random term, he will exploit this knowledge in forming his expectations about price changes such that

$$P_t^e = M_t^e \tag{13.22}$$

If the monetary authorities follow a simple rules approach to monetary policy such that

$$(M_t - M_{t-1}) = \gamma \tag{13.23}$$

then P_t would always be predicted with perfect accuracy except for the influence of any unexpected (and by definition unpredictable) shocks. Therefore,

$$P_t - P_t^e = M_t - M_t^e + \sigma_t \tag{13.24}$$

Substituting this back into the Phillips curve, when M_t^e is set equal to M_t,

$$U_t - U_{Nt} = -\frac{1}{\beta}(\sigma_t) \tag{13.25}$$

In other words *the only thing which can generate a deviation of unemployment from its natural rate is some unexpected and unpredictable shock to the system*. The staggering implication which this has for demand management policy is that there exists no systematic trade-off between inflation and employment – *even in the short run*. Thus shifts in *AD* only result in movements up and down a vertical *AS* curve. In figure 13.1 a policy-induced shift in *AD* from AD_1 to AD_2 to AD_3 simply means a movement $a \rightarrow c \rightarrow e$. In this schema the only way in which the authorities could alter unemployment and cause it to deviate from its natural rate is to use demand management policy in a wholly unpredictable and capricious manner such that all government action is consistently unexpected.[3] This is the case of the *surprise supply function* which was outlined in chapter 7 and which can usefully be re-examined here. In figure 7.9 *AS** is set by the natural rate of unemployment. The authorities could announce a policy of demand contraction, indicating their intention to shift AD_1 to AD_2. Agents acting rationally on this information revise their expectations of inflation and shift from *a* to *b*. Instead of actually contracting demand however, the authorities could do the opposite and shift AD_1 to AD_3. Employers reacting to actual prices respond to a fall in real wages by increasing their demand for labour. Employees on the other hand acting on the basis of expectations geared to AD_2 interpret any increase in money wages as an increase in real wages and increase labour supply. Consequently movement takes place from point *b* towards point *c*. Once however it is realized that prices are in fact rising more quickly than wages, labour supply contracts and movement is towards *d*. The locus *b* to *c* would be called a surprise supply function, because it relies on the dissemination of misleading

---

3 This conclusion follows even if a more sophisticated money supply rule is allowed for.

information which agents act upon, and are subsequently surprised by. The point is, however, that since agents act rationally they will sooner or later discover the facts regarding misinformation and act accordingly. Furthermore such capricious behaviour could not be followed systematically otherwise any 'rules' which were being followed would be discovered, and agents would condition their behaviour accordingly.

The implications of this line of reasoning are striking, to say the least, and the basis of the argument must be made absolutely clear. In general terms it is assumed that individuals are optimizing agents and that they therefore have an incentive to acquire and use information efficiently. Thus in an uncertain world, knowledge about economic regularities will be exploited in such a way that the implications of, for example, changes in government policy are quickly processed and acted upon. As Kantor (1979) puts it, 'rational expectations are profit maximizing expectations'. Individual agents are aware of how the system operates and cannot be systematically fooled.

If this is a reasonable representation of reality it has devastating consequences for demand management policy and policy evaluation. In the case of the former it means that monetary and fiscal policy cannot influence output, even in the short run. A decision, for example, to increase the rate of growth of the money supply will feed through immediately to inflationary expectations thereby affecting monetary variables but leaving real variables unaffected. The only role ascribed to monetary and fiscal policy is one of reducing uncertainty by providing a stable financial environment. In other words a rules approach to policy should be adopted whereby the rate of growth of the money supply is fixed, and a target is set for public borrowing which is consistent with this growth rate. It also means, as Lucas (1976) pointed out, that the conventional process of policy simulation–evaluation is undermined. One can no longer simulate the effects of various macroeconomic strategies because the exercise in effect assumes fixed expectations. The rational expectations doctrine revolves around the assertion that in fact expectations can be altered quite quickly. One cannot therefore compare simulations without allowing for changes in expectations.

Doubts Regarding the Rational Expectations Hypothesis

From this highly simplified presentation of the rational expectations thesis, the 'revolutionary' nature of its policy implications should be clear. They are quite distinctly neo-classical rather than neo-Keynesian and indeed go rather further in their denial of the role of stabilization policy than many 'orthodox monetarists' might be willing to go. The policy prescriptions associated with the analysis have an attraction of quite compelling simplicity in much the same way as those of the classical model did. Although there are some very obvious kindred features in the two systems (most obviously the real/monetary dichotomy, and the recommendation of non-discretionary intervention), the rational expectations thesis has a rather more sophisticated superstructure than the classical thesis.

As well as the compelling simplicity of its prescriptions, the approach has attractions because it conforms so closely with the predilections of *homo economicus*. It assumes that individuals are rational. It assumes that they have an interest in acquiring information and use that information efficiently in order to avoid making costly mistakes. It assumes that in the event that mistakes are made, they will not be systematic. It assumes that agents will not knowingly leave profitable opportunities unexploited. In sum it argues that agents are self-interested and act accordingly.

The thesis has not, however, been given anything like unqualified support. Criticism of the approach has centred on the following issues.

Ability of Agents to Process Relevant Information

Interpreted literally, the rational expectations (RE) hypothesis asserts that agents have the ability to process information in a manner which permits them to forecast all future paths of the economy. As Arrow (1978, p. 160) puts it:

> In the rational expectations hypothesis, economic agents are required to be superior statisticians capable of analysing the future general equilibria of the economy. (p. 160)

In other words a literal interpretation would mean that individual agents are sophisticated forecasters themselves rather than enjoying 'limited powers of information acquisition'.

Begg (1982) counters this criticism by contending that such a strong assumption is unnecessary. The information would in the main be processed by 'specialist' bodies, individuals and institutions whose comparative advantage lies in this practice and, indeed, who can process the changes in policy very quickly. Furthermore, Begg contends that it is not necessary to interpret the RE hypothesis in such a stringent manner. All that is necessary to obtain the RE results is to assume that individuals do not make systematic errors in their forecasting.

Costs of Acquisition of Relevant Information

A second criticism of the RE model is that information collection is a costly exercise and this in itself will limit the access which agents have to relevant information. If agents acquire information in an optimizing manner they would presumably obtain information up to the point where the marginal cost of acquisition is equal to the marginal benefit. Clearly the higher the marginal cost of acquisition, the less information will be collected.

This is certainly correct. A defendant of the RE approach might however respond by making two points. First, the marginal cost of information acquisition may be very low indeed. Economic forecasts are widely publicized and disseminated. Furthermore the unit of acquisition may be a labour union for which the benefit/cost ratio will be very much higher than a typical individual agent.

A variant on this argument is the point that agents, or groups of agents, might have differential access to information. Thus an agent may be much better informed about what is happening in his own market than what is happening at the macro level. This is certainly likely to be the case. According to Begg this need not undermine the RE approach; all it does is point to the need for models which emphasize differential access and explore further the implications of such behaviour for expectations formation. It is ultimately still consistent with agents forming expectations using all relevant information which they have on hand. The other way in which the argument may be cast is that government may have better access to information than non-government agents, which may provide them with a basis for responding more quickly and possibly even allow them a handle for stabilization policy. Governments invariably do have better access to relevant data since they tend to generate most of it. The lead time, however, in most cases is very short – probably too short to give them a stabilization handle.

Adjustment Lags and Credibility Problems

Agents may not respond instantaneously to any given change in the 'forcing variables' of the economic system. This may be true of many markets, and indeed the implications of different markets clearing at different speeds will be considered further. In the context of stabilization policy in a RE model there may be an adjustment lag associated with the time taken by individuals to realize that the 'rule' governing policy has changed. Thus, for example, when the incoming Conservative administration of June 1979 announced the medium-term financial strategy, there may have been a time lag before the precise implications of this change in policy rule were processed. This time lag might also have been lengthened by a credibility problem; that is, agents may simply not have believed that a given preannounced monetary and fiscal regime would be maintained. This would occur if for instance it were widely believed that the probability of a policy reversal or 'U-turn' were high or because the probability of changes in some other forcing variable were high, for example a widespread expectation of an incomes policy. In this event forecast inflation might be largely unaffected by changes in policy variables.

It is widely accepted that credibility can be a problem. The response of proponents of RE however is that this merely strengthens the case for preannouncement of policy intent, and regular statements to reinforce any particular policy stance.

The three previous criticisms relate to the assumption of rational expectations *per se*. To obtain the most devastating results for stabilization policy, one must combine an assumption of rational expectations with an assumption of efficient markets, that is, markets which clear relatively quickly and tend to equilibrium. The combination of these two assumptions is the hallmark of the new classical school. In addition to the criticisms of rational expectations *per se*, one can also object to the assumption of efficient markets and continuous market clearing, as follows.

Differential Flexibility of Prices Across Markets

One of the most serious general criticisms of the RE hypothesis is its assumption that markets clear quickly and efficiently. Whilst this may certainly be true of assets markets (an issue explored further in chapter 15), where the product being traded is very homogeneous, transactions costs are relatively low, the market is highly integrated, forward markets are highly developed and variations in the expected inflation rate affect forward prices very quickly, it may not be true in product and labour markets. In practice product and labour markets may be subject to quantity rather than price adjustment, in which case excess supplies could persist for relatively long periods. In the case of product markets this will vary with the nature of the product. Thus where perishables are concerned, price is likely to adjust relatively quickly compared with durables. As was seen in chapter 7, there are a number of well-documented reasons as to why labour markets may be quantity rather than price adjusters such that excess supply may persist for relatively long periods.

Some of the points made in chapter 7 can be repeated. As was noted there, the labour market is segmented by both occupational and geographical classifications. Since there are costs associated with occupational and geographical mobility, adjustment can be slow. One might argue that this is itself the outcome of market imperfections such as externalities (because the social costs of retraining or moving region are lower than private costs) or entry barriers (due perhaps to labour union apprenticeship rules); the solution is to correct the distortions present, by for example subsidizing retraining and/or relocation, relaxing union rules on apprenticeship, and so on. It was also noted in chapter 7 that the existence of contracts could induce wage rigidity. Although from a macroeconomic viewpoint such arrangements could be viewed as being inherently inefficient, from a micro-economic viewpoint there were justifications for their existence.

The Nature of Unemployment

It is implicit in most rational expectations models that unemployment is entirely voluntary. The labour market is assumed therefore to clear contin-uously, with recorded unemployment being largely those engaged in 'search'. The property does not necessarily follow from an assumption of rational expectations; in fact some RE models permit involuntary unem-ployment (see Begg 1982). The presumption is widespread, however, and it is controversial to say the least. It implies that individual agents view labour supply as an intertemporal decision. If the current real wage is 'too low' relative to what can be obtained from state support schemes, agents will engage in search for higher paid employment. If no such employment appears to be available, the agent will consume leisure now when its relative price is low, with a view to working later (for higher real wages) when the relative price of labour is higher. Some of the shortcomings of this view of unemployment have already been examined in chapter 7, and its relevance to current UK unemployment will be considered in chapter 19.

Empirical Evidence on Expectations

By now it should be clear that the manner in which expectations are formed has a crucial bearing on the existence or otherwise of a trade-off between inflation and unemployment, and in turn on the scope for stabilization policy. What light, if any, can empirical evidence shed on the issue?

There are very real problems in testing propositions relating to expec-tations formation. This is so for several reasons. First, expectations are essentially unobservable. With a few exceptions (such as sealed bids in an auction), it is rarely the case that one can directly observe expectations. Second, even if one can observe expectations, should one directly test the *assumption* of rational expectations, or the *prediction* of a zero trade-off between inflation and unemployment? Third, if one does test the trade-off proposition, one is essentially testing a joint hypothesis of both the natural rate hypothesis *and* the way in which expectations are formed. For instance, suppose one tests the zero trade-off proposition and rejects it. Is the hypothesis being rejected because expectations are not formed rationally, or because the natural rate hypothesis does not hold?

Despite these difficulties quite a number of tests relating to the formation of expectations have now been completed, both direct tests of expectations regimes, and tests of the natural rate hypothesis. Direct tests have focused on the way in which information is used and have attempted to establish whether information is used efficiently. This work does not provide convincing support for the assumption of rational expectations. For example, Aiginger (1980) summarizes a number of studies which compare 'expert' (that is, professional) forecasters with non-professional forecasters. Two points are particularly interesting. First, there appeared to be evidence of inefficiency in the use of information in the inflation forecasts of professionals; second, the professional forecasts appeared to outperform non-professional forecasts. The former finding sits uncomfortably with the proposition that individuals fully exploit all available information, the latter finding sits uncomfortably with the proposition that in a RE world 'we are all experts'. Non-RE proponents take these findings, in particular the latter, as evidence of the fact that different groups of agents have differential access to information, and different abilities to process a given information set. By contrast RE proponents would argue that empirical evidence which relies upon survey information, as these tests do, is inherently unreliable.

Tests of the trade-off between inflation and unemployment have proceeded in two different directions. Early work attempted to estimate the coefficient α in equation (13.18); more recent work has attempted to disentangle anticipated from unanticipated policy, and attempted to test the proposition that only unanticipated policy has any impact on real output levels.

Early studies for both the UK and the USA predicted the value of α to be less than unity (see Solow, 1969 and Parkin, 1970). Subsequent work completed in the 1970s for both economies provides a good deal of evidence for a unity coefficient. Gordon (1976) explains this by reference to a threshold effect – once inflation accelerates beyond a given rate of increase, agents pay more attention to ensuring that full compensation is sought for expected price changes. Despite this empirical support, the natural rate hypothesis has not gone unchallenged. In particular the coexistence of rising inflation and rising unemployment over long periods in the 1970s has attracted much attention. In the same way as efforts to maintain unemployment below the natural rate stimulate accelerating inflation, any maintenance of unemployment above the natural rate should stimulate accelerating deflation. This seems to conflict with the evidence. Opponents of the natural rate hypothesis view this as evidence of its fundamental weakness, whilst adherents of the hypothesis argue that in fact the natural rate has been rising over recent years.

Barro (1979) approached the problem in a different way. He distinguished between anticipated and unanticipated monetary policy, the distinction between the two being made by reference to a model of the money supply in the USA. He related both to changes in real output and concluded that only unanticipated policy exerted an impact on real output. However, this data set was also examined by Mishkin (1982) who assumed a different lag structure in the operation of monetary policy and concluded that in fact anticipated policy had a much more dramatic impact on real output than unanticipated policy!

One final point with regard to empirical work might be noted. If the new classical description of the world (that is, RE with efficient markets) is appropriate we ought to observe random deviations of real output, and in unemployment especially in recent years, we find serial correlation, that is, the persistence of relatively high levels of unemployment from one period to the next. This persistence is not easily explained in an RE context.

In summary, there is as yet no conclusive support for the assumption that expectations are formed rationally, although there is some evidence which can be viewed as consistent with the natural rate hypothesis. In chapters 18 and 19 we will consider the applicability of these ideas to recent inflation and unemployment experience in the UK.

Concluding Comments

In chapters 8 to 12 it was seen that there were a number of issues which could be cast in monetarist–Keynesian terms, one such issue being the determinants of inflation. This chapter has considered in more detail the possible initiating forces behind an inflation, and the dynamics of the inflationary process via a detailed analysis of the role of expectations formation. An analysis of the initiating forces is important since this determines to a large degree the policy prescriptions which one makes. As will be seen in chapter 18, a narrow demand pull view might dictate complete reliance on demand management, whilst a cost push view would see incomes policy of some form as being a necessary component of anti-inflation policy.

The reintroduction of expectations facilitated a clearer analysis of the possible limitations of demand management analysis, and it was found that many of the issues which were raised when the labour market was discussed in chapter 7 were again relevant. As was noted in that chapter, the way in which the labour market responds to various stimuli is at the heart of much current macroeconomic controversy. Clearly in this regard the part played by expectations formation is central.

Further Reading

There exists a voluminous literature on the determinants of inflation which has developed over the last 20 years in particular. The survey paper by Bronfenbrenner and Holzman (1963) summarizes developments to that date, and analyses a variety of models of cost push and demand pull inflation. The survey paper by Laidler and Parkin (1975) eschews the distinction between demand pull and cost push, and instead emphasizes the anticipated/ unanticipated distinction as their starting-point, which permits them to concentrate more fully on the role of expectations. Useful collections of essays are Heathfield (1979) and Laidler (1975) whilst Laidler (1982) provides an authoratative analysis of all aspects of the literature.

Phillips original (1958) paper has been reprinted in a number of volumes and can be found, along with Lipsey's (1961) paper, in Surrey (1975). Friedman's (1968) paper is also easily accessible. Non-technical introductions to the adaptive/rational expectations literature are given by Mayes (1981), Maddock and Carter (1982) and Shaw (1983a). A survey of the development of thought on rational expectations is provided by Kantor (1979), whilst one of the most authoritative reviews of the literature up to its year of publication is given in Gordon (1976). A number of texts on expectations have now been published, the most easily accessible and digestible being Shaw (1983a), and a more advanced treatment in Maddock and Carter (1985) and Attfield, Demery and Duck (1985). Notable volumes of collected readings are Fischer (1980), Lucas and Sargent (1981) and Lucas (1981). Fischer (1980) is a collection of papers covering theoretical and empirical aspects of expectations and stabilization policy; Lucas and Sargent (1981) concentrates on econometric applications and problems with rational expectations; and Lucas (1981) provides a collection of the author's papers on the subject. Finally a masterful, non-technical overview of the development of thought on expectations in a macroeconomic context is given by Laidler (1986).

14

Internal and External Balance

The closed economy system (whether Keynesian or neo-classical) is undoubtedly a valuable framework for analytical purposes. Clearly, however, it has one very obvious shortcoming, namely that *autarky* (that is no trade) is as likely to exist as perfect competition. In other words, countries engage in the process of international specialization and exchange – or more accurately, individuals exchange across national frontiers. Once allowance is made for a traded goods sector, a link is provided between the erstwhile closed economy and the rest of the world, a link through which economic impulses may be transmitted.

The extent to which the traded goods sector influences the domestic economy depends of course on the size of that sector relative to total output. For example, exports and imports account for around 30 per cent of GNP in the UK, whereas for the USA the figure is closer to 10 per cent. Other things being equal, therefore, economic activity in the UK would be expected to be more susceptible to external influences than in the USA.[1]

In this and the following chapter the models will be extended to allow for a foreign trade sector, whilst their relevance to UK experience will be evaluated in chapter 20. Initially some basic principles of exchange rate determination and balance of payments accounting will be reviewed. Following this, the external sector will be integrated into the *IS/LM* framework. The role of domestic expenditure policies on external balance will be examined, and finally demand management policies and exchange rate regimes will be analysed.

The Foreign Exchange Market

In order to participate in international exchange, individuals, corporate bodies and governmental agencies must have access to internationally

---

1 Other things are, however, rarely equal. In the present context, although the ratio of traded goods to GNP may be relatively low in the USA, in evaluating 'openness' the special role of the dollar as a key currency in the international monetary system would have to be borne in mind.

acceptable media of exchange. This may involve the acquisition of some generally acceptable asset (like gold or the US dollar), or it may involve the acquisition of the currency of the country with which one is trading. Either way a mechanism for the conversion of domestic currency is necessary. This mechanism is of course the *foreign exchange market*.

In this market, a demand for (supply of) foreign exchange (domestic currency) will be generated by importers, whilst a supply of (demand for) foreign exchange (domestic currency) will be provided by exporters.

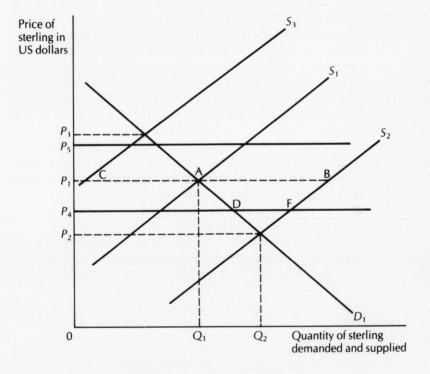

Figure 14.1 Exchange rate determination

Take for example the case illustrated in figure 14.1. Here a two-country world is assumed, the trading partners being the UK and USA. 'Foreign exchange' from the UK's standpoint refers therefore to dollars. D_1 and S_1 are the demand for and supply of sterling respectively. Both are expressed as a function of the price of sterling in terms of dollars, or the *nominal exchange rate*[2].

It is clear from the slope of the curves that the volume of sterling supplied per period is positively related to its dollar price, while sterling demand is inversely related to price. As the dollar price of sterling rises, the home currency price of imports will fall, the ensuing expansion in the demand for imports resulting in an increased supply of sterling. A rise in the dollar price of sterling would however raise the dollar price of exports, stimulate a contraction in the demand for exports, and hence a contraction in the demand for sterling.[3]

Where demand and supply intersect the market clearing exchange rate is established, in this case at P_1. As in any other market, this price will alter with shifts in demand and supply, assuming there is no intervention on the part of the monetary authorities. If for instance an increase in real incomes in the UK stimulates an autonomous increase in the demand for imports, S_1 would shift to S_2. At the initial exchange rate, there is clearly excess supply and price falls from P_1 to P_2 to clear the market. The same analysis would apply *mutatis mutandis* if the initial disturbance were a fall in real incomes in the UK.

In principle, therefore, if the exchange rate is permitted to float freely there will be an automatic tendency towards a market clearing price. Adjustment to any autonomous shifts in the underlying import and export functions will be continuous. In reality of course exchange rates are rarely permitted to float freely. Frequently the monetary authorities view a particular value, or range of values, of the exchange rate as a policy target.

At one extreme the exchange rate could be fixed, for example at P_1 in figure 14.1. Under these circumstances no *appreciation* (that is, increase in

---

2 The analysis is conducted entirely by reference to the *nominal exchange rate*, that is, the spot price of a currency in the foreign exchange market. Note, however, that in evaluating exchange rate movements through time much greater emphasis is placed on the *real exchange rate*, and the *effective exchange rate*. The real exchange rate is the nominal exchange rate adjusted for changes in price levels. The effective exchange rate is a trade weighted exchange rate, which is therefore more responsive to movements in the exchange rates of major trading partners compared with relatively minor trading partners. It is also possible to have a *real effective exchange rate*.

3 It is possible for the supply curve to be inversely related to the nominal exchange rate: this occurs when the home demand for imports is price inelastic. Given this condition, as the home currency price of imports rises, demand contracts less than in proportion to the price rise, and the volume of home currency on the market actually increases. For further analysis see Milner and Greenaway (1979, chapter 6).

price) or *depreciation* (decrease in price) would be permitted and the price of P_1 would be defended by official intervention. Thus in the event of a shift in supply from S_1 to S_2, rather than allow the exchange rate to depreciate to P_2 the authorities would soak up the excess supply by entering the foreign exchange market and purchasing AB of sterling, paying for this with holdings of dollars. In the event of a shift in supply to S_3, the opposite action would be taken. Instead of permitting the exchange rate to appreciate to P_3, the authorities would supply AC of sterling and acquire an equivalent volume of dollars, which would be added to their foreign exchange reserves.

Between these extremes of complete fixity and complete floating, there are many shades of flexibility which require varying degrees of management. For instance, the exchange rate may be maintained within preset bands, such as $P_4 P_5$. Intervention would then only occur when the rate threatened to fall below P_4 or rise above P_5. Management within pre-defined limits is a feature of many exchange rate systems, the European Monetary System being a good example.

The Balance of Payments

The balance of payments of a country is a systematic record of that country's international transactions. Abstracting from timing complications, it can be stated that the balance of payments will provide a monetary record of activities in the foreign exchange market over a given period.

Accounting conventions vary considerably from country to country (see Veil, 1975). Broadly speaking, however, three groups of transactions can be identified, namely *current transactions, capital transactions* and *balancing transactions*. The items which would typically be included in these accounts are listed in table 14.1. Note that the balance of payments is a systematic record of the value of the various transactions which a given country conducts with the rest of the world over a given period (usually one year). Thus when a balance of payments deficit or surplus is reported it is the nominal value of the imbalance which is reported, and indeed it is this magnitude which is important from a policy standpoint. In this respect the balance of payments is unambiguously a monetary phenomenon.

Whether the balance of payments is in surplus or deficit depends on whether the value of *credit* items in the current and capital accounts exceeds the value of *debit* items. Another way of stating this would be to say that it depends on whether *autonomous credits* exceed or fall short of *autonomous debits*. In stating it thus, it is assumed that all transactions recorded in the current and capital accounts are autonomous. This is not an uncontroversial assumption. As will be seen, there are occasions when monetary

TABLE 14.1
A Schematic Representation of the Balance of Payments

Credit	Debit
Current transactions	
Visible exports	Visible imports
Invisible exports	Invisible imports
Unilateral receipts	Unilateral payments
Capital transactions	
Official long-term inflows	Official long-term outflows
Official short-term inflows	Official short-term outflows
Private long-term inflows	Private long-term outflows
Private short-term inflows	Private short-term outflows
Balancing transactions	
Fall in official reserves	Increase in official reserves
Official foreign currency	Official foreign currency
borrowing	lending

policy is used deliberately to influence short-term capital flows.[4] Frequently, for instance, nominal interest rates are raised to relatively high levels in deficit countries, in order to attract short-term capital flows. Since these transactions are policy induced it becomes difficult to draw the line between autonomous and *accommodating transactions*. For the purposes of this discussion this complication will be ignored (for the present anyway) such that we can classify all transactions in the balancing account as accommodating transactions.

The balancing account is, quite literally, those transactions which make the balance of payments balance. Clearly if a country runs a net deficit on current and capital accounts, this implies indebtedness to its trading partners. This indebtedness would be settled by accommodating payments. In this case foreign exchange reserves would be disbursed. Thus a deficit (surplus) on current and capital accounts will be matched by an equal reserve outflow (inflow) in the balancing account. Thus, although in an accounting sense the balance of payments will always balance, the overall deficit or surplus situation will be reflected in the volume (and sign) of accommodating finance.

In figure 14.1 it can be seen that *in principle* payments imbalance will only arise when there is some degree of exchange rate management. In the example where the exchange rate is held at P_1 following a shift in supply

---

4 These flows are potentially enormous. At the time of writing the daily volume of short-term mobile capital on the foreign exchange markets is around $150 billion.

from S_1 to S_2, the distance AB gives an indication of the volume of accommodating finance, and of the magnitude of the balance of payments deficit. If instead of being fixed the exchange rate were maintained in the band P_4P_5, it would depreciate to P_4 and the resultant deficit would be DF rather than AB. If the exchange rate were free to float, abstracting from the problem of lags, it would depreciate to P_2 and no deficit would emerge.

From this relatively simple analysis *external balance* can therefore be identified as being a situation where there is a *net balance of zero on current and capital accounts*. In practice of course external balance may be rather more difficult to identify, in part due to difficulties associated with defining a time scale over which the accounts would be expected to balance, and in part because it necessitates some judgement about the relationship of external balance to internal balance. (This issue will be considered in greater detail when the UK balance of payments is analysed in chapter 20.) Using these definitions of the balance of payments and the exchange rate, we will now proceed to evaluate the implications of allowing for an external sector in our income determination models.

The Foreign Trade Sector and the Income Multiplier

Within the context of a simple IS/LM income determination model, exports are an injection into the system whilst imports are a withdrawal. The condition for equilibrium in the goods market within such a model is therefore revised to:

$$I + G + X = S + T + Z \tag{14.1}$$

where X and Z refer to *real* exports and *real* imports respectively. In the simplest models, real exports of goods and services would be regarded as exogenous (being determined by disposable income overseas) whilst real imports are positively related to the level of income:

$$X = \bar{X} \tag{14.2}$$

$$Z = zY \tag{14.3}$$

Substitution of equations 14.2 and 14.3 into equation 14.1 gives the equilibrium condition rewritten as:

$$\bar{I} + \bar{G} + \bar{X} = s(Yd) + t(Y) + z(Y) \tag{14.4}$$

Casual inspection of equation 14.4 reveals the first important implication of including a traded goods sector in a Keynesian IS/LM model, namely that the value of the multiplier changes. Specifically a further leakage from the system has been included. Thus the multiplier of chapter 4 is extended to:

$$dY = \frac{1}{s(1 - t) + t + z} \, dI + dC + dG \tag{14.5}$$

where s and t are, as before, the marginal propensity to save and the marginal tax rate, whilst z is the *marginal propensity to import*.

Clearly,

$$\frac{1}{s(1 - t) + t + z} < \frac{1}{s(1 - t) + t} < \frac{1}{s} \tag{14.6}$$

In the same way as the inclusion of a government sector introduced an additional leakage which reduced the value of the multiplier, the inclusion of an overseas sector does likewise. The apparent simplicity of this result should not detract from its importance. Within a Keynesian framework, it has a significant impact on policy prescriptions. Clearly if one is recommending a strategy founded on demand reflation, the implications of any injection of import demand have to be carefully considered. In an economy like the UK, for example, there have been occasions when the marginal propensity to import has been as high as 0.6 – that is to say, some 60 per cent of increased expenditure 'leaked' overseas. Such a situation is only sustainable in the short run and ultimately imposes a (balance of payments) constraint on expansion. This interpretation of the relationship between income expansion and the balance of payments has led one influential group to argue for general import controls to prevent additional expenditure from demand reflation in the UK from leaking overseas (see Cambridge Economic Policy Review, 1981). It is also this consideration which leads some commentators to prefer fiscal expansion via increased government expenditure, rather than via cuts in direct taxes.

It should be noted, however, that one important shortcoming of this simple multiplier model (and indeed policy prescriptions which follow from it) is that in a two-country or multicountry system exports of all countries are endogenized. There are therefore *respending effects* which must be considered – increased import demand generates income overseas, and ultimately increased demand for home exports. None the less, it generally remains true that the country initiating an income expansion will experience a worsening of its trade account despite an element of respending from abroad. This must follow when the overseas marginal propensity to import is less than one since under these circumstances only a fraction of the increase in income is respent. (For a formal demonstration of this point see Peacock and Shaw, 1976, pp. 48–9). For the moment respending will be ignored; the simplest possible case will be used to explore more fully the relationship between imports, exports and the level of income.

It must be emphasized that the simple income multiplier model deals with *real exports* and *real imports*. For policy purposes, however, it is the *value of exports relative to the value of imports,* measured in a common currency, which is the object of interest. In the event that, for a given level of real income, the value of exports (imports) exceeds the value of imports (exports) a balance of payments surplus (deficit) will be recorded. As will be seen in the next chapter, this apparent dichotomy between real and nominal exports and imports resulted, in the judgement of many neo-classical economists, in neglect of the monetary implications of the balance of payments. For the moment it must be remembered that in discussing balance of payments imbalance the magnitude is nominal.

Another, equally important, feature of this model which also may not be immediately obvious is that it only includes current transactions, that is, imports of goods and services which would be recorded in the current account of table 14.1. As will shortly be seen, this imposes important limitations on the policy conclusions of the model. However, although the simple income multiplier approach is restrictive, a number of interesting insights can be developed from it.

In the upper panel of figure 14.2, equality between the value of

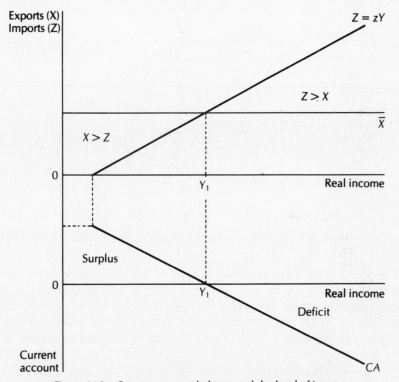

Figure 14.2   Current account balance and the level of income

exports and the value of imports is associated with a unique level of real income Y_1. Income levels below (above) Y_1 result in an excess of exports (imports) over imports (exports). This information permits the derivation of a current account schedule in the lower panel (CA). The CA schedule is negatively related to the level of income, indicating that other things being equal (in particular the exchange rate), increases (decreases) in the level of real income will result in a tendency towards a deficit (surplus) on the current account. The slope of this schedule is determined by the marginal propensity to import, higher values being associated with steeper CAs.

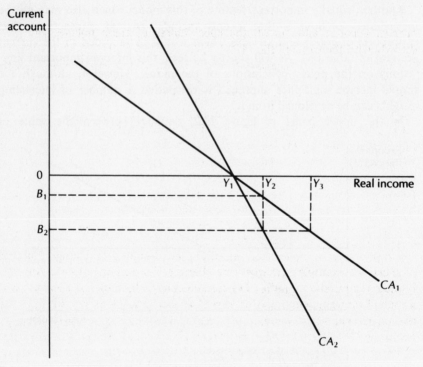

Figure 14.3 Current account imbalance and import propensity

Figure 14.3 therefore presents diagrammatically the deductions made above with respect to the marginal propensity to import (MPM) and the foreign trade multiplier. The higher the value of the MPM (the steeper the CA schedule), the larger the potential current account deficit associated with a given income expansion. Compare for example the deficits associated with CA_1 and CA_2 in figure 14.3 as income increases from Y_1 to Y_2. It can also be noted parenthetically that if income reducing policies are employed for

TABLE 14.2
Effects of Sterling Devaluation on UK Import and Export Prices

Before devaluation	After devaluation
£1 = $2.80 $1 = 35.7p	£1 = $2.40 $1 = 41.7p
$100 of US exports sells in UK at domestic price of £35.70p	$100 of US exports sells in UK at domestic price of £41.70p
£100 of UK exports sells in US at domestic price of $280	£100 of UK exports sells in US at domestic price of $240

current account adjustment, the effectiveness of these policies will vary directly with the value of the MPM. Refer again to figure 14.3 and compare the income reduction necessary to remove a payments deficit of B_2. Because of the lower MPM, a greater reduction in real income (from Y_3 to Y_1) is necessary for CA_1 than for CA_2 (from Y_2 to Y_1).

The CA schedule, which for present purposes can be taken as the analogue of the current account in table 14.1, is drawn simply as a function of the level of real income. In this respect it fits well in a Keynesian framework. It is of course constructed on *ceteris paribus* assumptions, and any given schedule could shift for a variety of reasons, in particular as a consequence of changes in the prices of domestic goods and services *relative* to goods and services produced abroad. Thus a general improvement in the competitiveness of domestically produced goods and services would shift CA to the right, facilitating payments balance at a higher income level.

Certain specific policy actions might be designed to change competitiveness, for example exchange rate changes. An exchange rate *devaluation* reduces the number of units of foreign currency which can be obtained with a unit of domestic currency (or looked at from the other side of the transaction, increases the number of units of domestic currency which must exchange for a unit of foreign currency). If these changes are translated into changes in the final prices of goods and services,[5] the domestic currency price of imports rises relative to import substitutes and the foreign currency price of home produced exports falls relative to competing products. Table 14.2 illustrates the way in which final prices can be affected by the devalu-

---

5 The changes in prices of goods and services need not fully reflect the devaluation. Exporters could for example increase their profit margins by allowing the overseas price of their goods to fall by less than the devaluation. Similarly, importers could allow profit margins to be squeezed by failing to increase the domestic price fully in line with the exchange rate change.

ation. Clearly if the home demand for imports and the overseas demand for exports are price elastic, the *CA* will shift to the right as a consequence of devaluation.[6] The same analysis applies *mutatis mutandis* to revaluation, and it should be obvious that this shifts *CA* to the left.

Changes in commercial policy can also shift *CA*. So far an absence of tariffs and non-tariff barriers (such as quantitative restrictions, voluntary export restraints and export subsidies), has been assumed. There is, however, a wide range of such instruments which may be implemented in order to shift X or Z. For instance an import tariff may be imposed to encourage import substitution. This would shift *CA* to the right (assuming no retaliation). Likewise an export subsidy would shift *CA* to the right. Other less obvious instruments might be employed with the same objective, such as discriminatory government procurement policies, administrative and technical barriers to trade and so on. Instruments like these have become increasingly common with the growth of the new protectionism in the 1970s (see Greenaway, 1983).

The *CA* schedule can be combined with the *IS* and *LM* curves to consider the interrelationships between external balance (as given by zero imbalance on the current account) and internal balance (as given by the intersection of the *IS* and *LM* schedules at the full employment level of income). In defining internal balance in this way, it may at first appear as if a retrograde step is being taken, given the discussion of the *IS/LM* framework and the analysis of expectations in the previous chapters. These limitations still apply. In the same way as the *IS/LM* framework proved useful for analytical purposes in the closed economy context, it has its uses here. Its limitations in the open economy context will be considered further in the next chapter.

---

6 For a devaluation (revaluation) to improve (worsen) the current account balance, the well-known Marshall–Lerner condition should hold, namely:

$$\sum dx + dm > 1$$

That is, the domestic price elasticity of demand for imports (dm) and the foreign price elasticity of demand for exports ($d\chi$) should sum to greater than unity. If they sum to less than unity, because the home demand for imports and the foreign demand for exports are price inelastic over the relevant range, the trade balance actually worsens following devaluation. It is not unusual to find that in the short run the condition does not hold as agents take time to adjust to relative price changes. This can give rise to the so-called 'J-curve' effect of a devaluation. Immediately following the devaluation the current account deficit deteriorates, then as agents react to price changes in the longer run it improves.

Internal and External (Current Account) Balance

The *IS/LM* framework requires only minor modification to accomodate exports and imports. To see this refer back to figure 10.2 where we derived the *IS* schedule with a government sector and taxation. Government expenditure was treated as exogenous and was incorporated into the model by way of a horizontal displacement of the *ID* function in quadrant (a). Since, as we can see from equation 14.2 we treat exports as exogenous, we can incorporate them into the model in exactly the same way. Other things being equal, a given amount of exports will displace *ID + G* to the right in quadrant (a), and therefore cause a rightward shift in the *IS* schedule (without affecting its slope). Because taxes were a function of income, we found in figure 10.2 that the inclusion of taxes into the model caused the savings function to rotate to the left. We now know from equation 14.3 that imports too are a function of income and can be incorporated into the model in the same way as taxes were. Inclusion of imports therefore causes the *S + T* function of quadrant (c) in figure 10.2 to rotate to the left. Other things being equal, this will result in the *IS* curve being steeper over the relevant range. In the remainder of this chapter we will assume that these adjustments are incorporated in the *IS* schedule.

In figure 14.4 simultaneous internal and external balance as defined above, or *twin balance,* could be achieved if the relevant schedules were IS_1, LM_1 and CA_1. The internal target of full employment (and price stability) is ensured by the intersection of IS_1 and LM_1 at Y_F whilst the external target of a zero trade balance is guaranteed by the intersection of CA_1 with the Y axis at Y_F.

Suppose, however, the relevant trade balance schedule were CA_2 such that at Y_F a trade deficit of $0B_1$ is recorded. There is internal balance but external imbalance, and if it is assumed that financing options have been exercised (that is, the country has run out of foreign exchange reserves and cannot borrow) the deficit has to be eliminated – *adjustment* must take place.

Adjustment action could be taken via *expenditure changing policies* and/or *expenditure switching policies* (Johnson, 1958). In the case of the former, policy would be directed at altering domestic expenditure in order to influence import demand; in the case of the latter, policy would aim to induce domestic residents and overseas residents to switch demand from overseas goods to domestically produced goods. Common expenditure switching policies are exchange rate changes and tariff/non-tariff interventions.

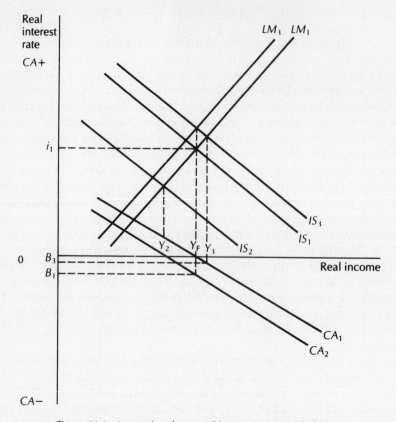

Figure 14.4   Internal and external (current account) balance

Within the context of figure 14.4, devaluation would raise the home currency price of imports whilst lowering the foreign currency price of exports. The resultant expenditure switches would push CA_2 to the right. It might appear that the required devaluation ought to displace CA_2 until it coincides with CA_1. Such a deduction would, however, be erroneous since it ignores the impact which exchange rate adjustments have on the goods market. If devaluation stimulates an increased demand for import substitutes and exports, IS_1 will be pushed to the right, increasing the income level to $Y_3 > Y_F$. Clearly, if twin balance is to be achieved, the devaluation has to be accompanied by policy action directed at reducing domestic expenditure at home, policy which would for instance shift LM_1 to LM_3. Ideally this expenditure reduction would *precede* the exchange rate adjustment, thereby creating excess capacity which will accommodate the secondary income effects caused by the devaluation induced shift of IS.

The analysis of figure 14.4 is of course a simple piece of comparative statics which abstracts from certain fundamentally important complications, like identification lags and reaction lags. It nevertheless serves to bring out an important principle of policy implementation, namely the *Tinbergen principle*. This asserts that if the relevant objective function embodies a number of targets, the number of independent instruments at the policy-maker's disposal should be at least as great as the number of objectives. Within the present context it can be seen that the application of one instrument (the exchange rate) to meet two targets simultaneously (internal and external balance) results in neither being met. As with any other rule there are exceptions, and it should be obvious from figure 14.4 that there are likely to be circumstances (under full employment and balance of trade deficit) when it may be possible to attain simultaneous internal and external balance via exchange rate adjustment only; these are so-called 'single policy' solutions.

Possible policy conflict can be highlighted within the context of figure 14.4 if it is assumed that the exchange rate is fixed, and international agreements forbid recourse to tariff and non-tariff interventions. CA_2 would therefore be fixed and external balance could only be attained by shifting IS and LM, that is through expenditure changing policies. For example fiscal contraction would shift IS_1 to IS_2. With an unchanged LM schedule external balance would be attained, but at the cost of internal balance since $Y_2 < Y_F$. Because the exchange rate is now viewed as a target rather than an instrument, the system is underdetermined in the sense that there are too few instruments for the given number of targets. As a result there is policy conflict, with current account balance acting as a constraint on the level of income which can be attained.

This scenario exercised the minds of a number of commentators in the early days of the Bretton Woods regime of pegged exchange rates (1948–71). It appeared that, because the exchange rate was fixed and the use of commercial policy instruments for balance of payments purposes proscribed under the GATT,[7] policy conflict was inevitable.

The simplest analyses of the stop–go cycle in the UK in the 1950s and 1960s can be cast within this type of framework. CA_2 was viewed as being immutably fixed because a sterling dollar exchange rate of £1 = \$2.80 was

---

7 The use of commercial policy for balance of payments reasons is not acually forbidden under GATT. Emergency action to relieve a payments deficit can be taken under Article XII.

regarded as a constraint on policy (up until 1967). Thus every time the economy appeared to expand towards its full employment level of output a current account deficit appeared. Deflationary policies designed to curb import demand and remove the deficit resulted in the level of income (and employment) falling. There seemed to be a trade-off between internal and external balance of the type depicted in figure 14.4.

Even such a simple Keynesian framework can therefore generate useful insights into policy conflict in an open economy setting. Figure 14.4 is, however, lacking in one very important respect; external balance is equated with a balanced *current account*, with the capital account being disregarded. In practice external balance is equated with zero imbalance on both current and capital account. Thus, for example, the current account deficit at Y_F in figure 14.4 could be 'covered' by a capital account surplus such that adjustment is unnecessary. As will now be seen, inclusion of the capital account alters the analysis quite radically.

Internal and External (Current and Capital Account) Balance

The policy options available for the simultaneous attainment of internal and external balance when the latter is defined to include capital transactions were rigorously analysed in a pair of classic articles by Mundell (1962, 1963). The focus here will be principally on the analysis incorporated in Mundell's 1962 paper.

This model is underpinned by a number of (essentially Keynesian) assumptions:

(1) Tax revenue and private disposable income vary directly with the level of real income.
(2) Consumption and investment expenditure vary directly with disposable income, and inversely with the rate of interest.
(3) The current account varies inversely with domestic expenditure.
(4) Money wages are constant in domestic money.
(5) Capital movements are interest sensitive.
(6) Constant terms of trade, constant productivity, a given commercial policy, and fixed exchange rates.

The targets in the model are internal balance (the equality of aggregate demand and aggregate supply at full employment) and external balance (a situation where the balance on current account equals net capital exports).

In the discussion of figure 14.4, expenditure changing policy was referred to as if it were a single policy instrument; indeed, policy conflict emerged for this very reason. Mundell argued, however, that it is crucially important to distinguish between different expenditure changing instruments, that is, monetary policy and fiscal policy, because these instruments may have a differential impact on the two targets.

In figure 14.5, fiscal policy is represented by the government budget

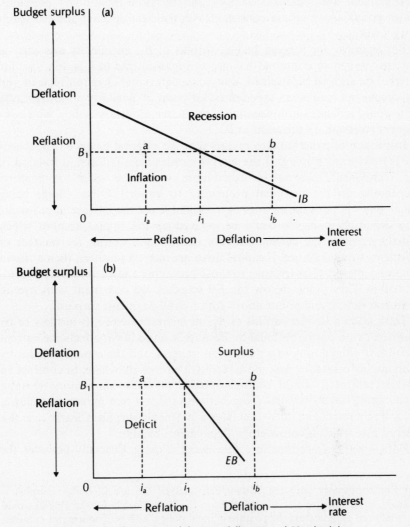

Figure 14.5   Derivation of the Mundellian *IB* and *EB* schedules

surplus[8] on the vertical axis, and monetary policy by the rate of interest on the horizontal. IB in panel (a) traces out those combinations of the budget surplus and the rate of interest which are consistent with internal balance. The schedule is downward sloping because any (reflationary) reduction in the budget surplus would have to be accompanied by a (deflationary) increase in the interest rate, otherwise aggregate demand would exceed aggregate supply. Points below IB are consistent with an excess of aggregate demand over aggregate supply, and therefore inflationary pressures, whilst points above IB are consistent with deficient demand and recessionary pressures.

For example, for a given budget surplus of B_1, an interest rate of i_1 is required to generate internal balance. An interest rate of i_a is 'too low' for internal balance to be attained, that is, monetary policy is too relaxed and inflationary pressures are experienced (at point a). Similarly an interest rate of i_b would indicate an unnecessarily restricitve monetary policy, with consequent recessionary pressures at b.

Inspection of panel (b) also reveals that the external balance (EB) schedule is downward sloping. If the budget surplus were reduced, a fraction of the consequent increase in expenditure would be spent on imports (depending on the marginal propensity to import). Other things being equal, this will push the balance of trade and hence the balance of payments into deficit. If a surplus could be induced on the capital account which exactly matched the current account deficit, then overall the balance of payments would balance. If capital flows are interest sensitive, then a rise in domestic interest rates (relative to those prevailing elsewhere) would accomplish this. Thus points below the EB schedule are consistent with overall payments deficit, and points above with overall payments surplus.

Thus, given a budget surplus of B_1, an interest rate of i_a is too low to be consistent with payments balance. Because it is too low it affects the current account by stimulating expenditure on imports, and the capital account by encouraging capital to seek more lucrative returns elsewhere. In contrast an interest rate of i_b would be high relative to one's competitors, thereby encouraging capital imports. Together with the fact that monetary policy is accordingly restrictive, this stimulates a payments surplus. Clearly i_1 is the interest rate which is consistent with payments balance.

Both schedules are therefore downward sloping. Crucially however the

---

8 For consistency with the Mundellian analysis the use of budget surplus is retained. In practice, of course, variations in the budget deficit (or the PSBR) would be monitored as indicating the posture of fiscal policy. This is of course not inconsistent with the use of the term 'budget surplus', since a budget deficit is simply a negative budget surplus.

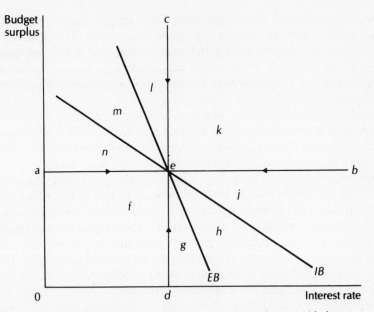

Figure 14.6   Internal and external (current and capital account) balance

EB schedule has a steeper slope. This follows from the assumption that international capital flows are interest sensitive. If both fiscal and monetary policy affected internal and external balance in precisely the same way, both schedules would have the same slope. By assumption both policies have qualitatively similar effects on internal balance but a differential impact on external balance. A change in the interest rate affects both the current account *and* the capital account of the balance of payments, whereas a change in the budget surplus only affects the current account.[9] Thus the *EB* schedule is more interest sensitive throughout its entire range than the *IB* schedule.

When the two schedules are combined as in figure 14.6 (if the schedules are linear throughout their range), there is a single unique point where twin balance is attained. If fortuitously the budget surplus and interest rate were set at levels consistent with point *e* then static equilibrium would be guaranteed and policy action unecessary. If the start were from any other point which represents some combination of internal and/or external imbalance, then some form of policy response would be in order. In a few special cases

---

9 As has been seen, modern monetary analyses emphasize the effects of changes in the budget deficit on interest rates. This indeed is one of the limitations of this analysis which will be considered shortly.

single-policy solutions are conceivable. Thus on the lines *ab* and *cd* the budget surplus and the interest rate are always at the 'desired' level, and twin balance is achieved simply by manipulating one of the instruments. The more usual case, however, would commence from a point in one of the segments labelled $f \rightarrow n$, and here manipulation of both policy instruments is necessary.

Mundell argued that from wherever one commences, it is possible to achieve both internal and external balance if one follows the Tinbergen rule, and if one solves the *assignment problem*. The Tinbergen rule has already been introduced. The assignment rule requires that each policy instrument should be assigned to the policy target on which it exerts the greatest impact. In the present model, both instruments have a similar effect on the trade balance (via changes in domestic expenditure). Monetary policy, however, has a relatively greater impact on the capital account because of the interest sensitivity of capital. Overall, therefore, monetary policy has a relatively greater impact on external balance and should be assigned to this target, whilst fiscal policy is assigned to internal balance.

Figure 14.7 illustrates the assignment problem more fully. Suppose the starting-point is *a*, where full employment is associated with a balance of

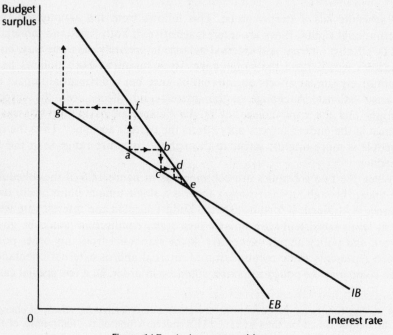

Figure 14.7   Assignment problem

payments deficit. If monetary policy is assigned to external balance, an increase in the interest rate deflates the level of income, reduces import demand and attracts a capital inflow. If the interest rate is raised sufficiently the result is point *b*, where the deficit is completely eliminated. The deflationary increase in the interest rate has, however, lowered income and employment and there has been a movement away from internal balance. To reattain full employment the budget surplus is reduced and there is movement from point *b* to point *c*. The reflationary fiscal expansion, however, disturbs external balance by attracting additional imports (given a positive marginal propensity to import). Note however that the deficit at *c* is smaller than the deficit at *a*. Another increase in the interest rate gives movement towards *d*, and further manipulation of monetary and fiscal policy ensures convergence on point *e*. If for some reason the policy instruments are misassigned, the result is divergence rather than convergence. Thus if fiscal policy is initially assigned to external balance there is a shift from *a* towards *f*. When monetary policy is used to remove the resultant unemployment there is movement from *f* towards *g*. Clearly, the movement is away from rather than towards *e*.

The analysis contends that twin balance can be attained from any disequilibrium point by judicious assignment of fiscal and monetary policy. As long as these policies are correctly assigned, even if they are apparently conflicting (with one being reflationary and one deflationary), the system will be stable and convergent progress to equilibrium is possible. Table 14.3 summarizes the combinations of fiscal and monetary policy which would be required for disequilibrium points in segments *f* through *n*, mapped out in figure 14.6.

This rather neat piece of comparative statics can also be conducted within the *IS/LM* framework, as was done when external balance was

TABLE 14.3
Policy Summary for Disequilibrium Points of Figure 14.6

Segment	Internal balance	External balance	Change in budget surplus	Change in i
f	Inflation	Deficit	+	+
g	Inflation	Deficit	+	+
h	Inflation	Surplus	+	−
j	Unemployment	Surplus	−	−
k	Unemployment	Surplus	−	−
l	Unemployment	Surplus	−	−
m	Unemployment	Deficit	−	+
n	Inflation	Deficit	+	+

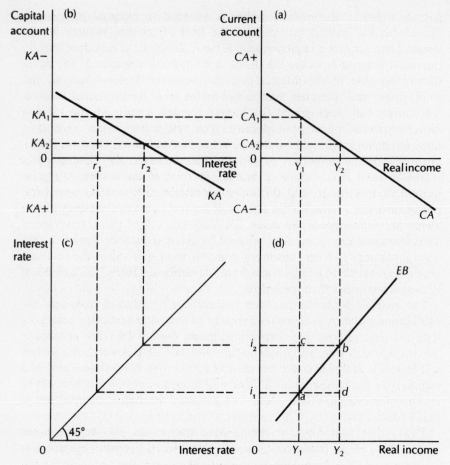

Figure 14.8   Derivation of the *EB* schedule

equated with a balanced current account. To do so, an external balance schedule has to be derived, where *EB* is a function of the rate of interest and the level of real income. This is done in figure 14.8. In quadrant (a) is reproduced the *CA* schedule, which was derived in figure 14.2. Quadrant (b) introduces a capital account schedule (*KA*) which is shown to be a function of the interest rate (or more accurately the domestic interest rate relative to that prevailing overseas). Note that capital account deficits are measured in the upper part of the diagram, capital account surpluses in the lower part. In this way the extent of any capital account deficit (surplus) which is required to cover fully a given current account surplus (deficit) can immediately be identified.

If for example the level of income is Y_1, a current account surplus of CA_1 would emerge. For overall payments balance this requires a capital account deficit of KA_1 which can be obtained with an interest rate of i_1. If the interest rate is taken through a transformation schedule as in quadrant (c) to transfer i from the horizontal to the vertical axis, it is found that the combination of an interest rate of i_1 and a level of real income of Y_1 generates overall payments balance; this point is a point on the EB schedule which lies somewhere in interest-rate/income space.

Consider now the higher income level of Y_2. Other things being equal, this would result in a smaller current account surplus of CA_2. To maintain overall payments balance, the capital account deficit would also have to be reduced from KA_1 to KA_2, this being accomplished by an increase in the interest rate from i_1 to i_2. If this is taken through quadrant (c) to quadrant (d), point b is another point on the EB schedule. Further changes in Y and i would result in EB emerging.

In quadrant (d) EB is positively sloped; this indicating that, if overall payments imbalance is to be maintained, increases (decreases) in the level of income which worsen (improve) the current account have to be accompanied by increases (decreases) in interest rates which improve (worsen) the capital account. Points above and to the left of EB are consistent with an overall payments surplus, whilst points below and to the right are consistent with overall payments deficit. If for example the level of income were Y_1 and the interest rate i_2, the latter would result in a capital account deficit which is smaller than the current account surplus, the result being overall payments surplus (at point c). Similarly with an income level of Y_2 and an interest rate of i_1 the capital account deficit exceeds the current account surplus, and the overall balance of payments is in deficit (at point d). The slope of the EB schedule is determined by the slopes of the CA and KA schedules. The former, as has already been seen, is determined by the marginal propensity to import. The latter is determined by the interest elasticity of capital flows. Thus, other things being equal, the higher the MPM the steeper the slope of the CA and EB schedules; the more interest elastic are capital flows, the shallower will the slopes of KA and EB be.

Having derived EB it is a simple matter to consider the adjustment process examined in figure 14.7; this is done in figure 14.9. IS_1 and LM_1 intersect at an interest rate of i_1, with income being at its full employment level Y_F. EB is however fixed at EB^*, since the exchange rate is fixed, and the balance of payments is therefore in overall deficit since point d lies below EB^*. The Mundellian solution is to assign monetary policy to the attainment of external balance and fiscal policy to the attainment of internal balance. LM_1 is shifted to LM_2, inducing an increase in the rate of interest (and a capital inflow) which reduces the payments deficit. The deflationary impact of the

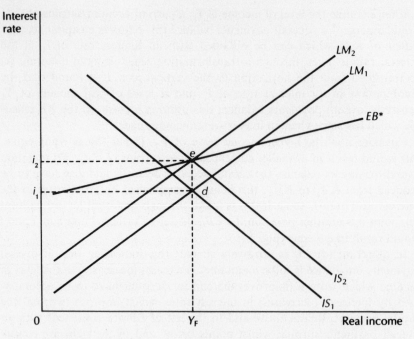

Figure 14.9   Internal and external balance in an *IS/LM* framework

policy results in a fall below the full employment level of income, however; this is countered by fiscal expansion that is, a rightward shift in *IS*. Eventually twin balance is attained at point *e* with income restored to its full employment level, and the interest rate at i_2.

The *IS/LM* framework then provides an alternative medium for outlining the Mundellian approach and can be applied to a variety of disequilibrium situations.

Limitations of the Mundellian IB/EB System

The Mundell model provides a framework within which it proved possible to derive some useful insights into the problem of simultaneously attaining internal and external balance when the exchange rate is fixed, or quasi-fixed, as it was for a very long time in the Bretton Woods system. The methodology has been frequently invoked (as will be seen in chapter 20) to explain UK attempts to achieve twin balance by financing current account deficits with capital account surpluses induced by relatively high interest rates. The approach has certainly had a lasting impact on the development of balance of payments theorizing over the last two decades. As a recipe for policy formulation, however, it suffers from a number of drawbacks which must be mentioned.

1. The policy mixing prescribed is essentially an exercise in *fine tuning*. As such it is subject to similar identification and implementation lags as other efforts at fine tuning. One might even use this as a basis for arguing that policy could be destabilizing rather than stabilizing, if circumstances have altered by the time any action has been taken.

2. It is implicitly assumed that any level of budget surplus or deficit, and any level of interest rates, is politically feasible. In practice of course political constraints invariably set upper limits on both magnitudes. In the examination of UK experience with monetary control in chapter 6 it was seen that on many occasions there has been an unwillingness to permit interest rates to reach unacceptably high levels. Likewise with the government budget. Budget surpluses generate pressures for increased expenditure; budget deficits, beyond a certain level, may likewise generate pressures for decreased expenditure.

3. A related assumption is that monetary and fiscal policies are independent instruments. As has already been seen, they are in fact interdependent; thus the scope for unambiguous assignment may be rather limited. For example in segment k of figure 14.6 the prescription would be a decreased budget surplus (or more probably an increased budget deficit) and a lower interest rate. If crowding out is important, execution of the former policy would increase interest rates, thereby frustrating the latter.

4. The model implicitly assumes that any current account deficit can be corrected by compensatory capital flows. Even if this is in principle possible, in practice the composition of capital and current account is likely to be an objective policy. In addition, the composition of aggregate demand may be an objective of policy. If the budget surplus is being altered by changes in government expenditure, then the composition of demand will be accordingly altered.

5. The most serious criticisms perhaps relate to the fact that the monetary implications of accommodating a current account deficit by attracting short-term capital inflows are largely ignored. Fausten (1981) has argued that it is possible to deduce monetary implications. The issue has, however, been rigorously addressed by recent work on the monetary approach to the balance of payments. It is also the case that the ability to conduct a completely independent monetary policy is assumed. As was indicated in

chapter 6, when the exchange rate is fixed monetary policies are interdependent rather than independent.

IS/LM Analysis with a Floating Exchange Rate

So far the exchange rate has been maintained at a fixed level, the implications of using monetary and fiscal policy to attain internal and external balance have been considered. Most of the models using this methodology concentrated principally on fixed exchange rate regimes (reflecting their period of development more than anything else). A few, however, have considered the problem within a floating exchange rate context (most notably Mundell, 1963) and indeed this is easily done. In fact all that has to be done is to permit the EB schedule to shift around in response to any tendencies towards payments imbalance, and allow for the fact that shifts in EB will induce shifts in IS and LM. For example, exchange rate depreciation in response to a payments deficit generates an increased demand for import substitutes and exports; this in turn will induce a shift in IS to the right. Figure 14.10 illustrates the process.

At the initial income level Y_1 and interest rate i_1 there is a balance of

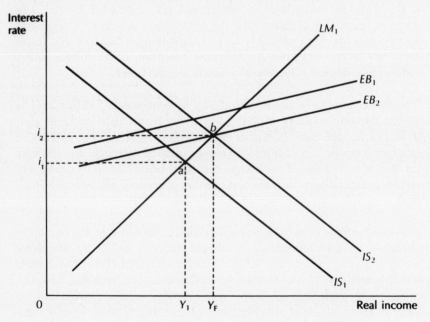

Figure 14.10   Effects of exchange rate depreciation

payments deficit. When the exchange rate is free to float it depreciates to clear the excess supply of domestic money on the foreign exchange market. EB_1 therefore shifts towards EB_2. As output and employment increase to meet the increased demand for import substitutes and exports, IS_1 shifts to IS_2 and twin balance is realized at point b. Of course the problem has been simplified by commencing from a position of less than full employment, but it should nevertheless be obvious that when the exchange rate is a policy instrument rather than a policy target, the attainment of twin balance is in principle more straightforward than when the exchange rate is fixed, simply because there is one more policy instrument at one's disposal.

Stabilization Policy Under Fixed and Flexible Exchange Rates

The final issue in this chapter is the relative effectiveness of fiscal and monetary policy under fixed and flexible exchange rates. Are there grounds for believing that fiscal policy is likely to be more effective at influencing real output than monetary policy when the exchange rate is fixed or flexible? This is an issue which papers by Fleming (1962) and Mundell (1963) addressed and, notwithstanding the earlier analysis of monetary–fiscal interdependence, it is an important facet of this present framework for analysing balance of payments problems.

This question will be considered within the Mundellian/neo-Keynesian framework already developed. Monetary policy will take the form of open market operations, fiscal policy a change in government expenditure financed by borrowing. The only additional assumption which will be invoked is that foreign exchange reserves are a form of high-powered money, and variations in foreign exchange reserves influence the domestic money stock. This is consistent with the treatment of the determinants of the money supply in chapter 6.

In figure 14.11 the effects of fiscal policy under fixed and flexible exchange rates are compared. Y_1 and i_1 are the initial income and interest rate levels. Initially, it will be assumed that the exchange rate is fixed; therefore EB_1 cannot shift. Expansionary fiscal policy is represented by a rightward shift in IS_1 to IS_2. This takes the form of an increase in government expenditure, which calls forth a multiplied increase in income and in turn an increase in the demand for transactions balances, which (with a fixed money supply) has to be met by a rundown of speculative balances. The resultant upward pressure on interest rates generates a capital inflow, a tendency to payments surplus and an accumulation of foreign exchange. The latter results in a multiplied expansion of credit and LM_1 shifts to LM_2. Ultimately, equilibrium is re-established at point b with the intersection of IS_2, LM_2 and

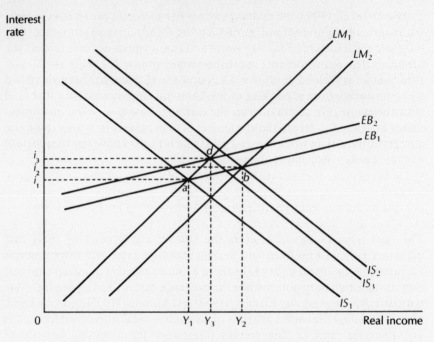

Figure 14.11   Fiscal policy under fixed and flexible exchange rates

EB_1. Both real income and the interest rate are higher than in the initial situation, at Y_2 and i_2 respectively.

Contrast this with a situation where the exchange rate is flexible. Here the same initial shift in IS_1 to IS_2 and the consequent upward pressure on the interest rate stimulates an exchange rate appreciation (that is, an upward shift in EB_1 towards EB_2). This follows because the increase in the domestic interest rate attracts a capital inflow. The resultant decreased demand for exports and import substitutes shifts IS_2 back towards IS_1. Ultimately equilibrium is established at the intersection of IS_3, EB_2 and LM_1. Income is higher than in the initial situation (Y_3 compared with Y_1) and the interest rate is higher (i_3 compared with i_1). Compared with the fixed exchange rate case, however, income is lower and the interest rate is higher (compare $i_3 Y_3$ with $i_2 Y_2$). This result follows from the fact that when the exchange rate is flexible, no reserve accumulation takes place, expanding the money supply 'by the back door'. Furthermore, because the exchange rate is flexible, exchange rate appreciation causes a reduced demand for exports and import substitutes and this chokes off some of the income expansion resulting from increased government expenditure.

Thus it seems that *the effect of fiscal policy on real output* (*and employment*) *is stronger when the exchange rate is fixed than when it is flexible.*

Figure 14.12 conducts a similar analysis for monetary policy. Take first the fixed exchange rate case. Open market operations result in an increase in the money supply which shifts LM_1 to LM_2 and pushes income towards Y_2. It should be clear, however, that the downward pressure on interest rates stimulates a capital outflow and creates a balance of payments deficit at *c*. In turn this causes a drain on the country's foreign exchange reserves and a multiplied contraction of the domestic money supply, pushing LM_2 back towards LM_1. Equilibrium would be re-established at the *initial* combination of income and the interest rate as given by i_1 and Y_1. The level of real income has been unaffected by the monetary expansion. Because of the effect of the increase in the money supply on foreign exchange resources it would seem that monetary policy is impotent in a fixed exchange rate regime.

When the exchange rate is free to float, however, the analysis is rather different. Assume the same initial shift in LM from LM_1 to LM_2, which places the same downward pressure on interest rates. On this occasion the capital outflow stimulates exchange rate depreciation. In turn this stimulates increased demand for domestically produced import substitutes and exports

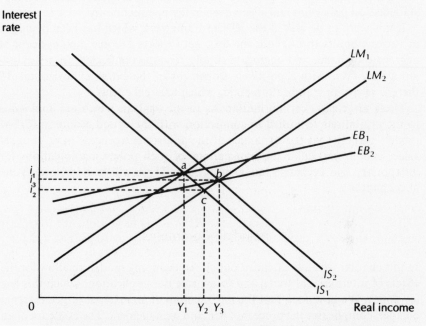

Figure 14.12   Monetary policy under fixed and flexible exchange rates

which pushes IS to the right. Eventually equilibrium is restored at point b with the intersection of LM_2, IS_2 and EB_2, the equilibrium interest rate and level of income being i_3 and Y_3.

In contrast to the case of fiscal policy then, it seems that *monetary policy is relatively more effective at changing the level of real income under flexible exchange rates than under fixed exchange rates*. Again this follows from an explicit recognition of the impact which reserve changes may have on the domestic money supply. In a world of fixed exchange rates monetary policies are interdependent and the domestic monetary authority can lose control over the domestic money supply. Permitting the exchange rate to float restores responsibility for monetary control to the central bank. This is a principle which, as will be seen in the next chapter, was formalized and stated more emphatically in the monetary approach to the balance of payments.

The conclusions of this analysis are then that the authorities can still use domestic stabilization policies to influence real output and employment even in an open economy. Its freedom of action may be constrained in so far as different instruments of financial policy may have differing degrees of potency under alternative exchange rate regimes. Nevertheless, judicious selection of policies, with greater emphasis being placed on fiscal policy if the exchange rate is fixed and monetary policy if the exchange rate is flexible, can mean that stabilization policy has real effects even in the open economy.

If this were to be cast in the AD/AS framework which has been deployed at various points throughout the text, net exports become a component of aggregate demand, and aggregate supply remains unaffected. In a Keynesian world, then, with a positively sloped (or in the extreme) horizontal AS there is scope for stabilization policy which has real effects.

There are clearly certain limitations to the analysis which are analogous to the limitations identified in connection with the closed economy IS/LM model; namely that the dynamics of the adjustment process have been set aside, and in particular the implications of such policy manipulations for inflationary and exchange rate expectations. These will be addressed in the next chapter.

Concluding Comments

In this chapter we have extended our closed economy models to allow for the effects of international trade, and to explore the implications which this has for policy. We have seen that the introduction of an external target, external balance, complicates the process of demand management. The existence of an external sector can create the potential for an external constraint on policy. When the exchange rate is fixed this constraint can, in principle, be relieved by a judicious manipulation of fiscal and monetary policy. However, the practical complications of this kind of fine-tuning may mean that it is only a useful guide to policy in the short run. When the exchange rate if flexible policy-markers appear to have an additional degree of freedom. Moreover, once the exchange rate is free to float, the relative efficacy of demand management policies may be different from what applies in a fixed rate context. Specifically, it appears that monetary policy may exert a greater impact on real output when the exchange rate is flexible than when it is fixed; by contrast, fiscal policy appears to exert a greater impact on real output when the exchange rate is fixed than when it is flexible. More recent developments with regard to flexible exchange rate models will be considered in the next chapter, whilst the relevance of these models to UK experience over the post-war period will be evaluated in chapter 20.

Further Reading

Most texts on international economics include chapters dealing with the balance of payments and the problems of simultaneously attaining internal and external balance; see for example Milner and Greenaway (1979, chapters 5 and 6) and Winters (1985, chapter 22). A thorough review of open economy macroeconomics is to be found in Rivera-Batiz and Rivera-Batiz (1985). The most rigorous and comprehensive analysis of open economy systems is that provided by Dornbusch (1980). A less rigorous but none the less useful survey of the Keynesian models is provided by Thirlwall (1980).

Mundell (1962) remains the most elegant and concise statement of the targets–instruments approach. This is well supplemented by Fleming (1962). Mundell (1963) extends the analysis to a floating exchange rate model. These and other relevant pages are reprinted in Mundell (1968).

Whitman (1970) offers a critique of the twin balance model whilst Fausten (1978) provides an interesting empirical analysis of the targets–instruments approach in the UK context.

15

Monetary Disturbances, Expectations and Exchange Rate Dynamics

If one were to summarize the view of the balance of payments taken by many Keynesian models, two features would figure prominently. First, the external sector is frequently viewed as being something which is linked to the domestic economy, but which if need be can be considered as separate for analytical purposes. Second, frequently balance of payments problems are viewed as essentially short-run problems which can be corrected by demand manipulation. In contrast much recent neo-classical work has taken a contrary stance by viewing the external sector as fully integrated with, rather than simply linked to, the domestic economy, and has viewed the balance of payments as a long-term policy problem.[1] Methodologically this has resulted in models of the balance of payments which emphasize these interdependencies to a greater extent and focus in particular on the monetary consequences of payments imbalance.

This chapter will examine in some detail recent work on the monetary approach to balance of payments analysis, as well as the implications of formally allowing for expectations in a floating exchange rate world. Prior to this, however, the *absorption approach* will be examined; as well as being the intellectual precursor to the monetary approach, this provides a bridge between neo-Keynesian and monetary (or neo-classical) analyses.

The Absorption Approach to the Balance of Payments

The absorption approach is the name given to a set of ideas about the balance of payments associated with the work of Meade, Alexander and Mundell, which was given most coherent expression in a classic paper by Johnson (1958). The approach is of interest because, by viewing the balance of payments as an economic aggregate rather than a subsector, it naturally

---

1 This applies not only to neo-classical/monetary approaches' but also to some approaches which claim to be neo-Keynesian, such as the views associated with the Cambridge Economic Policy Group.

tended towards a general equilibrium analysis of balance of payments imbalance. In addition, many of the ideas inherent in the absorption approach were subsequently refined into the monetary approach to payments imbalance.

If the familiar national income identity is taken,

$$Y = C + I + G + (X - Z) \tag{15.1}$$

and domestic expenditure $C + I + G$ is relabelled *absorption* A and, $X - Z$ payments balance B, then

$$Y = A + B$$

or

$$B = Y - A \tag{15.2}$$

such that

$$B \gtreqless 0 \quad \text{as } Y \gtreqless A \tag{15.3}$$

In other words, payments imbalance is the outcome of over- or under-absorption. If absorption exceeds income the result will be a balance of payments deficit; if absorption falls short of income then a balance of payments surplus results. The magnitude of absorption relative to income is determined by real factors like the average and marginal propensities to import, save and consume. Other things being equal, a relatively high average propensity to save would tend to result in a tendency towards under-absorption and therefore payments surplus. Likewise high consumption propensities in general and relatively high propensities to import in particular would generate a tendency to over-absorption and payments deficit. In this respect the approach has a distinctly Keynesian ring to it. As was seen in the last chapter, for example, a relatively high marginal propensity to import means that, commencing from a situation of payments balance, an increase in income generates a payments deficit. Likewise, within a Keynesian framework a loss of competitiveness could be seen as a source of rising import propensities and therefore a source of payments imbalance.

The absorption approach diverges from the standard Keynesian analyses, however, in a number of important respects. First of all it suggests that there are likely to be certain automatic adjustments associated with payments imbalance which, if allowed to operate, will mean that imbalance may be entirely self-correcting rather than necessitating (discretionary) policy action. Thus, the simple Keynesian income multiplier model and the Mundell (fixed exchange rate) IB/EB models assume that payments imbalance results from relative prices being out of line, and the imbalance will remain unless some discretionary action is taken to adjust or accommodate the imbalance. The absorption approach suggests that a *cash balance mechanism* may be operative which sets in motion certain automatic adjustment forces. The second distinctive difference is that the absorption approach suggests that even if policy action is taken (such as devaluation) it need not necessarily follow that such policy action will be successful, even when elasticities are appropriate (a possibility which was raised within the Mundellian framework but not fully analysed).

Cash Balance Adjustment in the Absorption Approach

Consider first the central role played by cash balance adjustments. In the event of a balance of payments deficit, for example, absorption exceeds income and therefore individuals and corporate bodies would find that cash balances were being depleted. This follows because cash balances must be leaking overseas via the balance of payments. Johnson (1958) argued that this cannot continue indefinitely if the money supply is fixed. There will come a point when the cash balances of corporate bodies and individuals will reach some minimum desired level. In order to maintain them at that level, expenditure has to decrease, that is absorption falls as savings increase. If this tendency is permitted to occur, the inequality between A and Y which was the original source of the deficit will ultimately be removed. Of course, if cash balances are continually replenished by the monetary authorities, that is to say if they allow the money supply to increase to accommodate the over-absorption, then any tendency to self-correction is frustrated. In terms of the IS/LM framework the process of adjustment can be illustrated by reference to figure 15.1. With an interest rate of i_1 and a level of real income of Y_1, a balance of payments deficit is being run at point a. Assuming the exchange rate is fixed, and the authorities maintain the nominal value of the domestic money stock constant, expenditure leaks overseas and depletes cash balances. In an attempt to maintain the real value of cash balances speculative balances are run down, putting upward pressure on interest rates. This results in a tendency towards capital account improvement. Simultaneously the loss of high-powered money through foreign exchange decumulation drives LM_1 towards LM_2, with payments balance being achieved at point b. Thus as long as the monetary authorities refrain from replenishing cash balances, adjustment will be automatic.

This cash balance mechanism is an important feature of the monetary approach since it directs attention towards some of the monetary implications of imbalance. This relationship was developed further by the monetary approach, and a final assessment of the mechanism will be deferred until discussion of the monetary approach.

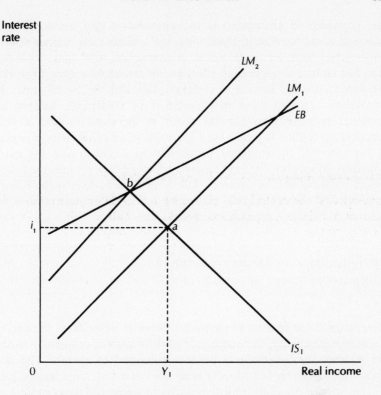

Figure 15.1   Cash balance adjustment in the absorption approach

Exchange Rate Adjustment in the Absorption Approach

Consider now a second contribution made by the absorption approach, namely the possibility that policy action may fail to eliminate payments imbalance. Prior to the absorption approach it had been assumed that, if import and export demand elasticities were appropriate, exchange rate devaluation would successfully eliminate a payments deficit. The absorption approach made it clear that this need not be so. The reasoning behind this is as follows.

Payments deficit results from over-absorption. The aim of a devaluation would be to reduce absorption relative to income. Given that

$$B = Y - A \tag{15.4}$$

taking first differences, a successful devaluation requires

$$\Delta B = \Delta Y - \Delta A \tag{15.5}$$

The increment to absorption is the outcome of two forces, an indirect income-induced increase in absorption and a direct cash balance effect. The former arises because, as was noted in connection with figure 14.4, devaluation has an income increasing effect as idle resources are put to work. It is this which accounts for the post-devaluation shift in the *IS* curve. But a devaluation can also result in an increase in absorption. As long as the 'marginal propensity to absorb' *a* out of increased income is positive, increased absorption is generated. (The value of this parameter is dependent on the value of the marginal propensity to consume and the marginal propensity to invest.) The cash balance effect *g* arises because the real value of cash balances will be squeezed following devaluation (as the home currency price of tradeables rises), and some reduction in absorption will take place in an attempt to maintain their real value. Thus

$$\Delta A = a\Delta Y - g \tag{15.6}$$

Substituting equation 15.6 into equation 15.5,

$$\Delta B = \Delta Y - (a\Delta Y - g)$$
$$= (1 - a)\Delta Y + g \tag{15.7}$$

The change in the balance of payments therefore depends on the magnitude of any income change, the magnitude of the marginal propensity to absorb, and whether the cash balance effect is permitted to operate. The latter is taken first, since this has already been considered at some length. Devaluation raises the prices of tradeable goods in home currency; as long as the nominal money stock remains fixed, there will be a reduction in the real value of cash balances. If their real value is to be maintained, absorption will be reduced. If the monetary authorities permit the money supply to increase following the devaluation, this mechanism is frustrated. This is an important consideration in practice. Other things being equal, a devaluation results in a cut in real incomes. If there is downward wage inflexibility (for any of the reasons discussed in chapters 7 and 13) there may be an unwillingness to accept the cuts associated with devaluation. Money wage demands might therefore increase and (if firms price on a cost plus basis) prices may follow, negating in part the effect of the devaluation. If this does occur then either unemployment results or the monetary authorities accommodate the process by allowing the money supply to increase.

The magnitude of the income change depends on the extent of any 'idle resources', that is, the amount of spare capacity. Income can only be generated if devaluation results in an expansion of the export and import substitute sectors; the latter can only be facilitated by the presence of idle resources. If for example a deficit country devalues whilst at full employment there would be little opportunity for the income effect to operate. A

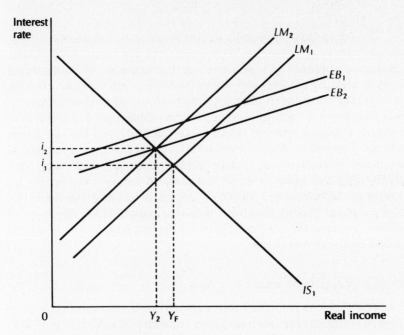

Figure 15.2   Devaluation without an idle resources effect

possible outcome is described by figure 15.2. Initially with an income level
of Y_F and a rate of interest of i_1 there is a balance of payments deficit.
Devaluation shifts EB_1 to EB_2. As a result of the increase in the price of
traded goods and the squeeze on cash balances, the real value of the money
supply falls and LM shifts to the left from LM_1 to LM_2. Payments balance is
ultimately attained at i_2Y_2. The move to payments balance is entirely
accomplished by direct disabsorption. Although there is payments balance
it occurs at less than the full employment level of income.

Clearly the absorption approach has certain kindred features with the
internal–external balance approach discussed in the previous chapter. After
all, the latter approach also pointed to the problems of taking policy action
to adjust to payments imbalance at full employment. Furthermore, it also
pointed to the impact which reserve accumulation/decumulation could have
on the domestic money stock. The innovatory features of the absorption
approach are in its emphasis on interdependencies between domestic
economic aggregates and payments imbalance, and its more explicit consideration of some of the monetary consequences of payments imbalance, via the
cash balance effect. Both themes are picked up and refined in the monetary
approach.

The Monetary Approach to the Balance of Payments

The monetary approach can be viewed as the extension of many closed economy monetarist precepts and principles to the open economy; indeed, theorizing along these lines is often described as 'international monetarism'.

The monetary approach is a generic term applied to a collection of models and empirical analyses which have emerged over the last fifteen years or so. There is no definitive monetary approach, rather a number of models/theories which share certain kindred features. It is these distinguishing features which will be concentrated on in building up an impression of the monetary approach. Concern is less with the characteristics of particular models than with the contribution which this body of thought has made to the analysis of external balance and the role of stabilization and exchange rate policy.

A Stylized Model of the Monetary Approach

The monetary approach to the balance of payments commences from the tautological statement that all transactions recorded in the balance of payments accounts are essentially reflections of monetary phenomena. Rather than focusing on the transactions themselves or any subgroup thereof (such as the current account or capital account), the monetary approach focuses on the role of adjustments in the money market in generating and sustaining imbalance. Thus the analysis of any change, whether policy-induced or not, commences from an analysis of how this change affects money market equilibrium. Another way of stating this is as follows. The approaches discussed in chapter 14 concentrated on 'above-the-line' transactions', that is, transactions in goods markets and assets markets which are recorded in the current account and capital account of table 14.1. The monetary approach shifts attention to 'below-the-line settlements', that is, the balancing transactions of table 14.1 which record the monetary implications of payments imbalance.

To illustrate, recall the equation for the money supply which was derived in chapter 6 (equation 6.7a):

$$M_j = \left(\frac{c+1}{c+r}\right) H_j \tag{15.8}$$

Where M refers to the money stock, H to the volume of high-powered money, c to the public's currency deposit ratio and r to the commercial banks' reserve ratio. Denoting the money multiplier by m, equation 15.8 can be written as

$$M_j = m_j H_j \tag{15.9}$$

or taking first differences

$$\Delta M_j = m_j \Delta H_j \tag{15.10}$$

In other words, the change in the money supply in country j is equal to some multiple of the change in high-powered money. In chapter 6 the change in high-powered money was identified with a domestically determined component, the issue of currency and the sales of securities to the clearing banks, and an externally controlled component, the change in foreign exchange reserves. If the former is referred to as D_j and the latter as R_j, equation 15.9 can be rewritten as

$$M_j = m_j(D_j + R_j) \tag{15.11}$$

(and similarly if changes are taken as in 15.10).

Assume now that, following the monetarist contention as outlined in chapter 5, the demand for money in country j is a stable function of a small number of variables, namely real income, 'the' domestic interest rate relative to 'the' world rate and expected changes in the price level,

$$L_j = f\left(Y_j, \frac{r_j}{r_w}, P_j^e\right) \tag{15.12}$$

Furthermore, assume that the government budget is initially balanced,

$$G_j = T_j \tag{15.13}$$

and that all markets are efficient and tend to clear quickly and smoothly.

If initially payments are balanced, exports would equal imports and the change in foreign exchange reserves would be zero. In equilibrium the only source of any monetary disturbance would be through variations in D_j. If the rate of growth of the money supply is set in line with the natural rate of growth of real income, then the economy would be in a steady state, with unemployment at its natural rate and with actual inflation equal to expected inflation. More formally,

$$X_j = Z_j \tag{15.14}$$

$$\therefore \quad \dot{R} = 0 \tag{15.15}$$

$$\dot{M}_j = \dot{Y}_j \tag{15.16}$$

and

$$\dot{P}_j = \dot{P}_j^e$$

$$\therefore \quad U_j = \bar{U}_j \tag{15.17}$$

Assume now that the authorities attempt to increase output beyond its natural level through domestic monetary expansion. The immediate impact of this disturbance is felt in the domestic money market in the form of a *stock* disequilibrium. Specifically, *actual* money balances exceed *desired* money balances. As has been claimed time and again, by monetary approaches this disequilibrium will be cleared through the markets for goods, services and securities. Since real output cannot be increased (because in equilibrium the starting-point is the natural rate of unemployment), the rate of change of prices rises in *j*, and domestic residents expend the excess money balances on goods, services and securities produced abroad. The outcome of this is a balance of payments deficit and, if the exchange rate is fixed, an outflow of foreign exchange reserves. The monetary shock therefore leads directly to a balance of payments deficit.

Implications of the Monetary Approach

The first important implication of the monetary approach is that, given time, adjustment to this imbalance will be automatic. It can be seen from equation 15.11 that foreign exchange reserves are an uncontrollable component of the domestic money supply. The balance of payments deficit causes reserve contraction at home (and simultaneous reserve expansion overseas) in turn this will induce domestic monetary contraction (and the reverse overseas).

Again it is adjustments in the money market which are emphasized. Reserve contraction and the resultant monetary contraction lead to a situation where actual money balances fall short of desired money balances. In other words, there is an excess demand for money in the domestic economy. In order to build up cash balances to their desired level expenditure on goods, services and securities contracts. (In the language of the absorption approach, disabsorption takes place.) This in turn slows down the rate of change of domestic prices and ultimately the deficit is eliminated. The entire process of adjustment to the deficit is therefore automatic.

A second implication of the monetary approach is that any attempt by the government to resist automatic adjustment is futile. For example, suppose during the process of adjustment the domestically controlled component of the money stock is further increased. This simply re-creates stock disequilibrium in the money market and re-creates the need for adjustment. It is argued that attempts by the monetary authorities to sterilize the effects of reserve outflows simply cause further inflation and further reserve outflows thereby maintaining disequilibrium.

It should be clear from this how the monetary approach extends the analysis of the Mundellian and absorption approaches. Considerable stress is laid on the links between the money market and payments imbalance, and the longer-run consequences of imbalance are emphasized. The approach asserts that under a regime cf fixed exchange rates, all balance of payments disequilibria are the outcome of differential rates of growth of real income which impact upon the demand for money and differential rates of monetary expansion. The central tenet of the approach is that since the reserve flows associated with imbalance cannot be sterilized in the long run, payments disequilibrium is necessarily a transitory phenomenon. The only circumstances in which an imbalance is persistent occurs where the rate of growth of the domestically controlled component of the money supply is continually in excess of (or below) the world average. Ordinarily this could not be sustained owing to the constraint of reserve loss and exhaustion of credit (in the case of a deficit country). One exception would of course be where the currency concerned was a 'key currency', i.e. is the principal asset for international exchange. Thus the rest of the world was for some time content to accommodate a persistent US deficit in the early 1960s in order to acquire dollars since the US dollar was the key currency under the Bretton Woods arrangements. It should be noted, however, that even this situation could not continue indefinitely. Persistent US deficits created a sharp deterioration in the USA's ratio of assets (gold and foreign exchange reserves) to liabilities (outstanding dollar claims). Ultimately this created a crisis of confidence in the USA's ability to honour these liabilities which contributed to the breakdown of the Bretton Woods arrangements in the early 1970s.

The final implication we should note of the monetary approach is the impotence of domestic monetary policy in a fixed exchange rate setting. Monetary policy is completely ineffective with regard to real income. As we saw in chapter 14 this is in fact an insight which was generated in the Fleming–Mundell approach to the balance of payments and is reaffirmed here.

The Monetary Approach and Flexible Exchange Rates

When the exchange rate is free to float the monetary approach has to be modified to allow for the fact that reserve flows no longer affect monetary growth. This is determined solely by the growth of the domestic monetary base. In terms of the above analysis, monetary expansion which creates a stock disequilibrium in the money market results not in a payments deficit but in exchange rate movements. This follows because any tendency towards payments deficit is corrected by exchange rate depreciation. This has the effect of restoring autonomy over domestic monetary policy to the domestic authorities in that a rate of growth of nominal income, and a rate of price inflation, which differ from the world average can be 'chosen'. If such a rate is chosen and domestic monetary policy adjusted accordingly, monetary expansion in excess of (below) the world average results in exchange rate depreciation (appreciation). An important implication of this is that domestic inflation is the cause of currency depreciation rather than vice versa as many Keynesian models predict.

Note further, however, that although autonomy over domestic monetary policy is restored to the domestic monetary authorities, the conclusions regarding the *effects* of monetary policy differ from the Keynesian model. In the monetary model, the long-run impact on real output and employment is still zero as in the closed economy model. Given the interdependence between monetary and fiscal policy this applies to fiscal as well as monetary policy. Thus in contrasting the Keynesian and monetary models it can be seen that the 'transmissions mechanism' for payments imbalance is different; Keynesian analyses emphasize expenditure flows whilst monetary models emphasize money market disequilibrium. In addition, as with closed economy systems, Keynesian models perceive a basis for demand management policies which have real effects, whilst monetary models simply reassert the neutrality of demand management policies.

Criticisms of the Monetary Approach

The monetary approach is therefore of interest because it stresses the longer-run interdependence between domestic financial policies and the external accounts. In so doing it delineates the limits of demand management policy in affecting the external situation. It is appropriate, however, to note that the analysis is subject to a number of general criticisms, criticisms which by and large tend to be levelled against monetarist philosophy in general. For example, the mechanisms described above rely on a stable money demand function. As Tsiang (1977) noted, this assumes that the variables to which money demand is related can be identified as well as the nature of the relationship. Although, as was seen in chapter 5, there are some difficulties in empirically analysing money demand, a growing literature does appear to suggest that, in the long run, money demand is stably related to income. There is more controversy with respect to interest rates.

A second area of controversy relates to the adjustment mechanism. This relies on efficiently and smoothly operating markets. In practice, of course, goods and factor markets in particular may clear relatively slowly. The implications of this when accompanied by assets markets which clear relatively quickly will be explored in the next section. Finally, in connection with the analysis of systems, note has been taken of the central question of exogeneity or endogeneity of the money stock. If it is determined by the level of money income (rather than determining it) then clearly the entire approach would be undermined.

Monetary Disturbances, Expectations and
the Exchange Rate

Towards the end of the previous section, brief comment was made on the implication of the monetary approach for a regime of flexible exchange rates. Following the *de facto* collapse of the Bretton Woods regime of pegged exchange rates in 1971, a much greater degree of exchange rate flexibility has been evident in the international economy. This has not meant that exchange rate targets have been entirely abandoned; they do appear to have been maintained by most Western authorities, even if only in the form of target ranges. Nevertheless it is the case that greater exchange rate flexibility has served to relax (and in some cases remove) the constraint of defending a particular exchange rate in many Western industrialized countries. Inevitably this has encouraged a reorientation of academic interest away from the relationship between domestic financial policies and the balance of payments towards the relationship between domestic financial policies and the exchange rate. This relationship has been closely scrutinized in the UK and USA in particular, where official attitudes towards the exchange rate in the later 1970s and early 1980s of 'non-intervention' and 'benign neglect' appeared to be associated with marked fluctuations in those exchange rates.

Our comparative static analysis of demand management policy under floating exchange rates in the Fleming–Mundell setting of chapter 14 implied that adjustment from one equilibrium exchange rate to another would be relatively smooth. Likewise the monetary approach implies that exchange rate movements will be driven by changes in relative inflation rates between one economy and another and it is implicit in that analysis that exchange rate changes will be stable and continuous. Smooth adjustment has not been a characteristic of exchange rate movements in the late 1970s and 1980s however. On the contrary, month-to-month, and even day-to-day fluctuations in many of the major exchange rates have been quite dramatic. In chapter 20 we will examine in detail the behaviour of the sterling exchange rate in recent years. For the moment we will evaluate the way in which expectations may influence exchange rate behaviour, as well as exploring a phenomenon known as exchange rate overshooting.

Purchasing Power Party and the Exchange Rate

A useful starting point for the evaluation of the role of expectations is the purchasing power parity concept. This is a simple explanation of exchange rate behaviour which we have in fact already introduced in our discussion of the monetary approach.

The purchasing power parity (PPP) doctrine asserts that in a world of floating rates exchange rate movements serve to equalize the purchasing power of different currencies after making due allowance for complications caused by imperfections such as transport costs and trade barriers. In a two-country world, for example, a rise in the rate of inflation in country A reduces the real value of country A's domestic money stock. The purchasing power of the currency on the home market would be reduced. In an open trading system, with fixed exchange rates, arbitrage in goods markets would ensure that a balance of payments deficit emerges. When the exchange rate is free to float, however, arbitrage results in exchange rate depreciation. Furthermore this depreciation would continue until the incentive to purchase goods had been removed, that is, when the depreciation of the exchange rate is just sufficient to offset the inflation differential. At this point *purchasing power parity* would be re-established.

Formally, if the current or spot rate of exchange is defined as the number of units of domestic currency D_c per unit of foreign currency D_f :

$$S_t = \frac{D_c}{D_f} \qquad\qquad\qquad (15.18)$$

such that

$\Delta S_t > 0$ denotes exchange rate depreciation

$\Delta S_t < 0$ denotes exchange rate appreciation

then according to the purchasing power parity theorem,

$$\dot{S}_t = \dot{P}_d - \dot{P}_w \qquad\qquad\qquad (15.19)$$

That is, changes in the spot rate are determined by the domestic rate of inflation $(\dot{P}_d)$ relative to the world rate $(\dot{P}_w)$, other things (such as relative rates growth) being given. This is essentially the monetary approach and sum-marizes the points which were made at the end of the previous chapter, that relative rates of monetary expansion, and therefore relative rates of inflation, drive exchange rate appreciation and depreciation.

This is the simplest possible statement of the PPP doctrine; it assumes that the spot exchange rate is determined by transactions which take place in the goods market. The speed and path of adjustment of the exchange rate to the change in the inflation rate is determined by how quickly agents in goods markets react to the latter. In terms of figure 15.3, a once and for all increase in the inflation rate between t_1 and t_2 (where t is time) might induce a once and for all depreciation of the spot exchange rate between t_2 and t_3. Alternatively, the adjustment could take place more quickly or

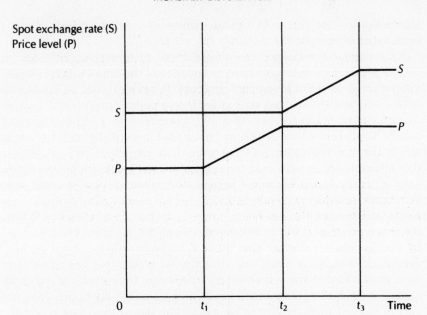

Figure 15.3   PPP and the exchange rate

more slowly. Ultimately, it depends on how smoothly and efficiently the markets concerned operate – how long it takes for the agents concerned to acquire, process and react to all relevant information about the change in the inflation rate.

Although the PPP doctrine is regarded by some as describing reasonably accurately the way in which exchange rates are determined in the longer run (see for example Friedman, 1980), it is not empirically well supported (see Winters, 1985). In addition a difficulty with the approach as we have outlined it is that it concentrates entirely on the components of the current account of the balance of payments; it is this which leads to the dominant influence of relative rates of inflation. In a world of relatively mobile capital flows the effects of capital transactions which take place in response to interest rate differentials can (and do) swamp the effects of current transactions in the short run. For example financial analysts estimate that in 1986 the *daily* volume of transactions in internationally tradeable assets amounted to around $150 billion. To put this in perspective, this amounts to about 8 per cent of the total *annual* value of world trade in goods. With the increasing volume of internationally mobile capital in the world economy, this is an effect which has been given an increasing amount of attention. Moreover note that it is not only *actual* capital transactions which are important but *potential* capital transactions – the threat of capital inflows or outflows might in many circumstances be sufficient to change the exchange rate.

Since capital movements can clearly exert an important influence on exchange rate movements, we need to understand the forces which influence international portfolio investment decisions. What motivates an invester to hold a sterling-denominated asset rather than a dollar-denominated asset, or to switch from holding a sterling-denominated asset to a yen-denominated asset? Clearly this will be determined by the riskiness of alternative assets as well as the expected returns on those assets. If, to simplify matters, we assume that all assets are equally risky (or riskless) we can focus wholly on relative rates of return. In the Fleming–Mundell model relative rates of return were determined solely by relative interest rates. If the exchange rate is fixed this is a permissible simplification. When, however, the exchange rate is free to float the return on an asset will be influenced not only by the interest rate, but also by changes in the exchange rate. Thus, if an investor is holding a sterling-denominated asset, exchange rate depreciation reduces the capital value of that asset. Thus, when individuals, corporate treasurers, or portfolio managers are making judgements about which assets to invest they look not only at interest rates on alternative assets, but also at how they expect the exchange rate to behave during the period they are holding the asset. The expectations of investors with regard to exchange rate movements has a crucial bearing on capital flows.

Expectations and Exchange Rate Movements

For simplicity, consider a model in which capital is perfectly mobile across frontiers. Information flows are smooth and efficient, and transactions costs are relatively low. Thus differences in expected rates of return will quickly be followed by capital movements which arbitrage these rates of return. The expected rate of return on an asset for which substitutes exist will be influenced by two elements. The first is relative rates of interest; *ceteris paribus*, a higher nominal rate of interest in country j will be associated with a higher rate of return. Second, any change in the capital value of the asset which is expected to occur will affect its rate of return. Exchange rate appreciation raises the value of the asset whilst exchange rate depreciation lowers it. The way in which agents in the market form their expectations is crucially important. Let us assume that agents form their expectations rationally. They are therefore well informed and use information efficiently. Although as we saw in chapter 13 there are reasons for doubting the appropriateness of the assumption of rational expectations in the labour market, it may not be an inappropriate assumption where the foreign exchange market is concerned. Agents in this market tend to be specialist transactors who are well informed.

To establish the relationship between capital inflows/outflows, interest rate differentials and expected exchange rate changes, consider first the circumstances for zero capital mobility. At the margin there will be no capital inflows to or outflows from the domestic economy when the expected rates of return on domestic and foreign assets are identical, that is, when

$$i_t^d = i_t^f + (S_t^e - S_t) \qquad (15.20)$$

where i_t^d and i_t^f refer to the current domestic and foreign interest rates respectively; S_t refers to the prevailing spot exchange rate and S_t^e refers to the expected spot exchange rate. Thus when domestic interest is equal to the foreign interest rate, plus the expected rate of depreciation of the domestic currency (over a given time period), rates of return will be equalized. Rearranging (15.20) we can put this slightly differently:

$$i_t^d - i_t^f = S_t^e - S_t \qquad (15.21)$$

This states that when the exchange rate is expected to depreciate ($S_t^e > S_t$) the domestic interest rate must exceed the foreign interest rate (and vice versa). The intuition between this equilibrium condition is quite straightforward. It simply states that where investors expect the exchange rate to depreciate, thereby lowering the capital value of a given asset, investors have to be compensated by a higher rate of interest. If they are not so compensated they will not hold assets in the domestic currency and a capital outflow will result. The contrary condition holds for a currency whose value is expected to appreciate. In this case domestic interest rates need to be less than those prevailing elsewhere to stem capital inflows.

This is a crucially important result which must hold for equilibrium where markets operate efficiently and investors form their expectations rationally. One interesting thing about the result is that, superficially it appears to contradict our findings in the context of the Fleming–Mundell model. There it was argued that an increase in the interest rate would induce a capital inflow whilst a decrease in the interest rate would generate a capital outflow. This seems to conflict with the proposition that a positive interest rate differential will be associated with exchange rate depreciation whilst a negative interest rate differential is associated with exchange rate appreciation.

Dornbusch (1976) argues that the two can be reconciled relatively easily once anticipated and unanticipated variations in exchange rates are allowed for. If agents have full information and therefore form their expectations of how the exchange rate will move rationally, a positive interest rate differential will be expected to be associated with exchange rate depreciation in order to equalize rates of return. It is the *expectation* of a capital loss (via depreciation) which stems the capital inflow otherwise a country with a positive interest rate differential would attract all mobile capital! Assume that some 'steady state' exists with a positive interest rate differential and a degree of exchange rate depreciation; some entirely *unexpected* policy change then raises the domestic interest rate to an *unexpectedly* high level, and makes assets denominated in the domestic currency appear *unexpectedly* attractive. What happens? Since assets denominated in domestic currency are *unexpectedly* attractive there is a capital inflow and exchange rate appreciation.

Thus the predictions of the efficient markets model and the Fleming–Mundell model can be reconciled. When interest rate differentials are known and fully anticipated a positive interest rate differential will be associated with exchange rate depreciation (and a negative interest rate differential with exchange rate appreciation). This is the prediction of the efficient markets hypothesis. When, however, some unexpected change occurs this relationship alters. If an exogenous shock occurs which makes the domestic currency unexpectedly attractive then a capital inflow results. For instance, if the domestic interest rate unexpectedly rises this results in a capital inflow and the exchange rate appreciates. This prediction is consistent with the Fleming–Mundell model.

This theorem is interesting not just because it introduces relative rates of return into the determination of the exchange rate but because it brings the role of exchange rate expectations into play, and in the same way as unexpected stabilization shocks can affect real output, it is found that they may also affect the exchange rate. As it is outlined above it is incomplete in so far as it has not been specified how relative interest rates are determined. Niehans (1975) and Dornbusch (1976) among others have developed these ideas within the context of complete macroeconomic models where the interest rate is determined by expected inflation. One very interesting and important idea which has developed from this work is that one may have certain markets which clear quickly (where expectations are formed rationally and institutional arrangements are amenable to price flexibility) – like the foreign exchange market – alongside markets which clear more slowly (where expectations are formed adaptively and institutional arrangements impede price flexibility) – like the labour market. When these conditions coexist it is possible to find a phenomenon termed *exchange rate overshooting* which, as well as being an interesting explanation of exchange rate behaviour, also provides a somewhat unexpected channel by which monetary policy can exert real effects in a rational expectations world.

Exchange Rate Overshooting

As noted above, one feature of exchange rate movements in recent years has been their sudden and erratic changes. One way of explaining recent

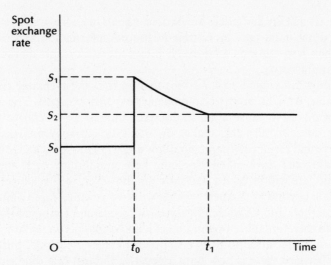

Figure 15.4   Exchange rate overshooting

movements is by reference to the process of exchange rate overshooting. This refers to the phenomenon whereby the exchange rate reacts to a change in economic circumstances not in a smooth transitional fashion, but in a rather abrupt and erratic manner. Specifically, instead of tracking towards its new long-run equilibrium value the exchange rate initially adjusts beyond its long-run value, then gradually converges on equilibrium. For example, if a monetary expansion occurs this leads to exchange rate depreciation. Initially, however, the exchange rate depreciates more than is necessary for full equilibrium – it overshoots its long-run value in other words. Having done so it then gradually appreciates back towards its final equilibrium value. Figure 15.4 illustrates the process. At t_0 the exchange rate is S_0. At this point in time a monetary expansion occurs. The exchange rate reacts by depreciating to S_1 immediately. Between t_0 and t_1 the exchange rate then appreciates until it reaches its final equilibrium value of S_2. If no further changes take place the exchange rate remains at S_2. If we compare S_2 with S_0 we observe that a depreciation has occurred in response to the monetary expansion. The adjustment path from S_0 to S_1 is rather odd however. The initial fall in the exchange rate is greater than that required for full equilibrium. This is the exchange rate overshoot. Let us consider more carefully the circumstances under which this phenomenon may occur and evaluate in more detail what is actually behind the overshoot.

Suppose that agents in assets markets and agents in goods and factor markets react at different speeds to monetary shocks. Specifically assume that agents in assets markets form their expectations rationally. Information flows are efficient, agents are able to process information about changed monetary conditions quickly and prices are flexible. Agents in goods and factor markets on the other hand take more time to process information and react. They form their expectations adaptively, prices are sticky and market clearing occurs more slowly.

Refer again to figure 15.4. Assume that up to t_0 the exchange rate is at its PPP value. At t_0 an unexpected monetary expansion occurs. The immediate effect of this is to cause a fall in domestic interest rates relative to foreign interest rates. In turn this makes the domestic currency unexpectedly unattractive and results in a capital outflow and a fall in the exchange rate. Once all adjustments have taken place the new equilibrium PPP value of the exchange rate will be S_2. In the short run, however, the exchange rate must depreciate beyond S_2. Remember that we have assumed rapid adjustment in assets markets and sluggish adjustment in goods and factor markets. In the short run therefore the entire burden of adjustment falls on the exchange rate. An initial depreciation to S_2 is insufficient to stem the capital outflow. This follows because there is now both a negative interest rate differential and a depreciating exchange rate. Returns on foreign assets still exceed returns on domestic assets. When will returns on the two assets be equalized? This will occur when the exchange rate has fallen sufficiently to ensure that future expected exchange rate appreciation compensates fully for the lower domestic interest rate. At this point the equilibrium condition of equation 15.21 holds again. In terms of figure 15.4 this is the appreciation which occurs between t_0 and t_1.

This may appear counter-intuitive. It must be remembered, however, that in the short run no adjustments are taking place in goods and factor markets. Agents in these markets take longer to adjust to the monetary shock. After a lag agents react to the exchange rate depreciation, demand for import substitutes and exports expands whilst demand for imports contracts. It is this which is behind the appreciation which occurs. If there were complete flexibility and rapid adjustment in goods and factor markets as well as in the foreign exchange market, the overshoot would not occur.

'Overshooting' is a phenomenon associated with assets markets in general and not just the foreign exchange market. It is a possibility which has been recognized for some time (for instance, Friedman, 1953b, discusses it). We have described the phenomenon in a highly stylized fashion and it should be noted that the overshooting model is subject to several theoretical objections. For example, instantaneous adjustment in assets markets may not occur. In addition the model ignores the fact that changes in the domestic price level will have wealth effects which will have real effects. Notwithstanding these objections many analysts believe that the basic insight provided by the overshooting model is of value in understanding recent exchange rate behaviour. For instance some commentators feel that the behaviour of sterling over the period 1979–82 is a dramatic example of the process. Here the process was opposite to that just described. An announcement of monetary contraction in the spring of 1979 was associated with a significant appreciation of the sterling exchange rate to a point where many commentators were convinced that it was overvalued. The exchange rate had overshot, and subsequently approached its long-run equilibrium level by depreciating – this being the mechanism whereby the holders of foreign assets were penalized for the positive interest differential in the UK, and the equality of equation 15.21 restored.

A glance forward to the sterling dollar exchange rate charted in figure 20.3 gives some idea of the behaviour of sterling over this period. Prima facie the evidence is not inconsistent with the overshooting hypothesis. It must be noted, however, that some commentators have invoked other explanations, such as the role of North Sea oil in conferring petrocurrency status on the UK. This question will be considered further in chapter 20. It might be noted for the moment, however, that if overshooting is a valid explanation of sterling's behaviour, one finds monetary policy having real effects via the back door – namely via its effect on the exchange rate. Sterling appreciation in 1979 and 1980 was one of the factors which influenced the dramatic deterioration in competitiveness documented in figure 20.4, which in turn squeezed UK industry in general and manufacturing industry in particular.

Concluding Comments

Chapter 14 was concerned primarily with the comparative statics of macroeconomic policy in a neo-Keynesian setting. This chapter has complemented chapter 14 by considering neo-classical models of the balance of payments which stress the monetary implications of payments imbalance. In addition, we have explored the role of expectations in a flexible exchange rate setting in order to evaluate some aspects of exchange rate dynamics. Our analysis in this chapter has provided us with a number of insights which complement those generated in chapter 14. We have seen that it is important to examine fully the monetary implications of payments imbalance. From a policy standpoint two particularly important points emerged from this examination. First, the possibility exists that payments imbalances may be self-correcting. Although this may be true in the long run however, as was pointed out, the period over which adjustment occurs may be so long as to be irrelevant from a policy perspective. Second, the impotence of monetary policy in a fixed exchange rate setting which was alluded to in the Fleming–Mundell model is reconfirmed here. Our analysis also extended to a consideration of exchange rate dynamics in a world where large volumes of internationally mobile capital exist. The possibility of sudden and erratic exchange rate changes being explained by exchange rate overshooting was explored. The most important insight which emerges from this analysis is that expectations play a crucially important role in short-run exchange rate changes.

We will return to many of these ideas in chapter 20. Then we shall look closely at UK balance of payments and exchange rate policies over the post-war period and consider the relevance of the models examined in chapters 14 and 15 to UK experience.

Further Reading

An overview of the absorption and monetary approaches can be found in most texts on international economics; see Milner and Greenaway (1979, chapters 5 and 6) and Winters (1985, chapters 20 and 21). For a much more sophisticated and rigorous analysis, see Dornbusch (1980, part 3) and Rivera-Batiz and Rivera-Batiz (1985, chapters 9, 10 and 11). Johnson (1976) provides a concise non-technical overview of the post-war development of thought on the balance of payments.

The two most influential papers on the absorption approach are Alexander (1952) and Johnson (1958); the latter makes especially worthwhile reading. There are a great many papers on the monetary approach; a representative paper is Johnson (1977). For the interested reader there are a number of symposia dealing with theoretical and empirical aspects of the monetary approach, namely Frenkel and Johnson (1976), IMF (1977) and Putnam and Wilford (1979). Critiques of the monetary approach are provided by Tsiang (1977) and Coppock (1978).

A classic paper on floating exchange rates is Friedman (1953b) and there are a number of useful papers in Corden (1977). The most important papers on expectations and the exchange rate are Black (1973), Niehans (1975) and Dornbusch (1976), whilst extremely useful review type articles are Frenkel and Rodriguez (1982) and Krueger (1983). Chrystal and Dowd (1988) provide an evaluation of the macroeconomic implications of overshooting. Empirical studies of PPP are provided by Frenkel (1981) and Branson (1981). Swoboda (1981) and Blackhurst and Tumlir (1980) provide empirical assessments of some of the macroeconomic implications of floating exchange rates. See also Baily, Tavlas and Ulan (1986). Finally the implications of the models reviewed in chapters 14 and 15 for international interdependence and policy co-ordination are evaluated by Frenkel (1986) and Hughes-Hallet (1988).

PART III

Macroeconomic Policy

The reasonable man adapts himself
to the world; the unreasonable one
persists in trying to adapt the world
to himself. Therefore all progress
depends on the unreasonable man.
George Bernard Shaw

Part III of this book differs from parts I and II in two very important respects. First, it is concerned with macroeconomic policy and thus with the attempt to intervene and change the functioning of the economy in order to improve upon the existing state of affairs. This involves making a normative judgement as to what constitutes a desired state of affairs and the need to be able to determine priorities amongst policy goals in the event of conflict. Thus these are fundamental questions of what *ought* to be, and nothing encountered in parts I and II of this book will be of assistance in determining these priorities. Second, the focal point of part III is very decidedly with policy and experience in the UK. The previous discussion of macroeconomic sectors and macroeconomic theories had a certain universal applicability, to the extent that this discussion was abstracted from the institutional framework; in the present section the concern is specifically with the success or otherwise of macroeconomic policy within the UK. Particular attention is paid, therefore, to schools of thought which have exercised influence in the UK and also the particular policy problems which have been the most acute for the UK authorities. Without any doubt, these have been and continue to be the problems of unemployment, inflation and until recently comparatively poor economic growth performance. In addition, considerable attention is given to balance of payments considerations, since these have acted as a constraint upon policy formulation under past regimes of fixed exchange rates and continue to carry implications for counter-inflation policy under flexible exchange rate regimes.

This part begins, however, with a detailed analysis of the objectives and instruments of macroeconomic policy and with a discussion of possible

345

alternative approaches to macroeconomic policy prescription. Some attention is also paid to the problems encountered in the attempt to formulate
macroeconomic policy under conditions of uncertainty where, for example,
the authorities may be uncertain about the future course of exogenous
variables – the price of OPEC oil providing a graphic case in point. It is
shown that, although uncertainty complicates the policy choice, one can
still derive optimal rules of policy intervention.

In dealing with the problem of inflation the micro- and macroeconomic
costs of inflation will be examined first since, in the absence of such costs,
inflation would be a matter of indifference. Alternative counter-inflation
policies are then considered, ranging from conventional demand management policies to wages and price controls. This analysis of the UK experience is concluded by looking at the case for indexation and the logic
underlying the medium-term financial strategy. In examining the problem
of unemployment in the UK particular attention is devoted to distinguishing between alternative forms of unemployment and the extent to
which they might respond to alternative policy measures, which in turn
reflect the differing viewpoint of the leading schools of thought. In the
analysis of the balance of payments and exchange rate policies of recent UK
governments, three distinct exchange rate regimes are distinguished; the
regime of fixed exchange rates which prevailed through 1950–67; the post-
devaluation period 1967–72; and the period of managed floating exchange
rates which has prevailed from 1972 to the present day. The British experience is also analyzed in relation to the European Monetary System (EMS)
which Britain has, thus far, refrained from joining. Finally, the book concludes by surveying the major constraints which have been advanced to
explain Britain's comparatively poor growth performance and by discussing
the policy proposals which have been put forward in an attempt to over-
come the constraints.

The book as a whole attempts to explain alternative theoretical positions,
the implications stemming from those positions and the policy recommendations and conclusions that might justifiably be drawn. It does not attempt
to come out with one particular viewpoint, either as to how the economy
actually operates or as to what the chosen economic policy should be. That
is hardly in keeping with the purposes that a macroeconomic text should
serve. Nor would it realistically be possible, since the authors themselves do
not share a common ground and one doubts that the present book would
have been enhanced had they done so.

16

Approaches to Macroeconomic Policy

Assuming that it is possible to define adequately the policy objectives and their order of priority in the event of conflict, the next step is to decide upon the approach to macroeconomic policy formulation. Broadly two general approaches may be distinguished, both of which spring from the theoretical and practical contribution of two Dutch economists. On the one hand there is what has become known as the *optimizing approach*, associated largely with the name of Henri Theil, whilst on the other there is the so-called *fixed targets approach*, intimately linked with the work of Nobel prize winner Jan Tinbergen. In what follows the essence of these diverse approaches will be sketched briefly before the problems arising from the existence of uncertainty are tackled. To this end it is convenient to reintroduce the short-run Phillips curve. For expository purposes it will be assumed that this summarizes the choice available to the policy-maker, an infinite number of inflation–unemployment combinations are potentially attainable; how does one select from this infinite range?

The Optimizing Approach

The *optimizing approach* to economic policy assumes that it is conceptually possible to specify *the social welfare function*. Once this is determined, and the preference pattern of society with respect to all possible outcomes of inflation and unemployment is known, the task of policy is simply to select whatever attainable combination will maximize welfare. Thus, for example, in figure 16.1 the objective function is summarized in the collective indifference curves in unemployment–inflation space superimposed upon the diagram. In this simple model, with only two policy objectives, the indifference curves indicate successively higher stages of collective well-being *as*

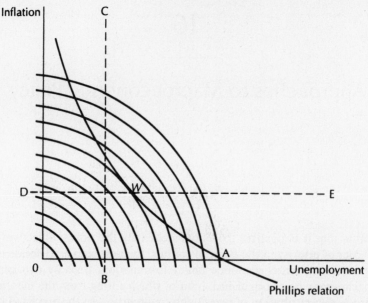

Figure 16.1   Optimizing and fixed targets approaches to macroeconomic policy formulation

they approach the origin.[1] Clearly the optimum position would be at the
origin where perfect price stability is reconciled with full employment.
However, the Phillips curve imposes a constraint by specifying all feasible
combinations of employment and inflation. The policy decision-maker must
select from this limited choice. If he is successful, he will juggle with alternative policy mixes to obtain a solution at point W, which maximizes the
well-being of society given the predetermined indifference map. Implicit in
this approach is the assumption that no one policy objective is sacrosanct:
objectives, as well as instruments, are flexible. It is the task of the policy-
maker to decide, in the light of all the available information, the extent to
which any one objective must be compromised to maximize total well-
being.

---

1 The community indifference curves are drawn concave to the origin for precisely the same reason that conventional indifference curves are usually portrayed as
convex – namely, that the marginal significance of one good in terms of the other
will normally increase the less one has of the one good and the more one has of the
other. In the present case, however, the indifference diagram portrays not goods but
positive 'bads' – inflation and unemployment. Thus, as successively higher rates of
inflation are encountered, the objective of price stability becomes more desirable and
further increments in inflation are only acceptable if progressively greater
increments in employment are offered. Hence the concavity of the indifference
curves.

In many ways the optimizing approach is theoretically appealing and being stated in terms of constrained maximization enjoys an affinity with conventional microeconomic techniques. However, its fundamental drawback is that it requires some theory of group decision-making in order to be able to determine with a reasonable degree of confidence the social welfare ordering. There are serious difficulties with this proposition. Modern welfare economics would suggest that transitive choice will not emerge from the simple majority voting principle as practised in the UK.

The Fixed Targets Approach

In many respects it may be contended that the *fixed targets approach* is a more pragmatic way of formulating macroeconomic policy. This approach to policy-making neatly sidesteps the difficulties associated with approximating social welfare functions. Instead, policy goals are stated as constituting fixed targets from which no departure is permitted. In effect, this is tantamount to the decision-making authorities intervening in the role of benevolent dictator in specifying what the social welfare function should be. Once the objectives have been determined, policy-making then reduces to the search for an adequate armoury of instruments to secure their attainment.

Assume, for example, that the decision-making authorities have decreed that the objective of price stability should be interpreted as no more than D percent inflation per year, whilst the goal of full employment is consistent with B per cent unemployed. In this case, the fixed targets limit the acceptable region of figure 16.1 to the area left of the vertical line BC and below the horizontal line DE. Moreover, given the Phillips curve, these twin objectives are incapable of being achieved simultaneously with the existing conventional tools of macroeconomic policy. The existing policy measures are able to achieve either goal at the sacrifice of the other. The introduction of new policy tools, therefore, is required in order to secure the additional policy objective, by affecting the appropriate inward shift of the Phillips curve. The Tinbergen principle was introduced in chapter 14; this derives from the fixed targets approach and concludes that successful policy execution necessitates having at least as many *independent* policy instruments as one has policy targets.

The Tinbergen approach has exercised considerable influence upon policy discussion and in reality this has been the approach favoured by policy-makers. This has arisen because in practice governments have chosen to accord priority to one objective to which the others have then been subordinated. Thus, for example, in terms of figure 16.1 this approach is akin to promulgating one target as fixed and letting the other be passively determined by the technical relationship underlying the Phillips curve. Different governments have chosen different fixed targets. The Wilson administration between 1964 and 1967, for example, looked upon the maintenance of an exchange rate of $2.80 to the £ as being the immutable objective to which other objectives, particularly employment, were subsequently sacrificed. One difficulty which arises with the Tinbergen approach to macroeconomic policy formation concerns the independence of the policy instruments. Recent theoretical work arising from the monetarist controversy and especially the analysis of the budget constraint has questioned the assumed independence of many of the major instruments. In any case it can be demonstrated that once uncertainty is allowed to enter the analysis the necessary equation between objectives and instruments is no longer sufficient; with uncertainty, optimum policy-making requires that more than one instrument must be directed towards each objective.

If one policy objective is accorded overriding priority, so that other objectives are passively determined as residuals, then the fixed targets approach can be simply illustrated by reference to an elementary national income model. Assuming a closed economy model of the form

$$Y = C + I + G \qquad (16.1)$$

where the symbols represent income, consumption, investment and government expenditures respectively, the policy objective can be represented by a target level of income Y^*. Assume that this target income level acts as a proxy for the ultimate policy goal, employment. Let consumption be a function of disposable income so that

$$C = bY_d \qquad (16.2)$$

where b is the marginal propensity to consume, and Y_d is disposable income and is equal to

$$Y_d = Y(1 - t) \qquad (16.3)$$

where t is a proportional rate of income tax. Let both private sector investment and government expenditure be exogenous so that

$$I = \bar{I} \qquad (16.4)$$

and

$$G = \bar{G} \qquad (16.5)$$

but with the latter being under government control and hence constituting an available policy instrument. Solving for the equilibrium level of national income,

$$Y = \frac{\bar{I} + \bar{G}}{1 - b + bt} \tag{16.6}$$

Given the model, and assuming that an estimate of the value of the marginal propensity to consume and a forecasted value of the exogenous variable $\bar{I}$ can be obtained, then the task of the policy-maker reduces to selecting values of the policy instruments, $\bar{G}$ and t, so as to secure the target income level Y^*. It will be appreciated that, in this simple case, one policy instrument is sufficient to secure the one objective. Holding government expenditures constant, t could be varied so as to secure Y^*. Alternatively, holding t constant the appropriate value of G could be determined so as to give the same result. Equally, however, the two policy instruments could be combined; indeed it may well be the case that in order to secure the target income level Y^* more than one combination of G and t is available. If this situation prevails, then the actual choice of G and t will be determined by reference to additional criteria – perhaps, for example, by the desire to minimize the budget deficit. Here the Tinbergen principle is seen at work. With just one policy objective, Y^*, either the expenditure tool or the tax tool was sufficient in itself. As soon as secondary objectives are allowed to enter the analysis, as in this case the size of the budget deficit, then the additional policy tool is required to provide the optimal policy mix.

Macroeconomic Policy and Uncertainty

Given the formal model result contained in equation 16.6, it has been seen that macroeconomic policy reduces to selecting that combination(s) of G and t consistent with the attainment of a target Y, Y^*. However, this rather *simpliste* approach tacitly assumes that the forecasted investment figure $\bar{I}$ is considered to be absolutely certain. In actual fact, purely exogenous variables are likely to be viewed with a considerable amount of caution with regard to their ultimate values. If uncertainty exists with reference to the purely exogenous values then equally uncertainty will prevail with regard to the values to be given to the control instruments G and t.[2]

To pursue this line of thought, assume that there are two possible values to be accorded the purely exogenous variable $\bar{I}$, I_A and I_B, where $I_A > I_B$.

---

2 In a world of uncertainty, there is a set of all possible states of nature denoted by the possible values of $\bar{I}$, a set of possible acts denoted by the possible values to be accorded to the instruments G and t, and a set of possible outcomes denoted by the possible values of Y. This terminology and related argument follows Peston (1982).

Table 16.1
Outcomes of Two Government Policies

	Outcomes		Values	
	I_A	I_B	I_A	I_B
Expansionary policy $G_A t_B$	Inflation	Y^*	85	95
Restrictive policy $G_B t_A$	Y^*	Unemployment	100	75

Assume also there are two possible levels of government expenditure $G_A >$ G_B and two possible rates of taxation $t_A > t_B$. For simplicity of exposition, the range of government policies are collapsed into two possible alternatives, an expansionary policy denoted by the combination $G_A t_B$ and a restrictive policy indicated by $G_B t_A$. All possible outcomes can then be illustrated as in the composite table 16.1, which also indicates the preferences of the policy-makers between the competing possibilities. Thus, for example, with the expansionary policy $G_A t_B$, if the event I_B occurs the target income level Y^* is established and the policy-makers award this a value of 95, whereas should event I_A occur then the outcome is inflation which earns a value of 85. Similarly with a restrictive government policy indicated by $G_B t_A$, if the event I_A occurs the target income Y^* is obtained with a value of 100, whereas should event I_B occur then the result will be unemployed resources which will be valued at 75. It will be noted that the securing of Y^* does not imply equal valuations; that is to say, the policy-maker will not be indifferent to the manner in which it is secured. Thus, in the present example, the policy-maker reveals a preference for securing Y^* *via* the 'restrictive' fiscal policy $G_B t_A$ as opposed to the 'expansionary' policy $G_A t_B$, presumably upon the grounds that the former implies a smaller public sector deficit.

It is now possible to examine alternative policy strategies. The optimal welfare value is secured only with strategy $G_B t_A$, but this is also the strategy with the greatest *potential* welfare loss. Assuming equal chances of I_A or I_B occurring, the mean value of this strategy is given as 87.5. In contrast, strategy $G_A t_B$ never secures the optimal 100 valuation but its mean value is 90. Moreover, this is also the strategy which avoids the worst possible outcome, namely that of unemployment. In these circumstances, it is quite feasible that the policy-maker will always opt for strategy $G_A t_B$. It never secures the maximum welfare but it is quite possible that the outcomes of the strategy are consistent with the retention of public office. In contrast, the worst feasible outcome associated with strategy $G_B t_A$ might guarantee certain electoral defeat. It will be noted that if the policy $G_A t_B$ is chosen then *ex post* it will always appear that a preferable alternative did exist. In retrospect, a higher valuation was always attainable had the value to be taken by $\bar{I}$ been known with certainty. It is in this sense that the optimal policy with uncertainty may differ from the optimal policy with certainty. In this manner, the existence of uncertainty acts as a constraint upon the design of optimal policy measures.

Admittedly, the preceding analysis is rather elementary. In particular, it assumes an equal chance of occurrence of outcome I_A and outcome I_B, and furthermore it restricts government policy intervention to one of two extremes. In principle, however, these restrictions can be readily dispensed with without modifying the essential conclusions in any fundamental way (see Peston, 1982).

The Principle of Certainty Equivalence

Largely because of the difficulties of dealing with uncertainty in macro-economic policy formulation, economists were quick to endorse what appeared to be a generally accepted principle, without arguably taking full account of the reservations which might reduce its applicability. This principle of *certainty equivalence* has exercised considerable influence both in the realm of pragmatic policy making and in academic circles. In keeping with the previous discussion it is assumed that the target level of income is Y^* and any departure from this income level will imply a welfare loss. Assume also, *in contrast to the previous example*, that the welfare loss is symmetrical about the target income level. This implies that a 2 per cent overshooting of the target income level generates the same loss of welfare as a 2 per cent undershooting. This situation is summarized with the aid of figure 16.2.[3]

Again, in keeping with the previous example, it is assumed that departures from the target level Y^* arise owing to the existence of uncertainty with respect to investment outlays, which may be either I_A or I_B. How is this difficulty dealt with? In principle, this question reduces to one in constrained minimization. Given estimated probabilities about events I_A and I_B, the task of the policy-maker is to select that combination of instruments, in this case G and t, so as to minimize the welfare loss. Pursuing this strategy may never result in attaining the desired income level Y^*, but it can be shown to be optimal in the sense that over time it will minimize the

---

3 Figure 19.3 implies that the welfare function is quadratic in that the welfare loss of departure from Y^* increases at an increasing rate. Thus 4 per cent unemployed resources is more than twice as bad as 2 per cent unemployment.

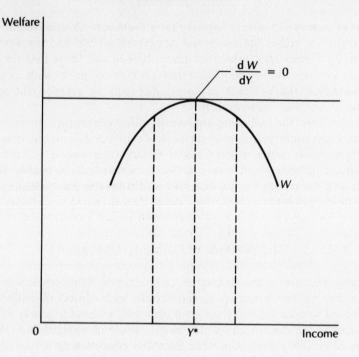

Figure 16.2   Welfare loss associated with departure from Y^* with quadratic utility function

welfare losses associated with *departures from Y^**. It may be demonstrated that the optimal policy mix is that combination of instruments which would secure the target level Y^* had the level of investment forthcoming been equal to the mathematically expected level of investment expenditures (see the appendix to this chapter). In the present example, if p is the probability of event I_A occurring then $(1 - p)$ is the probability of the event I_B and the mathematical expectation of investment is simply given by

$$ME = p(I_A) + (1 - p)I_B = \tilde{I} \tag{16.7}$$

If this value of $\tilde{I}$ is now inserted into the macroeconomic model so that

$$Y = \frac{\tilde{I} + G}{1 - b + bt} \tag{16.8}$$

where $\tilde{I}$ is now looked upon as a certainty, then the combination of instruments G and t can be chosen consistent with Y^*. That is to say, the values of the instruments are chosen to attain the targeted Y^* upon the assumption that the level of investment forthcoming is certain to be $\tilde{I}$. This is the principle of certainty equivalence. It provides a control guide to the policy-makers concerned with formulating economic policy. It may never succeed in generating the desired income level Y^* but it can be defended upon the ground that over time it will minimize the welfare loss associated with departures from Y^*.

The principle of certainty equivalence appeared to provide a control rule to guide rational decision-making. Moreover, part of its appeal doubtless lay in the fact that it was a proxy for what policy-makers had in fact been doing with their economic models which did not admit of uncertainty. Simply stated, elementary macromodels relied upon the forecasted values of the purely exogenous variables and these forecasts would normally coincide with their mathematically expected value. The principle of certainty equivalence not only provided a control guide to policy formation under certain conditions but it also provided a rationale for the existing code of practice. It is not surprising therefore that the principle was quickly endorsed. However, although the principle provided a useful insight into a difficult theoretical terrain, it is important to be aware of its reservations. First of all, its validity depends upon the crucial assumption that the utility function depicted in figure 16.2 is indeed symmetric about the target level Y^*. If this is not the case – if, for example, the welfare losses associated with unemployment exceed those associated with inflation so that the welfare function is asymmetric – then the analysis becomes decidedly more complex and the fundamental conclusion would no longer apply. Second, it is important to realize that the principle applies only to cases where uncertainty surrounds the purely exogenous variables. It cannot, for example, be extended to cases of uncertainty surrounding the estimated value of the parameter b – the marginal propensity to consume. It may well be the case that the major losses of welfare stem not so much from uncertainty regarding purely exogenous variables but rather from forecasting errors in the structural parameters determining national income multipliers.

Concluding Comments

In this chapter have been examined alternative ways of macroeconomic policy formulation. The optimizing and fixed targets approaches has been contrasted and the difficulties associated with each indicated. The difficulties created by the existence of uncertainty were then examined in greater detail and it was demonstrated that, even if one is unsure of the values taken by exogenous variables, none the less optimal decision rules still exist. This was illustrated by the principle of certainty equivalence, examined more formally in the appendix to this chapter. One consequence of uncertainty is that correctly conceived policies *ex ante* will almost always appear second-best solutions with the wisdom of hindsight. The macroeconomic policy-maker might justifiably conclude that economics is indeed the 'dismal science'.

Appendix: The Principle of Certainty Equivalence

Given the equation for the equilibrium level of income as

$$Y = \frac{\bar{I} + \bar{G}}{1 - b + bt} \tag{16.9}$$

simplify the analysis by assuming the tax rate to be invariant. That is, assume that the government seeks to attain the target level of income Y^* solely by the use of variations in the level of government expenditures. This gives

$$Y = k(\bar{I} + \bar{G}) \tag{16.10}$$

where k is the multiplier and is equal to $1/(1 - b + bt)$. If Y^* is the target income level, variations from Y^* are indicated by

$$Y^* - k(\bar{I} + \bar{G}) \tag{16.11}$$

that is, target income minus actual income levels. Assuming that the welfare function is symmetrical about Y^*, the welfare loss arising from deviations from Y^* can be expressed as

$$WL = [Y^* - k(\bar{I} + \bar{G})]^2 \tag{16.12}$$

The expected welfare loss depends upon the expected values of $\bar{I}$, so that

$$EWL = p[Y^* - k(I_A + \bar{G})]^2 + (1 - p)[Y^* - k(I_B + \bar{G})]^2 \tag{16.13}$$

This is the expression which must be minimized for maximum welfare. The task is to select the value of G consistent with the minimization of this expression. Differentiating with respect to G, and setting the result equal to zero to satisfy first-order conditions, yields

$$kpI_A + (1 - p)I_B + k\bar{G} - Y^* = 0 \tag{16.14}$$

Since $pI_A + (1 - p)I_B$ is the mathematical expectation of I, namely $\tilde{I}$, this reduces to

$$k\tilde{I} + k\bar{G} - Y^* = 0 \tag{16.15}$$

Accordingly,

$$Y^* = k(\bar{G} + \tilde{I}) = \frac{(\bar{G} + \tilde{I})}{1 - b + bt} \tag{16.16}$$

and

$$\frac{Y^*}{k} - \tilde{I} = \bar{G} \tag{16.17}$$

Thus the value of $\bar{G}$ consistent with the target income level Y^* is obtained by substituting into the equation for equilibrium national income the mathematically expected value of I, $\tilde{I}$ as if this value was assured with certainty. This is the principle of certainty equivalence.

Further Reading

Theil (1961) and Tinbergen (1952, 1965) are the seminal contributions on the optimizing and fixed targets approaches to policy formulation respectively. As was noted in the text, one of the principal difficulties with the optimizing approach is in identifying a social welfare function. Recent contributions in the theory of public choice have analysed this issue further. See for example the survey paper by Mueller (1976). The targets instruments approach has been applied to a variety of problems. One of the most tractable and interesting applications is the Mundellian internal–external balance model as outlined in Mundell (1962).

Brainard (1967) analyses the role of uncertainty, whilst a straightforward overview of the principle of certainty equivalence can be found in Peacock and Shaw (1976).

Most texts on macroeconomic policy review the issues in question, most notably Shaw (1977) and Peston (1982). For an overview of the development of thought on the subject see Peston (1985).

17

Macroeconomic Policy: Objectives, Instruments and Constraints

The design and formulation of macroeconomic policies presupposes the need for positive intervention and interference with the normal functioning of the macroeconomy. That is to say, it is implicitly assumed that the economy left to its own devices will not ordinarily attain a state consistent with the maximum well-being of its constituent members. This conclusion might be defended upon the Keynesian assumption that the economy possesses no inherent tendency automatically to adjust to a desired state of affairs following some autonomous disturbance; alternatively, invoking the classical view that there is an inherent tendency for the economy to approach 'natural' levels of employment, output, inflation and so forth, this conclusion may still be defended upon the grounds that the adjustment process is too slow and encounters too many artificial rigidities in the modern complex economy where atomistic competition does not always prevail.[1]

Recognition of the fact that it is possible, at least in principle, to improve the existing macroeconomic performance of the economy is of course only the beginning of macroeconomic policy. It then becomes necessary to specify the *objectives* of policy more precisely and to determine their *order of priority* in the event of possible conflict.

Determining the policy objectives and their priority rankings does not, however, advance the decision-taker very far. He will then be faced with the need to choose between alternative policy recommendations proffered by his economic advisers as a means of achieving stated goals. In some cases there may be genuine alternatives; more commonly, different recommendations will reflect differences in the way in which different economic advisers view the economy. In turn, this may reflect on the one hand fundamental differences in the intellectual attachment to opposing theoretical viewpoints and on the other differing assumptions of how the economy

---

1 Alternatively, intervention may be justified as a means of reducing uncertainty, as for example in the case of prescribing set rules for financial policies, money supply growth rates and so forth.

responds. Either form of difference may result in diametrically opposing conclusions as to the effectiveness of any given macro measure.

To summarize, therefore, macroeconomic policy involves three initial steps. The first is the determination of the policy objectives and their respective ranking in the event of conflict. This, it is assumed, is accomplished (doubtless imperfectly) via the political process. The second is the formulation of policies which are logically consistent with the attainment of the objectives, given a formal theoretical structure and set of assumptions which appear relevant to real world conditions. The third is some elementary cost–benefit calculation of policy effectiveness to ensure that net benefits outweigh the costs involved.

Policy Objectives

Although considerable differences of opinion exist with respect to the way in which policy objectives should be defined, and even greater differences emerge with regard to their relative ranking, there exists a remarkable consensus upon what broadly constitutes the macroeconomic objectives.

Employment

A high level of employment has been included amongst the objectives of government economic policy ever since the message of the Keynesian revolution suggested that employment lay within the domain of government control. The Keynesian view of employment is relatively simple; the involuntary unemployed can be divided into two categories, those who could be effectively employed by macroeconomic policies raising the level of aggregate demand and those who could not.[2] The latter category takes account of those who are seasonally unemployed or in the process of changing jobs, the structurally unemployed and the chronically unemployable. The goal of full employment, therefore, should be defined solely with respect to the former from the viewpoint of macroeconomic policy. The ratio of those unemployed owing to demand deficiency to those unemployed for other reasons has, as will be seen in chapter 19, declined in recent years. One major reason has been the secular decline in traditional industries such as textiles, shipbuilding and steel. Moreover, the difficulties have been compounded by a tendency towards regional concentration within these industries and by housing policies which have rendered labour geographically immobile. If unemployment is more the consequence of major struc-

---

2 This dichotomy derives from Keynes (see for example Kahn, 1976).

tural decline, then arguably the scope of conventional macroeconomic demand management policies has declined. Indeed, it is partly this reduced employment generating potential that has contributed to the greater degree of scepticism now accorded to Keynesian orthodoxy. An alternative view of the employment objective, associated with the monetarist school, would argue that macroeconomic policy is powerless to influence the long-term or 'natural' level of employment. The natural rate is determined by a host of influences including the level of unemployment benefits (in relation to the post-tax wage), the degree of regional and occupational mobility, and so forth – all factors which are essentially microeconomic. Thus, whilst the natural rate may be amenable to government policy it will not be amenable to macroeconomic policy measures in the long term. In the short run, however, this monetarist argument concedes that the actual level of employment may depart from its natural level – rising above it at the expense of increasing the rate of inflation, and falling below it to achieve a reduction in the rate of inflation.

Price Stability

Inflation is commonly defined to imply a *persistent* tendency for the aggregate price level to rise as measured by some acceptable price index. This immediately raises the question of which price index to use, for different indices may signal different outcomes and indeed may move in opposite directions on occasions. The *wholesale price index*, for example, is greatly influenced by changes in the terms of trade and in the rate of exchange and is perhaps the best index to invoke as a pointer to future changes in the level of industrial costs. In contrast, the *retail price index* indicates changes in the average cost of living for the representative family, and in contrast to the wholesale index is influenced by changes in the level of indirect taxation. A decision to effect a major shift from direct to indirect taxation, for example, would have an immediate impact upon the retail price index whilst leaving the wholesale index unchanged. The retail price index is dominated primarily by the costs of foodstuffs, transportation and housing and is the one most frequently invoked by trade unions in justifying wage increases. It is not, however, typical or representative of all income groups and may be positively misleading for special interest groups such as old age pensioners, students and the like. In recent years, the relevance of the retail price index to wage claims has been questioned upon the ground that it ignores changes in direct taxation which affect welfare whilst leaving price levels unchanged. It has been suggested that the *tax price index*, which takes into account both direct and indirect tax changes, would be a better indicator of the compensation needed to maintain real living standards intact.

Why is inflation such a major source of concern? The answer to this question derives from the belief that inflation imposes major costs upon society whilst conferring few benefits. As will be argued in more detail in chapter 18, many of the costs associated with inflation can be avoided if the rate of inflation is correctly anticipated. Since it is easier to anticipate the rate of inflation the more stable its rate, it could be argued that the policy objective should be to ensure stability in the rate of inflation over time rather than to seek its elimination, especially as the latter may imply strenuous adjustment costs. None the less, even if inflation is fully anticipated certain costs will remain which warrant consideration. First of all, there is the resource cost involved in adjusting to inflation contained in the time and inconvenience of changing prices, adapting to new prices, informing customers and sales staff and forcing changes to advertising projects. This is a real cost which depletes real net income and welfare. Second, as Friedman has frequently emphasized, inflation may be considered a form of taxation imposed upon the holders of money balances. This effectively transfers money from creditors in the private sector to the government as a net debtor in an arbitrary and unjustified manner. Moreover, this is a form of taxation imposed without regard to ability to pay and thus imposed without reference to the standard canons of equity. Third, inflation will carry consequences for those sectors engaged in international trade and in this event one encounters increased uncertainty as to future exchange rates, which in itself may impose transaction costs upon those engaged in trading.

Balance of Payments

The balance of payments objective is identified as the desire for long-run equality between international payments and receipts. It arises from the awareness that there are costs associated with any imbalance between payments and receipts. The nature of the costs involved, however, will depend upon the nature of the exchange rate regime.

In the case of a fixed rate regime the consequences of a payments surplus would be a potentially inflationary inflow of money. Alternatively, in the event of a deficit the domestic money supply would fall as money balances are run down in exchange for foreign currency holdings. It is for this reason that a distinction is sometimes drawn between the change in the money stock after allowing for these transactions and the change which would occur in the absence of such transactions. The latter, referred to as domestic credit expansion (DCE), is often looked upon as being a better indicator of monetary policy; the control of DCE is seen to appear crucial in meeting the balance of payments target.

If there were no limit to the extent to which a payments deficit could be financed by exchanging domestic currency for foreign currency *via* central bank mediation there would be no particular need to concern oneself unduly with the existence of a deficit. However, there will normally be a limit to the extent of foreign exchange reserves held by the central bank. Once these reserves are exhausted then the country becomes bankrupt in an international context and is unable to pay for its excess of imports which would quickly be curtailed. The choking-off of essential goods and imports of raw materials would have a profound and disruptive impact upon the economy; few economies have allowed matters to reach this stage but have preferred to correct the imbalance by resorting to deflationary measures. Such measures, often imposed by international agencies such as the IMF as a condition of aid, do themselves involve costs such as increased unemployment and a slowing down in the rate of economic growth. For these reasons, then, equality in the overall balance of payments is considered a desirable goal.

Nor is this conclusion altered by the adoption of a freely floating exchange rate. Under such a regime the consequences of a balance of payments surplus or deficit would be appreciation or depreciation of the currency with no change in official reserves.[3] Fluctuating exchange rates may generate uncertainty which, as was seen in chapter 15, may be intensified by a tendency for exchange rate movements to 'overshoot' and go beyond a range that would appear to be justified solely by reference to purchasing power parity. Temporarily high exchange rates can create competitive problems for both exporters and domestic producers alike, whilst temporarily low exchange rates raise import prices with discriminatory effects throughout the economy. All things considered, therefore, exchange rate stability is a logical goal of policy.

Economic Growth

The case for economic growth being included within the objectives of macroeconomic policy is clear and compelling. Increased real income per caput[4] permits the increased consumption of all goods including leisure and hence an increase in economic welfare as commonly understood. Second,

---

3 And in such a situation no distinction exists between the domestic money supply and the extent of domestic credit expansion.

4 This would be a generally acceptable definition of economic growth providing some possible dangers are recognized. For example, the sudden elimination of the retired part of the population would raise per caput incomes but one might hesitate to include this under the heading of economic growth. There are other similar distributional qualifications one might wish to make to the above definition.

with natural increases in the labour force combined with a tendency for economic activity to become increasingly capital intensive, economic growth becomes a necessary prerequisite for the maintenance of full employment and for the elimination of the social tensions which accompany unemployment. In addition, economic growth is the only feasible means of terminating poverty. This arises from the compounding nature of the growth process; in contrast, once and for all distributional transfers from rich to poor have but a relatively insignificant effect, and this is equally true of transfers effected by the tax transfer mechanism within an economy as it is of international aid grants between countries.

Although most economists would endorse this general desirability of economic growth, it should be emphasized that a consensus does not exist. There are also costs associated with economic growth including pollution, congestion, the tensions associated with living in a highly complex and urbanized society and the speeding up of structural change which generates displacement effects and regional decline. In addition, many economists have drawn attention to the impact of economic growth upon the depletion of natural resources, many of which are in finite supply, and also have pointed to the environmental and ecological damage inflicted by uncontrolled growth.

Regional Balance

Finally, one may justifiably include amongst the objectives of macroeconomic policy the desire to promote or maintain a relatively uniform spatial allocation of incomes and resources. It is recognized that labour is still relatively immobile and that there are severe costs associated with the secular regional decline of highly specialized industry. This is particularly the case with respect to traditional industries such as shipbuilding and textiles now facing intense Third-World competition, and it has led to the formulation of structural economic policies for specified industries, discriminatory fiscal treatment of the regions and interventionist government mediation. It has also witnessed the growth in importance of regional transfers in the EEC total budget.

Policy Instruments

Fiscal

Fiscal policy is defined to encompass any change in the level, composition or timing of government expenditures or any change in the burden, structure or frequency of the tax payment. Since fiscal policy normally influences the size of the actual public sector borrowing requirement (PSBR), changes in the latter are commonly looked upon as an indicator of the government's fiscal stance. Such a view, however, is essentially fallacious unless carefully qualified, since the size of the PSBR will vary in response to changing income levels quite independently of policy changes. Thus, for example, an exogenous movement into recession will deplete tax revenues and increase unemployment benefits leading to a widening of the PSBR without any conscious policy change upon the part of the fiscal authorities.

The essence of fiscal policy is that it is the means to influence expenditure *flows* in the economy whether directly through expenditure changes or indirectly through tax and transfer changes; such changes in flow magnitudes are seen to be a principal means of controlling the level of aggregate demand. In earlier Keynesian theorizing, such 'demand management' was looked upon as the principal means of maintaining demand at a sufficiently high level to provide full employment, and also as the primary means of 'fine tuning' the economy so as to smooth if not entirely eliminate the trade cycle. In this view, fiscal policy was the dominant macropolicy instrument and the monetary or budgetary consequences of fiscally induced deficits or surpluses were conveniently ignored. More recently, and partly as a consequence of the monetarist revival, more sophisticated Keynesian treatments, whilst still insisting upon the primacy of fiscal policy, have given an increasingly important role to the monetary and debt implications.

In examining the record of fiscal policy it would appear that the authorities have a marked preference for tax/transfer changes as opposed to expenditure changes as a means of macroeconomic control. There exists a number of reasons for this preference. First, expenditure programmes are the means of providing desired public services and meeting agreed social objectives; attempts to alter the volume of expenditure in line with macroeconomic goals will inevitably interfere with the attainment of these ends. Second, expenditure changes may, for administrative reasons, require time before they can be put into effect and may tend to be regionally concentrated in their impact. In contrast, tax changes can be speedily put into effect and will generally have a relatively uniform influence throughout the economy.

Monetary

The primary tools of monetary policy are the volume of money upon the one hand and the level of interest rates upon the other. These two are highly interdependent in that for a given PSBR the control of one inevitably implies loss of effective control over the other. In turn, both the money supply and the interest rate are intimately linked with fiscal policy. This is because, in the context of a closed economy, the increase in high-powered money is simply equal to the PSBR *minus* non-bank lending to the government by the private sector for a fuller discussion of this relationship refer to pages 127 to 129. Both non-bank lending to the government by the private sector and bank lending to the private sector will be a function, *ceteris paribus*, of the level of interest rates. Thus, for any given PSBR, there will be an infinite number of money supply/interest rate combinations consistent with financing the deficit. However, once the money supply target is specified so too will be the interest rate; alternatively, once the interest rate is decided upon so too will be the money supply, consistent with the given PSBR. If the government wishes to dictate both the money supply and the interest rate, then it must adjust fiscal policy to obtain a PSBR consistent with the desired money supply/interest rate combination. This is precisely the contention of the new classical position – namely, that if inflation is to be controlled without imposing excessively high rates of interest then the public sector deficit must be sharply curtailed. Hence the rationale of the monetarist assertion that fiscal policy should be rendered subordinate to monetary policy.

Faced with the choice between controlling either the money supply or the interest rate for any given PSBR, the authorities in the past have tended to opt for the interest rate target. In part this preference stemmed from the belief that too great a degree of fluctuation in interest rates, implying fluctuating government debt prices, would jeopardize the ability of the authorities to sell future government debt. In addition, high interest rates were considered politically undesirable especially because of their impact upon mortgage payments. Since 1976, however, this policy has effectively been reversed. Money supply targets were formally introduced for the first time and nominal interest rates were subsequently allowed to rise to record levels.

In addition to changes in the volume of money and the level of interest rates, monetary policy may also encompass selective controls over certain forms of credit – as, for example, hire purchase restrictions. These usually take the form of fixing minimum deposits and specifying the maximum period of repayment and generally exert a fairly immediate impact upon the level of aggregate demand. Although such forms of control were much in vogue in the UK during the 1960s they were virtually abandoned in the wake of the Bank of England's conversion to competition and credit control (1971). Whatever the virtues of competition and credit control in promoting competition, it did not serve as an effective means of controlling the money supply. Intense competition within the banking sector led to a sharp rise in loans to the private sector and hence a dramatic expansion of the M3 money supply. It was in order to regain control over the effective money supply that the experiment was finally abandoned in the attempt to control bank lending. In recent years UK governments have attempted a much firmer control of the effective money supply, reflected in their adoption of supplementary special deposits which commercial banks have to make with the Bank of England (the corset) and in a much greater willingness to accept the interest rate implications of financing by government debt sales to the non-bank private sector.

Price and Income Controls

Direct controls over prices and incomes have frequently been resorted to by British governments to supplement monetary and fiscal policy in a direct attempt to control inflation. As has already been indicated, Keynesians often argue that prices reflect costs, largely wage costs, and that the latter are determined mainly by sociological factors and are relatively immune to general macroeconomic control. Hence the need to impose direct controls over prices and incomes in order to meet the inflation objective. In contrast, monetarists view inflation as being determined almost entirely by monetary influences. Since trade unions cannot directly control the money supply they cannot generate inflation and thus controls over price and wage increases become an irrelevancy. This view was given its sharpest test during the 1973 OPEC-induced oil price rise. Monetarists contended that if the money stock were held constant then with a relatively stable demand for money function (stable velocity) the only consequence would be a rise in the *comparative* prices of oil intensive to non oil intensive products. From a purely long-term viewpoint, with unlimited price and wage flexibility, this may have been correct; however, in the short term, the comparative downward rigidity of non oil intensive product prices implied quantity adjustments with severe deflationary consequences for real income. Unwilling to accept such short-term changes, the monetary authorities attempted to cushion the blow by permitting a degree of monetary expansion and thus, in monetarist eyes, permitted a general rise in the retail price index.

Even if inflation is a purely monetary phenomenon in the long term, it is possible that price and wage controls have a useful role to perform. On the one hand they may condition expectations towards lower increases than might have been expected to emerge from the normal wage bargaining process, and to this extent to make the adjustment to lower inflation rates less painful than anticipated. In addition, it can be argued that the adoption of a monetarist approach, exercising a stringent control over monetary aggregates, requires an incomes policy, if only to ensure that sacrifices are made in a reasonably equitable manner. A rigid monetary squeeze in a completely free market environment would imply arbitrary changes in income distribution, with the expectation that the strong would benefit at the expense of the weak. Against these possible benefits must be offset the possible costs of resource misallocation as comparative prices and incomes are prevented from adjusting to the changing composition of demand. Moreover, it has been contended that income policies may operate in a decidedly perverse manner in that the ceiling rate becomes a minimum rate which arguably would have exceeded that determined by collective bargaining in many instances.

Exchange Rate

Exchange rate policy refers to the decision to adopt fixed or floating exchange rates and also, in the event of the former, to determine the appropriate rate of exchange and whether to alter the existing rate (revaluation or devaluation). Post-war UK experience would suggest that the authorities have placed little reliance upon the exchange rate instrument. Indeed, prior to 1971, under the Bretton Woods arrangements, the authorities identified the exchange rate not as a policy instrument but rather as a policy objective. In this view the confusion between objectives and instruments implied a welfare loss for society as a whole; the attempt to maintain a fixed and overvalued exchange rate for prestige reasons and to preserve an international role for sterling conflicted with the attainment of other policy objectives. In this perspective, the devaluations of 1949 and 1967 were not so much conscious policy decisions as events forced by the severity of balance of payments deficits.

Since 1971, the exchange rate has been allowed to float although not always without central bank intervention to 'manage' the exchange rate adjustments. In consequence, a new awareness as to the possible consequences of exchange rate movements has developed and the appropriate exchange rate policy, instead of being the 'great unmentionable', has become a lively topic of controversy.

The Public Sector Borrowing Requirement – An Intermediate Policy Target

The incoming Conservative Government of 1979 made the control of inflation its primary macroeconomic target. This was not merely a reflection of its views on the desirability of competing goals and a subjective preference for inflation vis à vis employment objectives; rather, it was founded upon the objective belief that the control of inflation was an essential prerequisite for the attainment of alternative goals, especially employment and economic growth.

If control of inflation was the primary objective of policy, control of the money supply was looked upon as the primary instrument by which to achieve it. It was believed that there was a strong and decisive relationship between the size of the PSBR and the money supply; the PSBR had become the intermediate policy target.

Does control of the PSBR imply effective control of the money supply? Needless to say, the empirical evidence is far from conclusive. None the less, the issues themselves are relatively clear. Conceptually, any projected positive PSBR can be financed simply by the expedient of the government issuing IOUs to the central bank and receiving cash in return, which is then put into circulation in the process of government expenditure. Alternatively, the government could sell bonds to the commercial banks and receive in turn an augmentation of its deposits with the banking system against which it can write cheques. Normally, this exchange will also imply an increase in the money supply. Equally, the government could offer its securities to the overseas sector and receive payment denominated in foreign currency, which it may then translate into £s sterling via the exchange equalization account in order to meet its domestic obligations. In order to conduct this transaction the exchange equalization account will be obliged to sell Treasury bills, implying that more Treasury bills have to be sold elsewhere. This additional sale will offset the sale of debt to the overseas sector, but the money supply is still increased by the event of the subsequent government expenditure. In each of these cases, therefore, there is a direct and immediate relationship between the financing of the projected PSBR and the money stock as conventionally defined.

However, there remains a fourth form of finance, namely bond sales to the non-bank private sector, upon which Keynesians have implicitly relied and which in their view leaves the total money supply unchanged. Here cash is transferred from private sector deposits to the government in exchange for increased bondholding by the non-bank private sector. The increased willingness to hold more government bonds upon the part of the non-bank private sector is explained in terms of enhanced yields on government debt. It is this increase in interest rates or the change in relative yields on financial assets which induces the non-bank private sector to adjust its portfolio and substitute bonds for cash.

The foregoing argument is now widely accepted in Keynesian circles, and implies that the relationship between the PSBR and the money supply is at best tenuous and uncertain; indeed the logic of the argument would lead to the conclusion that the authorities can minimize the monetary implications of the PSBR provided that they are willing to accommodate the required change in the level of interest rates. There may, of course, be all sorts of political difficulties and objections to accepting the interest rate cost, but in principle the choice remains.

Moreover, even if the entire PSBR translates into a money supply increase with no sale of government debt to the private non-bank sector, it does not follow that the increase is significant in terms of the increase in the total money supply. The latter includes bank lending to the private sector, and in recent years it has been the increase in lending to the private sector which has accounted for the vast bulk (on occasions some 90 per cent) of the increase in recorded M3. How then does one account for this monetarist emphasis upon the importance of the PSBR for the overall money supply?

The answer lies in the belief that there exists a reasonably stable relationship between the amount of public sector debt and the amount of bank lending to the private sector. Thus private sector borrowing from the banks is itself seen as a consequence of an enlarged PSBR. The rationale for this belief rests upon the proposition that the private sector seeks to maintain a given portfolio of financial assets related to its income and wealth, and that within this portfolio it wishes to maintain a given balance between cash and alternative financial assets, including government bonds.

More specifically, it is asserted that over the medium or long term there is a relatively constant relationship between the nominal public sector debt held by the private sector and national income. If this relationship reveals a short run-decline, say owing to the impact of inflation, it will establish the basis for further sales of debt as the private sector seeks to adjust its portfolio. Second, it is claimed that there is a relationship between bank lending to the private sector and national income. Although this relationship reveals short-run cyclical fluctuation and is distorted by interest rate changes and so forth, it is claimed that it is reasonably stable over the medium or long term.

Hence the claim that there is a strong and important relationship between the PSBR as a percentage of GDP and the total change in the M3 money supply. It is for this reason that monetary targets have often been approximated in terms of establishing a target PSBR figure as a percentage of GDP. The evidence remains far from conclusive; if such a relationship is ultimately established then a rationale exists for present government strategy. If it ultimately proves to be a weak relationship then the unavoidable conclusion must be that the government has chosen the wrong indicator by which to control the all-important variable (in its eyes) of the money supply.

Of course, even if one disagrees with the monetarist contention of a strong and dominant relationship between the money supply and the PSBR, one can still argue along Keynesian lines the need to reduce or constrain the rise in the latter. The greater the public sector deficit the greater, *ceteris paribus*, will be the pressure upon interest rates. Not only will this tend to crowd out a certain portion of private sector expenditures but also will it put upward pressure upon the exchange rate to the general detriment of the competitive position of British industry.

Constraints on Macroeconomic Policy

Both the objectives and the instruments of macroeconomic policy have been outlined, and the following is a consideration of the major constraints which might inhibit policy formulation.

International Agreements

One major constraint faced by all economies is the force of international commitments and agreements entered into with such bodies as the IMF, GATT and EEC. Such agreements will circumscribe the ability to alter tariffs, quotas, tax rates and structure and may also imply a commitment to money supply targets. The force of these constraints is not lessened by the fact that they were initially entered into by a government other than the one presently enjoying office.[5]

Non-macroeconomic Objectives

Other objectives of policy may conflict with the attainment of macro-economic goals. For example, belief in the desirability of a *laissez-faire* economy and the maintenance of a non-interventionist stance may inhibit the adoption of macroeconomic measures or render macroeconomic policy more difficult to effect. A recent example in the United Kingdom experience was the abolition of exchange controls, which arguably renders it more difficult to control the money supply, interest rates and the volume of domestic investment. Similar considerations apply to the adoption of certain competition policies, which may constrain the monopoly power of government, industry and the nationalized sector.

An extremely powerful non-macroeconomic objective which may constrain macroeconomic policy is the principle of equity. The need to establish an income distribution and a tax/transfer system which is accepted as 'fair' may significantly blunt incentives and impair the objective of economic growth. Lower growth today, to satisfy equity considerations, may

---

5 One might argue that such 'constraints' do no more than recognize the extent of international interdependence by placing 'limits to sovereignty'. Given free rider problems there have to be obligations as well as rights in any such international agreements.

imply lower overall incomes in the future, especially for the lower paid. Thus, a tax structure deemed progressive in the static sense may be regressive when viewed dynamically and vice versa.

Legislative Sanction

Virtually any macroeconomic policy with a sizeable impact will require legislative approval. The force of this constraint, and the extent to which it influences the modification of policy proposals, is determined by the relevant political institutions and systems of government. It is of considerable importance in the United States, where presidential policies may need the sanction of a Congress dominated by the alternative political party and where, in any case, political affiliation does not prevent opposition to the official party line. It is of decidedly less significance in the UK where the government of the day can, if it has an effective majority, virtually ensure the adoption of a given policy by invoking a three-line whip. None the less opposition can mean delay, and whilst the overall strategy may remain intact, piecemeal amendments can be made at the committee stage.

Uncertainty

Perhaps the single most important constraint stems from the existence of imperfect information and hence uncertainty as to the outcome of any given policy measure; the importance of this point is that it may dissuade the policy-maker from adopting the policy which *ex post* would have been optimal, and persuade him to adopt a policy which *ex ante* minimizes the risk of an unacceptable outcome. To illustrate this point, consider two alternative macroeconomic policy measures A and B. Policy A has a mean expected value which coincides with the target income level Y^*, but also possesses a standard deviation which implies that an unacceptable outcome remains a distinct if distant possibility. In contrast, policy B has a mean falling substantially below the target income level but its smaller standard deviation renders it a less risky policy. *Ex ante* the policy-maker who, electorally, will normally be risk averse will opt for policy B, although its chances of hitting the income level are comparatively remote. Such behaviour is, of course, perfectly rational; all that is emphasized here is that the existence of uncertainty renders the optimal policy *ex ante* different from the optimal policy *ex post* in the majority of outcomes. One consequence of such rational risk-averse behaviour is that in the majority of cases the chosen policy will appear in retrospect to have been wrongly conceived. That is to say, looking back, it will appear that a preferable alternative existed.

MACROECONOMIC POLICY

Concluding Comments

In this chapter the case for macroeconomic policy has been established – at least in principle – and the problems facing the individual or individuals charged with the decision-making process have been examined. The policy objectives and the instruments that can be employed for their attainment have also been surveyed. Whilst a broad consensus emerges with respect to the policy objectives – although not necessarily with regard to their ranking – considerable differences emerge with respect to the potency of policy instruments. Such differences reflect differences in opinion concerning the structure and functioning of the macroeconomy. Thus Keynesians and monetarists, for example, differ substantially with respect to the relative efficacy of monetary and fiscal policy and with regard to the relevance of prices and incomes policies, since they possess a different model analysis of the way in which the economy actually works. Finally, some of the constraints imposed upon macroeconomic policy formulation were examined, and it was indicated that perhaps by far the most important was the uncertainty of living in an uncertain world.

Further Reading

Since chapters 20 to 23 are concerned with the principal macroeconomic objectives, there is no need to provide detailed references on objectives at this stage. The further reading suggested at the end of those chapters provides an adequate number of references.

With regard to the policy instruments, Peacock and Shaw (1976) provide a thorough analysis of most aspects of fiscal policy, whilst Shaw (1977) offers a more concise review of the principal issues associated with the design and implementation of fiscal policy. Accounts of the principal instruments of monetary policy are provided in most specialist texts on monetary economics. Sound recent reviews which concentrate on UK experience are provided by Gowland (1982) and Artis and Lewis (1981). Prices and incomes policy is covered by Jones (1976) whilst a concise introduction to balance of payments policy can be found in Cohen (1971). A more specifically UK oriented balance of payments text is Thirlwall (1980).

The most valuable insights into the constraints on policy formulation are provided in accounts of experiences of policy formulation and implemented as for example in Peacock (1979) and Pliatzky (1982).

There are a number of texts on macroeconomic policy which cover most of the issues raised in this chapter. See for example Shaw (1977) and Peston (1982).

18

Inflation and Counter-inflation
Policy in the UK

Inflation as an object of policy interest has shifted to centre stage over the past seven or eight years, not only in the UK but also in many other developed market economies. The most obvious reason for this is the significant increase in inflation which has been recorded in the UK over the last decade (see table 18.1) and in other OECD countries (see table 18.2). The weighting given to control of inflation relative to employment and growth in the policy-maker's objective function has certainly increased in the UK.

The first question which will be addressed in this chapter is why recent governments have placed such a high priority on inflationary control. Their 'enthusiasm' presumably reflects a belief that inflation imposes real costs on society and a belief that the costs of 'squeezing inflation out of the system' are less than the benefits which will flow as a consequence. Following the review of the kind of costs which inflation *may* impose, a review will then be given of the policy instruments which can be deployed in order to reduce and/or stabilize the rate of inflation, with particular reference to UK experience with these policies over the post-war period.

Why Should Governments Control Inflation?

Macroeconomic Costs of Inflation

From various statements made by government officials it is quite clear that the government of 1979–86 saw the principal cost of inflation as being a macroeconomic one, namely that it generates unemployment. Take, for example, the following statement from Leon Brittan, a government minister:

> We have put at the forefront the goal of reducing inflation . . . because by doing that we are tackling the problem which has been at the heart of our trouble. It is not a question of choosing to tackle inflation rather than unemployment. It is rather a recognition that past inflation has been the *cause* of present unemployment. (Authors' emphasis)

TABLE 18.1
Inflation in the UK 1956–86

Year	% change in retail price index	Year	% change in retail price index	Year	% change retail price index
1956	2.0	1969	5.4	1982	8.7
1957	3.8	1970	6.4	1983	4.6
1958	3.2	1971	9.4	1984	4.9
1959	3.0	1972	7.1	1985	6.0
1960	1.1	1973	9.2	1986	3.3
1961	4.2	1974	16.1		
1962	1.6	1975	24.2		
1963	2.0	1976	16.5		
1964	3.2	1977	15.8		
1965	4.8	1978	8.3		
1966	3.9	1979	13.4		
1967	2.5	1980	18.0		
1968	4.7	1981	12.1		

Source: *Economic Trends* (various issues).

TABLE 18.2
Changes in Inflation for Selected Industrial Countries 1970–85

	1970	1971	1972	1973	1974	1975	1976	1977	1978	1979	1980	1981	1982	1983	1984	1985
Canada	4.7	3.2	4.9	8.4	13.8	10.8	9.7	7.0	6.4	9.9	10.3	10.6	10.4	5.3	2.8	3.2
United States	5.5	4.5	3.4	5.6	10.3	9.6	5.2	6.0	7.3	8.8	9.0	9.6	6.5	3.7	4.2	3.3
Japan	6.7	4.6	5.0	11.1	20.9	8.6	5.5	5.5	3.4	2.0	7.7	3.2	1.9	0.8	1.3	1.6
France	5.5	5.6	6.0	7.2	9.6	13.1	9.7	9.1	9.7	9.6	10.4	11.9	2.5	9.6	7.2	5.9
West Germany	7.1	7.9	7.9	5.9	6.6	6.7	3.2	3.8	3.9	3.8	5.0	4.0	4.4	3.2	1.8	2.2
Italy	6.6	6.6	5.9	10.3	16.3	17.4	18.0	18.9	14.0	15.1	18.5	18.3	17.8	14.9	10.8	8.8

Source: *IMF Annual Reports* (various issues)

In effect this is tantamount to arguing that in so far as a Phillips relation exists, it is *positively* sloped rather than negative or even vertical. This is a possibility which has in fact been posited by Friedman (1977) and merits further exploration.

One possible link between higher inflation and higher unemployment may be via disincentive effects on investment. This may occur as a result of greater uncertainty being associated with higher levels of inflation, especially in a regime of floating exchange rates. In taking a decision about whether or not to commit resources to investment one would have to make a judgement about how product prices will change relative to factor prices, and how the exchange rate will respond in consequence. If, as some have suggested, *higher levels* of inflation are associated with *greater variability* of inflation rates, then a greater element of uncertainty can be expected.

Investment might also be affected if, as part of the inflationary process, income is redistributed away from profit and towards wage income. This link is rather more tenuous, however. There certainly have been specific examples of such redistributions, but as with the uncertainty argument it is difficult to ascribe specific values to the effects involved. A third and more convincing connection between inflation and investment is via the effect which the former has on long-term nominal interest rates and short-term real interest rates. As a consequence of the significant increase in inflation in the UK over the 1970s, long-term interest rates have risen quite dramatically. Even as inflation has been falling in the 1980s these rates have remained high. For example, at the time of writing (early 1987), Minimum Lending Rate stood at 11 per cent whilst the inflation rate was of the order of 3.5 per cent, yielding a real interest rate of 7.5 per cent. By historical standards this is very high indeed. Given the wide variation in inflation rates which has occurred, investors have to be persuaded that any fall in inflation is permanent. As a consequence, short-term interest rates also remain high despite falling inflation, and relatively high real rates are recorded. High real rates are unequivocally a disincentive to investment. One might argue that this phenomenon is associated with variability in inflation rather than the actual level of inflation. Thus in the event that one had a relatively high *fully anticipated and stable* rate of inflation, relative interest rates would more accurately reflect society's rate of time preference. In this respect the cost (of output forgone) is a cost due to unanticipated and variable inflation, rather than inflation *per se*.

Another way in which inflation may adversely affect output and employment is through its effect on the demand for tradeables in an open economy. A relatively high rate of inflation at home would result in increased demand for import substitutes and a lower demand for exports. Unless the inflation differential is eliminated, unemployment results. Note again, however, that the variable of concern here is the *relative* rate of inflation rather than inflation *per se*. The most graphic illustration of this point can be seen if an examination is made of UK inflation rates in the 1960s, which were low in absolute terms but high relative to the UK's competitors such that balance of payments crises were frequent. One might contend that even this potential cost can be avoided by operating with a floating exchange rate. In a smoothly operating system the exchange rate will adjust in line with inflation differentials to maintain purchasing power parity and competitiveness. The effect which capital flows (and in the UK case) resource windfalls can have on the exchange rate are sufficient to call into question whether the link can be broken in this way. For example, despite a relatively high inflation rate in 1979–80 the sterling effective exchange rate *appreciated* rather than depreciated; despite a relatively low inflation rate in 1984–85, the sterling effective exchange rate *depreciated* rather than appreciated.

Microeconomic Costs of Inflation

It is traditional to comment on the (sometimes pernicious) income redistribution effects which inflation can have. Thus in the event that one agent borrows from another agent at a fixed *nominal* rate of interest and there follows an unexpected increase in inflation, there is a redistribution from creditor to debtor. Likewise, individuals on fixed income contracts find that real incomes are squeezed; students and pensioners are frequently singled out as cases in point. Such redistributions can and do take place. Note, however, that they result because fixed price contracts are agreed, and the inflation that is referred to is unanticipated. If inflation were fully and correctly anticipated contracts could be agreed which made allowance for inflation and thereby avoided redistributive effects. Furthermore there are administrative arrangements, such as *index linking*, which can be introduced to protect those on fixed incomes. Thus this cost is one which is associated with unanticipated inflation rather than inflation *per se*.

Another argument advanced in this connection is that as inflation increases it becomes more difficult for agents to distinguish between *absolute changes* in the price level and changes in the *structure of relative prices*. As well as generating uncertainty this may lead individuals to make mistakes, giving rise to resource misallocation. In referring to this argument, however, it must again be noted that the cost in question is not just of inflation *per se* but is rather associated with variable and essentially unanticipated inflation. The point is important because, as will be seen shortly, one might argue as a result of this and the previous point that the policy-maker's objective should be one of stabilizing inflation rather than seeking a reduction in the level *per se*.

Even when inflation is fully anticipated, however, there are likely to be other costs generated by the inflationary process, such as an increase in transactions costs. In an inflationary situation, nominal values have to be changed more frequently (wages, prices, taxes and income transfers). These transactions costs may be lower for one type of variable than another (for instance, compare the costs of a wage change for a large supplier of homogeneous labour with the costs of a supermarket chain altering prices). One thing is certain, however – these costs are positive. They are extremely difficult to quantify, although the paper by Minford and Hilliard (1978) does make an attempt to do so. The most surprising result of this study is that the costs turn out to be relatively low and somewhat insensitive to the level of inflation. Thus Minford and Hilliard estimate transactions costs as

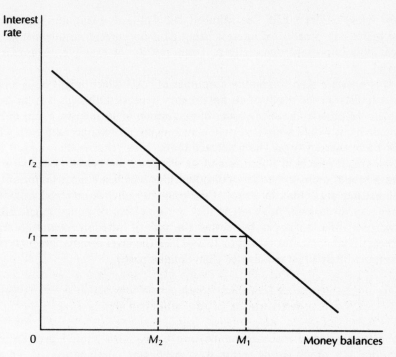

Figure 18.1   Inflation and the demand for real balances

0.06 per cent of GNP for a 2 per cent inflation and 0.11 per cent for a 30 per cent inflation. Even if these figures are accurate, 0.11 per cent of GNP is not an insubstantial amount. They are, however, almost certainly an underestimate since the proxy for the cost of price changes is the cost of new price lists, and that for the cost of wage changes is days lost in wage negotiations. As Gordon (1981) and (1982) shows, there are many more costs associated with price and wage changes respectively.

A specific type of transactions cost which may be associated with anticipated inflation and which has received considerable attention in the academic literature is the effect of inflation on holdings of money balances. Refer to figure 18.1. The demand curve refers to an individual's demand for real balances. As expected inflation rises, nominal interest rates increase from r_1 to r_2 and the demand for *real balances* contracts from M_1 to M_2 as individuals economize on money holdings and switch assets to interest-bearing near monies (perhaps switching from current accounts to deposit accounts). This involves the agent in costs; for example, he has to make more visits to the bank than formerly. Attempts have been made to estimate this cost and it turns out to be higher than the transactions costs which were listed earlier (again, see Minford and Hilliard, 1978), although given the increasing practice of interest being paid on current accounts it is not clear how important this really is. Tobin (1972), for example, regards it as trivial.

It is possible then to identify a number of costs which might be incurred by a society as the result of an inflationary process, although it is far from easy to be precise about the order of magnitude of such costs. From public statements it would seem that policy-makers are more concerned with what has been referred to as the macroeconomic costs, that is, the output and employment effects of inflation and its effect on the balance of payments, and it would seem to be these considerations which are most important in stimulating anti-inflation policy. One point which has emerged from the foregoing discussion, however, is that the objective of policy might be to lower not inflation *per se* but rather the rate of inflation *relative* to one's international competitors and/or to *stabilize* the level of inflation such that it is more likely to be anticipated than unanticipated.

Instruments of Anti-Inflation Policy

As with any other macroeconomic target, diagnosis should precede prescription. In other words, prior to a particular combination of policies being assigned to a given objective, the underlying causes of the problem concerned should first be identified. As we saw in chapter 14, this is far from straightforward in the case of inflation. For some years a good deal of controversy has surrounded discussion of its driving forces. Thus if one takes the view that all inflation is the manifestation of monetary mismanagement, then counter-inflation policy is 'simply' a case of keeping the rate of growth of monetary expansion within certain predetermined limits. Alternatively one might take the view that although inflation is generally demand determined, control of the rate of growth of the money supply is necessary but not sufficient for inflationary control. Monetary policy would have to be supported by a consistent fiscal policy. Another view might be that inflation is the outcome of some kind of 'social struggle' over the distribution of the national product and is basically therefore cost push. In this case the key to inflationary control is some form of incomes policy. Finally, instead of, or in combination with, all of these instruments one may attempt to minimize the damage done by inflation through the introduction of some form of indexation of wage contracts and transfer payments. Which combination of these policies is used, and the vigour with which they are applied, depends on the policy-maker's perception of the underlying causes, and the weight given to inflation in his objective function. All of these instruments have been deployed in the UK over the post-war period.

Inflationary Control in the UK 1950–86

The combination of policies chosen by any policy-maker depends in part on the prevailing economic orthodoxy and in part on his own particular philosophical inclinations. The complexion of the latter tends to change as governments change, whilst the former changes rather more slowly. One can trace particular switches in inflation policy to changes of government, and indeed if necessary one could compare the anti-inflation policies of alternating governments over this period. This, however, would be to ignore the thread of continuity which has run through policy for fairly long periods of time. Thus, despite the fact that different emphases may have been ascribed to different instruments at various times, it remains true that the prevailing orthodoxy from 1950 through to the mid-1970s was in the Keynesian tradition of emphasizing demand management manipulation as the basis to inflationary control, occasionally with the backing of direct controls. Since 1975 at least, a 'sea change' in orthodoxy has occurred (which is not incidentally confined to the UK) where monetary policy is seen as being the central instrument. In reviewing UK experience the discussion will therefore be structured around demand management manipulation, which dominated the post-war experience; the intermittent recourse to wage and price controls; and the recent primary reliance on monetary management, with particular reference to the medium-term financial strategy.

Demand Management and Inflationary Control

In discussing the use of demand management policies for inflationary control, two points must be borne in mind. First, that for most of this period the inflation objective was intertwined with the employment, balance of payments and growth objectives. Furthermore, with the discovery of the Phillips curve in 1958 it was widely accepted that a functional relationship between inflation and unemployment held. Employment policy will be considered specifically in the next chapter, but in discussing inflation it must be kept in mind that the two are related. Second, in covering such a lengthy period a great deal of detail will have to be omitted in order to focus on general issues.

The roots of the 'prevailing orthodoxy' on inflationary control in the 1950s and 1960s can be traced to three related pieces of policy analysis. First, there was the direct contribution of Keynes. The work of Keynes and others in the 1930s, and in particular the *General Theory*, had a profound effect on the way in which economic policy was formulated and executed in the UK. In the context of inflationary control, the Keynesian analysis of the inflationary gap is especially relevant. At its simplest this idea is expressed

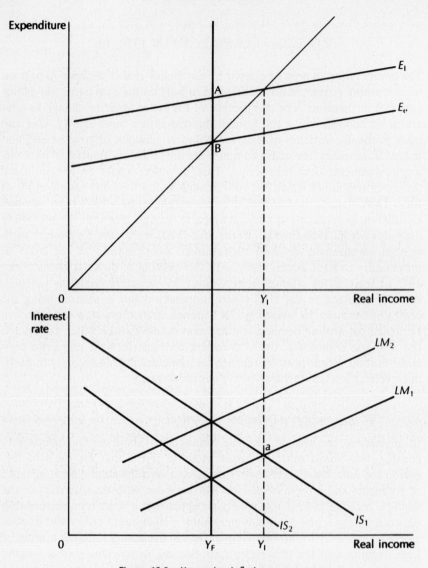

Figure 18.2   Keynesian inflationary gap

in figure 18.2. In the upper panel aggregate expenditure of E_1 results in an inflationary gap of AB. The resultant level of income Y_1 is in excess of the full employment level of income, and demand pull inflation ensues as increased expenditure is translated into increased prices rather than increased output. The prescription for removing such inflation is to restrict

the level of aggregate demand – precisely opposite to the case of the deflationary gap where the policy stance recommended was one of reflating
aggregate demand. This could be accomplished by engineering a shift in *IS*
and/or *LM* such that they intersected at the full employment level of
income rather than at point *a*. Since the authorities can shift *LM* by changing the money supply, and can shift *IS* by changing government expenditure and/or taxes, this is within their power.

The second strand which fed into the policy stance was the discovery of
the Phillips curve and the belief that a trade-off existed between inflation
and unemployment. This served to reinforce the inflationary gap type analysis by suggesting that reductions in inflation could only be attained by
increasing the level of unemployment, i.e. by manipulation of demand management.

This still leaves a missing link. Even if one believes that manipulations of
IS and *LM* are the key to inflationary control a question is begged; namely
is there any basis for relying on one policy option to a greater extent than
another? It is widely believed that Keynes firmly favoured reliance on fiscal
policy rather than monetary policy. Keynes himself, however, was in no
doubt as to the potency of monetary policy *especially* when it came to
inflationary control. The relative downgrading of monetary policy had
more to do with the inordinate amount of attention paid to his special cases
(of the liquidity trap and interest inelastic investment), and possibly the
third strand, that is, the publication of the highly influential *Radcliffe
Report* on the monetary system in 1959. The main thrust of this report was
to reinforce the view that monetary policy was likely to be of little help in
short-term demand management. Furthermore, by emphasizing the broad
supply of liquidity in the economy rather than any monetary aggregate, it
lent further support to the view that monetary manipulation affected final
expenditure principally through its effect on investment demand rather than
directly impacting on consumer expenditure.

Figures 18.3 and 18.4 give some information on the use of these policies,
in the former case from 1959 to 1974, in the latter for the entire duration of
the period. Figure 18.3 is taken from Price (1978) who tries to give an
indication of overall fiscal stance, that is, looking at the impact of both
expenditure and revenue changes. The diagonal which runs from north-west
to south-east traces out *neutral* budgetary positions. Points below and to
the left of this line are consistent with (fiscal) demand deflation, whilst
points above and to the right are consistent with (fiscal) demand reflation.
By comparing those years which lie below the neutrality line with the
information contained in table 18.1, it can be seen that these occur in years
following an acceleration of inflation. Here it will be recalled from chapter
17 that there are identification and implementation lags associated with the

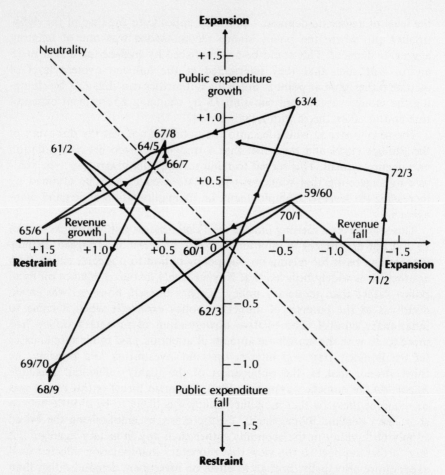

Figure 18.3   Changes in budgetary stance (with full employment corrections) 1959–60 to 1973–4. The corrections are changes in the ratios of weighted full employment receipts and expenditure to full employment GDP

use of most policy instruments. This is especially true of fiscal policy. One further feature of this experience can be noted from a comparison of figures 18.3 and 20.2. The periods of fiscal restraint are invariably associated with current account deficits and sterling crises.

Figure 18.4 documents changes in bank rate (later MLR) over the period. Again two important features of the pattern of changes can be deduced from a comparison with table 18.1 and figure 20.2. First, increases in bank rate (as a basis to credit restriction) coincide with periods of relatively high inflation. In other words it would seem that credit restriction was consis-

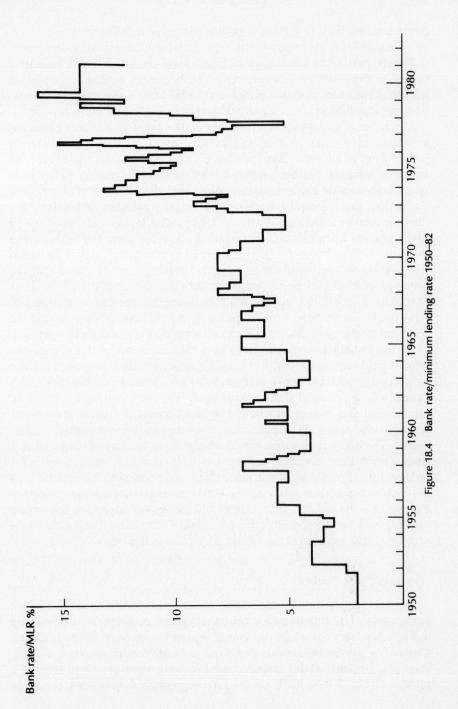

Figure 18.4   Bank rate/minimum lending rate 1950–82

tently a means used to try and close any perceived inflationary gap. Second, increases in MLR correspond with years in which the current account is in deficit, in part as an instrument of inflationary control but also to attract capital inflows (or more accurately to stem capital outflows). One other feature of the chart (and this comparison is notable) is that the implementation lags involved are quite clearly shorter than in the case of fiscal policy.

A number of comments can be made on the experience of using demand management policies in this way as the central plank in anti-inflation policy. First of all policy has been largely of a 'fine tuning' type; that is to say, once inflation has been reduced both fiscal and monetary policy have taken on a counter-cyclical posture. Note that the objective of policy over the period has principally been one of actually reducing inflation rather than necessarily stabilizing it around a particular level. Apart from one or two occasions when inflation was relatively high for particular reasons (like the Korean War boom of 1951–52), the level of inflation was in fact relatively stable through until the late 1960s. Further, it can be stated that the principal objective of policy was to reduce inflation relative to the rates prevailing in the UK's main trading partners. By the end of the period, however, it is quite clear that this approach to policy had failed to reverse the recurrent tendency of UK inflation to outstrip that of her main competitors. There are a number of reasons which have been advanced for this. On the one hand it has been argued that fine tuning was bound to fail because it did not control wage inflation – thus attempts to control inflation via incomes policy (which will be reviewed shortly) were made. On the other hand it could be argued that fine tuning was bound to fail because it created greater uncertainty and was itself responsible for a deteriorating competitive performance. The alternative which would emerge from this line of reasoning is a rules rather than discretionary approach to demand management. Yet another line of reasoning is that the policies were bound to fail because they did not strike at the roots of the problem, that is, excessive monetary expansion – the policy implication of this being that monetary control be uppermost. Together these last two points were instrumental in the change of attitude which occurred in the 1970s and persists in the 1980s.

Wage and Price Controls

A number of post-war governments have taken the view that the chronic tendency for UK inflation to exceed that of her competitors is essentially due to a tendency for wages per unit of output to rise faster in the UK than abroad. At source, inflation is perceived as being fundamentally cost push in origin. To 'correct' this there has been intermittent recourse to wage and price controls, that is, limits on the rate of growth of money wages and/or

TABLE 18.3
Wage and Price Controls in the UK 1969–77

Period	Restrictions	Status	Actual annual increase in average earnings during policy
1969–70	2.5–4.5% annual increase	Voluntary	7.5%
1971–2	$n - 1\%$ annual increase	Voluntary	11.1%
1972–3	Wages freeze	Compulsory	2.9%
1973	£1 + 4% (equivalent to an average of 5.5%)	Compulsory	13.7%
1973–4	£2.25p or 7% plus threshold payments (equivalent to an average of 7%)	Compulsory	18.5%
1974–5	'Social contract' voluntary restraint	Voluntary	25.0%
1975–6	£6 maximum (equivalent to an average of 12%)	Voluntary	18.6%
1976–7	5% plus £2.40p to £4.00p (equivalent to an average of 4.5%)	Voluntary	4.3%
1977–8	10% plus productivity agreements	Voluntary	19.0%
1978–9	5%	Voluntary	12.0%

Source: Various official publications, with data in column 4 and details of equivalent percentages in column 2 drawn from Batchelor et al. (1980).

prices. Wage control was used as an anti-inflation instrument as far back as 1948 but, as can be seen from table 18.3, has been especially 'popular' in the 1960s and 1970s. Controls can take a variety of forms. They may be statutory or voluntary; if voluntary they may or may not be backed with sanctions; they may impose a complete freeze on the rate of growth of money wages (and prices) or they may permit some increase; if the latter a percentage rate of increase might be permitted, or some lump sum amount; the 'norm' may or may not be related to productivity growth. Most of these options have been tried in the UK in various permutations.

The central objective behind wage and price controls is to run the economy at a higher level of employment and lower level of inflation than would be possible in their absence. There are a couple of cases where short sharp controls have been extremely successful in containing wage inflation. For example, the pay freeze imposed by Sir Stafford Cripps between 1948 and 1950 succeeded in limiting wage increases to just over 2 per cent per annum. An even better example is the effect of the Wilson–Callaghan voluntary policy in combination with *restrictive demand management policies* in reducing wage inflation from 33 per cent in the first quarter of 1975 to just over 10 per cent in the second quarter of 1977. In this respect complete freezes, or very low statutory norms, have the greatest chance of success. Such restraint cannot however be maintained indefinitely. Assuming productivity continues to grow during the period of restraint, there would follow an increase in the share of profits. Furthermore, in an open economy like the UK upward pressure on prices from imports can easily result in prices rising markedly more rapidly than wages. The most spectacular example of this is the introduction of Heath's three-stage policy, 1972–4, at a time when commodity prices were booming.

With regard to productivity growth it could be argued that allowance could be made in any norm for differential productivity growth, and indeed this has been attempted on various occasions, most recently in the latter part of the Healey–Callaghan *social contract*. Productivity is, however, an extremely fungible term capable of very wide interpretation and invariably provides a basis for getting around controls. Furthermore, because productivity gains can be more easily justified in activities which have a marketable output than in those which do not, the scope for exploiting any productivity loophole differs across activities. This often serves to generate resentment on the part of public service employees.

Another source of resentment which is frequently a concomitant of wage and price controls is the squeezing of differentials between skilled and unskilled workers. This is especially so when some kind of flat rate increase is set as a norm, like the £6 a week maximum set in stage one of Wilson's social contract (1975–6). At the other end of the salary scale one often finds that no increases are permitted at all – again under stage one of the social contract, those earning in excess of £8500 p.a. were allowed no increases. This has tended to encourage payment in kind with improved fringe benefits and perquisites being given in lieu of a salary increase.

To summarize these remarks, there is a good deal of evidence to suggest that wage and price controls generate distortions by disturbing the pattern of relative prices and incomes, and by encouraging the deployment of resources into avoidance activities (in the same way as was found with credit controls in chapter 6). Furthermore such controls can be extremely costly to operate, given the bureaucracy which has to accompany their implementation. One could argue that, nevertheless, wage and price controls could still be associated with net benefits if inflation falls as a result, and employment is higher than it otherwise would be. This brings us to the final point – how successful have wage and price controls been as an instrument of counter-inflation policy?

Evaluating the effect of such controls is not straightforward, largely because it can never be known exactly what would have occurred in their absence. It is, however, possible to use a wage equation to predict what may have happened in the absence of controls and then compare this to what actually occurred. A number of studies have attempted to do just this and there is a good deal of agreement on at least two points. First, there is evidence to suggest that temporary freezes do help to slow down the rate of change of money wages. There is a good deal of evidence to suggest that once controls are relaxed a little – for example, some provision is made for productivity gains – 'wage drift' becomes important (as a result of job reclassifications, bogus productivity awards and so on) and ensures that the actual out-turn on wages exceeds the 'norm'. This is well documented in table 18.3. There is a good deal of evidence to indicate that, once controls are removed, there is a catch-up period as labour unions attempt to regain some of the ground lost during the period of restraint. There are many such examples of this occurring in the UK. Many commentators, for example, would ascribe the wage explosions of 1969–70, 1974–5 and 1979–80 to a reaction to wage restraint in the years immediately preceding the explosion. Thus it would seem from UK experience that, although controls *may* have had beneficial short-term effects, any gains have been quickly eroded and the subsequent situation has been at least as bad as the precontrols period.

Indexation

Earlier in this chapter it was noted that many of the costs of inflation are associated with unanticipated inflation rather than inflation *per se*. It would seem reasonable to suppose therefore that if a mechanism could be found whereby the contribution of unanticipated inflation is minimized, then the costs of the phenomenon would be correspondingly reduced. For this reason indexation has often been recommended. If labour unions are guaranteed that the real value of their income will be maintained then they do not have to guess at the rate of inflation over the contract period. Furthermore, if all wages are indexed then the costs of arbitrary redistribution are eliminated, and in addition attempts to redistribute income towards any particular group are exposed to the public view. Against this, automatic indexation does mean that it becomes impossible to squeeze real wages as part of the adjustment to say a payments deficit. From the point of view of inflationary control, it also means that externally generated inflation feeds into the system extremely quickly. By the same token, however, the reverse also holds.

As inflation has reached higher levels in the UK the possibility of indexation has been widely discussed, and indeed a system of indexation was briefly in operation as part of the Heath phase III incomes policy. This permitted wage increases which would compensate for increases in inflation beyond a certain threshold (7 per cent). It is impossible to comment on the effectiveness of the system since it was simply not in operation long enough (barely six months) and it was introduced at a rather inauspicious time; shortly after its introduction the Yom Kippur war broke out and the price of crude oil quadrupled in a four-month period.

Experience of wage controls in the UK has therefore been somewhat less than entirely felicitous. Despite this, one major political alliance in the UK remains committed to their reintroduction (although in fairness what is envisaged here is a long-term policy aimed at institutionalizing the system of distribution and tempering the worst excesses of unfettered pay 'bargaining'). Their lack of success and a belief that they impose net costs on the economic system led to the Conservative administration of 1979–86 eschewing their use (although the use of 'cash limits' and 'guidelines' to public corporations and local authorities resembles to many a form of wage control). Instead the principal instrument for inflationary control has been monetary policy.

The Medium-term Financial Strategy

The transformation of anti-inflation policy from a fine tuning based regime (with or without an incomes policy) to the so-called medium-term financial strategy can be described as nothing short of revolutionary. The principles which underlie the medium-term strategy are a radical departure from previous practice in at least two important respects – first, the stress laid on monetary control as being both necessary and sufficient for the control of inflation, and second, the way in which monetary control has been administered, the practice of *preannouncement* of target ranges of growth. The former reflects the rise of monetarism in a general sense to the prevailing orthodoxy; the latter embodies a particular assumption about the manner in which expectations are formed, and is associated with the 'new classical macroeconomics' school.

The most graphic indication that orthodox monetarism had been accepted as the prevailing orthodoxy is given in a speech by the then leader of the Labour party in September 1976, when he said:

We used to think that you could just spend your way out of a recession by cutting taxes and boosting government spending. I tell you in all candour that that option no longer exists, and that in so far as it ever did exist, it worked by injecting inflation into the economy. And each time that happened the average level of unemployment has risen. Higher inflation, followed by higher unemployment. That is the history of the last 20 years.

In other words it was accepted that a relationship existed between government budgetary policies and inflation, and that the *natural rate hypothesis* held. Although Mr Callaghan did not spell out any relationship between budgetary policies and inflation, it is clear from subsequent statements and actions that the intermediate link was via the money supply – monetarism had arrived! Note, however, that as can be seen from table 18.3, although the Labour administration accepted this link it nevertheless still saw a role for wage and price controls. In other words, although it regarded monetary control as being necessary for the control of inflation, it was not viewed as being sufficient. This can certainly not be said of the Conservative administration of 1979–86 which pursued an altogether different brand of monetarism whereby, in the early stages at least, monetary control was viewed as being both necessary and sufficient for the control of inflation. It was felt, however, that in order to make monetary targets realistic, targets had to be set for the government borrowing requirement. Furthermore, there was an implicit premise that agents form their expectations about inflation rationally, and therefore the preannouncement of policy intent would allow them to revise their inflationary expectations quickly and more accurately.

The fullest statement of the medium-term financial strategy was provided in the March 1980 Budget White Paper. It is quite clearly stated here that the central objective of government economic policy was the progressive reduction in the rate of inflation between 1980 and 1984 to provide the basis for a sustainable (non-inflationary) growth in output. The mechanism by which inflation was to be reduced was a progressive reduction in the growth of the money supply, and targets for public borrowing were set which were consistent with the money supply objective. The target indicator selected for monetary control was initially sterling M3 (notes and coin in circulation, demand deposits and sterling time deposits held by UK residents). The targets set for the growth of £M3 are set out in table 18.4. As can be seen, target ranges were set in recognition of the difficulties of hitting a specific figure, and the idea was that there would be a staged reduction in the range. Table 18.5 details the government budget calculations which were forecast as being consistent with these target ranges. The target which was viewed as being important in this case was the *public sector borrowing requirement* (PSBR). Again the point to note in this table is that the PSBR was forecast to fall progressively, both in absolute terms and as a proportion of GDP. As well as facilitating attainment of the monetary objectives (by reducing the amount of money which is created to fund the borrowing requirement), it was envisaged that it would also facilitate a reduction in nominal interest rates (by reducing the amount which the government actually has to borrow). If these targets were met it was felt that inflation could be reduced to around 16 per cent by the end of 1980, with the possibility of single-figure inflation being attained by the end of 1981, and a progressive reduction thereafter.

This is really just an outline of the details of the 'mark I' version of the strategy, but a number of distinctive features should be noted. First, the entire strategy centred on two target variables, £M3 and the PSBR. Second, the fact that targets were set for both provided an explicit acceptance of the inter-dependence of monetary and fiscal policy and of a government budget constraint. Third, the strategy actually provided a statement of intent for up to four years ahead. Fourth, the inflation objective was divorced entirely from any employment objectives – labour markets were to be left entirely to themselves (in principle anyway).

TABLE 18.4
Target Ranges for the Rate of Growth of
the Money Stock 1980–4

Year	% change in £M3 during year
1980–1	7–11
1981–2	6–10
1982–3	5–9
1983–4	4–8

TABLE 18.5
Forecast 'Targets' for the Public Sector Borrowing Requirement (PSBR)
1978–84

Year	Government expenditure £bn	Tax revenue £bn	CGBR £bn	PSBR £bn	PSBR/GDP %
1978–9	74.0	65.0	9.0	9.3	5.5
1979–80	74.5	66.0	8.5	8.0	4.75
1980–1	74.5	67.5	7.5	6.5	3.75
1981–2	73.0	67.5	5.5	5.0	3.0
1982–3	71.0	69.5	4.0	3.5	2.25
1983–4	70.5	71.0	3.0	2.5	1.5

Source: Economic Progress Report, April 1980.

The targets reported in table 18.4 and 18.5 are those which were stated in the original medium-term financial strategy (MTFS). As we can see from the first two rows of table 18.6 these targets were overshot for £M3, the PSBR and inflation. We will comment on the reasons for this overshoot below. One point which can be noted here is that revisions to the targets took place as a consequence of these overshoots. This can be clearly seen by comparing, for example, the targets for £M3 for 1982–3 and 1983–4 (these being the original targets), with those for the same years in table 18.6 (these being the revised targets of 1982). As we shall see below, these and other revisions to the MTFS have led some commentators to argue that the 'strategy' was to all intents and

TABLE 18.6
Forecast and Actual Out-turns on £M3, PSBR and Inflation

	£M3		PSBR		Inflation	
	Forecast %	Actual %	Forecast %	Actual %	Forecast %	Actual %
1980–1	7–11	16.7	6.5	13.2	16	18
1981–2	6–10	15.2	5.0	10.5	9	12
1982–3	8–12	8.9	9.5	8.9	7.5	8.6
1983–4	7–12	10.3	8.5	9.8	4.5	4.6
1984–5	6–10	9.6	6.5	10.2	3.5	5.0

purposes abandoned at an early stage and replaced by a much more pragmatic approach to monetary control which relied principally on interest rate manipulation.

The first two rows of table 18.6 compare forecast and actual out-turns for 1980–1 and 1981–2. As can be seen, the targets for £M3 and the (nominal) PSBR have overshot the objectives laid down in the 1980 White Paper quite substantially. In no case did the growth of £M3 lie within its target range, and the nominal value of the PSBR has exceeded its target in all cases, although it must be pointed out that as a fraction of GDP it has been a little closer to its target. The obvious question begged is, therefore, why the targets were missed and what are the economic implications (in particular the effect on inflation). The easy answer is that aggregates like the nominal PSBR and £M3 are simply uncontrollable, the former because it is subject to cyclical and political pressures, the latter because the banking system can always find ways around controls. Although these aggregates are certainly difficult to control, it is unduly simplistic to argue that they cannot therefore be controlled. In the UK case there appear to have been a number of factors which have contributed to the initial targets being exceeded.

Take first of all the PSBR. It will be recalled from chapter 6 that this is essentially the difference between government expenditure and revenue which has to be funded. This being so, the out-turn on the PSBR is crucially dependent on unanticipated variations in expenditure and taxation. Thus, when the original targets were set for the PSBR insufficient allowance was made for the payment of comparability awards in the public sector, an election commitment inherited from the previous government and honoured within six months or so of taking office. Even more important, inadequate allowance was made for the impact of *automatic stabilizers*. As recessionary pressures intensified, government revenues automatically decreased (as a consequence of fewer people paying income tax, and decreased expenditure on taxable commodities), whilst expenditure automatically rose (as increased social security payments were made to the unemployed). Thus when the original targets were set for the PSBR, the forecast fall in output between 1979–80 and 1980–1 was 2 per cent; the actual fall in output turned out to be 4 per cent. The effect this had on expenditures and revenues accounted for a large portion of the PSBR overshoot.

It is tempting to go directly from an overshoot on the PSBR to the overshoot of £M3. After all, the economic theory on which the medium-term strategy is founded suggests that a stable and predictable relationship between the PSBR and the money supply exists. This, however, is an issue of some controversy; many, whilst accepting the existence of a longer-run relationship between monetary growth and price change, would deny the existence of any mechanistic link between the PSBR and monetary growth, emphasizing not only that this depends on the way in which the PSBR is funded but also the particular assumptions which underlie a mechanistic link (see Peacock and Shaw, 1981). As well as any contribution made by the PSBR to the growth of £M3, there are other reasons why it overshot its target, reasons which provide an interesting insight into the way in which fixing on one particular target can create problems.

In the first instance, although monetary control was the objective of policy, this was not administered by attempting to contract the monetary base but rather by interest rate manipulation. In other words, the authorities were attempting to slow the rate of growth of £M3, essentially through controlling the demand for credit. Given that one is effectively therefore guessing at the appropriate level of interest rates required to hit a given target, the technique is fundamentally imprecise. This has already been discussed in chapter 6, when it was noted that the use of interest rate manipulation as a basis for monetary control necessitates having the political will to permit nominal interest rates to rise to extremely high levels. As can be seen in figure 18.4, the Bank of England's minimum lending rate did reach historically high levels (17 per cent in 1979–80), but this was nevertheless consistent with low real interest rates due to high inflation. Furthermore, overdraft facilities were widely used to finance current expenditure as profit margins were squeezed and, given high nominal interest rates, frequently had to be extended just to service the initial borrowing. As was also seen in chapter 6, there were a number of *ad hoc* and distorting influences. Reliance on the supplementary special deposits scheme (the corset) had encouraged the growth of fringe methods of credit creation, like the issuing of acceptance credits. When the scheme was abandoned in 1981 these credits were converted, and as a result £M3 was increased by about 6 per cent. The increasing amount of mortgage business conducted by the banking system also resulted in £M3 growing faster than desired.

The response of the government to these targets being broached has taken several forms. The first and most obvious response was the rebasing of the monetary targets. Thus rather than sticking to the original targets and attempting to 'claw back' the overshoot, the overshoot was in effect written off and the targets rebased. In the circumstances this was probably quite sensible. As can be seen in figure 6.4, the monetary targets have now been revised on several occasions. A second response has been to redefine the monetary targets. Initially targets were set by reference to £M3 only. In 1982 this practice was altered with target ranges being set for M1 and PSL2 as well as £M3. The justification for this was that in order to gain a comprehensive view of monetary conditions, one had to have an eye to narrow and broad definitions of money. Critics of the MTFS argued that this particular change provided evidence of the failure of the policy. The authorities had failed to control £M3; in order to disguise this failure they included targets for other variables. Since, as we saw in chapter 6, these different measures of monetary control frequently provide different impressions of current monetary conditions, the authorities can select their monetary aggregate depending upon the story which it tells. There is something to be said for both views. On the one hand, given the complexities of monetary control, one should perhaps inspect information on both broad and narrow money. On the other hand, however, the proliferation of monetary targets is apt to cause confusion. Given the rationale behind the MTFS this is a fundamental criticism. After all, the whole point of targeting and pre-announcement is to clarify government intentions and provide a stable environment for private sector activity.

There is some evidence to suggest that a third response has occurred, namely the downgrading of explicit monetary targets to be subservient to an exchange rate target. In other words the laxity or tightness of monetary conditions is, at least in part, being judged by reference to the exchange rate. Other things being equal, exchange rate depreciation provides evidence of a 'market view' that monetary conditions are too lax and a tightening of conditions, via a change in the interest rate is in order (and vice versa for exchange rate appreciations). Even when sterling approached parity with the dollar in January 1985 the monetary authorities steadfastly denied the existence of an exchange rate target. Their actions suggest otherwise however.

This experience over the past few years had led many commentators to assert that the medium-term strategy has failed, and that this in turn is an indication of a wider disproof of monetarist beliefs. Although one cannot make any final judgement about the experience since we do not know what would have happened in the absence of the policy, a number of concluding remarks can be made. First, the medium-term strategy is not 'monetarist' in an orthodox sense, although it contains elements of monetarism (if that is taken to mean a belief in the natural rate hypothesis, and a belief in a systematic relationship between changes in the money stock and changes in inflation). Despite this a central role would not be given to the PSBR by many scholars who would ordinarily be dubbed 'monetarist' (such as Friedman and Laidler). Second, the experience has highlighted the technical difficulties of monetary control when this is administered via interest rate manipulation rather than monetary base control (whereby interest rates are then endogenous). Third, the experience cannot be used naïvely to assert that monetarism has been shown to be a failure. If one were to argue this on such frail grounds, then one could equally use the growth rate of M1 over the last few years to demonstrate that monetary restraint has been successfully administered (see table 6.3). Fourth, judged by reference to the narrow criterion of inflationary control, the strategy has had some measure of success, with the inflation rate having fallen from 18 per cent in 1980 to around 3 per cent in 1986–7. Moreover, the inflation rate has stabilized at around this level. Fifth, as we shall see in the next chapter, the dramatic fall in inflation has coincided with an even more dramatic rise in unemployment. There are a variety of reasons behind this increase which we will discuss in chapter 19. Here it might be noted that monetary contraction has probably contributed to the increase. This being so, the assumption of a zero trade-off between inflation and unemployment which was implicit in the original MTFS has been invalidated.

A Tax-Based Incomes Policy?

Earlier in this chapter we discussed the role of prices and incomes policies in inflationary control in the UK over the post-war period. The Conservative administration of 1979–86 has eschewed reliance on explicit incomes policy, arguing that it is merely a palliative which treats the symptoms rather than the cause of the problem and, given the distortions associated with incomes control, is a costly palliative at that.

Recently a role for incomes policy (in the wider context of a strategy for demand reflation) has been proposed by among others Meade (1985) and Layard (1986). These authors argue that demand reflation would help reduce unemployment, but concede that there are inflationary risks associated with any injection of demand. To contain inflationary pressure an incomes policy is recommended. When confronted with the evidence of past policies the authors argue that these have failed because they have been badly designed and badly implemented. What is needed is a new kind of incomes policy – a tax-based policy. Under this arrangement, norms for wage increases would be set. In the event that these were exceeded, the excess would be clawed back via a tax on employers. This, it is claimed, would provide an effective disincentive to firms to prevent them from conceding to inflationary wage demands. The idea is a novel one and would very likely provide a more effective disincentive than existed in previous policies, and would arguably be easier to police. However, whether it would be a straightforward policy to administer, and whether it would create much by way of by-product distortions are open questions.

Concluding Comments

It has been seen that there are costs associated with inflation, although these costs are largely related to unanticipated inflation or relative inflation rather than necessarily to inflation *per se*. Nevertheless they provide a rationale for inflationary control, although it is a matter for debate whether the objective of policy should be the elimination of inflation, the stabilization of its level, or its reduction to a level below that of one's competitors. For most of the post-war period it would seem that the latter objective has been uppermost, although the high and variable rates experienced in the 1970s have meant that this objective has become intertwined with one of stabilizing the level of inflation.

Policy in the UK has been a mixture of Keynesian fine tuning and/or wage and price controls for most of the period, and more latterly the setting of monetary targets with or without wage and price controls. The evidence appears to indicate that fine tuning failed to eliminate the phenomenon but rather helped it become an integral part of the stop–go cycle. Although there have been occasions when wage and price controls have been associated with reductions in inflation, overall they appear to have created more problems than they have solved. Monetary targets have been set for most of the last ten years or so. There have been very real practical problems associated with monetary control although it is reasonable to assume that it contributed to the reduction of inflation in 1978, and between 1981 and 1986. Monetary contraction over this period has probably contributed to the dramatic increase in unemployment which has occurred. This will be examined in more detail in the next chapter.

Further Reading

An extremely useful volume on all aspects of demand management policy in the UK over the period 1964–81 is Posner (1978). Here alternative (monetarist–Keynesian) assessments of UK economic performance are outlined, and their implications for particular targets assessed. Reviews of counter-inflation policy in the UK are also presented in Prest and Coppock (1982, chapter 1), Morris (1978, chapter 7) and Cross (1982a). An altogether more rigorous assessment of the determinants of UK inflation is given by the collection of papers in Parkin and Sumner (1978).

Dawkins (1980) provides a review of experience with incomes policy in the UK, whilst a more rigorous appraisal of the economic effects of incomes policy can be found in the papers edited by Parkin and Sumner (1972) and in Fallick and Elliott (1981).

A great deal of bank review space and rather less journal space has been devoted to the medium-term financial strategy. The strategy is originally set out in the Budget White Paper of March 1980. Important alternative views on its efficacy are to be found in the evidence to the Treasury and Civil Service Committee (1981).

19

Unemployment in the UK

In the 1970s and early 1980s, developed market economies in general, and the UK in particular, have experienced a dramatic increase in recorded unemployment (see figures 19.1 and 19.2). In the UK case, recorded unemployment has reached levels (both in absolute numbers and as a proportion of the labour force) which have not been experienced since the inter-war period. For many years it has been widely accepted that there are grounds for positive intervention in the labour market to reduce unemployment on both social and economic grounds. What has characterized recent debate, however, is a marked paucity of policy prescription with respect to what can or should be done. As with most (if not all) other economic problems there are a variety of diagnoses/prescriptions on offer which fill the spectrum from extreme rational expectations to Cambridge 'alternative strategy' proposals.

In this chapter the principal features of unemployment in the UK in the late 1970s and early 1980s will be examined in an attempt to build up some kind of picture of unemployment. This will then provide a basis for identifying possible 'causes' of the recent dramatic increase. Following this, alternative views will be considered on what the instruments of employment policy can or should be, with particular reference to policies which have been applied in post-war Britain.

Types of Unemployment

Chapter 7 distinguished between voluntary and involuntary unemployment. The former was found to be a feature of classical and neo-classical analyses of the labour market, whilst the latter tended to figure more prominently in Keynesian/neo-Keynesian analyses. In essence classical and neo-classical approaches emphasized the role of the rational optimizing agent who takes a deliberate decision to withdraw from the labour market and substitute leisure for work when real wages are regarded as being too low. Given the self-equilibrating nature of the system, all unemployment is therefore voluntary. Keynesian and neo-Keynesian analyses, on the other hand, stress the possibility of involuntary unemployment appearing as a consequence of money wage rigidity, the latter being an outcome of institutional features of the labour market such as labour unions or contracts.

This distinction is useful for policy purposes, as has already been seen in chapters 7 and 13. Thus, given the neo-classical emphasis on the equilibrium nature of the labour market and the stress placed on voluntary unemployment, the role for government policy would essentially be one of removing constraints to flexibility. This would permit the real wage to fall and allow the market to clear. There would be no role whatsoever for demand management policies. By contrast a neo-Keynesian prescription would take the source of the rigidity as a constraint on the grounds that there are good socioeconomic justifications for the existence of labour unions (or minimum wages) and/or there are sound microeconomic reasons for contracts. Policy prescription might then be a case of using monetary and fiscal policies to shift labour demand and absorb the involuntary unemployment. This is the world of the upward sloping AS curve.

This distinction between voluntary and involuntary unemployment can be usefully supplemented by a further distinction made by reference to the apparent source of unemployment (although arguably this only applies to involuntary unemployment), namely:

(1) frictional unemployment
(2) seasonal unemployment
(3) cyclical unemployment
(4) structural unemployment.

Frictional Unemployment arises simply as a result of timing differences which occur when a worker quits one job in order to take up alternative employment. It is conceivable that frictional unemployment is zero if the transition from one job to another is perfectly synchronized, that is one quits one job and starts another the following day. This may in fact be the norm for certain occupations, for example academic posts where it is usual to resign only when one has arranged alternative employment. In many unskilled and semi-skilled occupations, however, the norm is frequently one of quitting and registering as unemployed whilst one searches for alternative employment. In this case the worker is recorded as unemployed for the duration of his search. Even in the most smoothly operating of labour markets a certain amount of frictional unemployment is bound to be recorded.

Seasonal Unemployment arises because the demand for certain goods and services is seasonal. Note that this is only a necessary condition for seasonal unemployment to emerge. Take the case of coal, for example; demand is certainly seasonal, but the relative ease with which the commodity can be stored ensures that the demand for labour in the coal industry is not seasonal. The same cannot be said of ice-cream vendors or cricket players. Of course ice-cream vendors or cricketers could obtain winter employment which is seasonal, such as shop work; or the seasonal increase in demand could be met by temporary additions to the labour force from students, for example. Despite such offsetting tendencies, however, one invariably finds a certain amount of recorded seasonal unemployment.

Cyclical Unemployment arises during the downswing of the business cycle as a result of deviations in output from its 'full employment' level. As the economy runs through recession into depression, output falls and unemployment rises. The pattern of such unemployment would depend on which activities were cyclically prone. For example, construction services are often one of the first activities to 'suffer' in a downswing. Service industries where demand is income elastic find themselves in an exposed position. The point about cyclical unemployment is that once economic activity recovers and economic growth picks up, cyclical unemployment falls.

Structural Unemployment. Whereas cyclical unemployment is associated with the rundown and expansion of essentially similar activities, structural unemployment tends to be associated with the rundown of certain activities and their replacement by different activities which have essentially different labour requirements and/or are sited in different geographical locations. To take an extreme example, a shift in comparative advantage might result in the decline in shipbuilding on Clydeside and the emergence of computer manufacture in south-east England. There may as a result be an excess supply of labour in central Scotland and an excess demand for labour in south-east England. The two could coexist owing to a mismatch of skills and a mismatch of geographical requirements. The unemployment which is recorded would be referred to as structural unemployment.

Although it is far from easy to identify different types of unemployment from the data, the distinction between these alternative forms of unemployment is important from a policy standpoint. If one felt that there was a conclusive case for intervention the kinds of policy instrument applied would vary according to the type of unemployment one wished to alleviate. In the case of frictional unemployment, for example, policy would be directed at improving the efficiency of the labour market by way of providing Job Centres to make search activity easier; or it perhaps could take the form of subsidies designed to reduce the cost of search activity (like reimbursement of expenses incurred in attending interviews). In the case of seasonal unemployment, it might be felt that policy could be directed at encouraging activities to areas which are heavily dependent on commodities/services for which demand is seasonal, for example those areas heavily dependent on tourist-related services. One might feel that if cyclical unemployment is essentially transient then there is no need for policy intervention. This really depends, however, on the length of the cycle. In the event that recession is prolonged for years rather than months, one might feel that positive action is required to shorten the cycle and/or avoid some of the longer-term effects of prolonged cyclical unemployment – so-called *hysteresis* effects where cyclical unemployment essentially becomes structural. Structural unemployment emerges, as has been noted, essentially because certain factor-specific skills become redundant. One might argue that change is of the essence in a dynamic market-based economy, and if skills become redundant then workers will retrain for more productive employment. One might even argue that since the social cost of redundant skills is zero (on the principle that bygones are bygones), there is no case for any kind of policy. There are, however, a range of barriers to occupational and geographical mobility which may serve to frustrate the reallocation of labour from one activity to another. Furthermore these may be bound up with the fact that the private costs of retraining diverge from the social costs (as they undoubtedly do). The point is that, if policy is pursued, the kind of instruments with which one is dealing are the subsidization of retraining, subsidization of relocation and so on. In the event that structural unemployment is region specific one might feel that policies designed to stimulate investment in the regions concerned is the appropriate instrument to deploy.

These various instruments, and the extent to which they have been deployed in the UK, will be returned to in due course. For the moment the pattern of unemployment in the UK over the post-war period will be examined in greater detail in order to establish whether the relative importance of different types of unemployment has altered in recent years.

Patterns of Unemployment in the UK

Figures 19.1, 19.2 and 19.3 and tables 19.1, 19.2 and 19.3 summarize trends in and the pattern of unemployment in the UK over the post-war period. From this information it is possible to make a number of observations regarding the type of unemployment recorded, and its regional/occupational breakdown.

Take first of all figures 19.1 and 19.2. Figure 19.1 traces the trend in unemployment rates for the period 1964–86, whilst Figure 19.2 gives details of the absolute number of registered unemployed and recorded vacancies.

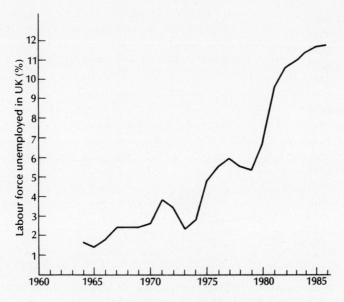

Figure 19.1   Unemployment in the UK 1964–1986

Although there are known to be a number of well-known defects associated with both unemployment and vacancy data,[1] which are acknowledged, the data will continue to be used here to identify trends. The first feature of these figures which may be noted is the cyclical pattern of unemployment. This is quite evident throughout the post-war period, and a glance at figure 19.3 confirms that this pattern is also evident in regional unemployment rates. In crude terms one could take the difference between the actual level of unemployment and the trough level (which would coincide with an output peak) as an indication of cyclical unemployment. Since the figures are seasonally adjusted, seasonal influences have already been ironed out. However, the data would include recorded frictional unemployment. Despite this one thing is clear, namely that the recorded swings in unemployment have been very much greater in the 1970s and 1980s than in the 1950s or 1960s – deviations from trend have been of a greater magnitude in

1 Basically, there are a number of distortions which tend to result in recorded unemployment and recorded vacancies understating actual unemployment and actual vacancies. In the case of unemployment it appears that certain groups simply do not bother to register as unemployed (for example, married women, casual labour). In the case of vacancies many firms have their own channels of dissemination which they rely on rather than report them to Job Centres.

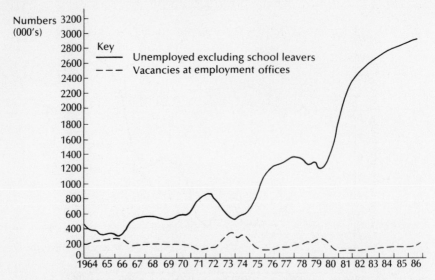

Figure 19.2 Unemployment and vacancies in the UK 1964–86. Three-month moving averages, seasonally adjusted. Vacancies at employment offices are about one-third of total vacancies

the 1970s and 1980s. A second feature of figure 19.1 is that the levels of unemployment associated with both peaks and troughs in the cycle have been rising since the late 1960s. With each successive recovery since 1965, unemployment has bottomed at a higher rate than in the previous cycle; whilst with each successive downswing unemployment has peaked at a higher level than before. This can be seen most emphatically by reference to 1985–6. Unemployment appears to have peaked and levelled off. It has done so, however, with in excess of 3 million people unemployed. This is taken by many commentators to be evidence of an increase in the natural rate of unemployment in the UK. In terms of the classification introduced above, we could take it as indicative of an increase in structural unemployment. A variety of explanations have been advanced for this.

Neo-Keynesian explanations revolve around the part played by exogenous forces and emphasize the involuntary nature of such unemployment (for example, world recession, the shift in comparative advantage in standardized manufactures, the crowding out effect of North Sea oil on manufacturing employment); whilst neo-classical commentators argue that the increase is endogenously determined, by a combination of real wages which are 'too high' and which have contracted the demand for labour, and real benefits which are 'too high' and have consequently contracted the supply

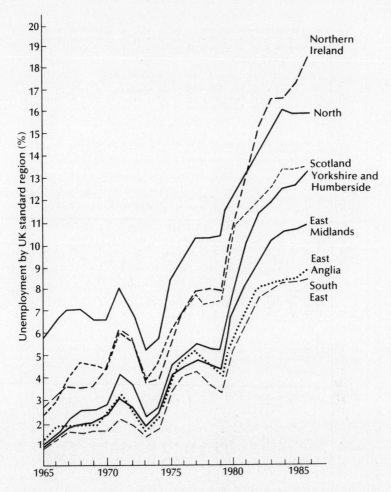

Figure 19.3   Unemployment trends for selected UK standard regions 1965–86

of labour. The essential feature of this line of argument is that unemployment is basically voluntary – agents leave the labour market of their own free will.

Table 19.1 and figure 19.3 reveal another important feature of UK unemployment, namely distinct regional disparities. The South East, East Anglia and the East Midlands have all had rates of unemployment consistently below the national average. On the other hand, the North, Wales, Scotland and Northern Ireland have recorded rates persistently in excess of the national average. Although all of the regions have been subject to cyclical

TABLE 19.1
Deviation of Regional Unemployment Rates from UK Average, 1965–81

	North	Yorks and Humberside	East Midlands	East Anglia	South East	South West	West Midlands	North West	Wales	Scotland	Northern Ireland
1965	+0.9	+0.4	−0.5	−0.2	−0.6	+0.1	−0.8	0	+1.1	+1.3	+4.4
1966	+1.1	+0.4	−0.5	0	−0.6	+0.4	−0.6	−0.1	+1.5	+1.3	+4.7
1967	+1.6	+0.3	−0.7	−0.5	−0.8	+0.1	−0.5	0	+1.5	+1.3	+4.7
1968	+2.3	+0.1	−0.5	−0.5	−0.9	0	−0.6	−0.1	+1.4	+1.2	+4.8
1969	+2.2	+0.2	−0.4	−0.5	−0.8	+0.3	−0.7	0	+1.5	+1.3	+4.3
1970	+1.8	+0.2	−0.3	−0.3	−1.0	+0.2	−0.6	+0.2	+1.1	+1.8	+4.1
1971	+2.3	+0.4	−0.7	−0.5	−1.6	−0.2	−0.3	+0.7	+0.9	+2.5	+4.3
1972	+2.3	+0.3	−0.7	−0.9	−1.5	−0.4	−0.3	+1.1	+1.0	+2.5	+3.6
1973	+1.6	0	−0.5	−0.7	−1.0	−0.2	−0.6	+0.6	+0.7	+1.5	+3.0
1974	+1.9	−0.1	−0.4	−0.5	−1.1	+0.3	−0.5	+0.9	+1.1	+1.2	+3.0
1975	+1.4	−0.2	−0.7	−0.7	−1.4	+0.6	+0.2	+1.1	+1.5	+0.9	+3.8
1976	+1.6	−0.4	−1.0	−0.3	−1.3	+0.8	−0.3	+1.0	+1.4	+1.4	+4.1
1977	+2.1	−0.3	−1.1	−0.8	−1.5	+0.7	−0.5	+1.2	+1.9	+1.9	+4.5
1978	+2.6	−0.1	−0.9	−0.9	−1.7	+0.2	−0.5	+1.2	+2.0	+1.9	+4.9
1979	+2.7	0	−0.9	−1.2	−1.9	−0.1	−0.1	+1.3	+1.9	+2.2	+5.2
1980	+3.1	+0.4	−0.9	−1.7	−2.8	−0.9	+0.9	+1.9	+3.0	+2.2	+6.4
1981	+3.2	+0.5	−1.1	−2.2	−3.1	−1.4	+2.2	+2.3	+3.0	+2.1	+6.2
1982	+4.3	+1.1	−1.0	−2.1	−3.0	−1.9	+2.5	+2.7	+2.6	+1.8	+5.1
1983	+4.7	+1.1	−0.7	−2.4	−2.9	−1.7	+2.5	+3.0	+2.4	+1.9	+5.8
1984	+5.2	+1.2	−0.6	−2.9	−3.1	−1.8	+2.3	+2.7	+2.6	+1.8	+5.4
1985	+5.0	+1.4	−0.5	−2.7	−3.0	−1.5	+2.1	+2.6	+2.6	+2.0	+5.9
1986	+4.9	+1.7	−0.6	−2.7	−3.0	−1.5	+2.0	+2.6	+2.6	+1.9	+6.9

Source: calculated from Economic Trends Annual Supplement, CSO 1982, pp. 106–9.

TABLE 19.2
Duration of Unemployment in the UK

	Number of weeks unemployed						
	<2	2–4	4–8	8–13	13–26	26–52	>52
Date	% of total						
Jan. 1985	5.8	3.3	7.6	8.5	18.1	17.4	39.4
Jan. 1984	6.0	3.6	7.8	8.6	18.4	18.4	37.1
Jan. 1983	6.1	3.6	8.1	9.2	19.0	19.8	34.3
Jan. 1982	4.8	3.8	9.2	10.2	19.8	22.7	29.5
Jan. 1981	7.6	4.5	11.9	13.6	23.7	19.9	18.8
Jan. 1980	8.5	5.6	13.5	12.6	19.6	16.0	24.2
Jan. 1979	8.7	5.7	12.4	12.2	19.1	17.7	24.1
Jan. 1978	7.8	5.5	12.0	12.8	20.7	18.6	22.5
Jan. 1977	9.0	5.8	12.9	13.2	20.1	18.5	20.5
Jan. 1976	8.7	7.8	15.2	14.7	22.4	16.6	14.6

Source: Employment Gazette, Department of Employment (various issues).

pressures, these disparities have been evident throughout the post-war period. Most commentators would agree that this phenomenon is bound up at least in part with structural change, namely the decline of the 'staple' industries (iron and steel, shipbuilding, cotton textiles and coal, until recently), which were predominantly located in the regions and the growth of light engineering and services located closer to the main markets, that is the South East and the Midlands.

Another feature of the data which might be noted from table 19.2 is the increase in the number of long-term unemployed. This has increased dramatically over the last few years and, by the end of 1985, over one and a quarter million individuals had been unemployed continuously for more than 52 weeks. This represents almost 40 per cent of the total number unemployed. This trend is viewed by most as the single most disturbing feature of current UK unemployment, not only because many of the debilitating effects of unemployment appear to be associated with long-term unemployment, but also because the probability of re-employment falls with length of unemployment. This is a consequence of so-called hysteresis effects, that is, lack of recent work experience and a depreciation of the human capital stock.

The final feature of the data that may be noted is the occupational structure of unemployment. As is clear from table 19.3, which provides illustrative figures for 1980 and 1981, this is heavily concentrated in unskilled occupational groupings with over half of total unemployment being accounted for by 'general labourers' and 'other manual'. The most obvious explanation of this phenomenon is that such workers lack much in the way of

TABLE 19.3
UK Unemployment by Occupational Group, 1980–1

		Managerial and professional	Clerical and related	Other non-manual occupations	Craft and similar occupations	General labourers	Other manual
		% of total					
1980	(1)	7.9	14.4	6.4	11.3	35.4	24.6
	(2)	7.3	14.2	6.2	11.6	35.9	24.7
	(3)	8.6	14.4	6.1	12.1	34.1	24.7
	(4)	8.5	13.1	6.0	14.1	32.5	25.9
1981	(1)	8.2	12.7	6.1	15.2	31.5	26.3
	(2)	8.4	12.5	6.1	15.4	31.5	26.3
	(3)	9.8	13.0	6.1	14.8	30.6	25.8
	(4)	9.5	12.6	6.3	15.0	30.2	26.5

Source: Employment Gazette, **90**(6), table 2.11.

human capital, and in a recessionary period it is easier for firms to lay off such workers rather than skilled workers. One might also argue that the 'replacement ratio' is highest for unskilled workers and therefore voluntary unemployment is higher. As will be seen, however, the support for this proposition is limited.

Employment Policy in the UK

One of the most forceful and unambiguous commitments to any target of economic policy was enshrined in the 1944 White Paper on Employment Policy. Following the traumatic experience of the inter-war period, when unemployment averaged 14.2 per cent between 1921 and 1938 (reaching a zenith of 22 per cent in 1932 and a nadir of 9.5 per cent in 1927), an undertaking was given by the government to 'accept as one of their primary aims and responsibilities the maintenance of a high and stable level of employment'. This commitment was adhered to by both Conservative and Labour administrations right up until the middle of the 1970s when, as was seen in the previous chapter, inflation took over as the 'primary' objective of government policy.

Over this quarter of a century from the later 1940s through to the early 1970s various threads of employment policy can be identified. On the one hand governments were quite willing to tackle what they viewed as cyclical unemployment by manipulation of monetary and fiscal policies. Whenever UK unemployment pushed much above 2 per cent of the total workforce (or in absolute terms around 0.5 million unemployed) an expansionary posture was invariably assumed on fiscal and monetary (or more accurately credit) policies. Deviations from the employment target as with the inflation, growth and balance of payments objectives were integrally bound up with the stop–go cycle of activity. The commitment to 'full employment' undoubtedly ensured that the authorities were willing to comply with (or acquiesce in) a stop–go pattern of activity and, for whatever reason, aggregate unemployment remained relatively low. One could argue that this was a measure of the success of fine tuning policy. Alternatively, one could point to the unprecedented expansion of trade which occurred over this period, and the increasing openness of the UK economy (in 1950 imports/exports accounted for around 12 per cent; by 1980 this had risen to 30 per cent). Both influences are relevant. Certainly, it appears to be the case that a short-run trade-off between inflation and unemployment did hold for at least part of this period, allowing the authorities some kind of handle for employment policy. As was seen in our discussions of expectations, acceptance of a Phillips relation means acceptance of a possible role for money illusion in the labour market or it relies on some other imperfection. Although money illusion is unreasonable as a long-run postulate, it may not have been inappropriate over periods such as the 1950s and early 1960s, for the simple reason that the average inflation rate was low in absolute terms and deviations around that average were also small. With inflation at such a low level, and deviations around the inflation rate being so small, it seems reasonable to suppose that individuals formed their expectations adaptively, and in many instances it is likely that expectations lagged behind reality facilitating a short-run trade-off. Even if it is accepted that the era is testimony to the efficacy of demand management manipulations, one might argue as Bacon and Eltis (1978) have done that the maintenance of a relatively high level of employment was achieved at a cost, namely a slowdown in the underlying rate of productivity growth. Bacon and Eltis argue that a high level of employment was maintained by expanding the share of public sector employment. In other words, as unemployment rose, fiscal expansion through increased government expenditure reduced unemployment by increasing employment in public services. Given that most such services are non-marketable, an increasing share of national product is therefore accounted for by non-market activity where productivity change is slow. The Bacon and Eltis thesis has been questioned (see Hadjimatheou and Skouras, 1979) but nevertheless provides an interesting view of the role which demand management may have played in employment policy.

As can be seen from table 19.1, a low average rate of unemployment continued to mask quite wide regional variations. It seems as if the 'depressed' regions were more susceptible to cyclical pressures than the 'prosperous' regions, as one can observe from the marked procyclical pattern of deviations from the average. Since, however, rates of unemployment were *persistently* higher for these areas it does suggest that a certain amount of structural unemployment was being experienced, unemployment bound up with the erstwhile dependence of these areas on heavy industry and subsumed under the euphemism of the 'regional problem'. Although this is not the place to explore this aspect of policy, it is nevertheless relevant to the discussion since one can view much of UK post-war regional policy as an extension of employment policy. Certain instruments were designed to take 'workers to the work', for example the availability of relocation grants. In the main, however, policy has been directed to try and encourage 'work to the workers', that is, a great many incentives have been made available to encourage investment in the peripheral regions. At times these have taken the form of tax incentives. Recently, however, greater use has been made of cash grants on plant and equipment. In the main subsidies have been given to capital, although there have been occasions when subsidies to labour have been offered (such as the regional employment premium).

All of these instruments can be viewed as attempts to alleviate structural rather than cyclical unemployment. There is some debate over the extent to which they have been successful (see Brown and Burrows, 1978). In evaluating such policy one faces the classic counter-factual problem; that is, it is simply not known what the situation would have been in the absence of intervention. Furthermore, extricating the effects of one policy from others is especially problematic in this case. Some evidence exists to suggest that regional policy type instruments have served to preserve *and* create employment in the peripheral regions. For example Moore and Rhodes (1973) contend that some 220,000 jobs were created between 1963 and 1970. Against this, however, it has been argued that regional policies have served to compound regional disparities and done little to alleviate structural unemployment, in part because they have encouraged relatively capital intensive activities, and, related to this, in part because they have discriminated against services activity. This line contends that since the UK economy (like many other developed market economies) is undergoing a process of tertiarization, service employment will expand relative to manufacturing employment. The explicit bias in UK regional policy towards manufacturing activity has served to prevent the peripheral regions from taking full advantage of the growth of the service sector. (see McEnery, 1981). According to this line of analysis, regional policy has served to encourage rather than reduce structural unemployment.

By way of summarizing policy over this period, two observations can be made. First, since the employment target was consistently hit up until the latter part of the 1960s, the overall level of unemployment was not really viewed as a pressing policy problem. If unemployment reached a critical level of around 0.5 million, demand manipulation was seen as the obvious and appropriate response. Second, in terms of long-term policy problems, the *distribution* of unemployment was seen as a more pressing issue and a variety of instruments were deployed to this end.[2]

Unemployment in the later 1970s and 1980s

There are two immediately striking features of unemployment in the UK in the later 1970s and 1980s. The first is the dramatic increase which has been recorded, and the second is the equanimity with which it has been viewed by both Labour and Conservative governments. This does not mean they have been unconcerned by the increase. Rather it is simply a comment on their resistance to the temptation of demand management as a means of reducing unemployment. In this section will be considered more fully alternative diagnoses of the underlying causes of this staggering increase in unemployment, and the policy prescriptions associated with each. To emphasize the poles in the debate, these will be examined first; the 'middle ground', which is occupied by many neo-Keynesians and monetarists, will then be discussed in rather more general terms.

New Classical View

At various points in part II the central features of the new classical macro-economics were outlined. It will be recalled that the foundations of this model are threefold. The first is that agents form their expectations rationally rather than adaptively. The second is that markets are efficient. The third is that the rate of change in prices is solely determined by the rate of change in the money supply and, given rational expectations, variations in the latter feed through to variations in the former with a very short lag and with minimal output/employment effects. If these assumptions hold, and if this is taken as a reasonably accurate description of the way the world works, there are a number of important implications for the explanation of current unemployment. In the more extreme models, for example, all unemployment would be viewed as voluntary or search unemployment. In terms of the classification introduced earlier, this view of the world would see

---

2 This should not be read to imply that there was continuity in UK regional policy. In fact, one of the problems with UK policy has been that Conservative and Labour administrations have favoured different instruments, and consequently one might argue that policy has been characterized by a distinct lack of continuity.

cyclical unemployment as relatively unimportant and frictional/structural unemployment as more important – the former because agents spend more time in job search, the latter because they simply perceive the costs of relocation/retraining as being too high. Thus the increase in unemployment in the UK would be explained by the interaction of a number of factors. One would be random cyclical pressures, like the 'second oil shock' of 1979. Another would be an increase in the natural rate of unemployment. This has occurred as a result of lack of incentive to work because the real value of welfare benefits are so high, and as a result of factor market distortions raising real wages and pricing people out of jobs. In an open economy this would be viewed as especially important.

The policy implications of this analysis are first of all that the natural rate of unemployment cannot be reduced by demand reflation – 'real' targets require 'real' policies. Thus to achieve a longer-run reduction in the level of unemployment, policy should be directed at the following. First, incentives to work should be improved. This could be achieved by reducing marginal rates of income taxation and reducing the real value of welfare benefits. Second, the operation of the markets allocative function should be improved by the removal of distortions, basically to encourage greater competition in product and factor markets. In product markets this would involve a more vigorous competition policy, whilst in factor markets it would involve proscribing the market power of labour unions. The role of government therefore is constrained to providing an environment within which markets can function efficiently (see Minford and Peel, 1981).

New Cambridge View

At the opposite extreme in the spectrum is the new Cambridge view. This view denies the validity of the rational expectations assumption and views inflation as essentially cost push in origin. In explaining unemployment it focuses on demand deficiency, and views unemployment as essentially involuntary rather than voluntary. In terms of the classification introduced earlier, unemployment would be viewed as largely cyclical and structural, the cyclical element being due to a combination of deficient domestic demand and deficient overseas demand; the former is seen as the outcome of contractionary fiscal and monetary policies, the latter as a consequence of world recession. Structural unemployment would be viewed as largely a result of competition from 'relatively successful' industrial countries, in practice other Western European countries and Japan. The policy implications of this analysis are, first, that active demand expansion is a necessary condition for a reduction in unemployment. In order, however, to ensure that increased expenditure does not leak abroad, fiscal expansion should be accompanied by general import controls. In this particular scenario, therefore, there is an extremely active role for government to play.

It should be noted that this description of the new Cambridge position is based on the strategy proposed up until April 1982, a fuller statement on which can be found in Cripps and Godley (1978), for example. It seems, however, judging from the April 1982 *Cambridge Policy Review*, as if the group have shifted ground and now argue that demand management policies can have no lasting effect on the level of unemployment. From the analysis in part II of this book, the reader might be struck by the similarity of this stance with the natural rate hypothesis.

Both these extreme analyses have shortcomings in explaining recent unemployment in the UK. The new classical analysis, for example, would have some difficulty in explaining the regional pattern of unemployment in the UK (table 19.1) as well as the huge increase in the long-term unemployed (table 19.2) which has occurred. Furthermore, some of their arguments regarding incentives simply do not square up with the facts. Thus, with regard to unemployment benefits, for example, in the UK these are only earnings-related for six months, flat rate for a further six months and are then replaced simply by supplementary benefit. Furthermore, although as can be seen from table 19.4 the ratio of unemployment benefit to average post-tax income (for a married man with two children) increased from 45 to 78 per cent between 1964 and 1971, it has since fallen back to around 60 per cent in 1981. This decline coincides with the most dramatic increase in unemployment. In addition, empirical analysis of the effects of unemployment and related benefits on recorded unemployment in the UK seem to indicate that as a causal factor this has a limited role to play. For

TABLE 19.4
The Ratio of Unemployment Benefit to Average Post-tax Income in the UK (for a Married Man with Two Children)

Year	Ratio (%)	Year	Ratio (%)
1964	45	1973	71
1965	49	1974	70
1966	69	1975	67
1967	73	1976	67
1968	73	1977	68
1969	71	1978	66
1970	73	1979	65
1971	78	1980	63
1972	74	1981	60

Source: Cross (1982a), table 12.2.

example, Nickell (1979) estimates that some 14 per cent of the actual increase in unemployment between 1964–5 and 1973 can be attributed to the increase in unemployment benefits relative to average after-tax income (the replacement ratio). Thus although there is evidence to indicate that this has made a contribution, it is not a pervasive explanation. This sits oddly alongside the increase in the long-term unemployed.

The most serious limitations of the new Cambridge view are the dissociation between demand reflation and inflation (prior to April 1982 anyway) and the limited role played by market forces or supply constraints. The latter are clearly viewed as important given the crucial role ascribed to import controls. Despite their shortcomings an examination of the extremes is useful if only to emphasize differing views on supply- and demand-based explanations. Most 'intermediate' views of unemployment emphasize these to different degrees.

Demand Deficiency

It is certain that demand deficiency has a part to play in the explanation of recent UK unemployment. On the one hand there are external pressures generated by the adjustment to the 1979 oil shock. The most obvious evidence of this is relatively high unemployment in other developed market economies (DMEs). On the other hand, as was seen in the previous chapter, the medium-term economic strategy of 1979–83 was explicitly directed at demand deflation. In a rational expectations world with a vertical aggregate supply curve a minimal effect on output and employment could have been anticipated. This does not seem characteristic of the UK economy and it seems as if fiscal and monetary contraction did contribute to the increase in unemployment. In other words, there has been movement some way along a positively sloped aggregate supply curve. How much of a contribution these two forces have made to present unemployment is difficult to say; it really depends which model of the economy is accepted as being most representative. Suffice it to say that those strategies explicitly founded on reflation forecast, at their most optimistic, a reduction in unemployment of around one million as a result of this kind of policy package. If these forecasts are accurate it indicates that more fundamental forces are at work than simply demand deficiency. This is implied by the picture of the long-run trend in unemployment conveyed in figure 19.1 where, as has already been noted, the unemployment rates associated with successive peaks and troughs of cycles in the post-1965 period has been increasing with each successive cycle, which implies that demand deficiency cannot in itself offer a comprehensive explanation for rising unemployment.

Supply Constraints

It has already been noted that the increase in the replacement ratio appeared to contribute to the increase in unemployment between 1964–5 and 1973. Since then the ratio has declined, yet unemployment has continued to increase. It would seem then that this is a less important causal factor, although some recent commentators have downgraded the importance of the replacement ratio *per se* and focused more on the role of high marginal tax rates and the poverty trap. At the very least this may have encouraged the growth of the black economy with the result that *recorded* unemployment is higher than *actual* unemployment.

Of more significance are developments in the labour market. Here employment protection legislation which makes it more difficult to vary employment demand in response to cyclical pressures has probably served to raise the natural rate. So too has the effect of labour unions on real wages. This is a factor which has been especially important over the last few years which, along with sterling appreciation, resulted in a quite extraordinary deterioration in UK competitiveness between 1979 and 1980, (see figure 20.4). Finally, at the 'micro' level there is some evidence to suggest that housing market imperfections have exerted an impact through their effect on labour mobility. In particular the presence of a large local authority housing stock, where allocation is administered via queueing rather than price, makes it difficult for local authority residents to move from one area to another. In this connection it is worth noting that Nickell (1980) finds that the unemployment rate for local authority residents in 1972 was higher than for non local authority residents. Of course it has to be conceded that local authority tenancy might simply be a proxy for other relevant influences like socioeconomic group, skill endowment or family circumstances. Nickell does, however, calculate that even on *ceteris paribus* assumptions the unemployment rate for local authority residents is still 60 per cent higher than for the 'standard man' of the study, a finding which can be interpreted as lending some weight to the mobility argument.

Although the micro–macro distinction is somewhat arbitrary, several developments can be identified which can reasonably be labelled macro. First of all there is the build-up in production of North Sea oil. It seems that this could have had a 'crowding out' effect on manufacturing through its effect on the external account – basically, since the balance of payments must balance with reduced oil imports, there are reduced exports of manufactures (see Forsyth and Kay, 1980). In so far as the presence of North Sea oil contributed to sterling appreciation it also helped reduce the competitiveness of UK manufacturing activity. Also on the macro side a structural change has been taking place in the world economy with a shift in comparative advantage in many standardized manufactures away from DMEs like the UK towards the so-called newly industrializing countries (NICs), namely Korea, Taiwan, Singapore, Hong Kong, Brazil, Mexico and so on. Although the NICs only account for around 10 per cent of total OECD imports of manufactures their exporting efforts have been concentrated in particular product lines which has caused adjustment problems in certain sectors (see Greenaway, 1983). Finally, on the macro side the process of tertiarization mentioned earlier has certainly been under way in the UK and may have been to some extent resisted, causing further adjustment problems

Co-ordination Problems

Finally, alongside these demand and supply forces might also be identified what could be described as co-ordination problems. These are the kinds of geographical and occupational mismatches of labour demand and supply that can result in structural unemployment. The influence of this factor has already been considered under the heading of labour market segmentation in chapter 7. There, it will be recalled, the emphasis was on the way in which segmentation can induce rigidities into the market and frustrate market clearing.

A mismatch of labour across sectors is especially likely during a period of high unemployment, given that depreciation of the human capital stock occurs. In other words, with over forty per cent of the total number unemployed suffering long-term unemployment, a large fraction of the excess labour supply has little in the way of recent 'on the job' experience which can help make them re-employable. Comment has already been made at length on the geographical mismatch of labour demand/supply which is such an integral feature of the regional problem in the UK.

Policy Implications of Present Unemployment

This stylized outline of the kind of forces which have interacted to generate such a high level of unemployment in the UK serves to emphasize one very important point, namely that there is no single factor which is unequivocally responsible, and therefore there is no single policy which can be unambiguously recommended to produce instant and/or lasting results. It is certainly the case that demand reflation *per se* would not be efficacious in the UK. This is implied in figures 19.4 and 19.5. In the former inflation is plotted against real output, in the latter inflation against unemployment, for the period 1966–86. Broadly speaking, the pattern traced out

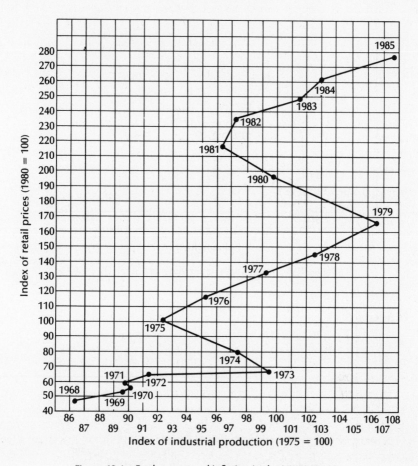

Figure 19.4   Real output and inflation in the UK 1968–85

in figure 19.4 can be viewed as a plot of aggregate supply. This appears to be consistent with the adjustment process described in figure 19.6. Shifts in *AD* temporarily raise output in a move along a short-run *AS* curve. Once adjustment has taken place, however, output returns to its natural level but the price level is jacked up further. In figure 19.5 a similar story appears to be being told. There is some evidence of short-run Phillips relations (as for example in 1972–3 or 1978–9) but adjustment occurs relatively quickly in the manner suggested by figure 19.7. Not only, however, does there appear to be a circling of the natural rate U^* (the mechanics of which were discussed in chapter 14), but U^* itself seems to be shifting to the right for reasons discussed earlier in this chapter. Although one cannot 'prove' anything from such statistical associations, as has been seen there is a good

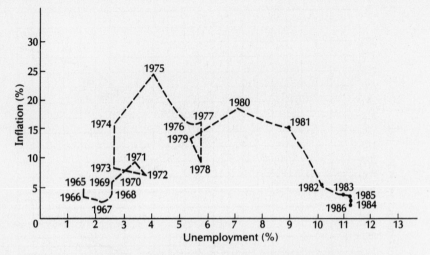

Figure 19.5   Inflation and unemployment in the UK 1965–86

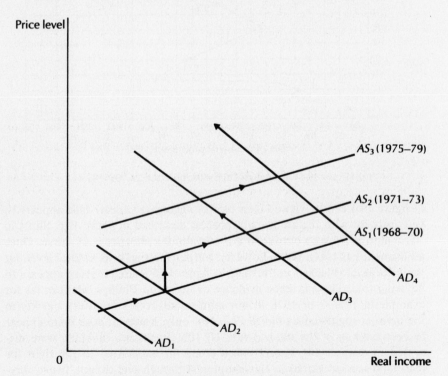

Figure 19.6   Adjustments in *AS* to demand stimuli

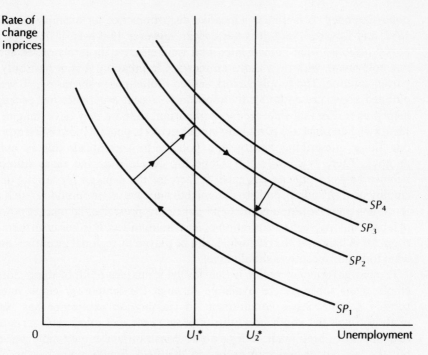

Figure 19.7   Movements around the natural rate

deal of perfectly respectable theory to back it up. The weight of empirical evidence does point to positively sloped AS curves in the short run, but places a question mark against any stable positively sloped long-run AS curve.

Despite this, advocates of intervention still see scope for judicious expansionary demand policy through public investment rather than public consumption, often with a commitment to income control of some form or other to try and alter any trade-off which is assumed to exist. Within the targets/instruments approach to economic policy discussed in chapter 17, one would be introducing an additional policy instrument (incomes policy) in recognition of the fact that wage bargaining is directed at two independent targets, namely clearing the labour market and deciding on the distribution of income. The introduction of some form of income control aimed at the latter is intended to match the number of targets and instruments. The problem is, of course, as was seen in the previous chapter, that all experiments with incomes policy in the UK demonstrate that this instrument also (adversely) affects the market clearing function of wage bargaining. As a consequence, much research effort has recently been directed at the design of an incomes policy intended to minimize allocative distortions (see for example Meade, 1982, and Layard, 1986). It is quite clear, however, that even if this type of policy response were implemented and were effective (in terms of reducing unemployment, with or without an increase in inflation) it is at best only a partial solution. The supply factors and co-ordination problems which were outlined above are undoubtedly important – recent experience has perhaps helped us realize that they are more important than we may have imagined. Identifying an objective of making labour markets operate more efficiently is one thing; prescribing appropriate policies to accomplish this is quite another. There is considerable scope for debate over the most suitable balance between policies designed to increase the demand for labour (like employment subsidies), policies designed to improve labour mobility (such as retraining and relocation grants) and policies to proscribe the market power of labour unions (such as limitation of legal immunities). Furthermore there is room for debate over the part which can be played by regional incentives and what form any incentives should take.

Present government policy is (inevitably) a mixture of all of these. Some employment subsidies are available through the temporary employment subsidy scheme. Some commitment to training/job experience has been made through the youth opportunity programme and other such schemes. Attempts have been made to legislate to constrain union monopoly power, but the law has an unhappy record in this field. Finally there has been a subtle but interesting change in regional policy. Many of the instruments which the 1979–86 Conservative administration inherited from the previous government have been retained, such as cash grants (although the number of areas eligible has been reduced), but there has been the creation of 'enterprise zones', areas where certain rules and regulations relating to planning and construction do not apply and where rates and so on are waived. Whether this has the desired effect of encouraging investment remains to be seen.

One other aspect of policy which ought to be mentioned is the encouragement given to small businesses. Most budgets between 1981 and 1987 provided a range of incentives to encourage the setting up of small firms in line with a government belief in the role which such (labour intensive) enterprises could play in any recovery.

These are the main strands of what might be termed employment policy. If they do have a common thread it is that they are essentially supply side oriented rather than demand side.

Concluding Comments

It is clear from the foregoing that unemployment in the UK increased dramatically between 1979 and 1981 and has remained stubbornly high since then. Some analysts argue that this is due largely to the deflationary impact of counter-inflation policies; others contend that it has more to do with market imperfections on the supply side of the economy. Both arguments have some relevance. It seems plausible that various supply side influences have combined to help raise the natural rate of unemployment. Estimates of what this rate may be vary. For instance Metcalf (1984) puts the range at 4–9 per cent. Even accepting the upper bound of these estimates suggests that the current unemployment level is beyond the natural rate by a significant degree. Quite what scope this offers for expansionary demand management policies is a matter of controversy. Many commentators feel that some non-marginal impact on the level of unemployment could be affected via increased public expenditure. The real concern here, however, is the implication of expansionary demand management policies for inflation. Layard (1976) argues that potential inflationary pressures can be defused by targeting assistance at the long-term unemployed where the pressures for wage inflation are likely to be at a minimum, and by introducing a tax-based incomes policy to contain any pressures which do result.

The present (1986) Conservative administration shows no inclination towards greater reliance on demand side policies, preferring to trust the (longer-term) supply side changes which have been so far effected. Whether such policies will ultimately be successful remains to be seen.

Further Reading

Data on unemployment in the UK are provided monthly by *Economic Trends*. This is a readily accessible source of information for aggregate and regional unemployment. A much more valuable source is the Department of Employment's monthly publication *Employment Gazette*. This provides detailed breakdowns by employment group, region, locality, duration of unemployment and so on, as well as regular special features on unemployment. More rigorous analyses of unemployment are provided by Nickell (1980) and the readings in Creedy (1981). The paper by Atkinson in the latter volume examines evidence on the disincentive effects of unemployment benefits, as does Nickell's (1979) paper.

A concise review of the new classical view of current UK unemployment can be found in Minford and Peel (1981). Brown and Burrows (1978) provide an overview of regional problems and their role in generating structural employment, as well as comparing UK regional unemployment problems with experience in other developed market economies. The Cambridge demand deficiency payments constraint analysis is outlined in most *Cambridge Economic Policy Reviews.*

For a comparative empirical study of the role of labour market institutions on output and employment, see Gordon (1982).

20

Balance of Payments and Exchange
Rate Policies in the UK

The balance of payments has occupied a central position in post-war UK macroeconomic debates. Recurrent sterling crises have been a feature of this period, which spans an era of both pegged exchange rates and managed exchange rates. In chapters 14 and 15 the interrelationships between internal and external balance, and the technical difficulties of simultaneously aiming to attain both, were considered. In this chapter the rather more specific issue of balance of payments and exchange rate policy in the UK will be considered.

As was seen in chapter 14 there are direct links between domestic expenditure policies and the balance of payments. Once a particular monetary/fiscal policy posture is adopted, there will be a given balance of payments outcome associated with it. This will be taken as given and, rather than examine further the links between domestic expenditure policies and the balance of payments which were extensively explored in chapters 14 and 15, the discussion will focus more sharply on those instruments which have been depolyed to alter a specific balance of payments situation. Moreover the discussion will take place against the backcloth of British experience over the post-war period.

The Meaning of External Balance

In chapter 14 external balance was equated with a situation where the sum of any surplus (or deficit) on the current account and any deficit (or surplus) on capital account is equal to zero. This would also be consistent with an absence of 'below the line' settlements. Such a definition was extremely convenient for analytical purposes as it permitted the tracing out of a locus of combinations of the interest rate and the level of income which were consistent with the sum of current and capital transactions netting out to zero. The *EB* schedule derived as a result was then used to explore the implications of various combinations of internal and external imbalance. When an attempt is made to transform this theoretical concept of external balance into a meaningful policy target, however, a number of difficulties are faced, in particular the time scale over which payments balance is expected to occur, the 'composition' of payments balance, and the relationship of external to internal balance.

Take first of all the question of time scale. Since the concern in chapters 14 and 15 was principally with comparative statics, this is a question which was largely ignored. Unless it is assumed that there are efficient markets throughout the system and freely floating exchange rates such that any tendency towards payments imbalance immediately alters the market clearing exchange rate, it is an issue which cannot be ignored. Even when exchange rates are relatively free, adjustment towards the market clearing rate invariably takes place in discrete steps. When, as is usually the case, some degree of exchange rate management is practised one has to be clear on the period over which one expects the accounts to balance. It would, for example, be quite absurd to aim at a target of daily, weekly or even monthly balance if only because of the complications caused by seasonal variations in demand for exports and imports. If, on the other hand, one were to view the relevant period as, say, a decade, then it could take an extremely long time to confirm any evidence of fundamental disequilibrium. In a famous tract Nurkse (1945) argued that a period of five to ten years would be appropriate for the identification of external balance. The reasoning behind this suggestion is that it would probably take this long for any cyclical influences to even themselves out and, according to Nurkse, cyclical influences should be treated in the same way as seasonal influences, that is, as self-equilibrating. This too is probably an excessive period and most commentators would accept that any surplus or deficit which persisted beyond a couple of years was evidence of payments imbalance and a candidate for policy action. There is in fact a good deal of qualitative evidence to suggest that the policy-maker's time horizon may be even shorter than this.

Even when one has identified the period over which the balance of payments should balance, the composition of the overall balance of payments may itself be viewed as an intermediate policy target. In other words there may be a preference for a surplus on current account matched by a deficit on capital account (or vice versa). It is of course likely that such a division will be primarily dictated by a country's relative resource endowments. Thus, in the UK it is usual to find a deficit on the trade account and a surplus on services, reflecting the fact that the UK is a resource scarce (notwithstanding the advent of North Sea oil) and capital abundant economy. This may not, however, prevent policy-makers from offering inducements to encourage the export of manufactures rather than services or capital. It may also mean that there may be an (implicit) limit on the volume of short-term capital which a country is willing to attract to generate a capital account surplus and overall payments balance.

This leads to a third important issue, namely the mix of domestic financial policies which is seen as being consistent with external balance. For example, a current account deficit could be matched, if necessary, by a capital account surplus if the authorities were willing to maintain the necessary short-term interest rate differential. This is familiar from the Mundellian *IB/EB* model. What was also noted in connection with that model, however, is that there may be political constraints on the use of interest rates which impose an upper limit on the extent to which the domestic interest rate can rise. Thus although payments' balance may in principle be attainable, in practice it may prove to be unattainable owing to an inability or unwillingness to mix the appropriate combination of policies.

For these reasons payments balance is rather more difficult to identify than say price stability or even full employment. For present purposes it will be taken to mean a tendency towards the current and capital accounts summing to zero over a period of a couple of years. As will be seen in the review of UK policy over the post-war period, this appears to be the kind of time scale within which most (vote maximizing) policy-makers operate.

An Overview of UK Balance of Payments

Figures 20.1 and 20.2 and table 20.1 describe the salient trends in the UK balance of payments over the period 1950–85. A number of distinctive features of UK payments can be noted from this information.

1. As is clear from figure 20.1 the UK traditionally runs a deficit on *visible trade* and a surplus on *invisible trade*. Between 1950 and 1985 the invisible account has been in surplus continuously. Visible trade has largely shown a deficit over this period with the important exception of the early 1980s, the period when the contribution of North Sea oil to the balance of payments was at its peak. These trends are largely the outcome of relative resource endowments. Until the discovery of North Sea oil the UK could be considered as a relatively capital-abundant resource-scarce economy. Although North Sea oil made a significant contribution to the visible surplus of the early 1980s, this is still largely true.

2. Figure 20.2 traces the behaviour of the current balance (that is, the sum of the visible and invisible balances) which follows a distinctly cyclical pattern, and certainly up until 1967 the cyclical pattern on the current account was integrally related to the stop–go pattern of economic activity which was such a prominent feature of UK experience. As was noted in chapter 14 monetary and fiscal policies are perforce related to one's payments situation. What is

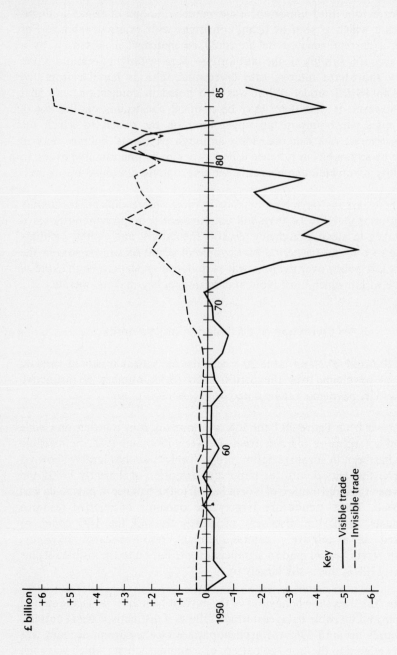

Figure 20.1   UK balance on visible and invisible trade 1950–85 (£billion)

Key
——— Visible trade
– – – Invisible trade

£ billion
+6
+5
+4
+3
+2
+1
0
1950
-1
-2
-3
-4
-5
-6

85

80

70

60

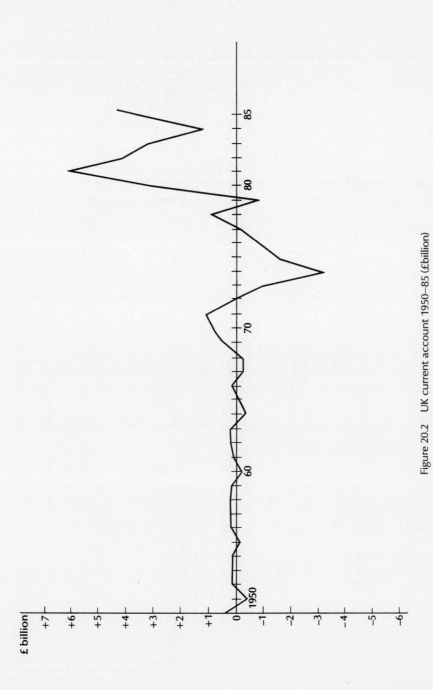

Figure 20.2   UK current account 1950–85 (£billion)

TABLE 20.1

Balance of Payments 1950–85: Summary (£m)

	Visible trade (balance)	Invisibles (balance)				Current balance	Special grants[2] and capital transfers	UK external assets and liabilities			EEA loss on forwards	Allocation of special Drawing Rights	Gold subscription to IMF	Balancing Item[4]
		Services[1]	IPD	Transfers[1]	Total			Transactions in assets[3]	Transactions in liabilities[3]	Net transactions[3]				
1950	−51	−30	396	−8	358	307	140	—	—	−447	—	—	—	—
1951	−689	6	342	−28	320	−369	43	—	—	−426	—	—	—	−100
1952	−279	106	252	84	442	163	—	—	—	−229	—	—	—	66
1953	−244	96	229	64	389	145	—	—	—	−177	—	—	—	32
1954	−204	80	250	−9	321	117	—	—	—	−174	—	—	—	57
1955	−313	9	174	−25	158	−155	—	—	—	34	—	—	—	121
1956	53	−9	229	−65	155	208	—	—	—	−250	—	—	—	42
1957	−29	87	249	−74	262	233	—	—	—	−313	—	—	—	80
1958	29	98	293	−60	331	360	—	—	—	−411	—	—	—	51
1959	−115	86	262	−61	287	172	—	—	—	−68	—	—	—	−46
1960	−401	8	233	−68	173	−228	—	—	—	−7	—	—	−58	267
1961	−140	21	254	−88	187	47	—	—	—	23	—	—	−32	−70
1962	−100	18	334	−97	255	155	—	—	—	−195	—	—	—	40
1963	−119	−31	398	−123	244	125	—	−534	494	−40	—	—	—	−85
1964	−543	−76	404	−158	170	−373	—	−542	925	383	—	—	—	−10
1965	−260	−98	449	−169	182	−78	—	−756	794	38	—	—	—	40

Year														
1966	−108	15	401	−181	235	127	—	−291	301	10	—	—	−44	−93
1967	−599	131	399	−216	314	−285	—	−369	535	166	−105	—	—	224
1968	−712	312	359	−223	448	−264	—	−1,120	1,773	653	−251	—	—	−138
1969	−209	368	531	−206	693	484	—	−1,336	476	−860	—	—	—	376
1970	−34	416	595	−182	829	795	—	−1,423	550	−873	—	171	−38	−55
1971	190	544	552	−196	900	1,090	—	−3,800	2,319	−1,481	—	125	—	266
1972	−748	618	595	−272	941	193	—	−872	1,331	459	—	124	—	−776
1973	−2,586	684	1,326	−443	1,567	−1,019	−59	−2,992	3,936	944	—	—	—	134
1974	−5,351	949	1,506	−422	2,033	−3,318	−75	−2,709	5,952	3,243	—	—	—	150
1975	−3,333	1,336	890	−475	1,751	−1,582	—	−1,534	3,315	1,601	—	—	—	−19
1976	−3,929	2,245	1,550	−786	3,009	−920	—	−3,723	4,317	594	—	—	—	326
1977	−2,284	3,038	238	−1,128	2,148	−136	—	−13,193	9,952	−3,241	—	—	—	3,377
1978	−1,542	3,478	820	−1,791	2,507	965	—	−4,628	1,506	−3,122	—	—	—	2,157
1979	−3,449	3,818	1,193	−2,279	2,732	−717	—	−39,515	39,445	−70	—	195	—	592
1980	1,361	3,868	−222	−2,078	1,568	2,929	—	−42,141	39,203	−2,938	—	180	—	−171
1981	3,360	3,826	949	−1,976	2,799	6,159	—	−49,581	43,071	−6,510	—	158	—	193
1982	2,331	2,607	960	−1,961	1,606	3,937	—	−31,023	28,506	−2,517	—	—	—	−1,420
1983	−835	3,652	2,421	−2,104	3,969	3,134	—	−30,815	26,142	−4,673	—	—	—	1,539
1984	−4,384	3,744	4,157	−2,305	5,596	1,212	—	−31,256	24,920	−6,336	—	—	—	5,124
1985	−2,111	5,812	3,400	−3,499	5,713	3,602	—	−50,021	42,725	−7,296	—	—	—	3,694

1 Prior to 1954, the coverage of general government services credits is likely to be incomplete, part remaining within general government transfers.
2 Grants to or from the United Kingdom government which, because they were of a non-recurrent financing nature, are not appropriate to the current account.
3 Prior to 1979 foreign currency lending and borrowing abroad by UK banks (other than certain export credit extended) is recorded on a net basis under liabilities.
4 For 1946 to 1951 very approximate estimates are given to the nearest £50 million for the 'balancing item' and the residual shown above as net transactions in external assets and liabilities.

Source: Economic Trends, Annual Supplement 1987, table 124.

evident from experience over the 1950–67 period in particular is that full employment and a balanced current account were incompatible.

3. The order of magnitude of recorded deficits and surpluses has increased quite dramatically in the 1970s and 1980s compared with the 1960s. This is in part due to the acceleration of inflation over this period and the effect which this has had on nominal values. This does not apply, however, to the deficits of 1974 and 1975, nor to the surpluses of 1980, 1981 and 1982. These, when expressed as a proportion of GDP, were high by historical standards. In both cases they can be explained by reference to specific developments – in the case of the former the 'oil shock' of 1973–4, in the case of the latter the build-up of North Sea oil production. These developments will be explored further shortly.

4. Table 20.2 outlines in broad terms the changes which have taken place in the commodity composition of UK trade over the last 20 years or so. Two features of this table are especially notable. The first is the increase in the relative importance of imported manufactures – a development bound up in the increasing importance of intra-industry trade, that is, the simultaneous import and export of commodities from the same product line.[1] The second is the change in the direction of trade away from North American and Commonwealth countries towards Western Europe – a development related to membership of EFTA and then the EEC.

In explaining these developments and trends it is helpful to break the period down into three sub-periods, 1950–67, 1967–72 and 1972–85.

1950–67: Pegged Exchange Rates and the Stop–Go Cycle

In 1948 the Bretton Woods arrangement regarding exchange rate movements was signed; it formed one of the bases of post-war international economic relations.[2] As a direct result of the Bretton Woods agreement a gold exchange rate system was introduced. Each country which participated

---

1 The importance of intra-industry trade has increased in most Western economies over the post-war period. Grubel and Lloyd (1975) document the magnitude of these changes. Greenaway (1983b) provides an econometric analysis of the determinants of intra-industry trade in the UK, whilst Greenaway (1982) discusses the sources of the phenomenon and Greenaway and Milner (1983) focus on measurement problems. Greenaway and Milner (1986) offer an evaluation of all aspects of the phenomenon.

2 The others being the GATT and the World Bank group. The former provided a framework of rates for the conduct of international commerce, whilst the latter was introduced specifically as a development agency.

TABLE 20.2
Area and Product Composition of UK Merchandise Trade, 1955–85
(percentages)

Area Composition	Imports				Exports			
	1955	1965	1975	1985	1955	1965	1975	1985
Western Europe	26	36	51	63	29	42	49	58
EEC	13	24	36	46	15	26	32	46
North America	20	20	13	14	12	15	11	17
USA	11	12	10	12	7	11	9	15
Other DMEs	14	12	8	8	21	15	9	5
Japan	1	1	3	5	1	1	2	1
CPEs	3	4	3	2	2	3	3	2
Oil Exporting LDCs	9	10	14	3	5	6	11	8
Other LDCs	29	18	11	10	32	20	15	10
Product Composition								
Food, Beverages and Tobacco	37	30	18	11	6	7	7	6
Basic Materials	29	19	9	4	6	3	3	3
Fuels	11	11	18	12	5	3	4	21
Semi-Manufactures	18	24	25	27	38	35	32	20
Finished Manu- factures	5	15	28	44	42	49	51	45
Miscellaneous	0	1	2	2	3	4	4	3

EEC   European Economic Community   DMEs   Developed Market Economies
CPEs   Centrally Planned Economies   LDCs   Less Developed Countries
Source: Adapted from *Economic Trends* various issues.

in the system fixed a *par value* for its currency against gold and this in turn bore a fixed relationship to the dollar (initially this was set at $35/oz). Thus the dollar was the *numeraire* in the system and all exchange rates were pegged against it. Only minor variations were permitted on a day-to-day basis, which amounted to a fluctuation around the par value (or central rate) of ±1.25 per cent. If the exchange rate threatened to fluctuate outside this band, support buying or selling was obligatory. In certain circumstances, the par value could be changed by devaluation or revaluation – this was permitted in the event of *fundamental disequilibrium*. In practice, exchange rate changes under the Bretton Woods regime were infrequent; to all intents and purposes there was a quasi-fixed exchange rate.

This is really background information but it is central to an understanding of the crucially important role played by the balance of payments in post-war UK policy, and proved instrumental in generating the ubiquitous

stop–go cycle to which reference has frequently been made.[3] It will be recalled that the combination of low productivity growth and relatively high
inflation together resulted in absorption exceeding income whenever the
economy expanded at a relatively healthy rate. Given the overhang of
sterling balances, balance of payments crises were relatively common, and
this period is characterized by the following factors:

(1) The balance of payments acted as a constraint on the rate of growth
of domestic output.
(2) Since the exchange rate was viewed as being *de facto* fixed, balance of
payments policy was largely a matter of expenditure reduction.
(3) As the years passed, crises occurred more frequently and were of
greater severity. This is partly a consequence of the increasing openness
of the UK economy, but also a result of the cumulative effects of relatively poor productivity growth.
(4) Related to the last point, the UK steadily lost ground in markets for
manufactures and semi-manufactures.

In terms of the models discussed in chapters 14 and 15 the experience of this
period can be thought of in the framework of the internal–external balance
setting of figures 14.4 and 14.9. Since the exchange rate was pegged the CA
schedule of figure 14.4 was fixed. Attempts to reflate the economy resulted in a
current account deficit which was remedied by deflationary shifts of *IS* and
LM. In terms of the Mundell–Fleming model of figure 14.9 the domestic
interest rate was manipulated on occasions in an attempt to secure external
balance. The persistence of current account imbalance through time,
however, illustrates one of the points made in criticizing that framework,
namely that such fine-tuning is merely a palliative and as such cannot
substitute for adjustment.

1967–72: Breaking the Mould of Pegged Exchange Rates

Given current attitudes to exchange rate movements, it may appear absurd
that devaluation was resisted for so long in the UK. Without doubt political considerations were paramount, with devaluation being viewed as a
symptom of national failure both at home and abroad. There were,
however, some genuine doubts about whether devaluation could result in a
permanent change in the UK's competitiveness – doubts about the way in
which money wages would react to devaluation, and reservations about
whether resources were sufficiently mobile to permit expansion of the

---

3 The stop–go cycle of growth is further analysed in chapter 21.

import substitute and export sectors. Notwithstanding these considerations, the domestic political palatability of a devaluation, given that it would have been the first since 1949 (which was also initiated by a Labour administration), and anxieties over the effect on overseas holders of sterling balances, appear to have been the principal forces behind resistance to devaluation (see Crossman, 1976). It is now a matter of historical record that a decision to devalue sterling by 14.3 per cent was finally taken on 18 November 1967. This reduced sterling's dollar value from $2.80 to $2.40.

As can be seen from figure 20.2, devaluation was followed by a turn-around from current account deficit in 1967–8 to current account surplus in 1969, 1970 and 1971. Two points should be noted here. First, the effect of the devaluation was recorded after a lag. Indeed, from observation of the impact on visible trade in figure 20.1 it is obvious that the deficit actually deteriorated before it improved. This is the so-called J-curve effect of devaluation which follows from the lags involved in adjustment – agents take time to respond to the higher domestic price of imports and the lower foreign price of exports, and as a result the trade balance initially deterio-rates. Following the reaction lag the trade balance improved strongly which, in terms of the analysis in chapter 14, implies that the Marshall–Lerner condition was satisfied; that is, the sum of import demand and export demand elasticities exceeded unity. The second point to be noted is that the turnaround on the current account was not only the result of devaluation. It will be recalled from chapter 14 that the absorption approach stressed the crucial role of idle resources; namely, even where elasticities are appropriate a devaluation may be unsuccessful if insufficient idle resources are available to accommodate increased demand for import substitutes and exports. In this particular episode the expenditure switching policy of devaluation was accompanied by an expenditure reducing package (of tax increases and public expenditure cuts). As well as helping to create the conditions in which devaluation might be effective, this undoubtedly had a direct effect on reducing import demand.

A number of econometric analyses of the effects of the 1967 devaluation have been completed (see NIESR 1972; Ball, Burns and Miller, 1972; and Artus, 1975). The general conclusion which can be drawn from these studies was that devaluation was a 'success' in transforming a current account deficit into a current account surplus. NIESR (1972) estimated that by 1976, devaluation had resulted in a 16.5 per cent increase in the value of imports but a 19 per cent increase in the value of exports; Ball, Burns and Miller (1972) estimated figures of 10 and 16.5 per cent, whilst Artus arrived at estimates of 7 and 18.7 per cent. All three studies suggest a change in export value of a similar order of magnitude, but differ on imports largely as a result of differing import demand elasticities employed.

It is also clear from figure 20.2 that the devaluation did not result in a permanent reversal of UK balance of payments difficulties. By 1971 the current account surplus was already declining, in 1972 it moved into deficit and remained in deficit for five years. This is in part related to specific events, in part due to an inherent difficulty of a policy of devaluation. To be effective it is necessary that the relative price effects of a devaluation are not quickly eroded by an increase in the rate of change of money wages. Devaluation raises the domestic price of imports and exportables. If labour unions suffer from money illusion then the change in relative prices can result in a permanent gain in competitiveness. If, however, attempts are made to maintain real wages by seeking compensatory increases in money wages, the competitive edge conferred by devaluation is transient. In the UK an attempt was made to hold the line on money wages with the introduction of an incomes policy in April 1968. With hindsight this could be said to have been completely ineffective in part because the upper limit (of 3.5 per cent!) was relatively generous, in part because of the scope for 'productivity' related increases. The ensuing wage inflation of 1969–71 contributed significantly to the erosion of the benefits of devaluation.

In addition, there are a number of specific developments which were important. First, there was the Smithsonian realignment of exchange rates in December 1971 which was effectively the death-knell of the Bretton Woods gold exchange standard. As a result of the exchange rate realignments which actually took place sterling was *revalued* by 8.6 per cent, with its dollar value rising from $2.40 to $2.60. Second, the incoming Conservative administration in 1970 engaged in an expansionary demand management programme in an attempt to reduce unemployment. All of these factors combined to help the current account back into deficit by 1972 and in June of that year a decision was taken to float sterling. This decision was as momentous in its own right as the decision to devalue; the former could not have been taken, however, without the latter. Devaluation in 1967 and the Smithsonian realignments of December 1971 broke the pegged rate psychology and opened the way to greater exchange rate flexibility. What followed is the longest period of exchange rate flexibility recorded in the UK, and it is to this experience that we now turn.

1972–86: The Managed Floating Experience

Figure 20.3 outlines the movements which have taken place in the sterling dollar exchange rate and the sterling effective exchange rate[4] over the

---

4 The effective exchange rate is a weighted average index of exchange rates between sterling and the UK's principal trading partners.

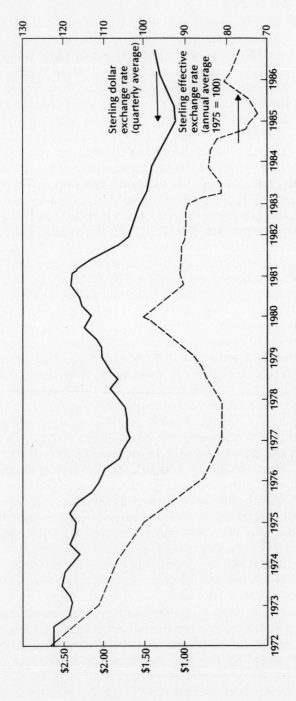

Figure 20.3   Sterling dollar exchange rate and the effective exchange rate

period 1972–86. In very general terms it can be seen that between June 1972 when sterling was floated and late 1976/early 1977, sterling's dollar value depreciated from $2.60 to around $1.60 (the actual nadir being $1.56 in November 1976). Between early 1977 and early 1981 an equally dramatic appreciation took place with the dollar value rising from around $1.60 to almost $2.40. Between 1981 and 1985 a further dramatic turnround occurred with the rate falling from $2.38 to $1.05 in January 1985. Since then some recovery has occurred and in March 1987 the rate stood at $1.57. The sterling/dollar rate is of course only one bilateral exchange rate and a clearer indication of sterling's relative strengths and weaknesses is given by the effective exchange rate. Although this shows the same pattern of depreciation between 1972 and 1976, it is greater than that implied by the nominal exchange rate, whilst the effective appreciation from 1977 to 1981 is less. In other words sterling depreciated relative to other currencies in addition to the dollar in the earlier period, but appreciated relative to fewer in the later period. When one examines the effective exchange rate after 1981 one sees evidence of further sustained depreciation. The extent of the change again implies depreciation relative to other currencies as well as the US dollar.

By historical standards these are extremely wide fluctuations. The simple theory of floating exchange rates might lead one to expect that they were associated with a continuous tendency towards payments balance. In fact, as perusal of table 20.1 and figure 20.2 makes clear, no such tendency can be observed. Indeed the absolute magnitude of payments imbalance increased (although its magnitude relative to GDP remained roughly constant). How then can these fluctuations be explained.

From chapter 15 it will be recalled that one view of exchange rate determination is the purchasing power parity (PPP) doctrine. This asserts that exchange rate movements will be determined by relative rates of price inflation. More specifically it argues that the rate of change of the exchange rate will be proportionately equal to the difference between domestic price inflation and the 'overseas' price inflation – the latter being a (trade) weighted average of the inflation rates of one's competitors. It is certainly true that over the period under discussion the UK's rate of inflation exceeded that of her major trading partners. A rule of thumb approach applied by Metcalfe (1980) can be used as a basis for evaluating whether this higher rate of inflation can fully account for the exchange rate depreciation which has occurred. This involves taking the effective exchange rate as broadly speaking equivalent to PPP and comparing movements in this with the change in UK inflation relative to her principal trading partners. Applying this rule of thumb reveals that the effective depreciation from 1972 to 1976 exceeded the depreciation which would have been predicted by PPP (by 16 percentage points), whilst the effective appreciation between 1978 and 1981 exceeded that predicted by PPP (by 8 percentage points).

This does not mean that PPP is entirely inappropriate when it comes to explaining movements in sterling over the last decade; rather it means that there have been other forces at work which have to be acknowledged:

EEC Accession. In January 1973 the UK became a full member of the European Community. With regard to the UK's external situation and the value of sterling this had two interrelated effects. First, there followed a significant shift in the direction of trade away from the United States and Commonwealth partners towards members of the EEC. Thus in 1975 UK imports from and exports to the EEC accounted for 36 per cent of total imports and exports respectively. By 1985, these shares had changed to 46 per cent of both imports and exports. Second, prior to accession UK tariffs were on average higher than the EEC common external tariff – they were therefore lowered to a greater extent during the adjustment period. These together with the budgetary implications of the common agricultural policy have resulted in the overall balance of payments effects of entry being negative. There is some debate over the precise balance of payments effects of EEC entry (see for example Morgan, 1980, and Winters, 1986). Here it may merely be noted that it accounts for some of the depreciation in excess of that predicted by PPP.

Oil Shocks. Between October 1973 and January 1974 the posted price of crude oil quadrupled, whilst in the summer months of 1979 it again doubled. Figures 20.1 and 20.2 tell their own story of the impact which these changes had on the current account, with the earlier of the two having the greater impact. Given the suddenness and magnitude of the first oil shock, and given that it was an experience shared with other developed market and developing market economies, the induced deficit was largely accommodated. Given the highly inelastic demand for oil, exchange rate depreciation to eliminate the deficit would have been quite inconceivable. In the event the oil-induced recession which followed served to deflate import demand and helped turn around the deficit. None the less this episode undoubtedly contributed to the exchange rate depreciation in excess of PPP which followed.

North Sea Oil. The second oil shock of 1979 did not have the same impact on the current account as the first oil shock, largely due to the cushion of North Sea oil. (It is also possible to argue that the expectation of North Sea oil coming 'on tap' eased adjustment to the first oil shock by providing collateral for foreign borrowing to accommodate the deficit.) The move towards self-sufficiency in oil and the contribution which this has made to payments surplus in the early 1980s are likely to have had an important effect on the effective appreciation of sterling which occurred in 1979–82. As with the effect of EEC entry on the exchange rate, the precise impact of North

Sea oil is a matter of some debate, although the direction of its impact is uncontroversial, as the current account surpluses of the early 1980s indicate.

Expectations and Capital Flows. In chapter 15 was stressed the role which expectations of exchange rate changes play in driving currency inflows and outflows. In this connection was discussed the concept of exchange rate *overshooting* which was associated with changes in macroeconomic policy – the idea that anticipated changes in PPP are quickly taken into account and exert an influence on the spot rate of exchange. All that was necessary for this to occur is an efficient foreign exchange market, where differences in rates of return in assets which are close substitutes for each other are quickly arbitraged. Given the magnitude of potentially mobile international capital in an economy like the UK, which has a well-developed capital market and for historical reasons is an attractive centre for short-term 'investors', this is undoubtedly a contributory factor. Between 1974 and 1976 the rundown of sterling balances (by OPEC holders in particular) was instrumental in driving the depreciation which occurred. Similarly the accumulation of sterling balances in 1979–80 (in anticipation of a falling rate of inflation, and because of sterling's petrocurrency status) played a significant part in driving exchange rate appreciation. Furthermore, the very dramatic depreciation of sterling in late 1984/early 1985 was stimulated by a substantial capital outflow.

There have thus been a number of influences as well as relative rates of inflation which have influenced exchange rate movements over the 1972–86 period.

Balance of Payments Policy 1950–86

In chapters 14 and 15 the distinction between balance of payments accommodation and adjustment was emphasized. The former, it will be recalled, referred to the practice of financing a payments deficit by foreign exchange decumulation, foreign borrowing or attracting short-term capital inflows by engineering relatively high interest rates (the analogues in the case of a surplus are foreign exchange accumulation, foreign lending or encouraging short-term capital outflows by maintaining relatively low interest rates). Balance of payments adjustment by contrast refers to the use of policies to remove the source of the payments imbalance. Thus to use the terminology of the absorption approach, adjustment to a payments deficit requires that domestic absorption be reduced relative to income. This in turn necessitates reliance on expenditure reducing policies and/or expenditure switching policies.

This distinction between accommodation and adjustment is crucially important in any evaluation of balance of payments policy. In principle the distinction between the two is quite clear. In practice, however, it can be somewhat opaque. The extent of any reserve decumulation (accumulation) or foreign borrowing (lending) can be adduced from the balance of payments accounts, but reliance on short-term capital inflows cannot since the latter is not broken down into autonomous and induced components. One thing is clear, however; accommodation is a short-term palliative which can only be expected to remove what Johnson (1958) referred to as *stock imbalances*. Since most payments imbalances are flows, accommodation can only be used to buy time (although the length of time which can be bought is invariably longer for a surplus than a deficit). This follows because reserves are finite, creditworthiness has its limits and there are political constraints on the limits which nominal interest rates can reach.

Over the last thirty years there have been many occasions when the UK has attempted to rely on accommodation rather than adjustment, in both the period of pegged rates and during the managed float. In the earlier period interest rates (as indicated by bank rate) were frequently raised when the balance of payments was in deficit and the sale of sterling balances was placing sterling under pressure (for example, 1951–2, 1955–6, 1960, 1964). In this regard a comparison of figure 18.4, tracing interest rate movements, and figure 20.2, charting the current account, is interesting. In addition, the authorities were willing to borrow on an extensive scale to finance payments deficits. A particularly good example of this in the era of pegged rates is the agreements reached between 1964 and 1967. Thus in December 1964 $1 billion was drawn from the IMF. This was supplemented by a drawing of $1.4 billion in May 1965. In addition, bilateral borrowing arrangements were made with other central banks (most notably the Federal Reserve Bank), in part to repay the IMF drawings but also to support sterling. In the end of course the parity was changed.

After 1972 one also observes the use of interest rate manipulation as a means of payments accommodation. Despite the fact that sterling has been floating, the authorities have been unwilling to permit it to fluctuate outside certain (unannounced) limits. For example the possibility that the sterling dollar rate might move significantly below $1.80 in the second half of 1981 was instrumental in stimulating a rise in interest rates. Likewise when sterling approached parity with the US dollar in January 1985, interest rates were increased dramatically to arrest the decline. One can also find occasions when accommodation via borrowing/reserve use has been important over the managed float period. The clearest example is during the period of the post-

OPEC deficit 1974–7. The oil-induced deficit of 1974 and 1975 would have required an unacceptable reduction in absorption and/or an unacceptable effective depreciation to remove them (always assuming that such interventions would have been successful). The deficits were accommodated in part by borrowings from the IMF, in part by borrowings from the Euro-currency markets (through encouraging UK public corporations to borrow in non-sterling currencies), and in part by the 'recycling' of OPEC surpluses. The latter was especially popular with many Western governments given the size of the OPEC surplus and their inability to absorb much of it on current consumption. In the UK case one finds that OPEC holdings of sterling balances rose from $1 billion in 1973 to $3.2 billion in 1974. Although this proved to be an essential expedient, the subsequent rundown of these balances in 1975 and 1976 placed sterling under considerable pressure.

Invariably this aspect of policy has tended to be a holding operation; adjustment action has had to be taken sooner or later. Over the period 1950–67 this took the form principally of expenditure changing policies, with only peripheral use of explicit expenditure switching policies (such as the travel allowance introduced in 1966, the export rebate of 1964–8, the import surcharge of 1964–6, the import deposit scheme of 1968–70 and efforts to reduce government overseas expenditure). Demand deflation through the use of restrictive fiscal and monetary policies (the latter via credit restrictions) was the principal instrument of payments adjustment. It has already been noted that this tended to be effective in removing the deficit but not the balance of payments constraint to growth – whenever the economy recovered and moved on to a growth path the deficit invariably returned. With the recognition that the UK was in fundamental disequilibrium and that an exchange rate of $2.80 could not be defended indefinitely, a greater willingness to use the exchange rate as an instrument rather than viewing it simply as a target has been evident.

It has already been noted that the devaluation of 1967 served to transform a payments deficit into a surplus, but its effects were relatively short lived. Between June 1972 and the end of 1976 a sustained depreciation occurred, with the effective rate for sterling being more than one-third lower at the end of the period compared with the beginning. As can be seen from figure 20.4, trade competitiveness did improve over this period but there is no more evidence of any permanent change in competitiveness than there was as a consequence of expenditure reducing policies. Furthermore, any gains were reversed in the late 1970s/early 1980s. As figure 20.4 demonstrates a dramatic deterioration in competitiveness followed as a consequence of accelerating domestic inflation, against the backcloth of an appreciating exchange rate. Subsequent exchange rate depreciation combined with a

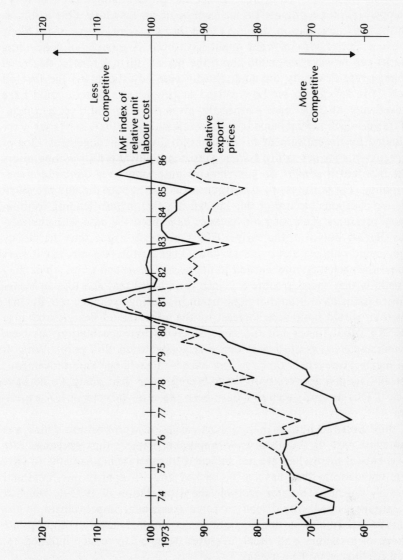

Figure 20.4   Indices of UK trade competitiveness 1973–86 (1980 = 100)

depreciating exchange rate have seen some improvement in competitiveness (relative to the 1979–81 period).

Evaluation of the floating experience in the UK (and indeed in other developed market economies) is far from being an easy task. One is not, as with the 1967 devaluation, dealing with a discrete event, where one is likely to have a clearer idea of what might have been. A number of concluding remarks can however be made about the period. First, a greater degree of exchange rate flexibility did undoubtedly ease adjustment to the first oil shock. It is difficult to see how a fixed or pegged rate system could have survived such an experience – especially given the high and divergent inflation rates which accompanied it. One might argue that the latter were facilitated by the movement to a (managed) floating arrangement. One of the arguments for a floating system consistently advanced by sympathizers is the fact that it confers on governments autonomy over domestic monetary policy. The corollary to this argument is that it may thereby provide a basis for irresponsible use of this instrument, this in turn leading to inflationary pressures. This may for instance have been the case with the infamous 'Barber boom' of the early 1970s. One might argue that the money supply could only expand by more than 20 per cent in two successive years because the exchange rate was left to depreciate. A second point which may be made is that there is some evidence to indicate that speculative movements of funds have been more important in causing exchange rate fluctuations than would have been forecast by the adherents of flexible exchange rates. Note that this is not the same as saying that speculation has been destabilizing. No conclusive evidence is available on this point. What it does mean, however, is that the *real* effects of exchange rate movements, especially sudden appreciations, have been greater than many would have forecast. This certainly seems to have been the case with recent UK experience.

A third point to note is that support exists for a proposition which was an integral part of the absorption approach, namely that exchange rate movements of themselves are not sufficient to generate adjustments to payments imbalance – they have to be backed up with appropriate fiscal and monetary policies. Thus for example the depreciation of 1975–6, which it was initially hoped would lead to some permanent improvement in the payments position, was not brought under control until an appropriate package of monetary and fiscal measures designed to reduce inflation restored confidence in the currency.

A fourth point is that although the relative price effects of devaluation and depreciation are theoretically identical in practical terms there is an important difference which hangs on the role of the expectations of traders. In a pegged rate system with relatively low inflation rates, one can be reasonably confident that discrete changes in par values will hold for a reasonable length of time. In a floating system, however, with high and divergent rates of inflation and where speculative flows are influential, the variance associated with exchange rate changes may be quite high. Thus traders may take rather longer to commit themselves to a particular investment decision.

As we noted earlier, it is extremely difficult to evaluate the managed floating experience, given the structural changes which have occurred during the period in question. It is certainly true that exchange rate fluctuations have been more dramatic than most commentators would have anticipated. To some this constitutes grounds for a movement towards greater official intervention to stabilize the exchange rate. Others argue that the sheer volume of potentially mobile international capital makes any hope of intervention futile. One thing is reasonably clear however. A more flexible exchange rate does not seem to have been the panacea which some expected. The evidence of the 1970s and 1980s suggests that the external constraint has not been removed.

Current Issues

In conclusion three specific issues must be mentioned. The first is the impact of North Sea oil on the balance of payments; the second, possible UK participation in the European Monetary System; and the third, import controls.

North Sea Oil

There has been considerable debate over the effects of North Sea oil on the UK economy. Discussion has focused particularly on the impact of North Sea oil on the balance of payments/exchange rate, and its impact on the manufacturing sector. In both cases there appears to have been a dramatic impact.

The build-up in the production of North Sea oil resulted in import substitution and the development of an export capability with the result that the UK was transformed from being a significant net importer of oil to a significant net exporter in a relatively short space of time. Table 20.3 provides details of the dramatic turnround. After the first oil shock in 1973, the UK's deficit on petroleum and petroleum products was close to £4 billion. By 1983 this had been transformed into a surplus in excess of £6.5 billion.

The effects of this turnround on the current account can be seen in table 20.2. As one would expect this movement into surplus placed upward pressure on the exchange rate, which in turn, as we can see from figure 20.4 reduced the competitiveness of British exports, especially manufactures. The exact interrelationship between North Sea oil, the exchange rate and the

TABLE 20.3
UK Balance of Trade in Petroleum
and Petroleum Products* 1973–85

Year	Trade balance (£m)
1973	−941
1974	−3,833
1975	−3,447
1976	−4,356
1977	−3,110
1978	−2,293
1979	−1,072
1980	+194
1981	+2,872
1982	+4,409
1983	+6,758
1984	+7,818
1985	+3,828

* Division 33 of the SITC.
Source: Monthly Digest of Statistics (various issues).

decline in competitiveness is a controversial one. For example, Buiter and Miller (1983) contend that the strong sterling appreciation of the early 1980s can largely be attributed to monetary contraction. By contrast Chrystal (1984) argues that North Sea oil was of much greater significance than monetary contraction. It is difficult to disentangle the precise effects of monetary contraction and North Sea oil. As we saw in chapter 15 the overshooting hypothesis provides us with a mechanism for explaining how monetary contraction may have initiated strong appreciation and a loss of competitiveness. Notwithstanding this, however, there is a strong case to be made for North Sea oil contributing to real appreciation and the associated loss of manufacturing competitiveness. Corden and Neary (1982) among others have shown how a real resource boom can result in a loss of competitiveness in tradeables. Crudely, since the balance of payments must balance, the oil surplus initiates a current account surplus; this in turn stimulates exchange rate appreciation which pushes other tradeable sectors (manufacturing in particular) into deficit. Although, as we noted above, it is difficult to disentangle the precise effects of monetary contraction and North Sea oil, there is strong presumptive evidence that the latter has had an important impact on the manufacturing sector.

As we can see from table 20.3 the balance of payments effects of North Sea oil were significant. What was the UK government's policy response? Basically the policy choice was between stabilizing the exchange rate (via

TABLE 20.4
UK Official Reserves 1965–86

Year	Reserves at end of period $m
1965	3,004
1966	3,100
1967	2,694
1968	2,421
1969	2,528
1970	2,827
1971	6,582
1972	5,646
1973	6,476
1974	6,789
1975	5,429
1976	4,129
1977	20,557
1978	15,694
1979	22,538
1980	27,476
1981	23,347
1982	16,997
1983	17,817
1984	15,694
1985	15,543
1986	21,923

Source: Economic Trends Annual Supplement. (various issues).

reserve accumulation and the encouragement of capital exports), and permitting sterling to appreciate to whatever level was required for balance of payments equilibrium. In the event policy has been a mixture of the two. As can be seen from table 20.4, substantial reserve accumulation occurred between 1977 and 1981. As well as facilitating the early repayment of accumulated debts (incurred during past payments crises), it must be assumed that this ameliorated the exchange rate appreciation. In addition, in 1979 exchange controls were abolished thereby making the export of capital from the UK easier. This particular policy change contributed towards an outflow of some £60 billion between 1979 and 1984. This too meant that the actual appreciation was less than what would have occurred in the absence of capital exports. Despite substantial capital outflows and reserve accumulation a significant appreciation of the exchange rate resulted during 1979–81. This, combined with relatively high inflation over the same period, resulted in a spectacular decline in UK trade competitiveness (see figure 20.4).

Over the last few years oil-induced pressures on the exchange rate have in fact been in the opposite direction. Global excess supply resulted in a substantial weakening of oil prices in 1985–6 (from around $30 per barrel to a low point of around $10 per barrel). This fall in price created uncertainty regarding the prospects for the UK economy, stimulating capital outflows and placing downward pressure on the exchange rate. As is clear from figure 20.3 a significant depreciation is evident in recent years. It is equally clear from figure 18.4 and table 20.4, however, that some official intervention to arrest the decline has occurred, both by way of interest rate manipulation and by way of support buying of sterling.

European Monetary System

An opportunity to stabilize the exchange rate was provided by the creation of the European Monetary System in 1979. The EMS is a regional system of pegged rates introduced as part of a long-term move towards monetary union in Western Europe. It was envisaged that participation in the scheme would help insulate Western European economies from dollar instability and would provide a means of generating a convergence of inflation rates. Furthermore, it was hoped that the stabilization of exchange rates would serve to stimulate trade expansion. In the event all member countries agreed to participate in a system (albeit on different terms)[5] apart from the UK. Although participation in the scheme has been raised from time to time since then, the UK has so far resisted joining.

British objections have revolved around a number of issues. It was felt for example that (as under the Bretton Woods system) there would be asymmetries in the incentives to adjust in the event of payments imbalance – with greater pressures being applied to deficit than surplus countries. The UK argued for a specific type of arrangement (a weighted basket of currencies as the *numeraire*) to avoid this, which in the event was not accepted.[6] Another aspect of this which caused concern was the effective removal of monetary policy as an independent policy instrument. In a system like the EMS, the rate of monetary expansion would effectively be dictated by the Federal Republic of Germany, given its absolute importance in Community trade and its relatively low inflation rate. The feeling of UK negotiators was that once the devaluation option was removed a deflationary bias would be imposed on the system. In the event that this was the

---

5 For example the Italian lira was permitted wider support margins than the other currencies.

6 This is not strictly true. A compromise was reached between the weighted basket (proposed by Britain) and the parity grid (proposed by France and Germany), although the final agreement resembles the latter proposal rather more than the former.

case the question of resource transfers became paramount, especially given UK sensitivity to her position as the largest net contributor to the Community budget. The final issue over which the UK was anxious was the position of sterling balances given the probability that, as under the Bretton Woods regime, one-way option speculation would again become a source of pressure.

Some of these fears have been shown to have some foundation. For example, it is possible for speculators to forecast exchange rate realignments, and this has encouraged one-way option speculation. In addition the financing of the Community budget and the entire question of resource transfers have not yet found a long-term solution. (Short-term arrangements have been made to provide 'rebates' to the UK as one of the largest net contributors to the budget, but no major restructuring of arrangements has taken place.) Against this, however, other fears have been shown to be without foundation. A number of exchange rate realignments have now taken place and it is clear that the devaluation option has not been removed. Nor does there appear to be any evidence to suggest that significantly greater adjustment burdens have been imposed on deficit countries than on surplus countries. Contrary to the predictions of some commentators, the system continues to function some eight years after its inception.

The wide fluctuations in sterling over the 1979–86 period have led to a revival of interest in British participation in the EMS. There is evidence of growing support for British entry in official circles. At the time of writing, however, no timetable for participation has been identified.

Import Controls

The one instrument which has not so far been mentioned, and which can be used to influence the balance of payments, is trade policy. The General Agreement on Tariffs and Trade (GATT), of which the UK is a Contracting Party, does permit the use of *temporary* trade controls for balance of payments purposes under article XII. Trade interventions can take a variety of forms. They may be fiscal instruments (like import tariffs or export subsidies) or direct quantitative restrictions; they may be overt (like tariffs) or covert (like voluntary export restraints). Within the framework outlined in the absorption approach, such instruments are expenditure switching; that is, they are intended to encourage domestic consumers to switch consumption from imports to import substitutes, and/or overseas consumers to switch purchasing from other countries exports to 'home' produced exports. In principle, therefore, commercial policy instruments can be used for payments adjustment.

GATT proscribes the use of commercial policy instruments for this purpose largely because they are inefficient relative to the alternatives (exchange rate adjustment or demand deflation). There is a well-founded body of theory, dating back to the work of James Meade (1955), which underpins this belief. In the main, recourse to article XII by developed market economies has been infrequent; indeed, the occasions when trade instruments have been temporarily deployed for balance of payments reasons are conspicuous by their presence – the Wilson import surcharge of 1964 and the Nixon import surcharge of 1971, for example.

Despite the presence of a well-developed body of theory (and a good deal of empirical evidence to back it up) which suggests that trade policy is an inefficient instrument for balance of payments adjustment because of the distortions introduced by their use, one school of thought has recently proposed that the most efficacious means of relieving the UK balance of payments constraint would be via general import controls. This has been a central feature of the analysis of the Cambridge Economic Policy Group. Although the proposal has been consistently propounded, as yet it has failed to persuade a governing party that it would be a superior instrument to relative price adjustment via exchange rate change or demand deflation.

It may be noted in closing that although the temptation of general import controls has been resisted there has been a widespread proliferation of selective import controls in the UK recently (as well as in other developed market economies), often in the guise of voluntary export restraints (a euphemism for import quotas). Most of these have been applied in response to pressure for employment protection in specific sectors (see Greenaway, 1983, and Greenaway and Hindley, 1985).

Concluding Comments

Balance of payments policy is much less easy to identify than inflation or growth policy simply because the balance of payments is integrally linked to domestic demand management policies. Nevertheless, governments do engage in balance of payments policy if only on a 'reactive' basis – that is, because they have a balance of payments problem.

During the period 1949 to 1967 such policies were primarily expenditure changing policies in the UK. Following devaluation, in 1967, and, more especially the floating of the exchange rate in 1972, exchange rate changes have played a much more important role than previously. It is probable that this greater degree of exchange rate flexibility facilitated easier adjustment to several major shocks, in particular the oil price rises of 1973–4 and 1978–9, and the discovery and exploitation of North Sea oil. Having said that, it is clear that exchange rate fluctuations have been more marked than many expected, so much so that some commentators believe that a return to a greater degree of exchange rate management is appropriate.

Further Reading

There are a number of treatises on UK balance of payments experience over the post-war period. Milner and Greenaway (1979) provide an overview of the difficulties of identifying payments 'policy' and a review of the institutional background to the 1950–67 period. Metcalfe and Green (1986) outline post-war UK experience as a whole, as does Sinclair (1978). Tew (1978) concentrates on the pre-1967 period, whilst Milner (1980) focuses on the post-1967 period. The two Brookings studies of the UK balance of payments are excellent analyses, Cooper (1968) covering the experience of the 1950s and 1960s and Dornbusch and Fischer (1980) covering the experience of the 1970s. The latter in particular is an exemplary piece of applied economics. A worthwhile international comparison of the experience with floating exchange rates is given by Swoboda (1981). Emerson (1979) concentrates on Britain and the European Monetary System.

A number of analyses of the effects of North Sea oil are available. The theoretical framework for evaluating 'Dutch Disease' effects is developed in Corden and Neary (1982). Forsyth and Kay (1981) provide estimates of the exchange rate effects of North Sea oil which are supported by Chrystal (1984). An alternative view which argues that monetary contraction was largely responsible for appreciation is provided by Buiter and Miller (1983).

A full statement of the argument for general import controls can be found in Cripps and Godley (1978) or Nield (1979), whilst critiques of this strategy are given in Scott, Corden and Little (1980) and Greenaway and Milner (1979). Greenaway (1983) documents the recent proliferation of non-tariff interventions as well as providing an economic analysis of their effects.

21

Policies for Economic Growth in the UK

Thus far, the policy issues we have examined with respect to the UK economy have been essentially short-term in nature and as such relevant to the concept of the political business cycle whereby governments may attempt to co-ordinate policies for electoral advantage (see Whynes, 1988). According to this thesis, which commends a certain amount of empirical support, governments have a tendency to adopt expansionary policies in the run up to an election to get unemployment down and then follow contractionary policies in the post-election period to deal with the resulting inflationary trends.

Now, however, we turn our attention to the long-term issue of economic growth – that is, with the question of what determines the trend growth of *potential* output over time. Actual output, of course, may fall short of the trend rate owing to a shortfall in the level of aggregate demand. Indeed, short-run demand management strategies for full employment may be regarded as an attempt to promote a convergence between the growth rate of actual output and the trend rate of potential output. The maintenance of such a convergence over time may itself be a factor impinging favourably upon the trend rate of growth of potential output so that demand management strategies, even if short-run in their conception, may none the less carry implications for the long-term growth rate of potential output. However, most economists would tend to give more prominence to what they regard as the fundamental determinants of the underlying trend of potential output whether these be the augmentation of factor inputs, the pace of technical progress and innovation, or changes in the prevailing socio-economic structure attitude and beliefs. The recognition of factors influencing the trend of long-run potential output is the first step in the devising of policies which may be invoked in raising the long-run future growth path of the economy. Whilst policy measures may have comparatively little effect when compared to the more fundamental determinants which may be realistically viewed as autonomous, they should certainly not be ignored. Such is the compounding nature of the growth process that even *minor* changes in the underlying growth rate can make for a profound difference to standards of consumption and welfare over a relatively short time span.[1]

The Sources of Economic Growth

Let us consider then, possible sources of economic growth. Assuming, for expositional simplicity, that full employment of both labour and the capital stock prevails, growth depends either upon an augmentation of factor inputs, or alternatively an increase in their productivity, or some combination of the two. To illustrate let us invoke the concept of the aggregate production function of the form

$$Q = A(L,K) \tag{21.1}$$

where Q is real output expressed as a function of labour and capital inputs, L and K respectively, and of a residual influence A. Output may be increased in consequence of either increasing labour and capital imputs, or alternatively by increasing the value of the coefficient A – which may be viewed as encompassing a host of non-factor influences, such as innovation and technical change, educational and cultural factors, fiscal influences and so forth. This dichotomy is useful in highlighting one of the controversies surrounding the current growth debate. On the one hand, there are those economists who point to the need for increased productive inputs, particularly capital inputs, as the driving force in economic expansion, whilst upon the other there are those who, emphasizing diminishing returns, are sceptical of factor augmentation and point to alternative 'environmental' influences.

In order to bring out some of the implications of this general approach let us simplify the argument by assuming that the production function is

---

1 To illustrate this point, invoking a rule-of-thumb procedure, consider two individuals born on the same day with the same per capita income and facing identical life spans of 72 years. Assume one can look forward to a constant increase in per capita income of 2 per cent per year whilst the other enjoys 3 per cent. At the time of his death the former will be enjoying an income approximately four times that he was endowed with but the latter would be more than twice as well off enjoying an income equal to eight times his initial endowment. Small differences in the rate of economic growth, therefore, are crucial in changing *comparative* living standards over the space of one or two generations. Moreover, it is this critical compounding nature of the growth process which render it the only possible solution to the elimination of poverty and destitution whether in advanced or Third World economies. In contrast, policies of income redistribution, whether internally or intra-country, and whilst arguably desirable upon grounds of equity, can exert little real beneficial effect when compared to the overriding importance of promoting a raising of the growth rate.

Cobb–Douglas and exhibits constant returns to scale. Such a production function implies that a doubling of the factor inputs, *ceteris paribus*, will lead to a doubling of the output, or alternatively a halving of the factor inputs will imply a halving of the final product. We may write such a production function in the following manner:

$$Q = AL^{\alpha}K^{(1-\alpha)} \tag{21.2}$$

The exponents α and $(1-\alpha)$ indicate the respective productivity of the two factor inputs. Constant returns production functions are commonly invoked in economic analysis primarily because of their great convenience and mathematical simplicity. However, it is perhaps necessary to note that they are also relatively biased against factor augmentation *per se* because they exhibit diminishing returns to any one factor input.[2]

The comparative impact of augmenting labour *vis-à-vis* the capital input depends therefore upon the exponents α and $(1-\alpha)$. The effect of factor augmentation upon output is given by the increment in the factor multiplied by its marginal productivity. Thus, for example, increased output arising from the augmentation of the labour input is given by

$$\Delta Q = \Delta L.MP^{L} = \Delta L\alpha AL^{\alpha-1}K^{(1-\alpha)} \tag{21.3}$$

whilst the corresponding increase arising from augmentation of the capital input is simply

$$\Delta Q = \Delta K.MP_{K} = \Delta K(1-\alpha)AL^{\alpha}K^{-\alpha} \tag{21.4}$$

---

2 To see this consider the marginal product of labour and capital respectively

$$\frac{\partial Q}{\partial L} = \alpha AL^{\alpha-1}K^{1-\alpha}$$

gives the marginal product of labour and

$$\frac{\partial^2 Q}{\partial L^2} = (\alpha-1)\alpha AL^{\alpha-2}K^{1-\alpha} < 0$$

implying that the marginal product declines with increasing augmentation of the factor input.

Likewise,

$$\frac{\partial Q}{\partial K} = (1-\alpha)AL^{\alpha}K^{-\alpha}$$

shows the marginal product of capital and

$$\frac{\partial^2 Q}{\partial K^2} = -\alpha(1-\alpha)AL\alpha K^{-\alpha-1} < 0.$$

An α value of 0.5 would mean that it was a matter of indifference whether one increased the input of labour or the input of capital upon total output. However, if α were to be approximately 0.75, implying a value of the capital exponent of 0.25, then a 10 percent increase in the input of labour alone would lead to a raising of the level of output by 7.5 per cent, whilst 10 per cent increase in the capital input alone would lead to a raising of the level of output by 2.5 per cent. A 10 per cent increase in the input of both factor inputs would, of course, raise output by 10 per cent. The values of the exponents 0.75 and 0.25 are not randomly picked out of the air; there are indeed very close to values suggested by the empirical evidence which accordingly questions the wisdom of policies concentrating solely upon the need for increased capital formation.

Some Growth Theory

This general scepticism concerning the efficacy of capital formation as a means to increased economic growth is reinforced by the general conclusions of what is probably the best-known theoretical growth model, the so-called neo-classical growth model. The general conclusion stemming from the elementary version of this model is that the ultimate determinant of the economic growth process is the rate of growth of population which to all intents and purposes is exogenously determined. Thus although there are policies which may be successful in promoting the pace of capital formation and thereby increasing the amount of capital per capita, they are relatively ineffective as a means of promoting a higher rate of growth of potential output. As always, elementary statements of complex theoretical positions are necessarily deficient and subject to considerable qualification and reservation. None the less, it is perhaps instructive to present this elementary proposition first. As a means of proceeding we borrow a diagrammatic analysis first proposed by Johnson (1966) in an influential paper which introduced monetary issues into growth models.

In figure 21.1 the vertical axis displays income per capita and savings per capita, the latter being assumed a constant proportion of the former. On the horizontal axis we illustrate the amount of capital per capita. The autonomous rate of population growth is shown by the slope of the ray On; an increase in the slope of On implies a raising of the pace of population expansion and vice versa. Given this framework the only possible long-term equilibrium solution is indicated at point T, implying a capital/output ratio of OK/OY. At T, the amount of saving per capita is just equal to the rate of population expansion. Accordingly, the rate of capital formation is just offset by the rate of population growth leaving the aggregate capital per capita ratio unchanged. To illustrate further, consider the consequences of a decline in the

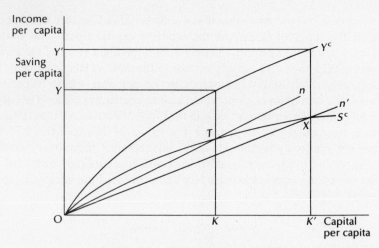

Figure 21.1   The neo-classical model

rate of population expansion as indicated by the ray n'. This would imply that at the initial equilibrium T, the rate of capital formation now exceeds the rate of population growth. The amount of capital per capita would accordingly increase and the increase must continue until position X is obtained when once again the rates of capital formation and population expansion are equated. Whatever the rates of population expansion or whatever the savings ratio there is always an indicated solution implied by the appropriate adjustment in the capital/output ratio. In the movement from T to X, for example, the capital/output ratio rises from OK/OY to OK'/OY' as the labour supply declines.

Once the equilibrium is attained it follows that the capital/output ratio is rendered a constant, the capital/labour ratio remains constant and moreover the level of income per capita is also invariant through time. Thus the economy expands at the predetermined rate of population growth n, but with no change in the level of income per capita. This 'golden age' solution implies constant real income being maintained over time – a vision of an eternally moving stationary state.

The policy implication of this result is well known: namely, that if the growth rate is autonomously determined by population expansion then it remains immutable to policy intervention. In particular, fiscal policy which by generating forced savings can influence the overall savings ratio, is powerless to influence the overall rate of growth. To see this consider figure 21.2. Restrictive fiscal policy is able to generate an increase in the aggregate savings ratio revealed as an upward shift of the savings per capita curve as indicated by the hatched line. The result is an increase in the amount of capital per

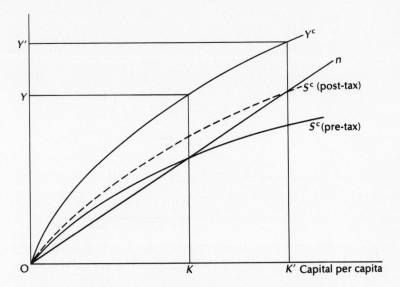

Figure 21.2   The effect of fiscal policy on the growth rate

capita, a changed capital/output ratio and an increase in the level of income per capita. But once the adjustment is complete the economy continues to grow at rate n. Thus fiscal policy is able to alter income per capita levels but not the actual growth rate of the economy.

One should note an immediate implication: whilst population expansion ultimately determines the growth rate in the neo-classical model it does not follow that the maximization of population growth is the desired objective even if it is assumed that population may respond to policy stimulus. *Ceteris paribus*, the higher the rate of population growth the lower the level of income per capita and vice versa. Nor should the objective be unquestioningly to maximize the level of income per capita. Rather the welfare maximizing condition resides in the maximization of consumption per capita – that is, the difference between the level of income per capita and savings per capita and there occur odd situations whereby such a goal is achieved by reducing the level of per capita income. The conditions generating the welfare goals of maximum consumption per capita are usually summed up in the concept of 'the golden rule of capital formation' implying that the rate of savings formation which together with the autonomously determined rate of population expansion so maximizes the level of consumption per capita.

This excursion into growth theory has suggested that the long-run steady state growth path is relatively immune to policy influence. However, this conclusion must be modified once allowance is made for technical progress.

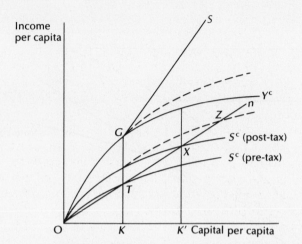

Figure 21.3   Technical change in the neo-classical model and the implications for fiscal
policy

In particular, if technical progress is incorporated into the investment act –
that is to say if technical progress is embodied in the act of investment
generating an upward shift in the aggregate production function then it may
be possible for transitional stages between differing steady state equilibria to
be transformed into a permanent condition whereby increased levels of
capital per capita imply not only increased incomes and consumption per
capita but also a raising of the growth rate of physical output. This type of
situation is portrayed with the aid of figure 21.3. Again we assume an initial
equilibrium at T and take account of a fiscally induced raising of the savings
ratio. In the absence of technological change the new equilibrium would be
indicated at X – fiscal policy would have attained a once and for all change in
per capita income without influencing the growth rate. Now, however, we
assume that the new investment needed to raise the capital/labour ratio
incorporates a degree of technical progress. Both the production function and
the savings function are shifted upwards – as indicated by the broken curves –
and a new equilibrium is again indicated at Z. But Z need never be attained.
Investment-induced technology may again occur and the upward shift of the
production function be made continuous. In this case the economy is moving
along a long-term growth path such as GS with per capita income continually
rising. The growth rate of the economy always exceeds that of population
growth.

The present analysis, where a once and for all fiscal change takes the
economy to the point where technological innovation becomes self-
sustaining, is clearly related to the Rostovian economics of the 'take-off'

(Rostow, 1960). At low levels of capital per worker, technological progress is inhibited; a certain capital intensity is required before innovation can occur. The task of fiscal policy is to force an increase in savings to transform existing methods of production and attain the required capital intensity. The difficulty faced by so many less-developed countries is how to pursue such a policy when faced with surplus labour resources and the consequent need to adopt labour-intensive methods for full employment.

Similar reasoning, and above all an awareness of the interdependencies between economic variables which are obscured in the more elementary models, does suggest a possible role for active interventionist policies to promote the overall growth rate. Alternatively, one can countenance the beneficial effects arising from identifying and then removing the obstacles to the attainment of the potentially feasible long-run growth path. This has been very much the attitude of recent governments in the United Kingdom stimulated by an acute awareness of the dismal record of UK growth when compared with other advanced industrial countries and in particular when compared with the growth rates attained by other member states of the EEC. Having already indicated the crucial importance of even small differences in growth rates when maintained over time the disturbing implication which emerges is that Britain will not only become the poorest nation in Europe but will stand in relation to Europe as many Third World countries presently stand. Table 21.1 summarizes some of the salient features of the recent UK comparative growth performance.

Policy and Experience in the UK

Concern with the consequences of such a comparatively poor growth performance has led to the attempt to identify the main causes of slow UK growth with a view to devising appropriate countervailing policies. Different diagnoses have generated different policy prescriptions and considerable controversy continues over the appropriate growth strategy; this controversy is reflected in the distinct policy stances of the two major political parties. In brief, it is possible to categorize the Conservative view of growth policy as encompassing a commitment to supply side economics with competition allowed free reign, and with government intervention and regulation reduced to a minimum. In contrast Labour politicians, and especially those on the left of the party, incline towards demand side policies, coupled with the need for considerable State intervention and direction including at one extreme, import controls. What follows will attempt to identify the rationale underlying the major explanations for Britain's poor growth performance, before comparing these opposing policy viewpoints.

TABLE 21.1
Growth, Investment, and Export Performance (average of yearly figures)

Countries	% change GDP constant price sum		% change gross domestic investment		% change in exports	
	1965–73	1973–84	1965–73	1973–84	1965–73	1973–84
USA	3.2	2.3	2.7	1.5	6.8	2.3
Canada	5.2	2.5	3.8	0.1	9.5	4.3
W. Germany	4.6	2.0	4.4	1.3	10.7	4.5
Netherlands	5.5	1.6	5.9	−2.0	12.7	2.9
Sweden	3.6	1.4	2.1	−1.5	7.9	1.3
France	5.5	2.3	6.9	0.4	11.4	4.4
Denmark	3.9	1.7	4.9	−2.4	6.6	4.8
Australia	5.6	2.4	3.7	0.7	9.3	3.0
Italy	5.2	2.1	5.9	−0.5	10.2	9.6
Switzerland	4.2	0.8	5.3	1.2	6.7	3.4
Norway	4.0	3.7	4.5	−2.1	8.3	6.4
Belgium	5.2	1.7	4.1	−2.6	10.3	3.1
Japan	9.8	4.3	14.1	3.0	14.7	7.5
Austria	5.5	2.5	6.9	0.7	11.2	6.1
UK	2.8	1.0	3.1	−1.0	5.0	4.2
S. Africa	5.1	2.7	—	—	—	—
Spain	6.4	1.6	6.7	−2.3	15.8	—
Finland	5.3	2.9	4.9	−0.2	7.6	5.1

Source: World Development Report 1986 Oxford, Oxford University Press for World Bank.

A Growth Sector?

Formal growth models frequently abstract to the point of assuming a one-sector, one-good economy, and where they extend to two sectors they are invariably consumption goods and capital goods sectors with a homogeneous input and output. Such models achieve great tractability by virtue of their necessary and justifiable simplifying assumptions, but in consequence they depart from the consideration of issues which may be crucial for policy purposes. One such issue which has attracted attention in recent policy debates turns upon the existence or otherwise of a vital or dominant sector in the growth process. Does such a sector exist? Is it the same sector for all economies, for relatively open economies as well as the relatively closed? Can the sector be identified, and if so can policies then be devised to assist and promote its development in order to hasten the overall rate of economic growth?

More recently, considerable attention has been focused upon the pre-dominance of the manufacturing sector in explaining disparate growth rates amongst advanced economies. This reflects the empirical observation that the fastest growing economies have experienced a rapid increase in the share of manufacturing expressed as a percentage of GDP. Overall output growth appears closely correlated with the growth rate of manufacturing output. In addition, however, it rests upon an assertion originally put forward by Verdoorn (1949) which has since been elevated to the status of Verdoorn's Law; this claims a positive linear relationship between the rate of output growth and productivity growth generally. Verdoorn's original findings were based on international comparisons of indices of industrial production, and thus strictly are applicable only to the industrial sector. Kaldor (1966) claimed to have verified this law for manufacturing, construction and public utilities, but with the correlation being weaker in the latter cases. Implicit in these findings is the notion not only that manufacturing industry enjoys increasing returns to scale in the conventional static sense, but also dynamic and non-reversible productivity gains stemming solely from the fact of expansion *per se*. This belief that the manufacturing sector is vital to productivity growth generally has influenced policy prescriptions as witnessed by the experiment with the selective employment tax, a form of payroll tax levied at positive rates upon the service sector but at negative rates upon manufacturing. Although considerable controversy surrounds the empirical findings relating to Kaldor's resurrection of Verdoorn,[3] it is none the less the case that growth policy has been predominantly concerned with influencing the manufacturing sector. As a point of departure, therefore, it is perhaps of interest to consider the arguments which suggest that British manufacturing industry has fared unfavourably in the post-war years when viewed in an international context.

Labour-Constrained Growth of Manufacturing Output

One of the most fashionable explanations of Britain's inadequate growth performance in the past has rested upon the proposition that the expansion of the manufacturing sector has been held back by the shortage of labour. This, it is argued, has seriously impinged upon growth rates because manufacturing is the most productive sector of the economy, enjoying increasing returns to scale. Moreover, and more importantly, the manufacturing sector is identified as the principal sector enjoying endogenous technical progress as a con-sequence of scale economies over time; *ceteris paribus*, overall productivity growth will be greater the greater the growth of manufacturing. Accordingly,

---

3 See in particular Rowthorn (1975) and McCombie (1981). For a review of the evidence see Stafford (1981).

productivity growth will be inhibited if constraints are imposed upon the movement of required labour resources into the manufacturing sector.

The initial version of this thesis was linked to the name of Kaldor (1966), who argued that the progressive contraction of the agricultural sector was traditionally the source of labour supply into manufacturing. For the economy of the UK, the first nation to industralize, this source of surplus labour had become exhausted long before it had been eliminated in competing nations and before productivity per head had attained high levels. Britain's comparatively poor recent growth performance is thus to be explained by being first in the field and the first to reach economic maturity.

More recently, an alternative version of the labour-constrained thesis has been advanced by Bacon and Eltis (1978). They suggest that the expansion of public sector employment in both central and local government has dominated the rise in non-industrial employment and constrained the supply of labour to the manufacturing sector. Moreover, they contend that this tendency has been much stronger for the UK than for major competing industrial nations. The evidence, however, does not support this contention as a primary cause of labour supply shortage to manufacturing, since much of the increase in public sector employment has been met by increases in the female participation rate.[4]

In addition, it is difficult to substantiate the general claim that manufacturing industry has suffered from a chronic labour shortage. Indeed, much of the more recent evidence points to the existence of considerable labour surpluses in the form of overmanning and in the failure of manufacturing industry to take up reserves of labour as they became available. It is for this reason that Kaldor (1975) subsequently abandoned his labour-constrained thesis of Britain's slow growth without, it should be added, abandoning the dominant role of the manufacturing sector.

Capital-Constrained Growth of Manufacturing Output

Assuming that the expansion of manufacturing is the key to productivity changes and economic growth, and assuming that this sector is not constrained by labour shortages, the question which suggests itself is whether the operable supply constraint rests with capital. Two issues are involved here – first, whether the overall investment/GNP ratio is too low (see table 21.1), and

---

4 See Thatcher (1979). It should be noted that this contention of the Bacon and Eltis argument is a relatively minor aspect of their overall thesis, namely that it is the impact of the relative growth of the non-market sector upon the investment and growth of the market sector which is responsible for Britain's recent disappointing performance.

second, whether capital has been misallocated into sectors having in-ordinately extravagant capital/output ratios.

There can be no disputing the observed correlation between high growth rates and high investment/GNP ratios. However, correlation need imply nothing about causation, and indeed high investment ratios may be the consequence of high economic growth persistently enlarging the need for additional capacity. Moreover, the crucial relationship is between the rate of economic growth and *net* investment, and this information is not readily obtainable from comparative international data. Small variations in aggregate investment/GNP ratios may conceal large variations in net investment/GNP ratios which render single-equation regression coefficients open to question.

Even if it were to be conceded that the lack of investment is a major factor inhibiting UK growth this would not, in itself, indicate the required remedy. The question which remains is whether the lack of investment is a con-sequence of a reduced prospect of profits from UK investment, or alter-natively stems from an inadequate flow of investable funds associated with inefficiency in British financial institutions. The former view is one favoured in the Bacon and Eltis thesis (1978), namely that the tax burden arising from the prolific expansion of the non-market sector serves to diminish post-tax profits and hence investment incentives. The latter view suggests that the peculiar nature of British financial institutions together with certain provisions for preferential tax treatment biases the investment choice towards land and property and away from productive industrial plant and equipment. Although there is some support for the latter view, which forms the basis for the left-wing advocacy that pensions funds, for example, might be commanded into certain investment channels by the State, it may be noted that the Wilson Committee (1977) did not conclude that this was a major cause of an insufficient flow of funds to the private investment sector.

An alternative explanation for Britain's poor growth performance also points to the misallocation of capital resources, but without attaching any particular blame to financial institutions. In this view, Britain's investment/GNP ratio, whilst relatively low, is not radically out of line with that experienced in the United States and other advanced industrial countries (see table 21.1). However, there is evidence to suggest that productivity of capital is low by international standards. In part, this springs from considerable opposition to multi-shift working, implying that expensive capital assets stand idle for considerable periods, but in addition it is a consequence of the fact that public sector investment has often been directed into sectors possessed of high capital/output ratios. In many cases, such investment reflects a concern with the social consequences of secular structural decline in traditional industries such as textiles, steel and shipbuilding. Regional concentration within these sectors, and the desire to minimize the unemployment consequences arising from increased Third World competition, has led to interventionist policies not always compatible with the aim of maximizing net returns.

The Slow Growth of Productivity Change

One feature which characterizes the British economy, and which has been singled out by many commentators, is the relatively poor growth rate of output per head in manufacturing, suggesting *inter alia* an inferior exploitation of technological progress. This failure, it should be emphasized, has occurred despite a high level of expenditure upon pure research and development.[5] It is not so much the lack of advances in knowledge as the failure to apply such advances in innovation which has been responsible for a limited pace of technological progress. How can such reluctance be explained? Here opinions differ markedly, often reflecting deeply ingrained political or class biases. The controversy and debate is not notably assisted by the fact that much of the evidence is inevitably qualitative in nature and thus cannot be resolved by resort to conventional empirical techniques. One school identifies the resistance to change in the conservative and generally non-professional nature of British management. Others point to the equally conservative practices of British trade unions and associated practices of overmanning and restrictive codes of conduct. In part, it is argued, these tendencies are reinforced by the practice of decentralized bargaining which characterizes British industrial relations (see Kilpatrick and Lawson, 1980). Other commentators have linked the lack of innovatory technical progress with the existence of a balance of payments constraint and the resort, at least in the period of fixed exchange rates, to stop–go policies. Such policies imply considerable uncertainty with respect to domestic demand pressure and thus considerable reluctance upon the part of industry to invest and innovate. This thesis contends both that technological change is embodied in the act of investment is itself inversely related to the degree of cyclical disturbance. It is upon this second point that the stop–go thesis has been scathingly attacked for, as Whiting (1976) demonstrates, the percentage deviations from trend of UK growth rates has been less than any other major OECD country, and yet none the less the UK has experienced the slowest rate of growth.

---

5 Caves's (1968) study found that expenditure upon research and development in relation to GNP was some 50 per cent higher in the UK than in the USA.

The Balance of Payments Constraint

Although the 'stop–go' thesis, in itself, cannot be accepted without considerable reservation as a major explanation for Britain's poor industrial performance, it can be argued that the overall constraint imposed by the balance of payments has been a major factor. Two distinct arguments can be mentioned in this connection. On the one hand it has been alleged that, primarily for political and historical reasons, the pound sterling has been overvalued – at least until the adoption of floating exchange rates. In turn, overvaluation of the currency generates an unwillingness to transfer venture capital into the export sector, which accordingly becomes even less competitive and renders the exchange rate ever more overvalued.

This general contention leads to a further view of the reasons for Britain's slow growth rate and emphasizes the vital role of exports. In this view, since the bulk of exports stem from the manufacturing sector and since it is the latter which is vital for productivity changes, any factor constraining export growth will inhibit productivity changes and hence dictate relatively low rates of economic growth. British exports are constrained by the level of unit labour costs, reflected in a falling share of world markets and increasing import penetration. British unit labour costs in turn reflect changes in labour productivity. But equally, the rate of change in British labour productivity will itself depend upon the rate of expansion of the manufacturing sector, since it is this sector which enjoys endogenous technical progress as a result of increasing economies of scale. In this scenario, largely identified with Kaldor (1977), the UK economy is caught in a vicious circle of low exports, slow expansion of the manufacturing sector, slow productivity change, increasing uncompetitiveness and hence low exports. Thus in Kaldor's new formulation of Britain's growth failure, the dominant role of the manufacturing sector remains unchallenged. What has changed is that, whereas in the past Kaldor considered the major constraint upon manufacturing to lie in the *supply* side constraints of inadequate labour supply, it is now firmly identified with the *demand* side constraint of inadequate exports. If this analysis is correct, then it follows that the appropriate remedy lies in what has become referred to as 'export-led growth'.[6]

---

6 Other adherents to the export-led growth thesis, or who are generally sympathetic to the external payments constraint thesis, include Beckerman (1965) and Thirlwall (1980).

Demand Side Strategies for Economic Growth

Demand side policies for economic growth may be caricatured in the following way. The government can, by subtle fiscal and monetary policies, ensure that a sufficient level of aggregate demand is forthcoming so as to guarantee that the potential equilibrium growth rate will be attained. In turn, invoking Verdoorn's Law, the expansion of actual output in line with potential output will maximize productivity changes and enlarge potential future output. Unfortunately, this strategy has never been put into effect and sustained over any appreciable period, and thus the policy has never been given an adequate test. The reasons lie in the inflationary and balance of payments consequences of expansionary policies. Thus, under the regime of fixed exchange rates, expansionary policy generated repeated balance of payments deficits which ultimately forced reversal of the expansionary strategy (see Shaw, 1967). In the period of floating exchange rates after 1971, expansionary policies have implied depreciation of sterling, accentuating inflationary tendencies and triggering off index-linked wage demands. To cope with these constraints, and to permit the demand strategy to be maintained, Keynesians have advocated recourse to one or more of the following: devaluation of the currency, the adoption of prices and incomes controls, and finally the imposition of import controls. The last policy prescription is closely associated with the new Cambridge variant of Keynesian economics spearheaded by Wynne Godley, director of the Cambridge Economic Policy Group. According to this formulation, which relies upon a peculiar and debatable behavioural response of the private sector with regard to saving and investment decisions, conventional demand expansion achieved through budgetary deficits will reveal itself principally in the form of a balance of payments deficit by attracting imports. Thus, paradoxically, the primary impact of fiscal policy designed to stimulate demand to the betterment of domestic industry will be upon industry overseas. If this is the case, and it should be emphasized that the 'alternative economic strategy' is still highly controversial, then demand management policies for economic growth can only succeed if accompanied by stringent measures of import control. Such controls, it is optimistically asserted, would not generate retaliation since they would not be designed to curtail imports from their existing level, but merely to prevent them from rising above current levels in the wake of fiscally induced expansionary economic growth. Whether these policies in themselves would be sufficient to promote growth, or whether they would need to be supplemented by positive government intervention and investment, is another facet of the debate on the alternative strategy where opinions understandably differ (see Greenaway and Milner, 1979; Scott *et al.*, 1980).

Supply Side Strategies for Economic Growth

In complete contrast, supply side policies for economic growth take a decidedly neo-classical view of the economy and see the overriding constraint to lie in the natural long-term augmentation of the productivity of factor inputs. Comparatively little can be done to influence their long-term natural growth rate, but steps can be taken to ensure that they are able to combine efficiently and that unnecessary obstacles are not allowed to impede their progress. In addition, scarce resources can be more efficiently allocated if incentives are provided and if competition is allowed to reign. Demand management policies are eschewed partly on the grounds that they generate uncertainty and hence deter investment and risk-taking. On the macro level, the best that can be achieved is to provide a climate of stability and relative certainty. In particular, it is desirable to contain and if possible eliminate inflation by a policy of gradually curtailing the money supply. The elimination of inflation is considered desirable because inflation generates wasteful resource costs, creates uncertainty and reduces international competitiveness. The primary stimulus to positive growth policy, however, resides in the field of micro-economics.

The fundamental point underlying supply side strategies is that long-run aggregate supply is completely unresponsive to aggregate demand conditions. Demand changes may, and indeed will, carry implications for the price level, but they will leave the 'natural' level of output and employment unaffected. This situation is depicted with the aid of figure 21.4, where the aggregate supply curve is shown to be completely inelastic with respect to price. However, the *position* of the aggregate supply curve will depend on a host of microeconomic influences which are amenable to policy choice and which can be manipulated to produce a favourable outward shift of the supply schedule – see figure 21.5. The major microeconomic factors that might happen should a shift occur can be briefly indicated as follows.

Increased Privatization

The private sector is regarded as being naturally more efficient than the public sector. Curtailment of public sector spending and a gradual return of assets to private ownership are seen as one means of increasing aggregate output. This thesis, that productive private sector undertakings are 'crowded out' by the

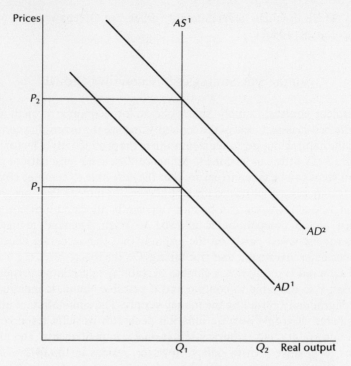

Figure 21.4   Non-response of supply to aggregate demand change

public sector, is of course closely linked to the Bacon and Eltis doctrine of the overriding importance of the market sector to economic growth.

Reduced Taxation

Decreases in the marginal rate of income taxation, combined with a shift in the mix of taxes from direct to indirect, is looked upon as a principal means of encouraging saving, risk-taking and work effort. This issue is closely linked to the need to reform the system of unemployment and welfare benefits which are held to be disincentives to work effort, especially in often cited cases of the poverty trap where marginal implicit tax rates may approach 100 per cent.

Increased Competition and Deregulation

Under this general heading may be grouped a number of diverse elements. The trade union movement, with its insistence upon restrictive practices and its ability to generate wages over and above what would prevail in a non-

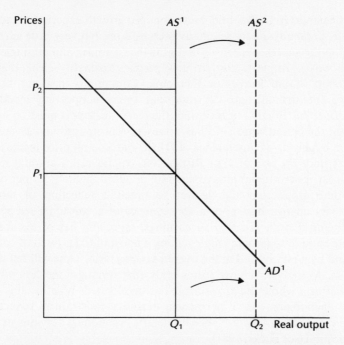

Figure 21.5   Altering natural output levels by supply side strategies

union situation, is looked upon as a cause of both inefficiency and unemployment. In addition, employment legislation, especially measures such as the Employment Protection Act of 1975, raise the cost of employing labour and therefore contribute to raising the natural level of unemployment. Other controls, such as rent controls, impede mobility as do certain private sector retirement pension provisions, all of which contribute to inefficiency and higher unemployment.

Measures such as the ones mentioned here by no means exhaust the arsenal of supply side economic strategies. They do, however, serve to indicate the flavour of the policy, and stress the important need to condition attitudes and expectations towards a more dynamic competitive climate. In short, supply side strategies may be considered a resurrection of Say's Law, in that they affirm the adage 'let competition prevail and demand will take care of itself'. By the very nature of the policies involved, many of these recommendations are essentially qualitative and do not lend themselves readily to empirical verification. Consequently, their espousal frequently requires an act of faith on the part of their advocates who usually, and not surprisingly, are to be found in the monetarist camp.

What emerges from this brief excursion into growth experience and policy in the UK are many diagnoses, many prescriptions, but very little agreement, apart from the general consensus that growth is complex and no single simple solution exists. In particular, it now seems reasonably clear that mere membership of the European Economic Community has not been the palliative for Britain's growth rate that many supporting membership believed it to be. Finally, in reviewing the recent history it must be borne in mind that the period since 1973 has witnessed a prolonged and severe world recession largely as a consequence of OPEC-induced oil price increases. It is true that since the end of 1981 Britain has experienced a gradual recovery with output recovering at an average rate of approximately 2.4 per cent per year. Some argue that this is not so much a reflection of long-term productivity change but more a consequence of a consumer-led spending boom financed by a rise in real earnings, especially net of tax for those fortunate enough to remain employed, by a boost in the growth of consumer credit and by a relative fall in the overall savings ratio. Time will tell whether this is so. Moreover, it now seems clear that amongst the less advanced economies as a whole the growth rate has decelerated. Whether this reflects cyclical phenomena, or a permanent resource-constrained reduction in economic growth for the advanced industrial economies remains as yet an open question (see Hicks, 1981).

Concluding Comments

The survey of the major policy problems confronting the British economy has been completed by examining the case of economic growth – or rather the comparative lack of it. It is clear that no broad consensus prevails as to the ultimate reasons for Britain's comparatively poor post-war growth performance. Rather, a host of factors and influences appear to interact and combine. This conclusion is frankly disturbing, for if there is no simple single cause of Britain's poor growth, then the obvious corollary is that there is no simple single cure. And whilst the current emphasis upon supply side economics may, if proved successful, generate a welcome once and for all increase in productivity it may not, of itself, generate an increase in the *rate* of growth. Neither the advent of North Sea oil nor membership of the European Economic Community appears to have disturbed the historically observed trend although it has to be conceded that since 1982 productivity growth in the UK has been relatively high compared to most of the post-war period.

Further Reading

One of the most influential empirical studies of comparative growth performance is Denison (1967). Denison (1968) concentrates specifically on UK growth performance over the period 1950–62. The finding from this (and other studies) has been, as noted in the chapter, that the UK's rate of growth has been relatively poor. The question of why it has been relatively poor has generated much controversy. Kaldor (1966) argues the case via slow employment growth in manufacturing, a view which is challenged by Beckerman (1965). The role of the balance of payments constraint is outlined in Thirlwall (1980), whilst Bacon and Eltis (1978) discuss the role played by the growth of the non-market sector. Shaw (1980) provides a concise appraisal of all of these competing explanations. More comprehensive reviews of alternative views are to be found in Peaker (1974) and Stafford (1981) (although the former is still quite terse). Giersch (1981) provides a compendium of papers directed at re-evaluating the determinants of growth.

Mishan (1967, 1977) and Beckerman (1974) are the most readily accessible sources on the debate about the net benefits of economic growth. See also Meadows *et al.* (1967) and Hirsch (1977) for further insights into the controversy. Matthews (1986) examines the possible role of institutional change as a positive (or negative) contribution to the growth process.

Bibliography

Ackley, G. (1961) *Macroeconomic Theory* New York, Macmillan.

Ackley, G. (1978) *Macroeconomics: Theory and Policy* New York, Macmillan.

Aiginger, K. (1980) Empirical Evidence on the Rational Expectations Hypothesis Using Reported Expectations. Paper presented to the World Conference of the Econometric Society, Aix en Provence.

Akerlof, G. (1979) 'The Case Against Conservative Macroeconomics' *Economica* **46**.

Alchian, A. (1955) 'The Rate of Interest, Fisher's Rate of Return over Cost and Keynes's Internal Rate of Return' *American Economic Review* **45**.

Alexander, S. S. (1952) 'Effects of a Devaluation on a Trade Balance' *IMF Staff Papers* **2**.

Alpine, R. L. W. (1985) 'A Pedagogical Note on Bond Financing of Government Expenditure' *Journal of Economic Studies* **12**.

Andersen, L. C. and Jordan, J. L. (1968) 'Monetary and Fiscal Actions: A Test of Their Relative Importance in Economic Stabilisation' *Federal Reserve Bank of St. Louis Review* November.

Ando, A. and Modigliani, F. (1963) 'The Life Cycle Hypothesis of Saving' *American Economic Review* **53**.

Arrow, K. (1978) 'The Future and the Present in Economic Life' *Economic Inquiry* **16**.

Artis, M. (1979) 'Recent Developments in the Theory of Fiscal Policy: A Survey' in Cook, S. T. and Jackson, P. M. (eds) *Current Issues in Fiscal Policy* Oxford, Martin Robertson.

Artis, M. and Lewis, M. K. (1981) *Monetary Control in the U.K.* Oxford, Philip Allan.

Artus, J. (1975) 'The 1967 Devaluation of the Pound Sterling' *IMF Staff Papers* **22**.

Aschauer, D. A. (1985) 'Fiscal Policy and Aggregate Demand' *American Economic Review* **75**.

Attfield, C., Demery, D. and Duck, N. (1985) *Rational Expectations in Macroeconomics* Oxford, Basil Blackwell.

Azariadis, C. (1975) 'Implicit Contracts and Underemployment Equilibria' *Journal of Political Economy* **83**.

Bacon, R. and Eltis, W. (1978) *Britain's Economic Problem: Too Few Producers* (2nd edn) London, Macmillan.

Bailey, M.J., Tavlas, G. S. and Ulan, M. (1986) 'Exchange Rate Variability and Trade Performance' *Weltwirtschaftliches Archiv* **122**.

Bain, A. D. (1976) *The Control of the Money Supply* (2nd ed) Harmondsworth, Penguin.

Ball, R. J., Burns, T. and Miller, G. (1972) 'Preliminary Simulations of the London Business School Model' mimeo.

Ball, R. J. and Drake, P. S. (1963) 'The Impact of Credit Control on Consumer Durable Spending in the U.K. 1957–61' *Review of Economic Studies* **30**.

Barro, R. (1976) 'Rational Expectations and the Role of Monetary Policy' *Journal of Monetary Economics* **2**.

Barro, R. (1977) 'Long Term Contracting, Sticky Prices and Monetary Policy' *Journal of Monetary Economics* **3**.

Barro, R. J. (1979) Unanticipated Money Growth and Unemployment in the United States: Reply. *American Economic Review* **69**.

Batchelor, R. *et al.* (1980) 'Inflation, Unemployment and Reform', in Blackaby, F. T. (ed.) *The Future of Pay Bargaining* London, Heinemann.

Baumol, W. (1952) 'The Transactions Demand for Cash: An Inventory Theoretic Approach' *Quarterly Journal of Economics* **66**.

Bean, R. (1978) 'The Determinants of Consumers Expenditure in the U.K.' *Government Economic Service Working Paper no. 4*.

Becker, G. S. and Baumol, W. J. (1952) 'The Classical Monetary Theory: The Outcome of the Discussion' *Economica* **19**.

Beckerman, W. (1965) *The British Economy in 1975* Cambridge, National Institute of Economic and Social Research and Cambridge University Press.

Beckerman, W. (1974) *In Defence of Economic Growth* London, Jonathon Cape.

Beckerman W. and Jenkinson, T. (1986) 'What Stopped the Inflation? Unemployment or Commodity Prices' *Economic Journal* **96**.

Begg, D. K. H. (1982) *The Rational Expectations Revolution in Macroeconomics* Oxford, Philip Allan.

Bickerdike, C. F. (1914) 'A Non-Monetary Cause of Fluctuations in Employment' *Economic Journal* **24**.

Black, J. (1979) *The Economics of Modern Britain: An Introduction to Macroeconomics* Oxford, Martin Robertson.

Black, S. (1973) *International Money Markets and Flexible Exchange Rates* Princeton Studies in International Finance no. 32, Princeton, Princeton University Press.

Blackhurst, R. and Tumlir, J. (1980) *Flexible Exchange Rates and International Trade* GATT Studies in International Trade no. 7, GATT, Geneva.

Blaug, M. (1981) *The Methodology of Economics* Cambridge, Cambridge University Press.

Blinder, A. S. (1981) 'Temporary Taxes and Consumer Spending' *Journal of Political Economy* **89**.

Blinder, A. and Solow, R. M. (1973) 'Does Fiscal Policy Matter?' *Journal of Public Economics* **3**.

Brainard, W. (1967) 'Uncertainty and Effectiveness of Policy' *American Economic Review* **57**.

Branson, W. H. (1981) 'Comment' *European Economic Review* **16**.

Branson, W. H. and Klevorick, A. K. (1969) 'Money Illusion and the Aggregate Consumption Function' *American Economic Review* **59**.

Breit, W. and Hochman H., M. (eds) (1968) *Readings in Microeconomics* New York, Holt Rinehart and Winston.

Bronfenbrenner, M. and Holzman, F. (1963) 'A Survey of Inflation Theory' *American Economic Review* **53**.

Brothwell, J. F. (1975) 'A Simple Keynesian's Response to Leijonhufvud' *Bulletin of Economic Research* **27**.

Brown, A. J. and Burrows, E. M. (1978) *Regional Economic Problems* London, George Allen and Unwin.

Brown, E. Cary (1950) 'Analysis of Consumption Taxes in Terms of the Theory of Income Determination' *American Economic Review* **40**.

Brunner, K. and Meltzer, A. (1973) 'Mr Hicks and the Monetarists' *Economica* **40**.

Buiter, W. E. (1977) 'Crowding Out and the Effectiveness of Fiscal Policy' *Journal of Public Economics* **7**.

Buiter, W. and Miller, M. (1983) 'Changing the Rules: Economic Consequences of the Thatcher Regime' *Brookings Papers on Economic Activity* **8**.

Burrows, P. (1974) 'The Upward Sloping *IS* curve and the Control of Income and the Balance of Payments' *Journal of Finance* March.

Burrows, P. (1979) 'The Government Budget Constraint and the Monetarist–Keynesian Debate' in Cook, S. T. and Jackson, P. M. (eds) *Current Issues on Fiscal Policy* Oxford, Martin Robertson.

Burton, J. (1986) *Keynes's General Theory: Fifty Years On: Its Relevance and Irrelevance to Modern Times* Hobart Paperback 24, Institute of Economic Affairs, London.

Cagan, P. (1956) 'The Monetary Dynamics of Hyperinflation' in Milton Friedman (ed.) *Studies in the Quantity Theory of Money* Chicago, University of Chicago Press.

Cambridge Economic Policy Group (1981) *Economic Policy Review*, Cambridge, Cambridge University Press.

Caves, R. E. (1968) *Britain's Economic Prospects* Washington, Brookings Institution; London, Allen and Unwin.

Chick, V. (1977) *The Theory of Monetary Policy* (2nd edn) Oxford, Parkgate Publishers.

Chick, V. (1983) *Macroeconomics After Keynes* Oxford, Philip Allan.

Chrystal, A. K. (1984) 'Dutch Disease or Monetarist Medicine? The British Economy under Mrs Thatcher *Federal Reserve Bank of St Louis Review* **66**.

Chrystal, A. K. and Dowd, D. (1988) 'Exchange Rate Overshooting and Macroeconomic Policy' in Greenaway, D. (ed.) *Current Issues in Macroeconomics* London, Macmillan.

Clark, J. M. (1917) 'Business Accumulation and the Level of Demand: A Technical Factor on Economic Cycles' *Journal of Political Economy* **25**.

Clower, R. (1975) 'Reflections on the Keynesian Perplex' *Zeitschrift fur Nationalokonmie* **35**.

Clower, R. and Johnson, M. B. (1968) 'Income, Wealth and the Theory of Consumption' in Wolfe, N. (ed.) *Value, Capital and Growth* Edinburgh, Edinburgh University Press.

Clower, R. and Leijonhufvud, A. (1975) 'The Coordination of Economic Activities: A Keynesian Perspective' *American Economic Review* **65**.

Cochrane, J. L. (1970) *Macroeconomics Before Keynes* Glenview, Illinois, Scott, Foresman.

Coddington, A. (1976) 'Keynesian Economics: The Search for First Principles' *Journal of Economic Literature* **14**.

Coddington, A. (1983) *Keynesian Economics: The Search for First Principles* London, George Allen and Unwin.

Coghlan, R. T. (1973) 'Special Deposits and Bank Advances' *Bankers Magazine* (216).

Coghlan, R. (1980) *The Theory of Money and Finance* London, Macmillan.

Cohen, B. J. (1971) *Balance of Payments Policy* Harmondsworth, Penguin.

Cook, S. T. and Jackson, P. M. (eds) (1979) *Current Issues in Fiscal Policy* Oxford, Martin Robertson.

Cooper, R. N. (1968) 'The Balance of Payments', in Caves, R. (ed.) *Britain's Economic Prospects*, London, George Allen and Unwin.

Coppock, D. J. (1978) 'Some Thoughts on the Monetary Approach to Balance of Payments Theory' *Manchester School* **46**.

Corden, W. M. (1977) *Inflation, Exchange Rates and the World Economy* Oxford, Oxford University Press.

Corden, W. M. and Neary, J. P. (1982) 'Booming Sector and De-Industrialisation in a Small Open Economy' *Economic Journal* **92**.

Corry, B. A. (1962) *Money, Saving and Investment in English Economics 1800–1850* London, Macmillan.

Creedy, J. (ed.) (1981) *The Economics of Unemployment in Britain* London, Butterworths.

Cripps, F. and Godley, W. (1978) 'Control of Imports as a Means to Full Employment and the Expansion of World Trade: The U.K.'s Case' *Cambridge Journal of Economics* **2**.

Cross, R. (1982a) *Economic Theory and Policy in the U.K.* Oxford, Martin Robertson.

Cross, R. (1982b) 'The Duhem–Quine Thesis, Lakatos and the Appraisal of Theories in Macroeconomics' *Economic Journal* **92**.

Crossman, R. (1976) *The Crossman Diaries* London, Jonathan Cape.

Crouch, R. L. (1970) 'Special Deposits and the British Monetary Mechanism' *Economic Studies* **5**.

Currie, D. A. (1978) 'Macroeconomic Policy and Government Financing: A Survey of Recent Developments' in Artis, M. J. and Nobay, A. R. (eds) *Studies in Contemporary Economic Analysis* vol. 1, London, Croom-Helm.

Currie, D. A. (1981) 'Monetary and Fiscal Policy and the Crowding-Out Issue' in Artis, M. J. and Millar, M. M. (eds) *Essays on Fiscal and Monetary Policy* Oxford, Oxford University Press.

Currie, D. (1984) 'Monetary Overshooting and the Exchange Rate' *Manchester School* **52**.

Currie, D. (1985) 'Macroeconomic Policy Design and Control Theory – A Failed Partnership?' *Economic Journal* **95**.

Darby, M. R. (1974) 'The Permanent Income Theory of Consumption: A Restatement' *Quarterly Journal of Economics* **88**.

Davidson, J., Hendry, D. F., Srba, F. and Yeo, S. (1978) 'Econometric Modelling of the Aggregate Time Series Relationship Between Consumers Expenditure and Income in the U.K.' *Economic Journal* **88**.

Dawkins, P. J. (1980) 'Incomes Policy' in Maunder, W. P. (ed.) *The British Economy in the 1970s* London, Heinemann.

Deaton, A. (1978) 'Involuntary Saving through Unanticipated Inflation' *American Economic Review* **68**.

Denison, E. F. (1967) *Why Growth Rates Differ: Postwar Experience in Nine Western Countries* Washington, Brookings Institution.

Denison, E. F. (1968) 'Economic Growth' in Caves, R. (ed.) *Britain's Economic Prospects* London, George Allen and Unwin.

Dennis, G. E. J. (1980) 'Money Supply and Its Control' in Maunder, W. P. (ed.) *The British Economy in the 1970s* London, Heinemann.

Dennis, G. E. J. (1981) *Monetary Economics* London, Longman.

Dillard, D. (1948) *The Economics of John Maynard Keynes: The Theory of a Monetary Economy* Englewood Cliffs, NJ, Prentice-Hall.

Dornbusch, R. (1976) 'Expectations and Exchange Rate Dynamics' *Journal of Political Economy* **84**.

Dornbusch, R. (1980) *Open Economy Macroeconomics* New York, Basic Books.

Dornbusch, R. and Fischer, S. (1980) 'Sterling and the External Balance' in Caves, R. E. and Krause, L. B. (eds) *Britain's Economic Performance* Washington, The Brookings Institution.

Dornbusch, R. and Fischer, S. (1981) *Macroeconomics* (2nd edn) New York, McGraw-Hill.

Duesenberry, J. (1952) *Income, Saving and the Theory of Consumer Behavior* Harvard, Harvard University Press.

Eckaus, R. S. (1953) 'The Acceleration Principle Reconsidered' *Quarterly Journal of Economics* **67**.

Eichenbaum, M. S., Hansen, L. P. and Singleton, K. J. (1984) 'A Time Series Analysis of Representative Agents' Models of Consumption and Leisure Choice under Uncertainty' Mimeo, Carnegie Mellon University.

Emerson, M. (1979) 'The United Kingdom and the European Monetary System' in Major, R. (ed.) *Britain's Trade and Exchange Rate Policy* London, Heinemann.

Fallick, J. and Elliott, R. F. (eds) (1981) *Incomes Policy, Inflation and Relative Pay* London, Allen and Unwin.

Farrell, M. (1959) 'The New Theories of the Consumption Function' *Economic Journal* **69**.

Fausten, D. K. (1978) *The Consistency of British Balance of Payments Policies* London, Macmillan.

Fausten, D. (1981) 'A Partial Rehabilitation of the Policy Mix Approach' *Kyklos* **34**.

Feldstein, M. (1982) 'Government Deficits and Aggregate Demand' *Journal of Monetary Economics* **9**.

Feldstein, M. (1986) 'Supply Side Economics: Old Truths and New Claims' *American Economic Review* Papers and Proceedings, May.

Fender, J. (1981) *Understanding Keynes: An Analysis of 'The General Theory'* Brighton, Wheatsheaf Books.

Ferber, R. (1973) 'Consumer Economics: A Survey' *Journal of Economic Literature* **11**.

Fischer, S. (ed.) (1980) *Rational Expectations and Economic Policy* Chicago, University of Chicago Press.

Fisher, I. (1963) *The Purchasing Power of Money Rev. Ed.* (1922) New York, Augustus M. Kelly.

Fleming, J. M. (1962) 'Domestic Financial Policies Under Fixed and Floating Exchange Rates' *IMF Staff Papers* **9**.

Fleming, J. S. (1973) 'The Consumption Function when Capital Markets are Imperfect: The Permanent Income Hypothesis Reconsidered' *Oxford Economic Papers* **25**.

Fleming, J. S. (1976) *Inflation* Oxford, Oxford University Press.

Forster, B. A. and Shaw, G. K. (1976) 'The Tax Mix and Aggregate Demand: A Respecification' *Public Finance* **31**.

Forsyth, P. and Kay, J. (1980) *The Economic Implications of North Sea Oil* London, Institute of Fiscal Studies.

Forsyth, P. J. and Kay, J. A. (1981) 'Oil Revenues and Manufacturing Output' *Fiscal Studies* **2**.

Frenkel, J. A. (1981) 'The Collapse of Purchasing Power Parties during the 1970s' *European Economic Review* **16**.

Frenkel, J. A. (1986) 'International Interdependence and the Constraints on Macro-economic Policies' *Weltwirtschaftliches Archiv* 122.

Frenkel, J. and Johnson, H. G. (eds) (1976) *The Monetary Approach to the Balance of Payments* London, Allen and Unwin.

Frenkel, J. and Rodriguez, C. (1982) 'Exchange Rate Dynamics and the Over-shooting Hypothesis' *IMF Staff Papers* 29.

Friedman, M. (1953a) 'The Methodology of Positive Economics' in *Essays in Positive Economics* Chicago, University of Chicago Press.

Friedman, M. (1953b) 'The Case for Flexible Exchange Rates' in *Essays in Positive Economics* Chicago, University of Chicago Press.

Friedman, M. (1956a) 'The Quantity Theory of Money: A Restatement' in Fried-man, M. (ed.) *Studies in the Quantity Theory of Money* Chicago, University of Chicago Press.

Friedman, M. (ed.) (1956b) *Studies in the Quantity Theory of Money* Chicago, University of Chicago Press.

Friedman, M. (1957) *A Theory of the Consumption Function* Princeton, National Bureau of Economic Research.

Friedman, M. (1968a) 'The Role of Monetary Policy' *American Economic Review* 58.

Friedman, M. (1968b) 'Money: Quantity Theory' *The International Encyclopaedia of the Social Sciences* vol. 10.

Friedman, M. (1969) *The Optimum Quantity of Money* London, Macmillan.

Friedman, M. (1977) 'Inflation and Unemployment' *Journal of Political Economy* 85.

Friedman, M. (1980) Prices of Money and Goods Across Frontiers: the £ and $ over a Century. *The World Economy* 2.

Friedman, M. and Schwartz, A. (1963) *A Monetary History of the United States 1867–1960* Princeton, Princeton University Press.

Friedman, M. and Schwartz, A. (1982) *Monetary Trends in the US and the UK* Chicago, University of Chicago Press.

Gibson, N. J. (1971) 'Competition and Innovation' *Bankers Magazine* 212.

Giersch, H. (ed.) (1981) *Macroeconomic Policies for Growth and Stability* Tübingen, J. C. B. Mohr.

Goldfield, S. (1973) 'The Demand for Money Revisited' *Brookings Papers on Economic Activity* Washington.

Goodhart, C. (1973) 'Analysis of the Determinants of the Stock of Money' in Parkin, J. M. and Nobay, A. R. *Essays in Modern Economics* London, Longman.

Goodhart, C. (1975) *Money, Information and Uncertainty* London, Macmillan.

Goodhart, C. and Crockett, A. D. (1970) 'The Importance of Money' *Bank of England Quarterly Bulletin* 10.

Gordon, R. J. (1976) 'Recent Developments in the Theory of Inflation and Unem-ployment' *Journal of Monetary Economics* 2.

Gordon, R. J. (1981) 'Output Price Fluctuations and Gradual Price Adjustment' *Journal of Economic Literature* 19.

Gordon, R. J. (1982) 'Why U.S. Wage and Employment Behaviour Differs From that in Britain and Japan' *Economic Journal* 92.

Gowland, D. (1982) *Controlling the Money Supply* London, Croom Helm.

Greenaway, D. (1982) Identifying the Gains from Pure Intra Industry Trade. *Journal of Economic Studies* 9.

Greenaway, D. (1983) *International Trade Policy: From Tariffs to the New Protec-tionism* London, Macmillan; New York, St Martin's Press.

Greenaway, D. (1983b) 'Patterns of Intra-Industry Trade in the UK, in P. K. M. Tharakan (ed.), *Intra Industry Trade* Amsterdam, North Holland.

Greenaway, D. (ed.) (1988) *Current Issues in Macroeconomics* London, Macmillan.

Greenaway, D. and Hindley, B. V. (1985) *What Britain Pays for Voluntary Export Restraints* Thames Essay 43, Trade Policy Research Centre, London.

Greenaway, D. and Milner, C. R. (1979) *Protectionism Again . . . ?* Hobart Paper 84, London, Institute of Economic Affairs.

Greenaway D. and Milner, C. R. (1983) On the Measurement of Intra Industry Trade *Economic Journal* **93**.

Greenaway, D. and Milner, C. R. (1986) *The Economics of Intra Industry Trade* Oxford, Basil Blackwell.

Greenaway, D. and Shaw, G. K. (ed.) (1985) *Public Choice, Public Finance and Public Policy: Essays in Honour of Alan Peacock.* Oxford, Basil Blackwell.

Grossman, H. I. (1972) 'Was Keynes a "Keynesian"?' *Journal of Economic Literature* **10**.

Grubel, H. G. and Lloyd, P. J. (1975) *Intra-Industry Trade* London, Macmillan.

Hacche, G. (1974) 'The Demand for Money in the U.K.: Experience since 1971' *Bank of England Quarterly Bulletin* **14**.

Hadjimatheou, G. and Skouras, A. (1979) 'Britain's Economic Problem: The Growth of the Non Market Sector' *Economic Journal* **89**.

Hagen, E. (1966) 'The Classical Theory of the Level of Output and Employment' in Mueller, M. G. (ed.) *Readings in Macroeconomics* New York, Holt, Rinehart, Winston.

Hahn, F. (1980) 'Monetarism and Economic Theory' *Economica* **47**.

Hall, R. E. (1978) 'Stochastic Implications of the Life Cycle–Permanent Income Hypothesis: Theory and Evidence' *Journal of Political Economy* **86**.

Hall, R. E. (1980) 'Employment Fluctuations and Wage Rigidity' *Brookings Papers on Economic Activity no. 1*, Washington.

Hansen, B. (1973) 'On the Effects of Fiscal and Monetary Policy: A Taxonomic Discussion' *American Economic Review* **63**.

Harcourt, G. C. (ed.) (1977) *The Microeconomic Foundations of Macroeconomics* London, Macmillan.

Heathfield, D. (ed.) (1979) *Perspectives On Inflation*, London, Longman.

Helliwell, J. F. (ed.) (1976) *Aggregate Investment* London, Penguin.

Henry, S. G. B. and Karakitsos, E. (1987) 'Inflation, Unemployment and Indirect Taxation' *Bulletin of Economic Research* **39**.

Hicks, J. R. (1937) 'Mr Keynes and the Classics: A Suggested Interpretation' *Econometrica* **5**.

Hicks, J. R. (1967) *Critical Essays in Monetary Theory* London, Oxford University Press.

Hicks, J. R. (1973) 'Recollections and Documents' *Economica* **40**.

Hicks, J. R. (1974) *The Crisis in Keynesian Economics* Oxford, Basil Blackwell.

Hicks, J. R. (1980) 'ISLM – An Explanation' *Journal of Post-Keynesian Economics* November.

Hicks, J. R. (1981) 'Are There Economic Cycles?' The Robbins Lecture, University of Stirling.

Hines, A. G. (1971) *On the Reappraisal of Keynesian Economics* London, Martin Robertson.

Hirsch, F. (1977) *Social Limits to Growth* London, Routledge and Kegan Paul.

HMSO (1981a) *National Income and Expenditure* London, CSO.

HMSO (1981b) *The National Accounts – A Short Guide* London, CSO.

Holmes, J. M. and Smyth, D. J. (1972) 'The Specification of the Demand for Money and the Tax Multiplier' *Journal of Political Economy* **80**.

Hudson, W. D. (ed.) (1979) *The IS/OUGHT Question* London, Macmillan.

Hughes-Hallett, A. J. (1988) Macroeconomic Interdependence and Policy Co-ordination' in Greenaway, D. (ed.) *Current Issues in Macroeconomics* London, Macmillan.

IMF (1977) *The Monetary Approach to the Balance of Payments* Washington, IMF.

Jackman, R. (1974) 'Keynes and Leijonhufvud' *Oxford Economic Papers* **26**.

Jackman, R. and Sutton, J. (1982) 'Imperfect Capital Markets and the Monetarist Black Box: Liquidity Constraints, Inflation and the Asymmetric Effects of Interest Rate Policy' *Economic Journal* **92**.

Johnson, B. M. (1971) *Household Behaviour*, Harmondsworth, Penguin.

Johnson, H. G. (1958) 'Towards a General Theory of the Balance of Payments' in Caves, R. and Johnson, H. G. (eds) *Readings in International Economics* London, Allen and Unwin.

Johnson, M. G. (1966) 'The Neo-Classical One-sector growth model: A geometric Exposition and Extension to a Monetary Economy' *Economica* **33**.

Johnson, H. G. (1970) 'Keynes and the Keynesians' *Encounter* January.

Johnson, H. G. (1976) 'Money and the Balance of Payments' *Banca Nazionale del Lavoro Quarterly Review* March.

Johnson, H. G. (1977) 'The Monetary Approach to Balance of Payments Theory and Policy: Explanations and Policy Implications' *Economica* **44**.

Jones, A. (1973) *The New Inflation: The Politics of Prices and Incomes* Harmondsworth, Penguin.

Jorgenson, D. W. (1967) 'The Theory of Investment Behaviour' in Ferber, R. (ed.) *Determinants of Investment Behaviour* New York, National Bureau of Economic Research.

Jorgenson, D. W. (1971) 'Econometric Studies of Investment Behaviour' *Journal of Economic Literature* **9**.

Jorgenson, D. W. and Siebert, C. D. (1968) 'A Comparison of Alternative Theories of Corporate Investment' *American Economic Review* **58**.

Junankar, P. N. (1972) *Investment Theories and Evidence* London, Macmillan.

Kahn, R. F. (1976) 'Unemployment as seen by Keynesians' in Worswick, G. D. N. (ed.) *The Concept and Measurement of Involuntary Unemployment* London, George Allen and Unwin.

Kaldor, N. (1966) *Causes of the Slow Rate of Growth of the United Kingdom. An Inaugural Lecture* Cambridge, Cambridge University Press.

Kaldor, N. (1975) 'Economic Growth and the Verdoorn Law' *Economic Journal* **85**.

Kaldor, N. (1977) 'Capitalism and Industrial Development: Lessons From British Experience' *Cambridge Journal of Economics* **I**.

Kantor, B. (1979) 'Rational Expectations and Economic Thought: A Survey' *Journal of Economic Literature* **17**.

Kay, J., Mayer, C. and Thompson, D. (1986) *Privatisation and Regulation – The UK Experience* Oxford, Clarendon Press.

Kern, D. (1978) 'An International Comparison of Major Economic Trends' *National Westminster Quarterly Review* **May**.

Keynes, J. M. (1923) *Tract on Monetary Reform* London, Macmillan.

Keynes, J. M. (1930) *A Treatise on Money* London, Macmillan.

Keynes, J. M. (1936) *The General Theory of Employment Interest and Money* London, Macmillan.

Keynes, J. M. (1937a) 'The General Theory of Employment' *Quarterly Journal of Economics* **51**.

Keynes, J. M. (1937b) 'Professor Pigou on Money Wages in Relation to Unemployment' *Economic Journal* **47**.

Kilpatrick, A. and Lawson, T. (1980) 'On the Nature of Industrial Decline in the U.K.' *Cambridge Journal of Economics* **4**.

Knox, A. D. (1952) 'The Acceleration Principle and the Theory of Investment: A Survey' *Economica* **19**.

Kohn, M. (1986) 'Monetary Analysis, the Equilibrium Method and Keynes's "General Theory"' *Journal of Political Economy* **94**.

Korilas, P. J. and Thorn, R. S. (1979) *Modern Macroeconomics* New York, Harper and Row.

Kreinin, M. (1961) 'Windfall Income and Consumption: Additional Evidence' *American Economic Review* **51**.

Krueger, A. O. (1983) *Exchange Rate Determination* Cambridge, Cambridege University Press.

Kuznets, S. (1946) *National Product Since 1869* New York, National Bureau of Economic Research.

Laidler, D. W. (1971a) 'The Influence of Money on Economic Activity: A Survey of some Current Problems' in Clayton, G., Gilbert, J. C. and Sedgwick, R. (eds) *Monetary Theory and Policy in the 1970s* Oxford, Oxford University Press.

Laidler, D. W. (1971b) 'The Phillips Curve, Expectations and Incomes Policy' in Johnson, H. G. and Nobay, A. P. (eds) *The Current Inflation* London, Macmillan.

Laidler, D. W. (1975) *Essays on Money and Inflation* Manchester, Manchester University Press.

Laidler, D. W. (1977) *The Demand for Money* New York, Crowell.

Laidler, D. W. (1982) *Monetarist Perspectives* Oxford, Philip Allan.

Laidler, D. (1986) 'The New Classical Contribution to Macroeconomics' *Banca Nazionale Del Lavoro Quarterly Review*, March.

Laidler, D. W. and Parkin, M. (1975) 'Inflation: A Survey' *Economic Journal* **85**.

Lane, T. D. (1985) 'The Rationale for Money-Supply Targets: A Survey' *Manchester School* **53**.

Layard, R. (1986) *How to Beat Unemployment* Oxford, Basil Blackwell.

Leighton Thomas, R. (1984) 'The Consumption Function' in Demery, D. *et al. Macroeconomics* London, Longman.

Leijonhufvud, A. (1968) *On Keynesian Economics and the Economics of Keynes: A Study in Monetary Theory* London, Oxford University Press.

Leijonhufvud, A. (1969) *Keynes and the Classics* Occasional Paper no. 30, Institute of Economic Affairs, London.

Lerner, A. P. (1944) *The Economics of Control* New York, Macmillan.

Lindauer, J. (1968) *Macroeconomic Readings* New York, The Free Press.

Lipsey, R. G. (1961) 'The Relation Between Unemployment and the Rate of Change of Money Wage Rates in the United Kingdom 1862–57: A Further Analysis' *Economica* **27**.

Loasby, B. (1976) *Choice, Complexity and Ignorance* Cambridge, Cambridge University Press.

Lucas, R. E. (1972) 'Expectations and the Neutrality of Money' *Journal of Economic Theory* **4**.

Lucas, R. E. (1973) 'Some International Evidence on Output Inflation Trade Offs' *American Economic Review* **63**.

Lucas, R. E. (1975) 'An Equilibrium Model of the Business Cycle' *Journal of Political Economy* **83**.

Lucas, R. E. (1976) 'Econometric Policy Evaluation: A Critique' *Journal of Monetary Economics* **1**.

Lucas, R. E. (1981) *Studies in Business Cycle Theory* Oxford, Basil Blackwell.

Lucas, R. E. and Sargeant, T. (1981) *Rational Expectations and Econometric Practice* London, George Allen and Unwin.

Lund, P. J. (1971) *Investment: The Study of an Economic Aggregate* Edinburgh, Oliver and Boyd.

Maddock, R. and Carter, M. (1982) 'A Child's Guide to Rational Expectations' *Journal of Economic Literature* **20**.

Maddock, R. and Carter, M. (1985). *Rational Expectations* London, Macmillan.

Marshall, A. (1920) *Principles of Economics: An Introductory Volume* (8th edn) London, Macmillan.

Matthews, R. C. O. (1986) 'The Economics of Institutions and the Sources of Growth' *Economic Journal* **96**.

Mayer, T. (1959) 'The Empirical Significance of the Real Balance Effect' *Quarterly Journal of Economics* **73**.

Mayer, T. (1972) *Permanent Income, Wealth and Consumption: A Critique of the Permanent Income Theory, the Life Cycle Hypothesis and Related Theories* Berkeley, University of Los Angeles Press.

Mayes, D. (1981) 'The Controversy Over Rational Expectations' *National Institute Economic Review* (96).

Maynard, G. (1982) 'Microeconomic Deficiencies in U.K. Macroeconomic Policy' *Lloyds Bank Review* July.

McCallum, J. (1986) 'Unemployment in OECD Countries in the 1980s' *The Economic Journal* **96**.

McCombie, J. S. L. (1981) 'What Still Remains of Kaldor's Laws?' *Economic Journal* **91**.

McEnery, P. (1981) *Manufacturing Two Nations*, Research Monograph 36, London, Institute of Economic Affairs.

McLean, A. A. (1978) 'The Direct/Indirect Tax Ratio and Effective Demand – A Comment' *Public Finance* **33**.

Meade, J. E. (1955) *Theory of International Economic Policy* vol. 2: Trade and Welfare. Oxford, Oxford University Press.

Meade, J. E. (1982) *Stagflation. Vol. I: Wage Fixing* London, Allen and Unwin.

Meadows K. (1967) *The Limits to Growth* London, Earth Island.

Meade, J. E. (1985) *Wage Fixing Revisted.* Occasional Paper 72. London, Institute of Economic Affairs.

Metcalf, D. (1984). 'On the Measurement of Employment and Unemployment' *National Institute Economic Review* no. 109.

Metcalfe, J. S. (1980) 'Foreign Trade and the Balance of Payments' in Prest, A. R. and Coppock, D. J. (eds) *The U.K. Economy: A Manual of Applied Economics* London, Weidenfeld and Nicholson.

Metcalfe, J. S. and Green, C. (1986) 'Foreign Trade and the Balance of Payments' in Artis, M. (ed.) *The UK Economy: A Manual of Applied Economics* London, Weidenfeld and Nicholson.

Middleton, R. (1982) 'The Treasury in the 1930s: Political and Administrative Constraints to Acceptance of the "New" Economics' *Oxford Economic Papers* **34**.

Mill, J. (1966) *Selected Economic Writings* (D. Winch, ed.) Edinburgh, Oliver and Boyd.

Milner, C. R. (1980) *Payments and Exchange Rate Problems* in Maunder, W. P. (ed.) (1980) *The British Economy in the 1970s* London, Heinemann.

Milner, C. R. and Greenaway, D. (1979) *An Introduction to International Economics* London and New York, Longman.

Minford, A. P. and Hilliard, G. (1978) 'The Costs of Variable Inflation' in Artis, M. J. and Nobay, A. R. (eds) *Contemporary Economic Analysis* London, Croom Helm.

Minford, A. P. and Peel, D. (1981) 'Is the Government's Economic Strategy on Course?' *Lloyds Bank Review* April.

Miron, J. A. (1986) 'Seasonal Fluctuations and the Life-Cycle–Permanent Income Model of Consumption' *Journal of Political Economy* **94**.

Mishan, E. J. (1967) *The Costs of Economic Growth* London, Staples Press.

Mishan, E. J. (1977) *The Economic Growth Debate: An Assessment* London, George Allen and Unwin.

Mishkin, F. S. (1982) Does Anticipated Monetary Policy Matter? *Journal of Political Economy* **90**.

Modigliani, F. (1944) 'Liquidity Preference and the Theory of Interest and Money' *Econometrica* **12**.

Modigliani, F. and Brumberg, R. (1954) 'Utility Analysis and the Consumption Function: Interpretation of Cross Section Data' in Kurihara, K. (ed.) *Post Keynesian Economics* New Brunswick.

Modigliani, F. and Steindel, C. (1977) 'Is a Tax Rebate an Effective Tool for Stabilization Policy? *Brookings Papers on Economic Activity* **2**.

Moggridge, D. (ed.) (1973) *The Collected Writings of John Maynard Keynes. vols XIII and XIV: The General Theory and After* London, Macmillan.

Moore, B. and Rhodes, J. (1973) 'Evaluating the Effects of British Regional Policy' *Economic Journal* **83**.

Morgan, A. D. (1980) 'The Balance of Payments and British Membership of the European Community' in Wallace, W. (ed.) *Britain in Europe* London, Heinemann.

Morris, D. (ed.) (1978) *The Economic System in the U.K.* (2nd edn) Oxford, Oxford University Press.

Morris, D. and Sinclair, P. (1985) 'The Assessment: The Unemployment Problem in the 1980s' *Oxford Review of Economic Policy* Summer.

Mueller, D. (1976) 'Public Choice: A Survey' *Journal of Economic Literature* **14**.

Mueller, M. G. (ed.) (1966) *Readings in Macroeconomics* New York, Holt, Rinehart and Winston.

Mundell, R. A. (1962) 'The Appropriate Use of Monetary and Fiscal Policy for Internal and External Balance' *IMF Staff Papers* **9**.

Mundell, R. A. (1963) 'Capital Mobility and Stabilisation Policy Under Fixed and Flexible Exchange Rates' *Canadian Journal of Economics and Political Science* **23**.

Mundell, R. A. (1968) *International Economics* New York, Macmillan.

Musgrave, R. A. (1959) *The Theory of Public Finance: A Study in Public Economy* New York, McGraw-Hill.

Muth, J. F. (1960) 'Optimal Properties of Exponentially Weighted Forecasts' *Journal of the American Statistical Association* **55**.

Muth, J. F. (1961) 'Rational Expectations and the Theory of Price Movements' *Econometrica* **29**.

Nagel, E. (1963) 'Assumptions in Economic Theory' *American Economic Review* **53**.

Nickell, S. J. (1979) 'The Effect of Unemployment and Related Benefits on the

Duration of Unemployment' *Economic Journal* **89**.

Nickell, S. J. (1980) 'A Picture of Male Unemployment in Britain' *Economic Journal* **90**.

Niehans, J. (1975) 'Some Doubts About the Efficacy of Monetary Policy Under Flexible Exchange Rates' *Journal of International Economics* **5**.

Nield, R. (1979) *Managed Trade Between Industrial Countries* in Major, R. (ed.) (1979) *Britain's Trade and Exchange Rate Policy* London, Heinemann.

NIESR (1972) 'The Effects of the 1967 Devaluation on the Current Balance of Payments' *Economic Journal* **82**.

Nurkse, R. (1945) *Conditions of International Monetary Equilibrium*, Essays in International Finance no. 4, Princeton, Princeton University Press.

O'Brien, D. P. (1975) *The Classical Economists* Oxford, Clarendon Press.

Okun, A. (1981) *Prices and Quantities: A Macroeconomic Analysis* Oxford, Basil Blackwell.

Parkin, M. (1970) 'Incomes Policy – Some Further Results on the Determination of the Rate of Change of Money Wages' *Economica* **37**.

Parkin, M. and Bade, R. (1982) *Modern Macroeconomics* Oxford, Philip Allan.

Parkin, M. and Sumner, M. T. (eds) (1972) *Incomes Policy and Inflation* Manchester, Manchester University Press.

Parkin, M. and Sumner, M. T. (eds) (1978) *Inflation in the United Kingdom* Manchester, Manchester University Press.

Patinkin, D. (1948) 'Price Flexibility and Unemployment' *American Economic Review* **38**.

Patinkin, D. (1951) 'Price Flexibility and Full Employment' in Lutz, F. A. and Mints, L. W. (eds) *Readings in Monetary Theory* New York, Blakiston Press.

Patinkin, D. (1955) *Money Interest and Prices* (1st edn) New York, Harper and Row.

Patinkin, D. (1959) 'Keynesian Economics Rehabilitated: A Rejoinder to Professor Hicks' *Economic Journal* **69**.

Patinkin, D. (1965) *Money, Interest, and Prices* (2nd edn) New York, Harper and Row.

Patinkin, D. (1969) 'The Chicago Tradition, The Quantity Theory and Friedman' *Journal of Money Credit and Banking* **1**.

Peacock, A. T. (1972) 'The Multiplier and the Valuation of Government Expenditures' *Finanzarchiv* **30**.

Peacock, A. T. (1979) 'Giving Economic Advice in Difficult Times' in Peacock, A. T. (ed.) *The Economic Analysis of Government*, Oxford, Martin Robertson.

Peacock, A. T. and Shaw, G. K. (1976) *The Economic Theory and Fiscal Policy* (2nd edn) London, George Allen and Unwin.

Peacock, A. T. and Shaw, G. K. (1978) 'Is Fiscal Policy Dead?' *Banca Nazionale Del Lavoro Quarterly Review* June.

Peacock, A. T. and Shaw, G. K. (1981) *The Public Sector Borrowing Requirement* Occasional Papers in Economics no. 1, University of Buckingham.

Peacock, A. T. and Williamson, J. (1967) 'Consumption Taxes and Compensatory Finance' *Economic Journal* **77**.

Peaker, A. (1974) *Economic Growth in Modern Britain* London, Macmillan.

Peston, M. H. (1971) 'The Tax Mix and Effective Demand' *Public Finance* **26**.

Peston, M. H. (1981) *Theory of Macroeconomic Policy* (2nd edn) Oxford, Philip Allan.

Peston, M. H. (1982) *The British Economy* Oxford, Philip Allan.

Peston, M. H. (1985) The Efficacy of Macroeconomic Policy in Greenaway and Shaw (1985).

Peston, M. H. (1986) 'The Elementary Macroeconomic Consequences of Differing Public and Private Sector Wages' *Public Finance*, **41**.

Phelps, E. S. (1968) 'Money Wage Dynamics and Labour Market Equilibrium' *Journal of Political Economy* **76**.

Phillips, A. W. (1958) 'The Relationship Between Unemployment and the Rate of Change of Money Wage Rates in the United Kingdom 1862–1957' *Economica* **25**.

Pigou, A. C. (1933) *The Theory of Unemployment* London, Macmillan.

Pigou, A. C. (1937) 'Real and Money Wages in Relation to Unemployment' *Economic Journal* **47**.

Pigou, A. C. (1941) *Employment and Equilibrium* London, Macmillan.

Pigou, A. C. (1944) *Lapses from Full Employment* London, Macmillan.

Pigou, A. C. (1952) *Keynes's General Theory: A Retrospective View* London, Macmillan.

Pissarides, C. A. (1978) 'Liquidity Considerations in the Theory of Consumption' *Quarterly Journal of Economics* **92**.

Pissarides, C. (1985) 'Job Search and the Functioning of Labour Markets' in Pissarides, C. *et al. Labour Economics* London, Longman.

Pliatzky, L. (1982) *Getting and Spending: Public Expenditure, Employment and Inflation* Oxford, Basil Blackwell.

Posner, M. V. (ed.) (1978) *Demand Management* London, Heinemann.

Presley, J. (1979) *Robertsonian Economics* New York, Holmes and Meier.

Prest, A. R. and Coppock, D. J. (eds) (1982) *The U.K. Economy* (9th edn) London, Weidenfeld and Nicholson.

Price, R. (1978) 'Budgetary Policy' in Blackaby, F. T. (1978) *British Economy Policy 1960–74* Cambridge, Cambridge University Press.

Putnam, B. and Wilford, D. S. (eds) (1979) *The Monetary Approach to International Adjustment* New York, Praeger.

Ricardo, D. (1951–55) *Works and Correspondence of David Ricardo* (11 vols) (P. Sraffa, ed., with M. M. Dobb) Cambridge, Cambridge University Press.

Rivera-Batiz, F. and Rivera-Batiz, L. (1985) *International Finance and Open Economy Macroeconomics* New York, Macmillan.

Rostow, W. W. (1960) *The Stages of Economic Growth* Cambridge, Cambridge University Press.

Robbins, Lord (1952) *The Theory of Economic Policy in English Classical Political Economy* London, Macmillan.

Robinson, J. (1969) 'Review of "On Keynesian Economics and the Economics of Keynes" by A. Leijonhufvud' *Economic Journal* **79**.

Robinson, J. (1973) 'What has Become of the Keynesian Revolution?' in Robinson, J. (ed.) *After Keynes* Oxford, Basil Blackwell.

Rousseas, S. W. (1972) *Monetary Theory* New York, Alfred A. Knopf.

Rowthorn, R. E. (1975) 'What Remains of Kaldor's Law?' *Economic Journal* **85**.

Salant, W. (1957) 'Taxes, Income Determination and the Balanced Budget Multiplier' *Review of Economics and Statistics* **39**.

Samuels, W. (1966) *The Classical Theory of Economic Policy* Ohio, Cleveland.

Sapsford, D. R. (1981) *Labour Market Economics* London, Allen and Unwin.

Sapsford, D. and Tzannatos, Z. (1988) *Current Issues in Labour Economics* London, Macmillan.

Sargent, T. J. (1978) 'Rational Expectations, Econometric Exogeneity and Consumption' *Journal of Political Economy* **86**.

Sargent, T. and Wallace, N. (1975) 'Rational Expectation, the Optimal Monetary

Instrument and the Optimal Money Supply Rule' *Journal of Political Economy* **83**.

Say, J. B. (1964) *Traite d'économie politique* (4th edn) (1803) translated by C. R. Prinsep, New York.

Scarth, W. M. (1975) 'Fiscal Policy and the Government Budget Restraint under Alternative Exchange Rate Systems' *Oxford Economic Papers* **27**.

Schumpeter, J. (1961) *History of Economic Analysis* (4th edn) Oxford, Oxford University Press.

Scott, M., Corden, W. M. and Little, I. M. D. (1980) *The Case Against General Import Restrictions* Thames Essay 24, London, Trade Policy Research Centre.

Shaw, G. K. (1967) 'Monetary–Fiscal Policy For Economic Growth and the Balance of Payments Constraint' *Economica* **34**.

Shaw, G. K. (1972) *Fiscal Policy* London, Macmillan.

Shaw, G. K. (1976) 'A Simple View of a Simple Keynesian: Comment on Brothwell's Strictures on Leijonhufvud' *Bulletin of Economic Research* **28**.

Shaw, G. K. (1977) *An Introduction to the Theory of Macro-Economic Policy* (3rd edn) Oxford, Martin Robertson.

Shaw, G. K. (1980) 'Economic Growth: Causes, Consequences and Constraints' in Grant, R. M. and Shaw, G. K. (eds) *Current Issues in Economic Policy* Oxford, Philip Allan.

Shaw, G. K. (1981) 'Leading Issues of Tax Policy in Developing Countries: the Economic Problems' in Peacock, A. T. and Forte, F. (eds) *The Political Economy of Taxation* Oxford, Basil Blackwell.

Shaw, G. K. (1983a) *Rational Expectations: An Elementary Exposition* Brighton, Wheatsheaf.

Shaw, G. K. (1983b) 'Fiscal Policy under the First Thatcher Administration 1979–1983' *Finanzarchiv*, **41**.

Shaw, G. K. (1987a) 'Fiscal Policy under the Second Thatcher Administration 1983–1987' *Finanzarchiv* forthcoming.

Shaw, G. K. (1987b) 'Rational Expectations' *Bulletin of Economic Research* **39**.

Shaw, G. K. (1987c) 'Macroeconomic Implications of Fiscal Deficits: An Expository Note' *Scottish Journal of Political Economy* **34**.

Shaw, G. K. (1988) 'Expectations in Macroeconomics' in Greenaway, D. (ed.) *Current Issues in Macroeconomics* London, Macmillan.

Shoup, C. S. (1960) *Ricardo on Taxation* New York, Columbia University Press.

Signer, A. (1978) 'The Direct/Indirect Tax Ratio and Effective Demand – An Extension and A Comment on a Respecification' *Public Finance* **33**.

Silber, W. L. (1970) 'Fiscal Policy in *IS–LM* Analysis: A Correction' *Journal of Money Credit and Banking* **2**.

Sinclair, P. (1978) 'International Economics' in Morris, D. (ed.) *The Economic System in the UK* Oxford, Oxford University Press.

Smith, Adam (1904) *An Enquiry Into the Nature and Causes of the Wealth of Nations* (2 vols) (E. Cannan, ed.) London, Methuen.

Solow, R. (1969) *Price Expectations and the Behaviour of the Price Level* Manchester, Manchester University Press.

Solow, R. M. (1980) 'On Theories of Unemployment' *American Economic Review* **70**.

Spiro, A. (1962) 'Wealth and the Consumption Function' *Journal of Political Economy* **70**.

Stafford, G. B. (1981) *The End of Economic Growth: Growth and Decline in the U.K. since 1955* Oxford, Martin Robertson.

Stein, H. (1949) 'Price Flexibility and Full Employment – Comment' *American Economic Review* **39**.

Surrey, M. J. (ed.) (1975) *Macroeconomic Themes* Oxford, Oxford University Press.

Swoboda, A. K. (1981) 'Exchange Rate Flexibility in Practice: A Selective Survey of Experience from 1973 to 1979' in Giersch, H. (ed.) *Macroeconomic Policies for Growth and Stability* Tübingen, J. C. B. Mohr.

Taylor, C. T. (1979) 'Crowding Out: Its Meaning and Significance' in Cook, S. T. and Jackson, P. M. (eds) *Current Issues in Fiscal Policy* Oxford, Martin Robertson.

Tew, T. H. B. (1978) 'Policies Aimed at Improving the Balance of Payments' in Blackaby, F. T. *British Economy Policy 1960–74* Cambridge, Cambridge University Press.

Thatcher, A. R. (1979) 'Labour Supply and Employment Trends' in Blackaby, F. T. (ed.) *De-industrialisation* National Institute of Economic and Social Research, London, Heinemann.

Theil, H. (1961) *Economic Forecasts and Policy* Amsterdam, North-Holland.

Theil, H. (1964) *Optimal Decision Rules for Government and Industry* Amsterdam, North-Holland.

Theil, H. (1965) 'Linear Decision Rules for Macro-Dynamic Policy' in Hickman, B. (ed.) *Quantitative Planning of Economic Policy* Washington, Brookings Institution.

Thirlwall, A. P. (1980) *Balance of Payments Theory and the United Kingdom Experience* London, Macmillan.

Tinbergen, J. (1952) *On the Theory of Economic Policy* Amsterdam, North-Holland.

Tinbergen, J. (1965) *Central Planning* New Haven, Yale University Press.

Tobin, J. (1947) 'Money Wage Rates and Employment' in Harris, S. E. (ed.) *The New Economics* New York, Alfred A. Knopf.

Tobin, J. (1958) 'Liquidity Preference as Behaviour Towards Risk' *Review of Economic Studies* **25**.

Tobin, J. (1972) 'Friedman's Theoretical Framework' *Journal of Political Economy* **80**.

Tobin, J. (1986) 'The Monetary–Fiscal Mix: Long-Run Implications' *American Economic Review*, Papers and Proceedings, May.

Townend, J. C. (1976) 'The Personal Savings Ratio' *Bank of England Quarterly Bulletin* **16**.

Treasury and Civil Service Committee on Monetary Policy (1981) Third Report, House of Commons, 27 February 1981.

Trevethick, J. A. and Mulvey, C. (1975) *The Economics of Inflation* Oxford, Martin Robertson.

Tsiang, S. C. (1977) 'The Monetary Theoretic Foundations of the Modern Monetary Approach to the Balance of Payments' *Oxford Economic Papers* **29**.

Turnovsky, S. T. (1977) *Macroeconomic Analysis and Stabilisation Policy* Cambridge, Cambridge University Press.

Veil, E. (1975) *Surpluses and Deficits in the Balance of Payments: Definition and Significance of Alternative Concepts* Paris, OECD.

Verdoorn, P. J. (1949) 'Fattori Che regolano lo sviluppo della produttivita del Pavoro' *L'Industria*.

Vines, D. (1986) 'Macroeconomic Policy after Monetarism' *The Royal Bank of Scotland Review* no. 152. December.

Whalen, E. H. (1966) 'A Rationalisation of the Precautionary Demand for Cash'

Quarterly Journal of Economics **80**.

White, W. H. (1936) 'Interest Inelasticity of Investment Demand: The Case From Business Attitude Surveys Re-examined' *American Economic Review* **26**.

Whiting, A. (1976) 'An International Comparison of the Instability of Economic Growth' *Three Banks Review* **109**.

Whitman, M. V. N. (1970) *Policies for Internal and External Balance* Special Papers in International Economics no. 9, Princeton, NJ.

Whynes, D. K. (1988) The Political Business Cycle, in Greenaway (1988).

Wicksell, K. (1934) *Lectures in Political Economy* Vols. I and II. Translated by L. Robbins.

Wilson Committee (1977) Committee to Review the Functioning of Financial Institutions *Progress Report on the Financing of Industry and Trade* HMSO.

Wilson, T. and Andrews, P. W. S. (eds) (1951) *Oxford Studies in the Price Mechanism* London, Oxford University Press.

Winters, L. Alan (1985) *International Economics* London, George Allen and Unwin.

Winters, L. Alan (1986) Britain in Europe: A Survey of Quantitative Trade Studies. *Discussion Paper no.* 110 London, Centre for Economic Policy Research.

Wright, C. (1969) 'Estimating Permanent Income: A Note' *Journal of Political Economy* **77**.

Index

492   INDEX

Tantonnement   185
Taussig, F.   180
Taxes *see* Fiscal policy, Government
    budget constraint, Government
    revenue
Taylor, C. T.   260, 483
Testing expectations   290–2
Tew, T. H. B.   447, 483
Thatcher, A. R.   458, 483
Theil, H.   344, 357, 483
Thirwall, A. P.   323, 372, 461, 467, 483
Thorn, R. S.   42, 477
Tinbergen, J.   312, 347, 349, 351, 357,
    483
Tinbergen principle   302, 312, 347, 351
Tobin, J.   97–100, 260, 264, 378, 483
Townend, J. C.   40
Transactions demand for money *see*
    Money
Transfer payments   67, 75, 77–8, 242–5
Trapp, R. S.   15
Trevethick, J. A.   267, 293, 483
Tsiang, S. C.   334, 344, 483
Tumlir, J.   344, 470
Turnovsky, S. T.   260, 483
Tzannatos, Z.   157

Ulan, M.   344
Unanticipated inflation *see* Inflation
Uncertainty and macroeconomic
    policy   351–3, 371
Unemployment
    benefits and unemployment   154–6,
        360, 410–11
    cyclical   399, 410–11
    duration of in UK   405–6
    frictional   399, 410
    occupational structure in UK   406

regional breakdown in UK   404–5
seasonal   378–9
structural   379–400
User cost of capital   60

Veil, E.   296, 483
Velocity of circulation   85–6, 97, 101,
    117, 200, 221–2
Verdoorn, P. J.   457, 458, 462, 483
Verdoorn's Law   458, 462
Viner, J.   180
Vines, D.   14
Voluntary export restraints   445
Voluntary unemployment *see*
    Unemployment

Wage and price controls *see* Incomes
    policy
Wallace, W.   150, 284, 479, 481
Walras, L.   185
Waterman, L.   xi, xii
Wealth and consumption *see*
    Endogenous income theories
Whalen, E. H.   88, 483
White, W. H.   64, 219, 483
Whitman, M.   323
Whiting, A.   460, 484
Whynes, D.   448
Wicksell, K.   172, 484
Wilford, D. S.   344, 481
Williamson, J.   80, 82, 480
Wilson, H.   385, 386, 446, 459
Wilson, T.   219, 484
Winters, A.   323, 337, 344, 435
Worswick, G. D. N.   479
Wright, C.   39

Yeo, N.   42, 472